Henry Barrow, Separatist (1550?-1593) and the
Exiled Church of Amsterdam (1593-1622)
by Frederick James Powicke

Powicke, Frederick James.   Henry Barrow, separatist(1550?–1593) and the exiled church of Amsterdam (1593–1622).
London *James Clarke* 1900.   46+363 p. O.   7s. 6d.

An essay upon the origins of congregationalism ; describes Barrow as founder of English congregationalism, his doctrine of the church and views of the ecclesiastical powers of princes ; with valuable chapters upon the church at Amsterdam, and criticism of Arber's Pilgrim Fathers, 1897.   For a general account of the early separatists see John Brown's Pilgrim Fathers, 1895.

Ath. 1901. 1:169 (unfav.).

W. Dawson Johnston, Je. 1901.

7/6 out

HENRY BARROW, SEPARATIST

HENRY BARROW

SEPARATIST

(1550? — 1593)

AND

THE EXILED CHURCH OF AMSTERDAM

(1593—1622)

BY

FRED. J. POWICKE, Ph.D.

Author of " John Norris of Bemerton," &c.

London

JAMES CLARKE & CO., 13 & 14, FLEET STREET

1900

TO
REV. ALEXANDER MACKENNAL, B.A., D.D.,
OF BOWDON,
IN RECOGNITION OF
HIS INTIMATE ACQUAINTANCE
WITH THE
"ORIGINS" OF ENGLISH CONGREGATIONALISM,
AND
IN GRATITUDE FOR
MUCH PERSONAL KINDNESS TO THE WRITER.

PREFACE.

THIS book has grown out of a series of twelve "Short Lectures on the Origin of Congregationalism," delivered to my own people during the winter months of 1896-7, in connection with the "Ter-centenary Celebration."

Two of them dealt directly with Barrow and the Amsterdam Church.

In preparing the one on Barrow, it struck me that his relative importance in the story of the Separatists had not been fully appreciated; and I thought that the best way to test the accuracy of this impression would be to undertake a fresh study, first of all, of his own writings. I hoped, at the same time, that investigation of the "sources" might throw new light on the course of his life and his personal character.

So far as a discovery of new facts is concerned, I cannot say that the result has quite answered expectation. Correction of some errors and clearer arrangement are, perhaps, as much as can be claimed here. But, as to Barrow's own position and influence, the result does seem to prove that he, rather than Robert Browne and John Robinson, deserves to be named emphatically the founder of English Congregationalism. Possibly such a judgment may be questioned; and whether it be sound or no the reader will decide for himself. Of one thing, however, I feel sure. No one will question the heroic quality of the man, his passionate devotion to an ideal end, his absolute single-heartedness. No one, moreover, will question that the worth of his example in these respects cannot be too strongly commended to his descendants of these later and laxer days.

When the lecture on the Amsterdam Church was due, Mr. Arber's "Story of the Pilgrim Fathers" had just come out. More than one paper of good standing praised it highly; and this, together with the writer's reputation for scholarly research, made me turn to it eagerly. I did not doubt his rather bold assertion that every item and statement in the book was of the nature of "solid rock"—"absolutely or morally certain": though it was rather startling to learn that the actual truth about the poor exiled Church was worse than one had imagined; that, under Francis Johnson and Ainsworth, Barrow's goodly company of saints had lapsed so swiftly into a mere "rebellious rout." Still more startling was it to behold Johnson himself "unmasked" as a "hypocrite," a "thoroughly bad man." It was, indeed, the feeling that perhaps Mr. Arber had unwittingly done injustice to Johnson which induced me to examine some of his references. What revealed itself was so surprising and disappointing as to shake at once my confidence in his trustworthiness. With a view, therefore, to getting at the facts I took pains to consult all the authorities which underlie his account of the exiled Church. The last chapter of the second part is the outcome.

Concerning the book as a whole, I will only venture to add that at least it is not "second-hand." Of course, much old ground has had to be traversed, and possibly there is little or nothing in it that is new. The "aftermath" could scarcely fail to be somewhat slight when reapers like Waddington, Dexter, Brown, and Mackennal have been in the field.

But even with regard to familiar facts and statements, it has been my aim to verify them wherever possible; while, in the case of Barrow himself and his contemporaries, I have striven to let nothing pass for which his own or their evidence could not be cited.

I had hoped to give a more definite place to John Greenwood, and had written a chapter on him, as well as another on his and Barrow's protagonist, George Gifford, of Maldon; but considerations of space ruled these out. The omission, however, is no real loss. For—if one knows the mind of Barrow, one may be said to know Greenwood's; and if one writes of Barrow one can hardly help including in the narrative the few transmitted details which pertain to his friend. As to Gifford, though he should be conspicuous—more so than he has been— in a history of the Puritans, the special significance of his relation to the Separatists may be easily gathered from the chapter on the "Reformists."

Most of the quotations from Barrow and others have been conformed to our present mode of spelling. There are those who make a great point of printing an old author exactly as he appeared at first; and sometimes this may be of importance, but not when the spelling is so arbitrary as it was 300 years ago. "For," as Dean Church remarks, "spelling in Hooker's (i.e., Barrow's) time, and for long afterwards, was not only anomalous, as ours also is, but anomalous with an apparent unconsciousness of the possibility of regularity. The spelling of the same word sometimes varies within two lines. The use of double letters, or the interchange of vowels and diphthongs in the same word, often seems a mere matter of haphazard."

I ought to say that I am indebted to my son, Mr. F. M. Powicke, B.A., of Balliol College, for the exhaustive index.

THE PARSONAGE,
    HATHERLOW, NEAR STOCKPORT.
        August, 1900.

CONTENTS.

	PAGES
INTRODUCTION	xiii—xlvii

PART I.

CHAPTER I.—Henry Barrow	1—82
NOTE I.—Was Barrow Marprelate?	82—5
NOTE II.—Comparison of Lists of Separatist Prisoners	85—7
CHAPTER II.—Barrow's Doctrine of the Church	91—127
NOTE I.—Barrow's Views as to the Ecclesiastical Powers of the Prince	128—9
NOTE II.—Barrow's Argument for the Destruction of Churches	129—131
CHAPTER III.—Barrow and the Reformists	135—157
CHAPTER IV.—The Bishops of Barrow's Day	161—181
CHAPTER V.—Archbishop Whitgift and his Ecclesiastical Polity...	185—197
CHAPTER VI.—Barrow and the Anabaptists	201—218

PART II.

CHAPTER I.—The Exiled Church	221—261
CHAPTER II.—The Question of the Eldership at Amsterdam and Leyden	265—284
CHAPTER III.—Professor Arber and the Amsterdam Church	287—325

APPENDICES.

No. I.—The Scholar of Oxford	329
No. II.—The Earliest Separatist Manifesto	330
No. III.—The Chronology of Barrow's Writings (and Greenwood's)	331—341
No. IV.—The Two Editions of "A True Description of the Visible Church"	342—347
No. V.—The Separatists' Seven Questions...	348—349
INDEX OF REFERENCES	351—353
GENERAL INDEX	355—368

μὴ εἰκῆ περι τῶν μεγίστων συμβαλώμεθα.

MOTTO OF HERACLEITUS.

INTRODUCTION.

I THINK it quite likely that anyone who may care to read this book will find himself wondering whether it was worth while to spend so much pains on such a subject. Certainly, the story is not, in itself, very attractive. We know too little of Barrow to make possible a full-length portrait of him; and what we do know, drawn as it is from the last few years of his life, presents him in connection with circumstances scarcely fitted to elicit the finer and sweeter elements of character. And as to the Amsterdam Church, when every effort has been made to do it justice, it still brings before us a somewhat sordid scene, nowise remarkable for loftiness of life, thought, or aim. Moreover, the things for which Barrow and his fellows contended and suffered may appear so trivial—not the central questions which concern the "spirit's true endowment," or its practical relations to life and godliness, nor yet the universal problems which ennoble the quest of philosophy, but the structure and government of a Church! No doubt Barrow evinced the courage of a martyr; but martyrdom, it may be said, becomes a vain self-sacrifice if it be not inspired by some adequate motive; and, seeing that he held the common faith of Christians in all other respects, was he right to "strive and cry" and throw away his life for the poor remainder? John Smyth said, as he neared the end of his brief and stormy career, "My desire is to end controversies among Christians rather than to make and maintain them— especially in matters of the outward Church and ceremonies; and it is the grief of my heart that I have so long cumbered myself and spent my time therein; and I profess that differences of judgment for matters of circumstance, as are all things of the outward Church, shall not cause me to refuse the brotherhood of any penitent and faithful Christian whatsoever." Not a few must read such words with keen sympathy. There are some, indeed, who realise so vividly the evils that have flowed from ecclesiastical controversy—its withering influence on the springs of true Christian love and service—that they are more than tempted to deplore the very existence of Churches; and to believe that the purpose of Christ for individuals and for the world would stand a better chance of fulfilment if every form of "organised Christianity" were dissolved. But experience soon steps in to correct any dream of that sort. The social instinct, which operates as imperiously among human souls as attraction among the molecules of a crystal, renders an isolated life impossible. Men whose hearts beat with devotion to the same object cannot long remain apart. One in spiritual sympathies, they crave, and cannot but seek, conscious fellowship; and then the steps taken to ensure and express such fellowship land them, almost before they know it, into an organised society. Hence it is, in fact, that stern protests against sectarianism have so often issued in the creation of more sects.

We shall reach a wiser result if we reflect that controversies about the Church have been a necessary outcome of historic conditions; and that there is, perhaps, within our reach "a conception of the Church which may be recognised as in harmony with its essential principle."

I. At the time of the Reformation the Church of Western Europe had held possession of the field for a thousand years. Its ideal was uniformity of doctrine and discipline under the absolute rule of Pope and bishop. On the whole its ideal had been achieved. But not entirely. Quite apart from heresies like that of the Albigenses, which might obviously deserve the name of Protestant, there was from early days a Protestant force within the Church itself. This force was Monasticism.

The common notion is that Monasticism embodied the inmost temper and tendency of the Romish Church; and it is true that the monastic orders were the usual champions of orthodoxy as well as unfailing supporters of the Papacy. But the fundamental motive of Monasticism is what we are concerned with—a motive which prevailed through all changes and corruptions. And its fundamental motive was man's unquenchable desire—a desire ignored or overridden by the priestly system of the Church—"to secure the knowledge and to cultivate the sense of immediate and personal relation to God in order to the attainment of salvation."[1]   Its keynote was individualism—the plea that "the individual man" is "greater than the institution," is "greater than any temple which man can build or wherein he may worship."[2]   Jerome, "the most distinguished and typical representative of early Monasticism," sounded the note when he refused to serve "under compulsion, beneath the shadow of Episcopal authority, men whom we do not choose to obey"; when he declared that as an unordained presbyter he was the equal of a bishop; that bishop and presbyter were originally the same; that bishops might be necessary to the wellbeing of a Church, but not to its existence; and that the function of prophecy or preaching of the Word was higher than the gift of administration.[3]   A similar note had been sounded, in a shriller key, by the Montanists.   "Montanism had been subdued, but it was not without a succession of its own. Novatianism, as it was called, was a schism of the third century which reasserted the fundamental principles of Montanism—its theory of discipline, its doctrine of the Church and of its relation to the world, its antagonism to the Episcopal régime. If the Novatian schism yielded under the vigorous policy of the Catholic Church, it was only to be followed by another movement known as Donatism, which set up in the towns and villages of North

[1] Allen's Christian Institutions, p. 155. (International Theological Library.)
[2] Ditto, p. 156.
[3] Ditto, pp. 139-141.

xvi   INTRODUCTION.

Africa a rival Church to the Catholic Church, resembling it in outward organisation, but with an inward motive which points to an antagonism to Catholicity, which neither argument nor persuasion, kindness, nor even the force of the State could overcome. The Montanist, the Novatian, the Donatist were all alike in this respect, that they did not believe that salvation depended on adherence to the Catholic Church, that Church out of which there was no salvation as Cyprian had maintained, and as Augustine at a later time asserted with equal emphasis. In this conviction Monasticism also shared, putting the conviction into practical form by fleeing to the desert or the cell, in order to cultivate the religious life, and attain reconciliation with God."[1] The point we wish to make is, that the impulse which gave birth and strength to Monasticism was essentially one with that which created the spiritual revolt of the sixteenth century. "In a most direct and vital way it . . . prepared for the Protestant Reformation as if it had been the end of all its labours." Wycliffe, fierce "malleus monachorum" as he was, foresaw and hailed the development. "I anticipate that some of the friars whom God shall be pleased to enlighten will return with all devotion to the original religion of Christ, will lay aside their unfaithfulness, and with the consent of Antichrist, offered or solicited, will freely return to primitive truth, and then build up the Church as Paul did before them."[2] In Martin Luther, himself a monk, the forecast came almost literally true.

In the sixteenth century individualism was the spirit of the age. Beneath its influence, the fettering frost of tradition was melting from the mind of Europe. Renaissance, newness of life, with a corresponding temper of freedom and adventure, was manifest on all sides. In literature and philosophy, in science and art, in the sphere of morals and politics, its animating breath was felt. It was felt also in the Church. At first, as one might expect, its effects were

[1] Allen's Christian Institutions, p. 142.   [2] Ditto, p. 173.

negative. It nerved men to criticise. It inspired doubts. It
dissolved one after another the old creeds. It encouraged every
man to believe what was right in his own eyes. But the individualism thus claimed and exercised was, for the most part,
lawless. Men did not relate it to its true ground. They did
not discern the principle which at once dignifies, develops and
restrains it. How Luther found his way to that principle is
well known. We know how, in studying the experience and
teaching of Paul, it broke upon him as light from heaven that
the tie between God and himself was immediate and intimate;
that the work of salvation was throughout a spiritual process,
based on God's unbought love to him and his own unforced
faith in God; that the need, therefore, for any external agency
was done away. So the Church dropped from its unique place
and lost its unique functions. The individual soul became its
own temple, its own altar, its own sacrifice, its own priest. It
ceased to be a slave regulated in its service of God by dictation
from without; and regained the status of a son, responsive to
an inward light, capable of a free obedience, responsible for
its doing or misdoing to God alone.

Here is the kernel of that great modern movement
which we are accustomed to date from Luther. It was a
recovery by the individual of his lost spiritual rights. Its
purpose and effect was to bring the soul face to face with
God. It meant for every man not merely the right but
the duty to know God for himself; to rest in His personal
love and lead; to shape life in harmony with His will. And,
obviously, such a right and duty, once realised, must stand
first. Every other claim, however ancient and august,
must be deemed inferior. Henceforth conscience was free.
As to the Church, for example, it was free to raise the general
question, whether Christ intended the construction of a
Church at all. It was free, and was bound, to ask what
He intended His Church to be. It was free to judge how
far any existing institution which called itself the Church

carried out Christ's thought.   It was free to consider if its
defects and corruptions were such as to make it right for
him to retain communion with it or not.   It was free,
finally, to dictate separation, if necessary.   The consequence
might be external divisions and even confusions.   But
if the principle of individual responsibility was sound the
price had to be paid.

Perhaps the gravest charge which can be laid against
the sons of the Reformation is that they have so generally
upheld the soundness of the principle in theory and denied
it in practice.   In this respect their fault is greater than
that of the Romish Church.   For the Romish Church has
never formally admitted the rights of individual conscience.   It
has been consistent.   Its seat of authority, the ultimate and
absolute criterion of all things to be done and believed, has
always been itself.   It has boldly assumed the place and power
of Christ on earth, has claimed to know and interpret His
whole mind, and so has been able to represent revolt against
itself as identical with revolt against Christ.   But the Protestant Churches have shrunk before the consequences of
consistency.   They have taught as a first principle that the
only infallible oracle is the living voice of God within the soul;
that attention to this voice and obedience to its deliverances is
the soul's most sacred privilege and obligation; and then, in
view of the conflicting opinions and practices which were sure
to follow from the fact that conscience exhibits different
degrees of enlightenment and loyalty in different men, they
have gone on to contradict their own lesson by demanding
and enforcing uniformity.   Luther, who broke away from
Rome in the strength of his own private conviction of right
which would suffer him to "do no other," could not endure
that men, following the same inward gleam, should break away
from himself, or from the Church which he persuaded the
State to establish and defend.   Calvin, having reformed
the Church after what seemed to his own interpreting

reason the true Scriptural pattern, straightway made submission to it compulsory where he had the power; and,
where his personal authority did not reach, made his
disciples no less eager than himself to employ the secular
arm in putting down Dissent. The framers of the English
Church, themselves schismatics from the rest of Christendom on grounds which they defended as intrinsically
reasonable, so involved their Church with the State that
refusal to obey its ordinances could be construed as a political
crime and the recusant be punished as a felon or traitor.
And even Barrow, clamant though he was for the inviolable
rights of his own conscience, could not quite see that the
liberty to render unreserved obedience to what he took to
be the will of Christ was a liberty which must be granted
to every man; that to require the Prince to "clear the
ground" of error and "compel" men to hear the truth,
however clear and certain the truth might be, was to call for
the infliction on others of the very wrongs under which he
himself was suffering.

Thus it is that the history of Protestantism has been
largely a history of intestine strife, flaming out often in
persecuting violence. We are told that such strife and
violence are a natural and inevitable product of the individual-
istic principle; that when you commit men to the guidance of
their own conscience the differences thence arising cannot but
lead to angry contention. But, in fact, the proper issue of
the principle is tolerance, not contention. For as soon as you
name conscience you name a tribunal where God and God
alone can be judge. To God and God alone can the individual
be answerable for the opinions at which he arrives, and for
the process through which he reaches them. How far he is
honest and sincere God alone can say. If he is honest and
you compel him to speak or act otherwise than he believes, you
bring him under the condemnation of Paul, that "Whatsoever
is not of faith is sin." If he is dishonest, to his own Master

he standeth or falleth. His difference from you may be due, as you plainly see, to his mistake; and you may fairly use the instruments of persuasion to bring him into your fuller light. But you are bound to respect the sanctity of his plea that as yet he "can do no other"; and so the selfsame appeal to conscience which is the ground of difference is the ground likewise of forbearance and charity.

It is, however, far easier to recognise the truth of a principle than to comprehend its scope. Ages may be needed to evolve in men generally the power to see, and the courage to apply, all its implications. And as regards the principle under consideration, the hindrances to courage and vision have been specially great. Chief among them, perhaps, has been the presumed necessity to confront the discredited authority of a Church with an authority equally visible and more obviously Divine. Hence the dogma of an infallible Book and the war-cry—"the Bible and the Bible only is the religion of Protestants." No doubt the results of the change, in some directions, have been good, and certainly have been effectual for controversy. But, in relation to the individual conscience, it has worked disastrously. Had Scripture and conscience been allowed to co-operate freely in mutual and sympathetic alliance; had Scripture been suffered to speak for itself and conscience to judge for itself, the former would have revealed its truth to the latter with continually-increasing clearness, and the latter would have been trained to discriminate with ever finer insight between the chaff and the wheat, between the relative and essential in the former. Then, too, the age-long antagonism between the natural and the revealed, between the claims of reason and the claims of faith, could scarcely have arisen. For who speaks of antagonism between light and the eye, or between music and the ear?

In particular, the Christian conscience would have come to see that the doctrine of the Church, though important, is a derivative of something more important still; that the

Church cannot be an end in itself, but is subordinate to a greater end; that, therefore, the merits of a Church must lie not in the degree of its conformity to all the details of a fancied "pattern given in the Mount," but in the measure of its adaptation to the purpose it was designed to serve. Thus the Church as a subject of contention for its own sake would have passed out of sight. But the dogma of an infallible Book, by expunging distinctions of great and small, made this—*inter alia*—impossible. Everything in Scripture, and therefore its references to the Church, must be on the same plane of importance! An exact "description of the visible Church" must be there; and being there must be discovered; and being discovered must be copied; and being copied by the few to whom its features have been unveiled must be substituted, if necessary by force, for less perfect models! Such an assumption could not fail to entangle the mind with vain scruples, as Barrow's case will show.

II. Thus it would appear that, in view of the historic conditions, controversy about the Church has been inevitable. And now it remains to give reasons for believing that Barrow witnessed for "a conception of the Church" which is in closer harmony than any other "with its essential principle." After what has been said, we shall not be suspected of holding a brief for Barrow. But we speak of the ideal which, more or less clear to his own mind, began to take shape in his practical directions, and has been winning its way to fuller expression ever since. And ideals are far from worthless. "Human life and conduct are affected by ideals in the same way that they are affected by the example of eminent men. Neither the one nor the other are immediately applicable to practice, but there is a virtue flowing from them which tends to raise individuals above the common routine of society or trade, and to elevate States above the mere interests of commerce or the necessities of self-defence."[1] So, too, the ideal of the Church as con-

[1] Jowett's Introduction to the "Republic," p. 229.

ceived by Barrow has not been found immediately applicable ;
it has encountered many strong impediments from the dull
" actual " ; but, at the same time, there has been a virtue flowing from it which has imparted to the majority of Congregational churches an elevated aim, has made them contributory
to the best life of city and State, has always quickened them to
newness of aspiration and endeavour when they have become
cold and dead.

What, then, was Barrow's ideal ? Substantially it was
the Apostle Paul's : "A glorious Church, not having spot
or wrinkle or any such thing " . . . a Church "built
upon the foundation of the apostles and prophets, Jesus
Christ Himself being the chief corner-stone : in whom each
several building fitly framed together groweth into a holy
temple in the Lord " ; a Church which is the " body of Christ,"
" fitly framed together through that which every joint sup-
plieth, according to the working in due measure of each several
part," and so making " increase of the body unto the building
of itself in love."   In a recent article it has been said that " he
who would know the mind of the ever-living glorified Redeemer,
our Lord and our King, our Priest and our Head, should use
all these terms " which are applied to the Church, such as the
Kingdom of God, the people of God, the vine of God, the flock
of God, the city of God, the house or temple of God, the household or family of God, the spouse and body of Christ ; and should
" endeavour to construct them into a harmonious and sym-
metrical whole.   There is in such a method much fruit for the
future use of Christ's Church."[1] This is really what
Barrow aimed to do. " Most joyful, excellent, and glorious
things are everywhere in the Scriptures spoken of this
Church. It is called the city, house, temple, and mountain
of the eternal God, the chosen generation, the holy nation,
the peculiar people, the vineyard, the garden enclosed, the

[1] Article on "The New Testament
Doctrine of the Church," by Chas. A.
Briggs, D.D., in *American Journal of
Theology*, January, 1900.

spring shut up, the sealed fountain, the orchard of pomegranates with sweet fruits, the heritage, the Kingdom of
Christ, yea, His sister, His love, His spouse, His queen,
and His body; the joy of the whole earth.''[1]   And it should be
noted that when he speaks of the Church he includes the
churches.   For he had learned from Paul that " the churches
are the local embodiments of the Church; the distribution of
the one into many is purely geographical.   The unity remains
unaffected.   There is no other Church of God.''[2]   Moreover,
this Church though ideal is not invisible—is not what is
known as " the Church mystical, the mystical body of Christ,"
which " cannot be distinguished or reckoned up or circum-
scribed by man.''[3]   He rightly held that the distinction
between visible and invisible has no New Testament support,
and did not emerge until the Church, having corrupted itself,
sought an excuse for its degraded state and for the continuance
of it.   What is the visible Church ? asks Hooker.   " Plain and
large," he answers: ' " All who own Christ as Lord and
embrace the faith He published, and have been baptized, are
members of His visible Church.   They may be impious,
idolatrous, heretical, wicked, excommunicate, and still, if they
have these three notes, if thus they are by external profession
Christians, they belong to the Church."   What then of
the New Testament description ?   So far as it is allowed
any present force, it must belong to the Church invisible,
is the answer. Not so, says Barrow. ' On the contrary.
It is an ideal toward which the true visible Church is
incited, by its very constitution, perpetually to advance.
It is, therefore, the condemnation of the Church as you
understand it that, by contentedly enfolding all sorts of the
unworthy, it surrenders the ideal and renders such advance
impossible.'

[1] A True Description of the Visible
Church. See Appendix iv.
[2] Article "Church" in Encyclopædia Biblica.

[3] Dean Paget's Introduction to the
Fifth Book of Hooker's " Ecclesiastical
Polity," p. 106.
[4] Ditto, p. 107.

We will note two central elements of Barrow's doctrine which make for the ideal.

i. It holds by what we have already indicated as a mainspring of the Reformation. In other words, it secures his indefeasible spiritual rights to the individual. Individualism has been called an entirely disintegrating principle. And so it is, if it be taken to stand for the tendency to separate from the fellowship of others on the ground simply of private opinion or taste or caprice. In this sense individualism is hostile not only to the Church, but to any society whatever. Those who enter into social relations must be prepared to accept some standard of opinion, action, or life in common. Anarchy is the alternative. But still a society becomes a tyranny if it seeks to cancel the individual as such; if it strips him of all personal worth; if it requires him to forget that he has a mind or soul of his own and to live for itself alone. Nay, the nearer such a society comes to success the nearer it comes to being an absolute curse. In the very process of annulling the individual it annuls its own power of doing any public good. In fact, the individual is prior and superior to the society. He does not exist for it, but it for him. In the family, for example, the means are social, the end is individual. It best achieves its purpose when authority and obedience are partners in service, when each member of the household lives for all, and all for each, so that their several personalities may be not only conserved, but developed and enriched. And the family is a type for other societies. It is a type, we may say, to which humanity itself will conform when the more mechanical bonds which unite men have done their work and been transcended.

Why should the Church be an exception? Certainly Christ did not depreciate the individual. Quite the contrary. He assumed and honoured in every man a power of reason and conscience. He aimed to elicit its spontaneous activity. He encouraged private judgment. He called for acts of faith which should be intelligent and free. He trained His disciples by methods and influences which were all calculated to disengage and educate latent capacities. He even based His summons to self-sacrifice on the fact that the self to be lost and won through sacrifice was of greater value than the whole world. "The Gospel everywhere individualises men as if one single human soul were valuable enough in the eye of God to account for Calvary, as if Christ would have died to save one solitary individual man."[1] And if at the very moment of revealing and exalting the individual He claims his undivided allegiance; if He liberates him from other masters only to lay upon him the yoke of His own authority, it is still in the name of truth, and because He is conscious of Himself as "the Light which lightens every man that cometh into the world."

We can be sure, then, that if He founded a Church He would not sacrifice the individual to the society. He would wish it to consist of free men—men drawn together by a common devotion to Himself, by a common purpose to learn and do His will, by a common enthusiasm for Christian service. He would wish the individual to be at one with the society in all things possible; to defer, as far as might be, to its control; to revere the legitimate claims of those whom it might choose for rulers and teachers; to cast his special gift of nature or grace into the treasury of its life. But He would also wish the society to remember that the individual must be treated as a being related directly to Himself, called to live and think and act in the light of his own conscience, accountable for the making of his own character and the working out of his own salvation. And this, we find, is what He actually did. He laid the first stone of His Church in the voluntary faith of one man. In virtue of a like faith He added to its foundation the other apostles. It was the same formative principle which, under their direction, governed the upbuilding of the earliest Christian communities. These all consisted of "living stones," free

[1] Allen's Christian Institutions, p. 157.

"slaves" of Christ, self-dedicated personalities—men whose union with the Church, whose respect for its ordinances, whose participation in its labours were acts which expressed a spontaneous submission to the one Lord. He alone was the Master. To Him alone they stood or fell. To win resemblance to Him was their aim. As the Church helped them to this and gave them scope for helping others to this, it was good. If it grew into an institution which hindered this, who can doubt that the first disciples would have pronounced it bad? In other words, individual perfection, promoted through the influence of mutual edification, was the Church's law.

Barrow, then, did but revert to the primitive type when he defines the Church as "a faithful people gathered by the Word unto Christ, and submitting themselves to Him in all things"; and goes on to say that "all the members have a like interest in His Word and in the faith. They altogether make one body unto Him. All the affairs of the Church belong to that body together. All the actions of the Church be the actions of them all jointly and of every one of them severally. . . . All the members are jointly bound unto edification and unto all other helps or service they may do unto the whole. All are charged to watch, exhort, admonish, stir up, reprove, &c., and hereunto have the power of our Lord Jesus, the keys of the kingdom of heaven, even the Word of the Most High."

And such a Church, we say, makes for the ideal. For what is contemplated is a community which shall really answer to the apostle's figure of a living body where head and hand and foot are alike honourable, alike necessary, alike subservient to the health and growth of the whole organism. Indeed, the result would be a community of the kind toward which all who understand man's nature and needs are directing thought and effort, with whatever phase of associated human endeavour they are concerned—a community combining the achievement of its own specific purpose with the production of a rich and varied individual life.

We are stating what the idea of Congregationalism demands—not, of course, what all its churches have attained. Probably few have done more than follow it afar off. But with full allowance for practical shortcoming, it might be easy to show that a chief glory of the Congregational Church has been its ability to develop full-grown men; men disciplined both to serve and rule; men quick to read the signs of the time; men made wise, by constant use of the spiritual sense, to discern what is the good and acceptable and perfect will of God. Obviously such men could not live to themselves. They have taken their place and fulfilled their calling in the circles of business, society, and the State, as well as in their own little brotherhood. What these departments of human activity have owed to them can seldom, perhaps, be traced. But their contribution to the streams of so-called secular life has never failed to reinforce its elements of integrity, energy, enterprise, and enlightenment. In a recent address Dr. Mackennal mentioned, as one illustration of this, the large proportion of men trained in Congregational churches who were found ready to take up the burden and discharge the duties of municipal life when, in the early decades of the present century, local self-government was so rapidly extended. As our churches become more alive and loyal to their ideal, it will be seen that the nation has reaped little more, in this respect, than the first-fruits of a noble harvest.

ii. Barrow's doctrine demands the spirituality of the Church. What makes the Church spiritual? One answer is given by the Sacerdotalists. They tell us that the notes of spirituality are two, priesthood and the Sacraments—a priesthood rightly ordained, and the Sacraments rightly administered. Here the organs of spiritual grace are a clerical order; its channels are narrowly defined; its recipients are mere laymen. Admit this, and the door is opened to all the evil with which the name priest has become associated.

We turn for an answer to Christ, and He tells us that the Church is spiritual in a real sense through the possession of His own Spirit ; and that His Spirit is a gift which all its members may—nay, must receive, if the privileges promised to the Church are to be enjoyed, or the duties expected from it are to be discharged. He is the Vine, they are the branches. Union between Him and them is a personal relation mediated, not by priest or Sacrament, but by a sustained exercise of faith. There is no corporate relation which supersedes the personal. It is the personal which precedes and conditions the corporate. The Church is dead, so far as its branches are dead. Their several measures of life blend to form its fulness.

We turn to the earliest Christian societies, and we note at once that of priest and Sacrament word there is none, but that apostle, elder, deacon, and the whole company of believers were of one heart and mind, were of a new heart and mind, because all alike had been endowed with the one spirit of love and truth.

We turn to Paul, and we find that for him all the members of a Church are called to be saints; that the Church as a whole is a sanctuary of God ; that to each one is given the manifestation of the Spirit to profit withal ; that he has all the " saints " in mind when he prays that the Father " would grant you, according to the riches of His glory, that ye may be strengthened with power through His Spirit in the inward man . . ." So we see that there is no room in the Church for a priestly caste, and that it was not presumption on Barrow's part, as Dr. Andrews thought, when he, a layman, claimed to have " the same Spirit with the apostles," though not in equal measure yet " in that measure that God hath imparted unto me " ; and that he was right to declare " the people of Christ are *all* enlightened. To them and every one of them God hath given His holy sanctifying Spirit to open unto them, and to lead them into, all the truth ; to them He hath given His Son to be their King, Priest, and Prophet, who hath made them unto Him kings and priests."

Moreover it should be emphasized that this demand for the true spirituality of the Church is not a minor point. Much depends upon it. In particular, the capacity of the Church to accomplish its true work depends upon it. For its true work is not, as the Sacerdotal theory would insist, to furnish a formal guarantee to trusting souls of spiritual safety here and hereafter. Its true work is twofold. It is, on the one hand, to perfect holiness in the sight of God within itself. It is, on the other, to be an agency for the salvation of the world. " By the Christian Church," says Arnold of Rugby, " I mean that provision for the communicating, maintaining, and enforcing of this knowledge (*i.e.*, the knowledge of God in Christ), by which it was to be made influential, not in individuals, but in masses of men. This provision consisted in the formation of a society, which by its constitution should be capable of acting both within itself and without, having, so to speak, a twofold movement, the one for its outward advance, the other for its inward life and purification; so that Christianity should be at once spread widely and preserved the while in its proper truth and vigour, till Christian knowledge should be not only communicated to the whole world, but be embraced also in its original purity, and bring forth its practical fruit."[1] Arnold wrote as the advocate of a comprehensive National Church, but his words might have come from a Congregationalist. And, indeed, he would have agreed to the inference which they suggest, that the efficiency of the Church for its twofold purpose must be in direct proportion to its real spirituality.

Cromwell wished to beat the King's troops. But at his " first going out " he saw that the Parliamentary forces " were beaten on every hand." He showed his friend John Hampden the reason. " Your troops," said he, " are most of them old decayed serving-men and tapsters, and such kind of fellows,

---

[1] Fragment on the " Church," p. 4.

and their troops are gentlemen's sons. Do you think that the spirits of such base and mean fellows will ever be able to encounter gentlemen that have honour and courage and resolution in them? You must have men of a spirit that will go on as far as gentlemen will go." Hampden thought it "a good notion, but an impracticable one." Cromwell said he thought he could do "somewhat," and before long he had "two thousand brave men, well disciplined. No man swears, but he pays his twelve pence; if he is drunk he is set in the stocks, or worse; the countries where they come leap for joy of them, and come in and join with them." Nor were they "ever beaten."

When we come to the passages in Barrow which burn with what may seem an excessive zeal for discipline, it will help us to do him justice if we remember that their inspiring motive was a sentiment very similar to Cromwell's. He beheld the Church beaten on every hand. He realised that it could never be otherwise, until the Church ceased to compromise with the enemy, and became whole-hearted. He therefore urged that the Church should be reformed on a new basis or model. The principle of selection should be a passionate devotion to the cause of Christ. Those who did not make conscience of this, who were not heart and soul with Christ, should be excluded or rejected. All care and watchfulness should be used to keep up the first enthusiasm, to keep the sacred fire ever burning, to increase faith and love and a good courage. To this end united prayer, mutual exhortation, preaching and teaching, the communion of the Lord's Supper, and every other "means of grace" commended by the Word, or approved by experience, should be faithfully employed. Everybody in connection with the Church should be bent on the supreme end of sustaining his own and the Church's spiritual vigour. And thus would the Church become an instrument in the Lord's hand, charged with irresistible force for the "casting down of strongholds," and the establishment of His kingdom throughout the earth.

We can afford to admit that this new model did not prove

a success in its first embodiments. Any one inclined to vote it "impracticable" might well deem his opinion confirmed by the story of the Church in London or Amsterdam. The failure was a natural consequence, partly of the strange conditions under which the venture was made, partly of the defective spiritual intelligence which rendered it so difficult for the Separatists to distinguish at first the great from the small, the weightier matters of the Gospel from its anise and cummin. It has been said that the American constitution outlines a not far from perfect political state, but that the American people have even yet scarcely found out the way to make the best of it; and that the first years of their national history were largely a record of mistakes and follies such as might seem to put it to an open shame. But a wise man does not say so. He considers rather that what is true abides unshaken by human error and folly—nay, that these may be even a stage through which clearer views of the truth are gained and a plainer path to it disclosed.

So the only question is whether Barrow's new model is the true model; and if what has been said as to the mission of the Church be admitted there can be but one answer. For as little might a church of unspiritual persons be expected to spiritualise the world as a diseased body to communicate health. What else did Jesus teach when He said to the new society at its birth, "Ye are the light of the world, ye are the salt of the earth"? What else but a pure church was the subject of His prayer, "I pray not that Thou shouldest take them out of the world, but that Thou shouldest keep them from the evil"? What else but a solemn warning against the persistent danger of moral decay was conveyed in the words, "Salt is good, but if the salt have lost its savour wherewith shall it be salted? It is thenceforth good for nothing but to be cast out and trodden under foot of men"? The truth, then, lay with Barrow; and the failure of his immediate followers, or the repeated failure of their descendants, can be no excuse for surrendering it.

Surrender is the worst of failures. No doubt it is a high, even a heroic endeavour, to which Congregationalists are dedicated. They are, one may dare to say, the Sir Galahad of the "Table Round," and the "Holy Grail" is far to seek. But what has to be laid to heart is that as soon as they unloose their grasp on the fact that spirituality belongs to the essence of a church and must at all cost be secured, their glory is departed, the main reason and justification of their existence are gone.

iii. There are two sure consequences of the two principles just stated. One is that Congregationalism, the truer it becomes to its ideal, must be increasingly on the side of intellectual progress; the other is, that it must nourish a spirit of tolerance.

(a) One of the names Christ gave to Himself was the Truth, and one of the promises He gave to Christians was that through Him a Spirit should come to them and be their guide into all the Truth. No doubt His primary reference was to the truth enshrined in His own Person, words and life; the truth about God and His saving purpose, and man's spiritual relations to Him; truth theological and ethical. And in this respect experience has confirmed the promise. The history of the Church is, on the whole, a history of developing power to understand and interpret the mind of the Master. "The old analogy of the tree of existence, Ygdrasil, which was daily watered by the Nornen from the fountain at its root, is a true figure of the progressive life of Christianity." Its fulness has never been reached at any one time. Age after age has had its great teachers, its favourite dogmas, its special points of view, and all have added something to the gradual advance; but if they have claimed finality the claim has been disowned by time. Whole systems of faith which aimed, and were taken, to be complete have been found too small for expanding knowledge, and have either ceased to be or have had to be transformed. And still the light is breaking in from all sides. "The progress of civilisation, the increase of secular knowledge, the influence of art and industry, the spreading of the people of the earth over its surface, the growth of political and social institutions," all are found to have some part to bear in the unfolding of Christian truth. They "give it forms of thought, modes of application," or they "expand its meaning." But the promise of a revealing Spirit cannot be confined to truth specifically Christian. It is a promise related to truth generally, however it may come to light, or whatever may be its character. The guidance which widens and clears the thoughts of men in their study of history and the physical universe, of human life and its conditions, of the ultimate realities that are the problem of philosophy, is always Divine. Science in every form, so far as it means real knowledge, depends for its progress on "the inspiration of the Almighty" which "giveth man understanding." His success in discovering the true origins of the earth, the actual constitution of the heavens, the law of gravitation, the fact and scope of evolution, is at bottom a process of revelation. It is the product of the reason in man, co-operating with the Eternal Reason, the Word, the λόγος, which is active alike in man and his world. Its claim, therefore, to be welcomed—at least, by Christians—is imperative. Contradiction between it and the mind of Christ can never be more than seeming.

It is well when there is nothing in the constitution of a church that need hinder the recognition of this fact. And, ideally, such is the case with a Congregational church. Given a church whose members are all free, and pledged, to consult the will of Christ; to study His mind; to keep an open door to the breath of His Spirit, and have you not here a church which offers no internal obstacle to the acceptance of truth? Nay, have you not here a church urged by the highest motives to seek and pursue it? Of course, it cannot be denied that many a church nominally Congregational has shown itself the home of stagnation and reaction.

c

Nor is the fact surprising when we bear in mind that if once the consciousness of its ideal be lost, it has no defence. It may then fall under the sway of its own narrowest prejudices. It may submit to be bound hand and foot by the clauses of a creed outworn. It may follow the dictation of the loudest voice or the strongest will. It may thus become "a little republic" permeated with the worst spirit of conservatism and intolerance.

There have been periods in the course of Congregational history when such a calamity, the result of such a loss, has seemed to overtake the churches generally. And other causes more creditable have worked sometimes in the same direction. Stagnation and reaction may be the issue, for example, of a great emotional experience like that of the Evangelical revival. Religion is spirit and life; it makes its most direct appeal to the conscience and heart; the appeal may be made in the name of a few simple doctrines which attest their practical efficacy by the turning of thousands to repentance and righteousness. Naturally, therefore, these doctrines come to be accounted as at once true in themselves and identical with the form through which they have done their work. Moreover, they may come to be accounted as "the sum of saving truth," and whatever lies outside them—the hundred and one questions which may be raised by speculation, criticism, or science—are eyed askance, are deprecated, are even labelled dangerous. Something like this was the feeling created by that mighty wave of spiritual enthusiasm which sprang from the preaching of Wesley and Whitefield. Succeeding as it did an age of theological free-thinking combined with spiritual coldness — an age when churches were "schools of philosophic discussion," and when the preacher was almost "constantly employed upon the out-works of religion, proving to people why they ought to believe, and showing them the legitimate way to arrive at faith, instead of producing the faith itself in their hearts by appeals to their inmost convictions and deepest sympathies,"[1] we cannot wonder that the moral of the Evangelical movement was taken to be that intellectualism in religion was a snare, that openness of mind was rationalism, that certitude on certain points and a glowing heart were all in all. So it came to pass that when the "glowing heart" had grown cold the "certain points" remained, with a strong prejudice in their favour as the test of orthodoxy.

The late Dr. Samuel Davidson stood in the wake of this reaction when he was called to pass through his ordeal (1857) at Lancashire College. A few years before (1852) he closed his lectures on "The Ecclesiastical Polity of the New Testament" with a chapter on the Congregational system, which is still one of its best apologies. Believing its principles, he says, "to be of heaven and founded on the constitution of man, we look on them as pregnant with the seeds of future success. As reason prevails and the world becomes wiser, they will assuredly be exalted in the estimation of thinking men. Every advance in the state of society, every step it takes in enlightenment, is conducive to their growth. In proportion as sound sense, freedom of thought, unfettered conscience, and the study of the Bible prevail, so do we expect the essential advancement of them among men." He does indeed note one lack—the lack of an educated ministry and so of an educated people. "The eye of learning has cast its beautiful, brightening glances but niggardly through the ranks of our ministry." "Our ministry" is deficient in men who have that "large, sound, roundabout sense" which can take a full view of questions connected with the high destinies of man, in lovers of truth wherever it is found, in rational assertors of liberty." But he does not think that this is a fatal objection to the system. It is only one of the many "oppressive influences" which warrant the statement that "the system has never had full room for its inherent strength to move in." His fiery trial, however, in-

[1] Tayler's "Retrospect of the Religious Life of England," p. 258 (2nd Edit. 1876)

duced a complete change of mind. He lost faith in the possibilities of a voluntary church. Eleven years later (1868) he writes, [1] "I believe theological learning cannot arise or be nurtured in any Church but one that is established. Voluntary Churches cannot take much part in the search for truth, or the honest declaration of it. The voice of the multitude will soon drown the voice of the teacher who adduces new views or new aspects of old ones, as long as he is dependent for daily sustenance on such as are more ignorant than himself. And as doubt is known to be dangerous, doubt of beliefs inherited or instilled by education, the temptation of falling into different beliefs, a temptation that might possibly prove too strong amid honest inquiry, is turned aside." Again, " I fear that voluntary religious associations, held together by a rope of sand and developing a narrow isolation, are not fit to cope with the great problems of theological science at the present time. They neither rear men of learning nor do they encourage them in their midst. . . . It is only within an establishment that a great work in defence of some doctrine commonly received in Christendom is produced. . . . In the ranks of Dissent learning is withered by neglect or starves. On the whole, the advantages are on the side of ecclesiastical endowment which does not necessarily involve bondage, or restrict individual freedom."

Some statements of fact here might be questioned and some granted. It might be questioned, for example, whether a voluntary Church " neither rears men of learning nor encourages them in its midst." It might be questioned, again, whether an established Church (at least, as we know it) "alone provides for learning and progress within its pale." On the other hand, it might be granted that " the voice of the multitude " is too often lifted against " new views or new aspects of old ones "; that fear of that voice too often deflects the preacher from honest

[1] Autobiography, p. 96.

inquiry or utterance; and that, therefore, the preacher may run grave risk of ceasing to be a student or thinker. But what we would insist upon is, that so far as a Congregational Church, or its leaders, or any association into which they may enter, set up mere "views," be they old or be they new, and call them orthodox, and refuse to test them or have them tested, and impose them on others, they are recreant to themselves and to Christ. For such an attitude implies at least want of faith in what is central to the Congregational idea—that Christ is the living spring of intellectual as of spiritual progress; that His hand it is which opens all doors and holds the lamp that illumines all rooms. Realise this, and there can be no fear of the question, "What is truth"? or reluctance to seek the answer with simplicity and seriousness. Least of all can there be any necessary reason for holding fast supposed facts which increased knowledge may have shown to be doubtful or fictitious. We can see, for instance, how the very idea of sacerdotalism demands the rejection by its adherents of the fact, now made abundantly clear, that the earliest records of the Church give no support to the theory that the power to dispense and transmit spiritual grace is the prerogative of a particular class of men. Theory and fact are here so vitally connected that destruction of the one entails total collapse of the other. Thus a certain clear result of historic research has become for the Sacerdotal Churches a matter of life or death. In like manner Rome's "pretension of infallibility compels it to adhere to its every dogmatic decision as a truth which no subsequent investigation can change." But a Church whose "idea" summons it first and last to follow the mind of Christ—a mind coincident with all truth—can have no need to fear facts of any kind. On the contrary, it can afford to look them all in the face; yea, is bound to give them all hospitable welcome.

Is there reason to think that we are now more fully awake

to this? Many would at once say "Yes." But some may be pardoned if they admit the suggestion of a doubt. It is certainly the case that during recent years there has been much intellectual advance—or, at least, much intellectual movement. No college committee now would wish to deprive a professor of his Church for expounding and employing the critical methods which, in Dr. Davidson's day, seemed so dangerous. Not a few of his conclusions are now deemed harmless or have even become current coin. Views which fifty years since were supposed to be sapping the foundations of faith are now exerting an unquestioned influence far and wide through pulpit, Bible-class, and press. Nor is Dr. John Hunter singular in his experience that at the present time "intelligent and thoughtful people are generally not slow in welcoming and supporting an honest and bold ministry; and that the most independent preaching of modern times is found, as a rule, in churches that depend on voluntary support." The signs, indeed, are manifold and manifest that the former frigid orthodoxy is fast breaking up in our churches under the action of a more liberal spirit. But perhaps just this phenomenon, while a reason for thankfulness on the whole, is what may occasion some concern. For the question arises, Whence has come this new freedom and boldness of theological thought? Has it to any great extent flowed from the contagion of fashion, or from intellectual shallowness, or from a decay of reverence? All these are possible causes of change, but they are not of a kind to guarantee genuine progress. Genuine progress takes place only when the cause of change is unalloyed love of truth, whether truth new or old; whether truth residing in a doctrine of the fathers, or first put forth in a theory of yesterday. New and old together, fulfilment not destruction, is the law of a true growth as it is the law of Christ. Unintelligent preference for the new as new is no less alien from His mind than blind attachment to the old. In fact, the spring of progress is neither with a stubborn adherent of the old nor with an easy favourer of the new. It is much rather with him whose convictions of truth, no matter to what they may cleave, are deep and sincere. For in his case it is the truth that is really loved, even though the present object of his devotion should turn out to be false. And where truth is loved the fuller inflow of light is only a matter of time.

We think of Barrow. He was, we admit, a dogmatist of the dogmatists. But who would deny, remembering what he suffered and sacrificed, that he had a passion for truth? With great pains he sought it, with a great price he bought it, and not for the whole world would he consent to sell it. He might, and did to some extent, mistake its sources and signs. He sought it where it could not be found and seemed to find it where it did not exist, but it was for him the one pearl of infinite value. "God knows," he cries, "at whose final judgment I look hourly to stand, that I hold not anything in these differences of any singularity or pride of spirit." His most ardent desire is to make sure "whether as men and simple souls we be deceived by any false light, or else as His dear children (for so we hope) honoured and trusted with the first view of, and faithful standing in a cause of holiness and righteousness." Such a temper—earnest, devout, single-eyed—will rise clear of all errors in the end.

May it not be said of Congregationalists that to such a temper they are specially called; is it not certain that its result would be that best of blessings, a disciplined reason and conscience, open to every approach of truth, and yet quick to distinguish the gleam that is Divine from the glamour that leads astray?

(b) Further, the Congregational idea, so far as realised, cannot but nourish the finest tolerance. There are two stages in the history of tolerance. The first is achieved when the pretensions of the State to control or check the doctrine or life of the Church have been abandoned. The second will be achieved as soon as there has disappeared within

the Church itself the last trace of a disposition to persecute
men for differences of opinion. Congregationalism has borne a
conspicuous part in bringing about the former. It ought to be
foremost in promoting the latter. For the basis of its unity is
not agreement in a system of opinions. We are one with
Barrow. But the ground on which we stand side by side with
him, and with those who have upheld the Congregational tradition from his day to our own, is in asserting the sufficiency of
personal devotion to Christ, as Prophet, Priest, and King, for
the maintenance of the Church, the unfolding of Christian
character, the development of faith. And this is more than a
mere opinion; it is a principle of life. A thousand defunct
trust-deeds tell us how imperfectly the principle has been
grasped; how ready the fathers have been to bind themselves
and their children within a meshwork of " sound words." And
we may not have learnt even yet how futile as well as inconsistent are such attempts to lay a dead hand on the vital
energies of growth. But there the principle is—the root and
centre of all—pleading for full recognition and waiting to be a
means of harmony with all Christian souls. For where we
differ from other Churches is not in presuming to claim a
monopoly of devotion to the common Lord, but in being content
to entrust everything to the power and guidance of that
devotion. At present other Churches cannot quite agree with
us in this respect. They hold their various systems of polity
and doctrine to be necessary or at least expedient. It may be
a long time before they think otherwise. And, meanwhile, we
would not, even if we could, do what Barrow desired—make a
clean sweep of such systems that our own simpler and (to us)
more spiritual system might take their place. We may believe
that the free and natural expression of the Christian life is
hindered by them, and by some of them is hindered greatly.
But it is not for us to censure or condemn. So far as visible
unity is possible, the Spirit of truth, working through experience, will sooner or later bring it to pass. What we must do

however, is to withdraw the emphasis from the outward to the inward; is to insist on the paramount importance of the spiritual relation which we all sustain to Christ compared with the things which divide.

To declare the fact of this relation, to indicate and welcome its signs, to foster whatever will tend to deepen the sense of it, to exalt it as the central and unchanging basis of communion—this is to make a home for true tolerance, and to do this belongs, in a special degree, to the calling of a Congregational church.

"The irresistible conviction is winning its way into all candid and tolerant minds, that the essential spirit of religion may exist under wide theological divergencies; and that, though good men may differ—and differ greatly—in doctrinal forms of belief, there is something deeper which unites them. The essence of religion is something more catholic than its creeds. The theological schools to which they belong were very far apart, but who can doubt that between the religion of St. Bernard and Thomas à Kempis and Savonarola and Fénelon and Pascal, on the one hand, and the religion of Cranmer and Latimer and Jeremy Taylor and Hooker and Leighton, on the other, there was a deep and essential harmony? In modern times could dogmatic differences be wider than those which separated Newman from Arnold, or the author of 'The Christian Year' from Frederick Robertson, or all of these from Chalmers and McCheyne; yet, can we hesitate to think that there is a something profounder than ecclesiastical and dogmatic differences in which, as religious, as Christian men, these good men were really at one? And could we say what that something is—call it spiritual life, godliness, holiness, self-abnegation, surrender of the soul to God, or, better still, love and loyalty to Christ as the one only Redeemer and Lord of the spirit—could we, I say, pierce deeper than the notions of the understanding to that strange, sweet, all-subduing temper and habit of spirit, that climate and atmosphere of heaven in a human breast, would not the essence of religion be in that, and not in the superficial distinctions which kept these men apart?"[1]

iv. It is plain that in proportion to the clearness with which the essence of Congregationalism is discerned the easier will it be to mark off from it the accidental and allow free play to the latter.

Brethren among one another; prophets, priests, and kings toward God; called to worship Him "with open face," to experience the inspirations of His free Spirit, to exercise self-rule in His fear and love—here is the pith of the matter; and whatever threatens to destroy this must be accounted evil.

Any encroachment, for example, of a sacerdotal or masterful spirit demands instant and incessant resistance. It may be expedient that as a rule public worship should be conducted and the sacraments administered by one who has been ordained; but if the custom should lead to a feeling on the part of people or pastor that there is a validity in the spiritual acts of an ordained person which is absent from those by a "layman," then the oftener a "layman" is invited to officiate the better. Indeed, of all Churches the Congregational might be expected to give freest scope to lay agency; and if it be true that to a great extent the fact is otherwise, it is one of the signs which betray the existence still of a lurking priestly leaven.

Expediency, then, cannot be made an excuse for customs or changes which limit or lessen the spiritual rights of the people. On the other hand, expediency may be justly pleaded in behalf of whatever custom or change is fitted to preserve and expand those rights, or to make the worship of the Church more edifying, or to render its agencies more effective for realising the will of Christ in relation to the exigencies of time and place.

[1] See Caird's University Sermons, pp. 20-23.

"True catholicity," we are told, "is that Divine quality in the Christian Church which enables it, and indeed forces it, to adapt itself to the changes of time and environment in order the better to fulfil its mission."

In this sense of catholicity a Congregational church can, if it will, take the lead. Of course, if we were obliged to admit with Barrow that the New Testament has prescribed to the Church a particular copy of what it should be and do for all time and under all circumstances, adaptation would be very difficult. But Barrow was deceived. Christ laid down principles, not rules. The Church as much as the individual is left to deduce the latter from the former, face to face with the pressures of actual need. "Some lay great stress on extemporaneous prayer as though it were a part of Congregationalism, declaiming against liturgies and all prescribed forms as unscriptural or prelatic. But should a particular church think it right to adopt occasionally written forms of prayer, judging them most conducive to devotional feeling, nothing in the system is opposed to that arrangement. The worshippers may agree to do so or they may not, according to their ideas or experience of subserviency to edification—since the Scriptures determine nothing absolutely on the point."[1] So with regard to externals generally. These are very seldom "a part of Congregationalism." Sentiment, more or less intelligent, may have attached itself to them, and suggestions of change may cause a shock; but, if a church should resolve to modify, or even, perhaps, remove them, it may safely do so, as a rule, without infringing any vital principle; and conceivably might often do so with an appreciable gain to its spiritual life and service. Even the institution of pastor and deacons, though sanctioned by long usage as an almost exhaustive "formula" for the ministry, is not "a part of Congregationalism." There is no reason, outside the domain of expediency, why a church should not decide to revive the order of prophets,

---

[1] Davidson's Ecclesiastical Polity of the New Testament, p. 314.

as understood by Barrow; or to add other officials to the traditional two, such as the deaconess, the teacher, or, in some form, the diocesan bishop.

Still less reason is there, from the point of view of principle, why a church should guard its independency to the extent of lapsing into what has been called " an over-driven individualism." Some time ago a correspondent of *The British Weekly* declared that " Independency is a principle of weakness and division, and is contrary to our true relation of dependence on God and on one another." "All our efforts to improve our organisation as Congregationalists have been wrecked on the sandbank of independency." "Let us, then, modify the principle of independency, whilst we maintain the democratic and Christian principle of church government by members." There is wisdom in these words. Independency in the sense of isolation *is* a principle of weakness. A church is certainly right to guard its own liberty so far as to refuse external dictation and control. But a church starves its best life when it practically builds a wall around itself, and shuts out the free winds of the Spirit which blow across the wide spaces of social life. Churches maintain their vigour, widen their outlook, develop their resources through mutual intercourse, consultation, co-operation for common ends. They are free communities, and may, if they like, manifest their freedom by declining to enter into fellowship or to contribute their units of force to the current of organised effort. But they are also free to do the reverse. There is a limit to the complexity of organisation to which they may consent, and it is reached when the tendency to organise begins to be tyrannous. It is a mistake, however, to suppose that organised independency is a contradiction. As a society of free and responsible personalities is the highest, so is an organisation of free and responsible societies. And the promise holds good for churches as for individuals : " Give, and it shall be given unto you ; good measure, pressed down, and shaken together, and running over, shall men give into your bosom. For with the same measure that ye mete withal it shall be measured to you again."

v. Barrow was a pioneer, and, as pioneers are apt to do, he sometimes lost his way. But his feet took the right direction. He made no false "discovery" when he set forth the true nature of Christ's "visible Church." Then and now and for ever it must be so, that a society which, by its very idea, exists for the learning and doing of His will, the embodiment of His life, the furtherance of His kingdom, was meant to consist of spiritual persons, persons who have "sanctified Him in their hearts as Lord." Barrow both saw this distinctly and, what is more, had the heroic temper which made him obedient to his vision. It may be that we lack his heroic temper even if we have not lost his vision. It may be, in other words, that we confess the truth and beauty of his idea, but are disposed to admit that it is all "too high and good for human nature's daily food." It may be, therefore, that we are content to let go his enthusiasm for a pure Church; his jealous care to begin, continue, and end its worship and service, its schemes and tasks, by sole reference to the holy will of Christ. It may be that we are becoming reconciled to the "practical" conditions of success which demand that members of the Church need not be members of Christ; that the "narrow" distinction between members and seat-holders shall be erased; that the latter equally with the former shall decide what old-fashioned notions have hitherto reserved for the spiritual judgment of the church-meeting alone; and that in general the cash-nexus shall be substituted for a communion of saints. It may be that, in some such way as this, the Christocracy of our churches is in danger of passing into a democracy whose votes are guided by taste, or passion, or caprice. But if so, then the issue will surely be that they will remain churches only in name. They may continue to serve a useful purpose as benevolent or social agencies, but they will have degenerated really into clubs with nothing more distinctive than the habit of keeping a flag waving which, in spirit and truth, they have disowned.

No; the call is for a heroic temper. Our churches are summoned to great tasks. One of these is to lead the way in effecting a severance of the legal chains which bind a particular Church to the State. We are to do this on the high ground, and on no other, that the intrusion of political power into the sphere of spiritual life is a fruitful source of corruption to the latter. But with what face can we address ourselves to so lofty an argument if, while urging the claims of spiritual religion in one direction, we are ceasing from the effort to maintain them within our own borders ? Can we, in such a case, escape the rebuke : "Thou hypocrite, first cast out the beam out of thine own eye; and then shalt thou see clearly to cast out the mote out of thy brother's eye." Another task presented to us is that of working toward a time when sectarianism, masking under the name of Christianity, shall no longer be favoured by the State in its treatment of elementary and other day schools. But how can we dare to advocate a scheme of universal secular education if at the same time we are failing to conserve and increase the spiritual energy which more than ever will be needed when the children have to depend for their spiritual training almost exclusively on the Churches ?

No doubt the heroic temper is hard to win or to keep. It means a readiness on the part of a church, from the pastor downwards, to forego not a few superficial attractions; it means concentration on the simplicities of faith and worship; it means severe self-discipline; it means patient endeavour to create enthusiasm for a spiritual ideal in all its members, particularly in the young ; it means firm emphasis on Christian character as the requisite for Christian service ; it may mean, consequently, a sacrifice of outward expansion for the sake of inward enrichment.

But great would be the recompense of the reward. Possessed of such a temper, our churches would suffer no check to the reality, though they might to the apparent rate, of their progress.

They would win in power more than they lost in popularity. They would be athrill with a Divine life, and all around would feel its magnetism. They would be, collectively, as Barrow dreamt they might be: " A heavenly army of the saints—marshalled here on earth . . . under the conduct of their glorious Emperor Christ, that Victorious Michael . . . peaceable in itself as Jerusalem, terrible to the enemy as an army with banners, triumphing over their tyranny with patience, (over) their cruelty with meekness, and over death itself with dying."

PART I.

HENRY BARROW.

What shall we say? There hath seldom any truth come to light
but it hath cost some blood; and that should teach men to love it
the better.   MILES MICKLEBOUND (1611).

Eine Jede Idee tritt als ein fremder Gast in Die Erscheinung,
und wie sie sich zu realisiren beginnt, ist sie kaum von Phantasie
und Phantasterei zu unterscheiden.

GOETHE, SPRÜCHE IN PROSA, 566.

HENRY BARROW.

HENRY BARROW[1] was a native of Shipdam, Norfolk,[2] and was born about the year 1550. His mother, Mary Bures, was daughter and co-heiress of Henry Bures, of Acton, Suffolk. His father's name was Thomas, and Henry was the third son. It has been conjectured that Judith Bures, who became the wife of Aylmer, Bishop of London, was a sister of Barrow's mother, and that so Aylmer was his uncle. This may have been so, and I have found nothing to contradict it. But it is at least strange that no mention of such a relationship occurs in notices of the family. We hear[3] of a sister, Anne Bures, who married Edmund Butts, third son of Sir William Butts (of Barrow), chief physician of King Henry VIII. Nothing, however, is said of the (socially) more important fact that there was another sister, Judith, who married a famous bishop. But if we cannot be quite certain about his relation to Aylmer, there is no doubt that he was related, in a degree, to Lord Bacon. For his cousin Agnes,[4] daughter of Anne Bures and Edmund Butts, was wife of Sir Nicholas Bacon, of Redgrave, eldest son of the Lord Keeper of the Great Seal, and brother of the great Francis. He was thus, in a very remote degree, related even to Lord Burghley, whose wife, Mildred, was a sister of Anne Cooke (daughter of Sir Anthony Cooke), wife of the Lord Keeper. Lord Bacon, then, may be supposed to have spoken from personal knowledge when he once described

[1] Often spelt Barrowe—and so by himself, sometimes, but usually Barrow.

[2] Near Thetford; a village now of 1,471 inhabitants. There is another Shipdam in Somerset.

[3] History and Antiquities of Suffolk. By John Gage, p. 26.

[4] Ditto.

Barrow as " a gentleman of a good house." He was connected, indeed, by birth " with many noble and eminent families."[1] And having said this we have said all there is to say. Barrow himself never refers to his kindred, except once to his father. There is no reference to him in the county histories, though there are references enough to the Barrows. There is no trace of him in any local register or tradition. The " family " would hardly care to keep his memory green as a gibbeted " separatist," and other motives for doing so did not exist. Details, therefore, of the kind that usually survive to throw light on the early life of famous men are entirely lacking. We can ascertain nothing of the years he spent as child and boy in his father's house. We know that he was one of a large household,[2] and we may imagine that its daily character corresponded to that of any other country gentleman's household of the period. But we get no answer when we ask what he was in appearance, what schooling he received, what influence his parents—especially his mother—had upon him, how he fared among his brothers and sisters. The book of his history is a blank till we turn the page at the year 1566 and find him at Cambridge. Here he matriculated at Clare Hall as a fellow commoner on November 22[3] ; and here he graduated B.A. in 1569-70. The four years between are again a blank. Of his conduct as man and student we can only guess. But Lord Bacon's allusion to his " vain and libertine youth " suggests a

---

[1] Strype's words (Aylmer's Life, p. 174), said in connection with Judith Bures, wife of Aylmer. Strype mentions Joan, a daughter of *Robert* Bures, who married (1) Thomas King, (2) Sir John Buck; " From which match or matches sprang many noble and eminent families of the Mordaunts, Barrows, Bacons, Bucks, &c." There was also a *Henry* Bures, who married Anne, daughter of Sir George Waldegrave, of Smalbridge. Judith may have been a daughter of this Robert or Henry. Barrow's coat-of-arms was

" S, two swords in Saltare A, hilted O, a bordure gobony, A and G."

[2] The children were—" (1) Thomas, (2) William, (3) Henry, (4) Edward, (5) John, (6) Ann, (7) Bridget, (8) Elizabeth."—Harleian MSS., 5,189, p. 31.

[3] Quidam Henricus Barrowe aulae clar conv; admissus est in Matriculam Acad., Cant., Nov. 22-23, An. 1566. Alter Hen. Barrowe Coll. C.C. (Corpus Christi) Conv. 2, admiss. in Matric. Acad., Cant , Mar. 15, 18, An. 1577.— Harleian MSS., 7,042, 57 (34).

strong suspicion of misspent days which is confirmed by
Barrow's own words. His tone in speaking of the Universities
has a personal ring in it, and is always hostile or scornful. He
ridicules the notion that such places could possibly produce
good ministers, whether you take good to mean rightly
instructed or truly religious. You see, he exclaims, what kind
of men are actually in possession of Church offices, and "if the
tree be knowen by the fruit," then "let the religion and
priestes of the land show what kind of seminaries and colledges
these Universities are." His own experience, indeed, had
revealed them to him as "a miscellaneous rout of very young
men, for the most part, and boys together, leading their lives
in vanity, folly, idleness; living neither in the fear of God nor
in any well-established order of the Church, neither in any lawful calling in the commonwealth."[1] They are "the seminaries
of Anti-Christ, the bane of the Church, the corruption of all
youth in the land."[2] There is exaggeration here, no doubt, as
there is in Travers's even stronger description of the different
colleges of Cambridge as "the haunts of drones, the abodes of
sloth and luxury, monasteries whose inmates yawn and snore
rather than colleges of students; trees not merely sterile but
diffusing a deadly miasma all around."[3] The case was not so
bad as this. Against so "gloomy" and "morose" a picture
one needs to weigh a contrasted statement like that of Richard
Cox, Bishop of Ely,[4] that there is an "abundant crop of pious
young men" in the two Universities; and of Whitgift that
"Cambridge alone had turned out fully 450 competent
preachers since the beginning of Elizabeth's reign."[5] But the
case was bad enough. When, e.g., Dr. Caius—founder of the
college which bears his name—visited Cambridge in 1558, he

[1] Discovery of the False Church, p. 175-6.
[2] Plain Refutation of Mr. Gifford, p. 124.
[3] 1574, quoted by Mullinger in History of Cambridge, p. 263.
[4] In letter to Mullinger (1568), quoted by the latter's namesake as above.
[5] In letter to Archbishop Parker a few months before the latter's death, 1574.

deplored the disappearance of "the poor, modest, diligent
student of former times, with narrow means but lofty aims,
rising before dawn to commence his studies, living on scanty
fare, reverently doffing his cap in the streets and courts to the
grey seniors, among whom he found his best friend and counsellor." The undergraduates no longer "spent their pocket-
money on books"; their minds were no longer given to study.
Money and mind alike were "devoted to dress and the adorn-
ment of their chambers. They wandered about the town,
frequenting taverns and wine-shops; their nether garments
were of gaudy colours; they gambled and ran into debt."[1]
And Clare Hall is noted as a specially troublesome haunt of
misrule. It was one of the three colleges which "took up
most time" when in 1549 governmental commissioners made a
visit of enquiry, and issued statutes forbidding students to
frequent "fencing-schools" and "dicing-taverns," to "wander
about the town," or to play cards except at Christmas.[2] We
get a glimpse at what was popular in the colleges in the following. The students wished to hold up a mirror to the magnates
of the town in which they might see their weaknesses duly
featured. So they were induced, under some flattering pre-
text, to attend the performance of a "merry (but abusive)"
comedy called "Club Law." The performance took place in
Clare Hall, and the students made a ring around the mayor,
his brethren, and their wives, riveting them in whilst "some
town privacies" were being "lively personated" before them.[3]
Yet Clare Hall is described as "that ancient and religious
house." Its fellows were all theologians. It was founded
expressly for the study of God's Word. And a scheme, by
which it and Trinity were to be dissolved in order to form a
college for the study of civil law, met with indignant and
effectual resistance, particularly on the part of Bishop Ridley,
the martyr, because it was "a very sore thing" and "a great

[1] Quoted by Mullinger, pp. 94-96.   [2] Mullinger, p. 430.
[3] Mullinger, p. 118.

scandal" to divert a college from the study of God's to the study of man's laws![1]

Barrow, then, may have had no reason to think of Cambridge gratefully.[2] He may well have contracted there those tastes and habits, which earned for him the reputation of being "licentious and a gamester" in London. Was it in London that he spent the six years between his leaving Cambridge and his entering at Gray's Inn? We should like to know, but we can only suppose it likely. He seems never to have been without money; his temper and tendencies would naturally incline him to the freedom and gaiety of city life; and the fact of there being about the Queen one or more whom he might consider friends or kinsmen would open his way to a footing at Court. Anyhow, he did "follow the Court," and got no good. No good was to be got at Elizabeth's Court, so far as character was concerned. The Queen herself, however serious in her state-craft, was given over to vanity in social life. Her favours were the guerdon, not of merit, but of flattery; or, of a "fine personal appearance and elegant manners." Christopher Hatton, *e.g.*, a young student of the Inns of Court, attracted the Queen's attention by his elegant dancing at a masque. He left the study of law, and became a courtier. In due time he was rewarded by no less an office than that of Lord Chancellor.[3] Such examples of capricious advancement were food for the hopes of many a brilliant youth. Perhaps Barrow was one of them—neglecting study, pursuing pleasure, dreaming of some happy time which should lift him to honour. Perhaps, too, the bitterness of disappointment which Spenser describes was his :—

> To feed on hope, to pine with feare and sorrow,
> To fret thy soul with crosses and with cares,
> To eate thy heart through comfortlesse despaires :
> To fawne, to crouche, to waite, to ride, to roune,
> To spend, to give, to want, to be undonne.

[1] Mullinger, pp. 134-6.
[2] Robert Browne also speaks of that "woful state of Cambridge whereunto those wicked prelates and Doctors of Divinity have brought it." — Mullinger, p. 300.
[3] Macaulay's Essay on Lord Burleigh.

Barrow could do nothing by halves. His passions were strong, and equally strong was the will which directed them. When he turned to the right way he trod it with impetuous haste. So long as he gave himself to the wrong he gave himself altogether. But, in such cases, the pleasures of sin are apt to be short-lived. The more eagerly they are devoured the sooner they begin to turn into "apples of Sodom." Disgust and weariness lay hold on the heart—driving it, at first, to worse excesses ; but leading at length to deeper reactions of secret shame and remorse. Thus the "way of the Lord" is prepared; and His Spirit, working through some seemingly accidental circumstance, may win an easy victory. Is not this the right point of view from which to read the story of Barrow's conversion ? "Walking in London one Lord's day with one of his companions, he heard a preacher very loud as they passed by the church. Upon which Mr. Barrowe said unto his consort, 'Let us go in and hear what this man saith that is thus earnest.' 'Tush,' saith the other, 'What! shall we go to hear a man talk?' But in he went, and sat down. And the minister was vehement in reproving sin, and sharply applied the judgments of God against the same, and it should seem, touched him to the quick in such things as he was guilty of, so as God set it home to his soul, and began to work for his repentance and conviction thereby, for he was so stricken as he could not be quiet, until, by conference with godly men, and further hearing of the Word, with diligent reading and meditation, God brought peace to his soul and conscience, after much humiliation of heart and reformation of life. So he left the Court and retired himself to a private life, sometime in the country and sometime in the city, giving himself to study and reading of the Scriptures and other good works very diligently ; and being missed at Court by his consorts and acquaintances, it was quickly hinted abroad that Barrow was turned Puritan."[1] Friends and acquaintances were astonished at the sudden change. "He made a leap from

---

[1] Young's Chronicles, p. 484.

a vain and libertine youth to a preciseness in the highest degree, the strangeness of which alteration made him very much spoken of."[1]

No man had seemed farther from virtue than he, or less likely to turn Puritan. So Paul had seemed the last man likely to turn Christian. But if the Balm of Gilead be offered to a conscience already sore wounded by kicking against the pricks, little wonder if it yield itself gladly to be healed.

In his first examination before Whitgift, when Barrow complained that his arrest by the Keeper of the Fleet had been " without warrant by the law of the land," the Archbishop asked him scornfully, Know you the law of the land ?

B. Very little ; yet was I of Gray's Inn some years.[2]

If we may assume, as almost certainly we may, that Barrow withdrew from Gray's Inn at the same time that he withdrew from his London life generally ; and if the expression " some years " may be taken to cover three or four years at least, then 1580 or 1581 would be the date of his conversion.

In the same examination Whitgift asks : Of what occupation are you ?

Barrow : A Christian.

Archbishop : So are we all.

B. I deny that.

A. But are you a minister ?

B. No.

A. A schoolmaster ?

B. No.

A. What, then, of no trade of life ?

Barrow refers him to a description of himself in some letter of his which Whitgift had seen.

A. You are then a gentleman ?

B. After the manner of our country, a gentleman.

---

[1] Bacon's Observations on a Libel.
[2] He became a member of Gray's Inn in 1576; he was never called to the Bar.—Harleian MSS., 6,848.

A. Serve you any man ?

B. No; I am God's free-man.

A. Have you lands ?

B. No, nor fees.

A. How live you ?

B. By God's goodness and my friends.

A. Have you a father alive ?

B. Yea.

A. Where dwelleth he, in Norfolk ?

B. Yea.

A. Where dwell you ?   In London ?

B. No.

Whence it may be gathered that Barrow, after his conversion, ceased to live permanently in London, although he might return now and then on a visit; that his means of living were derived mainly from his friends, *i.e.*, his kindred (particularly his father), and that these, therefore, had so far not disowned him. We may think of him as retiring to the old home at Shipdam, there to work out quietly the new thoughts and purposes which so great a spiritual change involved. Did he work his own way to Separatism ? Possibly. But, on the other hand, we remember that he was now within reach of John Greenwood. Greenwood's University course at Corpus Christi College, Cambridge, had come later than Barrow's at Clare Hall by more than ten years.[1] He had then been ordained both deacon and priest,[2] and had held a benefice. But he was now a Puritan Chaplain,[3] and fast drifting into Separatism. What influences had been acting upon him ? We cannot be sure; but the circumstances of his Cambridge life

[1] Sizar, March 18, 1577–8; B.A., 1581.

[2] "I was first made a deacon by London (Aylmer); after (was) made full priest by the Bishop of Lincoln." —Conference with Cooper.

[3] To Lord Rich, at Rochford Hall, Essex. "Aylmer had a long and troublesome business with a certain nobleman, Lord Rich, who, about the years 1580 and 1581, had exercises of religion after their way (the Puritans) in his house in Essex, one Wright being the preacher"(Strype's Life of Aylmer, p. 83). Greenwood is said to have been employed by Robert Wright.

strongly suggest first, the followers of Cartwright; next, Robert Browne. During Barrow's period of residence, the Puritan movement was in its infancy—concerned mainly about clerical attire or the "Vestiarian Controversy." Even then, Cambridge was one of its strongholds—witness the scandal of 1565 in St. John's College, when "the students came to chapel on a festival day without their hoods and surplices, to the number of three hundred, and continued to do so for some time"[1]; witness, too, the petition of the same year against Archbishop Parker's injunctions—signed, among other Heads of Houses, by John Whitgift.[2] But after 1570—with Cartwright's repudiation of Episcopacy in his Lectures as Margaret Professor of Divinity; with the uproar occasioned by these; with the first and second Admonitions to Parliament, wherein the whole existing Church-order was condemned; with Cartwright's defence of the same against Whitgift; with his translation of Travers's "full and plain declaration of ecclesiastical discipline," and its rapid circulation among the students—Cambridge might truly be deemed the mainspring of Puritan activity. And this it continued to be. Numerically, we are assured, the Puritans were never in a majority; but what they lacked in numbers was made up in talent, character, and earnestness. As Cartwright, Travers, Dering, Aldrich, left the scene, their place was filled by others who avowed their doctrines with equal boldness.[3] Emmanuel College arose, "notoriously designed as a school of Puritan teaching." The commonplaces of Musculus—an armoury for the Puritans—supplanted the "Sentences" as theological text-book. "Calvin and Beza were cited as of authority, inferior only to that of Scripture itself, while the names of Ambrose, Jerome, Augustine, often served but to raise a half-contemptuous smile."[4]

[1] Neal, Vol. I., 196.
[2] Strype's Whitgift, p. 9.
[3] Mullinger's Cambridge, pp. 298-300.
[4] Bancroft's Survey of the Holy Discipline, p. 64.

Such was the atmosphere breathed by Greenwood in his undergraduate days. And, if we may suppose that the divers misdemeanours in manners and doctrines in his own college (Corpus Christi) of which Archbishop Parker complained to Burghley in 1565 were also significant of the Puritan spirit; and that "the suspected books" for which he enjoined strict search to be made there were of a Puritan character, then it is clear that Greenwood's daily life was spent in a centre of Puritan influence. But further: no doubt we are bound to believe Greenwood and Barrow when they assert, emphatically and frequently: "We never had anything to do with Browne." And, as regards Barrow, there is no reason to think that Browne ever crossed his path. Browne, indeed, was in London[1] while Barrow was. He was living, however, in quite a different place and sphere.[2] And it would be near the time of his leaving for Middelburg when Barrow reappeared in his native county. But in the case of Greenwood some personal knowledge of Browne can scarcely have been avoided. Of course, he did not meet him at Corpus Christi, where Browne finished his course (1570-72) four years before Greenwood's began. But between 1578 and 1580 Browne was again in Cambridge, and making a stir there. He held a "cure" in the town (probably St. Benet's); here, and in the villages round, he preached for months. As a rousing preacher of strange doctrines he became famous. He attracted still more attention by the eccentricity of his conduct—e.g., by sending back the money his people (at St. Benet's) wished to give him for his support, on the ground that they were not as yet so rightly grounded in Church government as they should be; by refusing and flouting the bishop's licence to preach, and continuing to preach without it "wherever he had opportunity," until publicly inhibited. Greenwood, therefore, must have

---

[1] He was there between 1572 and 1578, when he returned home by order of his father.

[2] At Islington, as schoolmaster and "open-air' recusant preacher.

heard of him. Nay, it is hard to believe that he did not make
an effort to hear him, and learn for himself the drift of his
teaching—if, at least, the desire to know the truth about the
burning question of Church government had already come to
life in him; or even if he had an average share of curiosity.
The first impression may have been repellent; and repulsion to
the teacher may never have been overcome. But sometimes
the mind receives seed unconsciously; lets it grow more or less
insensibly; and only fully awakes to its presence when it has
taken complete possession. Even so, seeds let fall by Browne—
especially his central doctrine that the kingdom of God was not
to be begun by "whole parishes, but rather by the worthiest,
were they never so few"—may have worked in the mind of
Greenwood, prepared as it was by Puritan influence to give
it room. Doubts and questions may have been set going which
determined resistance could not silence; which circumstances—
perhaps actual experience of ministerial work, above all—made
more and more importunate. They drove him from his cure.
They would not let him rest in the half-way house of a private
chaplaincy. They beckoned him outside the gate—outside the
Established Church for good and all; and, with whatever slow-
yielding reluctance, he felt compelled to follow. In review the
whole process might seem to him Divine. The grace of God,
he would say, gave him "repentance of his sin in submitting to
episcopal ordination and led him to degrade himself from the
'false' ministry." But the grace of God is apt to work
through means, and what other means were available than the
teachings of Browne it is not easy to perceive. Certainly he
came within their range—directly at Cambridge; directly or
indirectly at Norwich, where Browne is found in 1580, with his
fellow-collegian, Robert Harrison; possibly also at Bury St.
Edmund's, where assemblies "of the vulgar sort of people"
"to the number of one hundred at a time" met in private
houses and conventicles, and "greatly depended on him."[1] In

---

[1] Bishop Freake's Letter to Burghley, April 19, 1581.

the autumn of 1581 Browne migrated to Middelburg, and, some
time before, Greenwood withdrew to Rochford Hall.[1]   But between this year and 1586 he had thrown in his lot with the
London Congregation.   Here, again, echoes of Browne's voice
would greet him and traces of his fiery personality would come
before him—if the story may be received which tells how
Browne "used to preach in the open air in defiance of the
rector of Islington, in whose parish it was that his auditors
assembled."   For some of these auditors, at least, and the
separatists must have been the same people.   We may agree,
then, that Greenwood was "deeply impressed by Browne," first
by what he had seen and heard; and then, perhaps, by his
books,[2] when these began to steal rapidly into circulation
after 1581.

But what of Barrow?   We have seen that he does not
appear to have had equal chances of coming into contact with
Browne, though he, too, may have read his books.   Two facts,
however, are clear.   One is that he and Greenwood became
intimate friends some time previous to 1586; the other is that
Barrow, like his friend, knew the brethren of the separation in
London.[3]   And we conjecture that the two men met first in the
neighbourhood of Shipdam, or possibly at Lord Rich's house in
Essex; that Greenwood's was the hand which conducted Barrow

[1] One would welcome precise dates,
but there is a clue. Lord Rich died in
1581, so that Aylmer's trouble with
him must have occurred before then,
and Greenwood is not likely to have
remained at the Hall after then.

[2] Three treatises were printed
during those two years (1582–3) from
the pen of Browne, and two from that
of Harrison. They "arrived at the
dignity of drawing a special proclamation from the Queen," while "two
men (Copping and Thacker) were
hanged for dispersing, and another
(Gybson) nearly hanged for binding
the same" (Dexter's Congregationalism, p. 74).

[3] (1) He recognised twelve of the
brethren amongst a great number of
other attendants in the ante-room of
the Lord Chancellor's Chamber at his
examination, July, 1588. (2) In the
Conference (March 18, 1590) his words
to Andrews—"So sweete is the harmony of God's graces unto me in the
congregation, and the conversation of
the saints at all times"—are evidently
reminiscent of former meetings with
the Church. (3) We read in the preface to the first series of Conferences
that "the prisoners *under their own
hands have made relation hereof unto
the Church*," as it behoved them to do
according to Acts iv. 23. This implies
that they were members and leaders
of the Church, yet at the same time
subject to it.

across the border of Puritanism into Separatism; that he it was who introduced Barrow to the secret assemblies in London, where, as a "layman," the latter could take no part except by way of prophesying, but where, by virtue of his natural force, eloquence, and earnestness, he soon came to the front. Thus, in this case, as in one more famous, Greenwood may be conceived as being, to some extent, a Barnabas who first took the lead and then gladly fell behind.

But in this case there was never the hint of a quarrel. "Greater love hath no man than this, that a man lay down his life for his friend." And Barrow did this for his, as Greenwood would have done for Barrow, nor do we ever hear the breathing of a word to suggest that Barrow grudged the sacrifice. One Lord's day—so runs the story—while reading the Scriptures in a friend's house, in the parish of St. Andrew-in-the-Wardrobe, St. Paul's Churchyard, Greenwood was surprised by the Bishop of London's pursuivants, and hurried away to the Clink. The date is given as "the autumn of 1586." But it is possible to be more precise. For Barrow's fatal visit took place on November 19, 1586. Then—we are told—for the next twenty-four weeks he lay in the Gatehouse. At the end of this time, however, Greenwood had been in prison thirty weeks,[1] which (taken literally) makes October 7 the date of his arrest. Barrow just then was in the country, and hearing what had befallen his friend came up to see him. His visit was an act of courageous devotion. But apparently he was not aware of any reason to fear extraordinary danger. He did not know that the Archbishop had been informed of his coming, and was on the watch for him. He learnt presently how the information had been conveyed. For at the end of the account of his second examination he adds this note:—"There was an article against me in the Bill for saying that I thought Elders were Bishops, and

---

[1] See paper containing "The names of sundry faithful Christians imprisoned, &c.," printed by Arber in his "Introductory Sketch to the Marprelate Controversy," p. 38.

Philip. 1. 1 was produced. Hereby I plainly discover mine accuser to be Thorneby, of Norwich, with whom 1 had communication at Ware, as 1 rode to London, and never talked with any other about this matter." What happened is best told in his own words :—" This 19th' being the Lord's day, between nine and ten of the clock in the forenoon, Mr. Hull and I went into the Clink to visit Mr. Greenwood and the other brethren there imprisoned ; where we had not been the space of one quarter of an hour but Mr. Shepherd, the keeper of the prison, came up, rebuked Mr. Greenwood and stayed me, saying he had commandment from his lord's grace so to do. I demanded a sight of his warrant. He answered that if I were wronged I might bring an action. So he locked me up in prison, and forthwith went to his lord's grace to Lambeth." He returned with two pursuivants about four o'clock. Barrow was then "put into a boat and carried to Lambeth." "By the way one of the pursuivants, called Watson, drew out of his bosom a letter from the Court of Lambeth unto me, saying how he had a long time sought me. I told him his pains deserved thanks neither at God's hands nor mine; I refused his letter, and said that I obeyed neither it nor him, neither would I read it, showing how I was under the arrest of the keeper of the Clink who sate by me. Well, we arrived at Lambeth, where, after I had perused the Bishop's state, I was brought into his presence-chamber. Yet not until this Watson had prevented me and showed his master what had passed in the boat."[2] Then the Archbishop addresses him :—

First Examination, Nov. 19, 1586. Lambeth Palace.

A. Barrow, is your name Barrow ?

B. Yea.

A. It is told me that you refuse to receive or obey our letter. Know you what you do? It is from the High Commissioners, and this man a pursuivant.

B. I refused to receive or obey that letter at that time.

[1] November, 1586.
[2] Besides Whitgift the Archdeacon of London (Mollins) and Dr. Cosin were present.

A. Why so?

B. Because I was under arrest and imprisoned without warrant and against law ; and, therefore, now it was too late to bring the letter.

A. Why, may not a councellor commit to prison by his bare commandment (alledging how the Aldermen of London do dayly).

B. That is not the question—what a councellor may do— but whether this man may do it without warrant by the law of the land ? (Pointing to the keeper of the Clink.)

A. Know you the law of the land ?

B. Very little; yet was I of Gray's Inn some years. (Then his two Doctors and he derided mine unskilfulness.) Let this pass; 1 look for little help by law against you; I pray you, why have you imprisoned me, and after this manner sent for me ?

A. That you shall know upon your oath; will you swear ?

A book is held toward him and he is bidden to lay his hand upon it.

B. To what purpose ?

A. To swear.

B. I use to swear by no books. . . .

A. Why, man, the book is no part of the oath, it is but a ceremony.

B. A needless and wicked ceremony.

A. Why, know you what you say ? Know you what book it is ? It is the Bible.

B. I will swear by no Bible. . . .

A. Will you lay your hand in my hand and swear?

B. No.

A. Will you lay your hand on the table and swear ?

B. No.

A. Will you hold up your hands toward heaven and swear ?

B. That is not amiss; but I will use my liberty.

A. Why, you hold it lawful to lay your hand on the table and swear ?

2

B. Yea, so it be not commanded and made of necessity.

A. Why, the Book is the like ; it is nothing of the oath, but a thing indifferent. . . .

B. If it be so, there is no power can bring me in bondage to my liberty.

A. Where find you that ?

Barrow says, "In St. Paul, 1 Corinthians," and tried to recall the exact place. He looks for it "in a little Testament in Greek and Latin which was brought" him, but cannot find it. "Great fault was in my memory, neither, indeed, could I bethink me where to find it, they so interrupted me."

A. Your divinity is like your law.

B. The Word of God is not the worse for my ill memory.[1]

A. I would like it well if you cited your place in *Greek*[2] or Latin.

B. Why, you understand English. Is not the Word of God in English ?

The talk glances off on a remark of Dr. Cosin about recognising him as a Cambridge man.[3]

A. Were you, then, of Cambridge ?

B. Yea ; I knew *you* there.

He said he was there before I was born.[4]   I said it might be.

Thus many things being alleged to and fro by us, the Archbishop commanded Cosin to record that I refused to swear upon a book.

B. Yea, and set down also that I will not swear thus at random, but first I will know and consider of the things I swear unto whether they require an oath.

A. Well, when were you at church ?

[1] The place he wanted was 1 Cor. vi. 12, and no sooner was he out of the house than it came to him. But here, in presence of the scoffing Archbishop and his Doctors, he is at a loss.

[2] Note this with reference to Whitgift's alleged ignorance of his Greek Testament.

[3] Richard Cosin (1549?–1597) was of Trinity College, Cambridge. He was a member of the High Commission ; Dean of Arches and Vicar-General of the Province of Canterbury ; a great authority in Canon Law.

[4] Whitgift was at Cambridge from 1548 to 1576.

B. That is nothing to you. . . .

A. Have you said (as reported) "That there is not a true Church in England"?

B. When you produce your witness I will answer.

Then came the questions and answers already quoted;[1] and, finally, he is asked if he can find surety for his good behaviour. He offers a gentleman of Gray's Inn, named Lacy. But being told that his bond will include the obligation to attend church, he says, promptly, "I will enter no such bond."

A. Will you enter bond to appear on Tuesday next at our Court, or on Thursday if not on Tuesday; and will you be bound not to depart until you be dismissed by order of our Court?

B. No.

A. Then I will send you to prison.

Accordingly he was committed to the Gatehouse. Eight days later he is again at Lambeth "to make appearance before the High Commissioners, and "found a very great train without;" "a goodly synod of Bishops, Deans, civilians within;" and as many "well-fed, silken priests" as might beseem "the Vatican." The first thing he hears—to his "no small grief"—is "a schoolmaster deny his Master Christ." Then his own case comes on. "Canterbury, with a grim and angry countenance," relates how Barrow, at their first meeting, had refused to swear, and demands whether he will swear now. Barrow answers that he must know at least to what he is swearing. Thereupon a list of charges is read, Aylmer[2] declaring that thus to acquaint him with his indictment is a favour which the Archbishop "doth not show to many." But Barrow will not take the oath after all. Canterbury then loses patience, and exclaims, "Where is his keeper? You shall not prattle here. Away with him; clap him up close, close; let no man come at him. I will make him tell another tale ere I have done with him."

Second Examination, Nov. 27 Lambeth Palace.

---

[1] See pp. 9, 10.   [2] Bishop of London.

Third Ex-
amination,
March 24,
1587.
Lambeth
Palace.

Five months elapse—spent in the Gatehouse. Then, on March 24 (1587), he is summoned before the High Commissioners again. "A great Bible in folio fair bound" is brought, which the Archbishop would not have. They bring him a smaller one, and he hands it to Barrow. The latter begins to open the Book instead of swearing by it. His intention is to ask "if the Apocrypha-Scripture and notes" are the Word of God, and to argue the point. This Canterbury cuts short, and demands again if he will swear. No, he will swear by none but God Himself: the Eternal Word who is more than any books or Bibles. At the same time, says he, "By God's grace I will answer nothing but the truth." Whitgift, weary of disputing the point, gives way. "A Christian man's word ought to be as true as his oath. We will proceed with you without your oath." He takes up from the table "a paper of interrogatories." Barrow desires leave to write his answers, and leave is granted. These questions and answers need not now detain us. But we may note that there was a marked difference between the temper of the bishops and the civilians.[1] When Barrow said, e.g., that[2] "no prince, neither the whole world, neither the Church itself, may make any laws for the Church other than Christ hath already left in His Word," there was much interruption, and Aylmer, in particular, was forward "in slanders, evil speeches, and blasphemies." But the Chief Justice said he thought Barrow answered "very directly and compendiously." When, again, he was asked whether the prince might "alter the judicial law of Moses according to the state of her country and policy"; and when he answered that he thought not, but that it was a question of

---

[1] *The civilians* present were the two Lord Chief Justices, the Master of the Rolls, the Lord Chief Baron, with another Baron of Exchequer. *The bishops* were Aylmer and Cooper (of Winchester), besides Whitgift.

[2] *Cp* Plain Refutation of Mr. Gifford,

p. 206, where it is said: Mr. G. hath picked out "a certain answer made by me Henry Barrowe to three great Bishops of the land (i.e., Whitgift, Aylmer, Cooper) to this effect (as I remember), that "no Prince, &c."—a proof that the Bishops did not keep the examinations a secret.

"great doubt and controversy"; that he wished to be "wise in sobriety"; and that he was always ready to change his mind if any man could better instruct him out of the Word of God, the Chief Justice, remarks Barrow, said "I spake well," but "the bishops, because my answer fitted not their turns, as I think, commanded the question and answer to be blotted out."

At the close of the main examination he was "dismissed for a time (while certain of my brethren were examined) then" again called and asked by Whitgift:—

1. Will you "take an oath according to the Statute of Supremacy"? No, said Barrow; but I am "ready to give and perform as much unto my prince as any true subject ought to do."

2. May the Church of Christ, if the prince "deny or refuse" to rectify abuses, reform them "without staying for the prince"? Yes, may and ought though all the princes in the world should prohibit the same upon pain of death.

3. May the Church of Christ excommunicate the Queen, and, if so, who is to do it? Yes, said Barrow, and it is to be done by the pastor.

"The Register," adds Barrow, "not myself, wrote down my answers to these three questions"; and then "was I sent again (to the Gatehouse) with more commandments yet to keep me more straitly." About six weeks later (or early in May, 1587) Barrow from the Gatehouse and Greenwood from the Clink were "indicted" at "Newgate Sessions for refusing to communicate with" a "false ministry and worship. . . . And this upon the statute made for the Papists." Their "judge and accuser" was the Bishop of London. They were condemned; and "other trial or conviction than this, either of error or crime, we never hitherto had or could obtain by any means."[1]

The Statute referred to was the first of the Recusancy laws

A Few Observations to the Reader of Mr. Gifford's Last Reply.

under Elizabeth. It came into force in 1581, when the Jesuits had grown active and dangerous. Its title is "An Act to retain the Queen's Majesty's subjects in their due obedience"; and is aimed at "all persons whatsoever which . . . shall by any ways or means put in practice to . . . withdraw any of her Majesty's subjects . . . from their natural obedience to her Majesty, or to withdraw them, for that intent, from the religion now by her Highness's authority established . . . to the Romish religion." The prisoners protested that the Statute did not apply to them, and undoubtedly the Puritan Parliament of 1581 had Papists chiefly in their thoughts. But there was one section, the fourth, which might be extended to such a case, viz.:—"Be it also further enacted that every person above the age of sixteen years which shall not repair to some church, chapel, or usual place of common prayer . . . and so for-bearing by the space of twelve months . . . shall for his or her obstinacy (after certificate thereof in writing made into the King's Bench by the ordinary of the diocese, among others) be bound in two sufficient sureties in the sum of £200, at the least, to good behaviour; and so continue bound until such time as the persons so bound do conform themselves." Thus they could be tried with an air of legality. With Aylmer on the bench, their conviction and subjection to the extremest penalty was a matter of course. He ordered them to find a surety of £260 apiece, and to lie in the Fleet till the sureties were forth-coming.[1] To the Fleet, then, they went, the one human con-solation being that now for the first time they would be near each other, and perhaps in the same room.

Old London prisons were all bad enough, but the Fleet seems to have been the worst. We get a good idea of its miseries from a "true report of Master (Bishop) Hooper's enter-tainment in the Fleet, written with his own hand January 7, 1555." He tells us that he was to have had "liberty of

[1] See paper of "names" already cited (Arber, p. 88). £260, says Mr. Arber = £2,000 of present money. As they "lay upon execution" of the surety, it is plain that the money could not be had.

the prison "; and, for this, " within six days paid £5 to
the warden for fees, but all the same was committed to
close prison one quarter of the year in the Tower Chamber,"
and " used very extremely." For a time, " by means of a
good gentlewoman," he was " suffered to come down to
dinner and supper; " but at the time of writing he had long
" been in the wards "—" having nothing appointed to me for
my bed but a little pad of straw and a cotton covering, with
a tick and a few feathers therein, the chamber being vile
and stinking. . . . On the one side of the prison is the
stink and filth of all the house ; and on the other side, the town
ditch, so that the stench of the house hath infected me with
sundry diseases." . . . Whilst sick " the doors, bars, hasps,
and chains being all closed, I have mourned, called and cried
for help. But the warden—when he hath known me many
times ready to die, and when the poor men of the wards have
called (him) to help me—hath commanded the doors to be kept
fast, and charged that none of his men should come at me,
saying, ' Let him alone; it were a good riddance of him.' "[1]
The experience of Barrow was similar. Again and again he
speaks of being shut up in a " miserable and close prison "—
" excluded from the air, from all exercise, from all company or
conversation with any person." Some nine or ten months after
his trial at the Session of Newgate, a " lamentable petition "—
which by internal evidence may well be assigned to Barrow's
pen—was presented to the Queen, and describes the sufferings
of the imprisoned in moving terms. Some (for Barrow and
Greenwood were only two of many) were lying in " cold and
noisome prisons," bound hand and foot " with bolts and fetters
of iron "; some the bishops had " cast into the ' Little Ease ';
some they had put into the ' myll,' causing them to be beaten
with cudgels in their prisons "; some had been done to death—

---

[1] True Report of Master Hooper's
Entertainment in the Fleet, written
with his own hand January 7, 1555.
Foxe's " Martyrs," Vol. VI., Part II.,
p. 647, 8.

two aged widows, *e.g.*, seized "for hearing" Greenwood, had
"died of the infection of the prison"; so had Nicholas Crane,
a man of sixty-six, taken for the same offence; so had John
Chandler, "having a wife and eight children." As to Barrow
and Greenwood their lot was little better. At first it would
seem they had enjoyed "benefit of the liberty of the houses,"
i.e., were free to walk within its precincts; but at the date of the
petition (March 13, 1588) they had been "again shut up close
prisoners these thirteen weeks to the great empeachment of our
health and hazard of our lives, and so still remain—no cause as
yet showed thereof." Perhaps it was in consequence of this
petition—which brought these facts directly to the notice of the
Queen, and besought her to have "some Christian consideration
and speedy redress of the outrageous wrongs and most extreme
injuries wherewith sundry of your most faithful and true-
hearted subjects have been a long time, and are at this present
especially, oppressed by the bishops of this land, but principally
by the Bishops of Canterbury and London. . . ."—that less
than a week later (March 18) he was "sent for in all post haste
by one Raglande, a gentleman of my Lord Chancellor's (Sir
Christopher Hatton)." This time his examination took place
not at Lambeth before the Court of High Commission, but
before "the council" in Hatton's chamber "at the Court of
Whitehall." "In a withdrawing" room he found "twelve of
the brethren amongst a great number of other attendants."
But without being able to have "any one word" with them, he
was "forthwith sent for into the chamber." At the upper end
seated about a table were Whitgift and Aylmer—both in their
"pontificalibus," or full episcopal dress—Hatton, Burghley, and
Lord Buckhurst, the Queen's cousin.[1] At the lower end stood
Doctor Some and Richard (Justice) Yonge, with others.

Barrow had now the opportunity he coveted. He was, in
a manner, face to face with the Queen, for the Sovereign was
always supposed to be present in the Privy Council. The Lord

Fourth
Examina-
tion,
March 18,
1588. Be-
fore the
Privy
Council at
Whitehall.

[1] Froude, ix. 368.

Chancellor was presiding. Lord Burghley, the man of all Elizabeth's Councillors most esteemed for justice and moderation, was his chief examiner. The Bishops were comparatively in the background. It is a pity that Barrow did not use the occasion to the better advantage of his cause and himself. He showed none of the wisdom of the serpent. A little of such wisdom would have made him restrained in language and circumspect. There was no need to say all he thought, still less to deliver his views about the Church and its representatives in a style so excited and extreme as to suggest merely an arrogant and embittered state of mind. Never was it more needful for him to subdue his spirit and bridle his tongue; but he did neither. He was particularly anxious to conciliate the favour of Burghley. But whatever chance there was of doing this, he lost at once. His answer to Burghley's first question led the latter to say: "Thou art a fantastical fellow, I perceive." His answer to Burghley's second provoked the remark: "Indeed, I perceive you have a delight to be an author of this new religion": you are glad to find reasons for putting away the old and setting up the new. The Treasurer's impression was not changed by Barrow's dogmatic statement that, "to keep a memorial of the Saints in the Church is idolatry, and that to say ' Sunday, Monday,' &c., is contrary to 'the Book of God.' " "The Lord Treasurer said I had a hot brain, and, taking in his hand a Book of Common Prayer which lay on the board, read certain Collects of the Saints, and showed that the Epistles and Gospels were part of the Scriptures, and asked what I could mislike therein."

B. I misliked all, for we ought not to use the Scriptures or prayer *so.* . . .

Lord Treasurer : But what is here idolatrous?

B. All, for we ought not to use the Scriptures *so.*

To a man of sober opinions like Burghley this was irritating. Said he :—" You complain to us " (in the Petition, no doubt), " of injustice; wherein have you wrong ? "

B. My lord, in that we are thus imprisoned without due trial.

L. Treasurer. Why, you said you were condemned[1] upon the Statute (made for Recusants).

B. Unjustly, my lord. That Statute was not made for us.

L. Treasurer. There must be straiter laws made for you.

This was an unexpectedly hard word, coming from such a quarter; and Barrow's answer had a pleading sadness in it. "My lord, speak more comfortably. We have sorrows enough."

But the Lord Treasurer is untouched. "Indeed, thou lookest as though thou hadst a troubled conscience."

B. No, I praise God. But it is a woeful thing that our prince's sword should be drawn out against her faithful subjects.

The Lord Treasurer "answered that the Queen's sword was not as yet drawn against us."

Dr. Some,[2] it will be remembered, was in the chamber, standing near the entrance and listening. We know him best as the author of two so-called "Godly Treatises," one meant to be decisive of certain questions "moved of late by Anabaptistical Recusants," with particular reference to Penry; the other directed mainly against "the execrable fancies given out and holden by Henry Barrow and John Greenwood." The former bears date May 6, 1588,[3] and so was in hand at this very time. The latter came out a year later, May 24, 1589. They were means to an end—the end being the light of Whitgift's countenance. For, till recently, he had figured as a rather conspicuous defender of Cartwright; and a sermon of his had

---

[1] In the preceding May.

[2] 1542–1609.

[3] This is the date of the second edition. In the first Some deals with questions moved of late in London, and "touching the ministry, Sacraments, and Church." Penry answered this in the second edition of his "Humble Supplication to Parliament" on behalf of the country of Wales. Thereupon Some added a defence "of such points as Mr. Penry hath dealt against," and charged him with as many as sixteen "gross errors and Anabaptistical fancies." The appendix is nearly five times the length of the original Treatise. 36 + 164 pp.

even drawn from Dr. William Chaderton,[1] president of his college (Queen's), that it was "a specimen of the licentious tone and dangerous doctrine" then prevailing at Cambridge—doctrine having for its purpose "to overthrow all ecclesiastical and civil governance that now is, and to ordain and institute a new-found policy." Dr. Some soon saw reason to seek a place of repentance—and has found it. Next year (1589, May 11) he will be appointed, through Whitgift's influence, Master of Peterhouse. Then he will become, through the same influence, Vice-Chancellor of the University; and then he will (in the common belief) sting the hand which has exalted him by assailing Whitgift from the University pulpit.[2] Just now, however, when we see him in the Council Chamber, his fortunes hang somewhat in the balance; and he is the Archbishop's very humble servant. It appears that he was one of several who had been sent to confer with Barrow in prison. Their report was that he had "mocked them." Barrow denies this, and says, "We mock no creature"; and as to Master Some, "he was with me indeed, but never would enter disputation. He said he came not therefore, but in questioning manner—to know somewhat more perfectly."[3] "Some was then, by the Archbishop, called and demanded whether he had conference with me or no." This point being settled in a sense agreeable to Whitgift, Master (Justice) Yonge—one of those who, at a later time, condemned Penry—"came uncalled and accused me of arrogant and irreverent speeches against my lord's grace (of Canterbury) at my first conference with Some in my chamber." Barrow then "beseeched" the lords "to grant a public conference." But the Archbishop "said

[1] Not Lawrence, first Master of "Emmanuel," but William (1540?—1608) successively Bishop of Chester and Lincoln. He followed Whitgift as Lady Margaret Professor of Divinity, 1567; became Regius Professor in 1569; and President of Queen's College in 1568. See the un-

pleasant story about him in Strype's Parker, Bk. IV., cap. 40.
[2] His text was Acts iv. 6—"John" being supposed to mean Whitgift. This Some vehemently denied.
[3] It is plain where Some got the material for his "Treatise" against B. and G.

in great choler we should have no public conference. We had published enough already, and therefore I committed you close prisoner."[1] Up to this time, so far as we know, Barrow had published nothing; but Whitgift treated him as a representative of those who had — perhaps Browne especially, whose writings had for years been in circulation. Presently Barrow repeated his entreaty for "a conference and that in writing." He felt so sure—poor impracticable visionary !—that he could prove his case from the Scriptures, whose authority all alike confessed; and that his case once proved there would be no further resistance or even indifference. He made no allowance for such stubborn facts as prejudice and selfish interests ! He believed, and went on believing, that Canterbury—who again denied his request "very princely "—alone stood in the way of a general peace; and thus came under the wrath of God. Meanwhile, Burghley has been glancing through a paper which lay on the table "among the Bishop's evidences against me "; a paper compiled by Dr. Some out of what Barrow had said to him in the prison. He reads there that Barrow "held it unlawful for the Parliament to make a law that the ministers should live by tithes or the people pay them." Is this so ? Barrow answers that tithes " are abrogate and unlawful ; " that ministers should live " *ex pura elemosina*, of clean almsdeeds," as Christ and the apostles did; that if the people will not give they prove themselves " profane "; and that to such people none ought to stand as minister. Burghley asks eagerly for Scripture proof, and Barrow quotes Heb. xii., Gal. vi. 6. But if the minister is not to have a *tithe* of any goods, what then ? " Wouldst thou have him to have all ? " Barrow : " No, my lord, but I would have you to withhold none of your goods from helping him ; neither rich nor poor are exempted from this duty." " Further," adds Barrow, " I showed that if the minister had things necessary to this life, as food and raiment, he ought to hold himself content,

[1] In March, 1587.

neither ought the Church to give him more." The passages quoted brought up the word " priest," and the Lord Chancellor showed his ignorance of Greek by remarking that presbyter is *Latin* for a priest.

Barrow corrected him. " It is no Latin word, but derived ; and signifieth the same that the Greek word doth, which is an elder."

Possibly to cover some confusion of face at this exposure, the Chancellor "asked me if I knew not these two men, pointing to Canterbury and London."

Barrow. Yes (my lord), I have cause to know them.

Lord C. But what ? Is not this the Bishop of London ?

B. I know him for no bishop, my lord.

Lord C. What is he then ?

B. His name is Elmar, my lord. The Lord pardon my fault that I laid him not open for a wolf, a bloody persecutor, and an apostate. He was thinking, we may suppose, of that " Harbour of faithful subjects," in which Aylmer had once " prophesied saying, come down you bishops from your thousands and content you with your hundreds ; let your diet be priestlike and not princelike."[1] It was no tenderness for Aylmer which restrained Barrow ; but by the time he was ready to speak, " the warden's man was plucking him up " from his knees ; and the Lord Chancellor was putting another question. " What is *this* man ? " (Pointing to Canterbury.)

" The Lord gave me a spirit of boldness, so that I said : He is a monster, a miserable compound ; I know not what to call him. He is neither ecclesiastical nor civil—even the second beast that is spoken of in the Revelation."

Lord Treasurer. Where is that place ? Show it.

" So I turned to the place, chap. xiii., and read verse 11. Then I turned to 2 Thess. ii.—but the Beast arose for anger, and gnashed his teeth, and said, ' Will ye suffer him, my lord ? ' "

" So I was plucked up from my knees by the warden's man "

[1] Marprelate's " Epistle," p. 5.

. . . "and led" back to prison "by another way than I came in, that I might not see the brethren nor they me." As he was leaving the chamber he made a last request—made it to Burghley as to the one who had the power to help him if he would—that he might not be confined again to a cell, but might have the " benefit of the air."

Burghley gave him no answer. Indeed, Barrow's un-chastened tongue had undone him. He felt this himself. " The Lord pardon mine unworthiness and unsanctified heart and mouth, that can bring no glory to the Lord or benefit to His Church." In the solitude of his prison he had regretful thoughts. He recalled the Lord Treasurer's admonition that he "took the Lord's name often in vain "; and confessed its justice, and prayed earnestly that he might learn to " set a more careful watch before " his " lips." But though this discloses the spirit of a humble and lovable man, the mischief was done. He had made Whitgift, if he was not so before, an implacable foe ; and he had alienated whatever degree of sympathy the civil lords might have been disposed to cherish. He still put his hope in the Lord Treasurer. He appealed to him more than once afterwards—in the impressive dedication, e.g., to his " Plain Refutation of Mr. Gifford's Treatise." But it is evident he was leaning on a broken reed. Burghley, in fact, was a man in whom the Separatists, and even the extremer Puritans, were certain to be disappointed. "Like the old Marquess of Winchester, who preceded him in the custody of the white staff," he "was of the willow and not of the oak." " He paid great attention to the interests of State, and great attention also to the interest of his own family. He never deserted his friends till it was very inconvenient to stand by them, was an excellent Protestant when it was not very advantageous to be a Papist, recommended a tolerant policy to his mistress as strongly as he could recommend it without hazarding her favour, never put to the rack any person from whom it did not seem probable that useful information might be derived, and was so moderate in his desires that he left only three hundred distinct landed estates, though he might, as his honest servant assures us, have left much more "if he would have taken money out of the exchequer for his own use, as many treasurers have done."[1]

Macaulay's sarcastic description may be too severe, though the facts are not few which seem to bear it out. The "worldly elements" were, indeed, stronger in Burghley than he was aware.[2] And if this also be thought too severe, we can, at least, say that he was one who sedulously pursued the middle way. All extremes were abhorrent to him, whether illustrated by the conduct of Mary in relation to Protestants; or Whitgift in relation to Puritans; or Puritans in relation to moderate Churchmen; or Separatists in relation to all alike. The only exception, perhaps, may be found in his sympathy with the treatment of Catholics; and this rested not on religious, but on political grounds. He could not understand the enthusiast, the idealist, the devotee of a scrupulous conscience. Why should a man commit money, position, success, fame, life even, to the keeping of an "opinion"? And if a practical application of the "opinion" meant a shock, a revolution in the existing order of things, what else could its holder be than mad?

Tradition says that Greenwood obtained his liberty for some time in the course of 1588. And this seems to be confirmed by what we read in the introduction to the first Conference, when Greenwood speaks of himself as "prisoner in the Fleet, having been kept close now a year and a-half by the Bishops' sole commandment." This was on

---

[1] Macaulay's Essay on Burghley.

[2] Cf His advice to his son—the very counterpart of Polonius's—Be sure to keep some great man thy friend, but (1) Trouble him not for trifles. Compliment him often, and (2) Towards thy superiors be humble, yet generous; with thy equals familiar, yet respective; towards thy inferiors show much humility and some familiarity; as to bow thy body, stretch forth thy hand, and uncover thy head, and such like popular compliments; and (3) Serve God by serving of the Queen; for all other service is, indeed, bondage to the devil. — Strype's Annals, Vol. IV., pp. 478-80.

March 9, 1590; and takes us back to September, 1588; and
implies that for awhile, at least, previous to that date, his
confinement had not been close. Tradition says, though less
confidently, that Barrow also obtained some liberty at the
same time. But here we can quote Barrow's own assertion to
the contrary. For on March 18, 1590, in his first conference
with Hutchinson and Andrews, he speaks of "having been two
years and well-nigh a-half kept by the Bishops in close
prison." Whatever liberty, then, Barrow may have had took
place in the autumn of 1587. Did such liberty amount to
freedom in the sense of being allowed to "live out of prison
on bail"? I think not. I think the facts were these. On
November 19, 1586, he was arrested. Early in May he had
his trial at Newgate. If we say May 6, this gives an interval
of exactly twenty-four weeks—the period, definitely named,
during which Barrow was "close prisoner" in the Gatehouse
"at the Archbishop's commandment for not taking an oath
administered unto him ex-officio." After "conviction" at
Newgate, he and Greenwood "lay in the Fleet upon an
execution of £260 apiece." Here, however, Barrow (and presumably Greenwood also) "enjoyed that liberty of the house
which the law" allowed. But for thirteen weeks before the
delivery to the Queen of the petition of March 13, 1588, this
privilege was taken away, and they were "again shut up close
prisoners." As regards Greenwood, this privilege was restored
between March and September; perhaps the "liberty" even
extended to a brief deliverance "on bail." As regards Barrow,
on the other hand, the privilege was never restored. On
March 18, 1590, he had been "close prisoner," as we have
seen, "two years and well-nigh a-half," the "well-nigh
a-half" answering, in his "frail memory," to the odd
"thirteen weeks." Early in 1591, when he issued his "Plain
Refutation of Mr. Gifford" he had been, "now more than three
years in miserable and close prisons," secluded "from the air,
from all exercise, from all company or conversation with any

person, from all means so much as to write. . . ." [1] And
in the spring of 1592, when the " Few Observations " (supple-
mentary to the Plain Refutation) were penned, he could say that
" We are and have been four years and three months without
trial or relaxation kept by the Prelates in most miserable and
strait imprisonment." [2]   Later in the year (1592), Greenwood
not merely regained the " liberty of the prison," but was at
large.   This is certain.   John Edwardes—*e.g.* (a witness in
Penry's case), deposed that " a little before Christmas, 1592,
he was at a Garden-house at the Duke's place, near Aldgate,
when Penry did preach, and (as he doth remember) Greenwood
did preach there also." [3]   He appears, too, at Christopher
Bowman's wedding in "Penry's house," when " Settle did
pray "; [4] and in September, at the house of Fox (in Nicholas
Lane), when the Church was officered with himself as teacher. [5]
His arrest, therefore, on December 5, came after some months
of freedom.   But there was no freedom, or relaxation of his
rigorous treatment, for Barrow.   Greenwood was reputed to be
only " a simple man; " and the reputation turned to his
advantage.   Barrow was reputed to be dangerous; he was
the man in the eyes of the ecclesiastics; and he suffered
accordingly.   He tells how " all means so much as to write "
were denied; how "ink and paper were kept from " him, and
" a diligent watch kept " by his " keepers "; how, moreover,
" continual searches " were made "upon one pretence or
another," when he was " rifled from time to time " of all his
"papers and writings " that could be found. [6]   Yet, somehow,
he learnt much of what was passing outside; somehow, books
and pamphlets came to him; and the amount he managed to
write is amazing.

But he did not write all he is said to have done.   For
one thing, he did not write the Marprelate Tracts.   These—

[1] In the Dedicatory Epistle to Burghley of the "Plain Refutation."
[2] A Few Observations to the Reader of Mr. Gifford's Last Reply.
[3] Harleian MSS., 7,042, f. 27 (19).
[4] Harleian MSS., 7,042, f. 35.
[5] Harleian MSS., 7,042, f. 60, 61, 63.
[6] A Few Observations, p. 237.

six or seven altogether—flew through the country between the end of 1588 and the autumn of 1589; the first, called the "Epistle," appearing in November; and the last, called the "Protestation," in September. The story of them and the secret migratory Press is well known. At the time, suspicion attached most strongly to John Penry as the writer; and recently his authorship, jointly with that of his friend and coadjutor Job Throckmorton, has been as good as proved.[1] There are still those,[2] however, who assert Barrow's claim—first seriously advanced by Dr. Dexter; and so one or two of the main arguments on which it is made to rest are considered in a detached note.[3]

After his recommittal in March, 1588, he remained in prison till the end came, five years later. It appears that he underwent a further examination about March, 1589, before "a great Commission." He speaks of it very bitterly. Thus, in his account of the first "Conference," a year later, we read:—

Hutchinson. I was at a great commission a year ago when you did set down with your own hand your own answers.

Barrow. Then did you see the bishops offer me the greatest wrong that I suppose was ever offered to any Christian in any age. I was brought out of my close prison, and compelled there to answer of a sudden unto such articles as the bishops in their secret council had contrived against us. I could not be admitted any further respite or consideration, neither any present conference with any of my brethren, neither yet so much as a copy of mine own answers, though I most earnestly and humbly besought the same; but have ever since been kept in most strait imprisonment without company, air, or comfort, never hearing of any kind of conference until now; but have, in the meanwhile, been grievously slandered, blasphemed, and accused by

Fifth Examination, March, 1589.

[1] By Professor Arber in his "Introduction to the Marprelate Controversy," 1895.

[2] Dr. Guinness Rogers, *e.g.,* says, "His intimate connection with the Marprelate Tracts forced him into public notice" . . . "the probability being that he was Martin himself."—Tercentenary Tracts, No. IV., p. 7.

[3] See Note I., p. 82.

sparsed articles, printed privileged books, in their pulpits, in open session, and unto our honourable magistrates.

On this occasion the bishops again took the lead, and behaved, it would seem, with less than their usual fairness. Barrow had to answer, then and there, a series of privately concocted articles. He was required to answer in writing. A copy of his answers was refused him. He was put into solitary confinement, separated even from Greenwood. He had heard nothing since, except rumours that he was being held up to obloquy in pulpit and Press. Thus he was an object of strict attention during the year 1589. Some's Treatise, published in May, would contribute to this. Still more would the "sparsed articles," by which he had been grievously slandered, blasphemed and accused.[1] These would furnish Puritan and Prelatist alike with a good text for railing; and were indeed of just the kind to evoke disgust. Marprelate, too, was in full career, and the wrath which could not be wreaked on him was not unlikely to find its way to the prisoner in the Fleet. But, strange to say, his intercourse with friends outside did not cease. A copy of the "sparsed articles" was brought to him; and he was able to write an answer. Almost as soon as the "Brief of Positions holden by the new Sectorie of Recusants" came to the hands of the preachers whom it concerned, he was served with a copy of this also. And probably, at the very moment of his complaint to Mr. Hutchinson, Barrow had these documents somewhere in his room with answers prepared to both. At any rate, in the spring of 1590 the two sets of articles and the two sets of answers, including a full narrative of the first four conferences, were in the printer's house at Dort.[2] It was an astonishing achievement. But Barrow had trusty agents —particularly Robert Stokes, so long as he remained a Separatist. He visited Barrow and Greenwood "at the prison." He took charge of the MS., carried it over to

---

[1] See Appendix iii.

[2] See "Egerton Papers" (in Camden Society Publications), p. 171.

Holland; had about five hundred copies of it printed at his own charges by one Hanse of Dort; conveyed them over into England; and disposed of them "to the matter of about 200 or 300," according to the author's directions. Thus side by side with the Marprelate Tracts, though in a far smaller circle, they went their round.

The contents of the volume were—"A collection of certain slanderous articles given out by the bishops, &c.," also "The sum of certain conferences," &c., and, in addition, "A brief answer to certain slanderous articles and ungodly calumniations sparsed abroad by the bishops . . . to bring them into hatred both with prince and people."[1]

This was not the first of the "prison" publications. Some time before the same Robert Stokes "caused a little thing of one sheet of paper" to be printed "by their procurement . . . called (mistakenly)[2] the Destruction of the Visible Church." It has the merit of being simply expository. It says little or nothing against opponents, but states calmly and clearly the marks of a true Church, with Scriptural proofs.[3] Though so brief, it is remarkably complete, and most of what the authors wrote later is but an expansion of its main points. Historically it is important for the proof it yields that Barrow's views were truly "congregational," even prior to 1589.[4]

At the same time and place as the "Collection of certain Slanderous Articles" was printed, also by Robert Stokes, Greenwood's "Answer to George Gifford's Pretended Defence of Read Prayers."[5] But the next publication which concerns us here is "A collection of certain letters and conferences lately passed between certain preachers and two prisoners in the

---

[1] The two sets of "Articles" are distinct. The one was for private use on a definite occasion; the other for popular reading. The latter was out and abroad weeks or months before the former, if indeed this was ever "abroad" at all.—Appendix iii.
[2] The correct title appears to have been "A True Description out of the Word of God of the Visible Church." See Appendix iii.
[3] This calmness of tone suggests the comparatively "free" time which succeeded the Newgate trial in March, 1588, as the most likely time for the writing of it.
[4] See Appendix iv.
[5] See Appendix iii.

Fleet." This was printed "about midsummer," 1590. Robert Stokes was again the intermediary—he and one Robert Bowle (or Bull). Barrow and Greenwood—who at the time were prisoners together in one chamber—collected "the letters and conferences"; sent them forth and had them "delivered"—to whom they could not remember, their memory "being so decayed."[1] But Bull was the man; and he acted under Stokes's orders, who told him "whatsoever Barrow and Greenwood should direct him to do, the same Bull should do it at this examinate's charges." Accordingly Bull had the printing done at Dort, "by one Hanse"; had two or three hundred copies printed;[2] had them put as they came from the press into Stokes's "clock-bag"; and then the latter (meeting all costs) "brought them into England and delivered sundry of them to one Mychens, there to be sted." Women also played a part. For Greenwood could not deny that perhaps his wife had smuggled out the MS., and that his maidservant, Cycely, may have smuggled in the printed book.

About Christmas, 1590, the MSS. of two other books went through a like "eventful history." These were Barrow's "Brief Discovery" and his "Plain Refutation of Mr. Gifford's Book." Here, too, Stokes "procures" them indirectly from the author; has them printed at Dort to the number of three thousand; and defrays all expenses. But on this occasion there was a mishap. For all the volumes "were taken at Flushing and Brill." Fortunately, however, the original MS. at least of the "Brief Discovery," was safe. In connection with this Daniel Studley comes on the scene.[3] Examined on the subject, he said that *he* received the original of the book, "sheet by sheet at Mr. Henry Barrow's study in the Fleet, when-as he and one Andrew Smyth had letters from the Archbishop of Canterbury to have access unto him." He, in turn, delivered it sheet by sheet to one James Forrester, who

1 See Appendix iii.
2 Stokes says about 500.

3 "Egerton Papers," March 20, 1592-3.

copied it out; and, "as one sheet was written, the same was taken away, with the copy thereof, and new brought." Then, apparently when the whole had been written out, the copy was sent to Barrow; and, after correction, returned by one " Padry " for printing. Forrester became the copyist by arrangement with Barrow personally, to whom he also found access; and once more Stokes is the friend in need at whose " charges " " Forrester did copy it out." Forrester, however, was not the only copyist, for he saw " Studley to write one copy thereof for himself." But Studley did not get his copy completed. Something interrupted him. He lost sight of the original, and what became of it he did not know.

One circumstance in the story is rather remarkable. Studley and Forrester would seem to have had small difficulty in finding admission to Barrow's chamber. Are we to think, then, that the " close " imprisonment of which he speaks was not so close after all? Scarcely: for it is not implied that Barrow himself could leave his chamber, it is only said that others now and then might come to him. And when we remember that Studley, Forrester, and Andrew Smyth belonged to the brotherhood and were fellow-prisoners —the two former in Bridewell,[1] the last in the Clink— the natural inference is that though they enjoyed some degree of liberty, even to the extent of visiting comrades in another prison, he had none at all! Still it lightens the gloom a little to find that close and miserable confinement did not mean an absolute seclusion from the sight of friendly faces.

We must now retrace a few steps. So far as we know, after his fifth examination in March, 1589, the bishops— mainly Whitgift and Aylmer—dropped him out of their thoughts for eleven or twelve months. Probably this was the

---

[1] James Forrester was in Newgate —in February, 1589-90; one of three to be conferred with by Dr. Bancroft. Studley, at the same time, was in the Fleet, one of two with whom Dr. Saravia and Mr. Gravet were to confer. Andrew Smyth was one of two to be conferred with by a namesake— Mr. Smyth.

darkest year of his life—"kept," as we have heard, "in most strait imprisonment, without company, air, or comfort." The sure effect of such an experience on the temper of his mind ought to be realised. Highly-strung, passionate, imaginative, energetic, he was a man for whom nothing could be worse than unrelieved confinement and solitude. Under similar circumstances men of similar temperament have gone mad. He was saved from madness by his religious faith. But, in brooding day after day on his own thoughts, on his wrongs, on his swiftly passing life, on his helplessness, one of two results was certain—if he was a weak man he would admit doubts, and probably let them drive him to renounce his convictions; if a strong man his convictions would gradually fasten upon him with fanatical intensity. What happened in Barrow's case—as we might anticipate—was the latter; and, with it, came that overpowering sense of exasperation and bitterness which fanaticism always tends to develop. And so, when the signs of this unbalanced mental state meet us in many a virulent passage or epithet of his later writings, we have not the heart to blame him. Blame melts into pity; and pity into admiration, when we picture him in his dark, squalid room, writing on with indomitable perseverance as best he can.

At length the dreary monotony is broken. For one thing, Greenwood and he are permitted to be together again.[1] For another, the bishops have again turned their thoughts to them, and Aylmer issues a mandate, signed February 25, 1589-90, to his "loving friends Mr. Archdeacon Mollins, Mr. Dr. Andrews, Mr. Cotton, Mr. Hutchinson, and the rest of the preachers in and about London within named." His action was in consequence of an order "received from my lord's grace of Canterbury, with the advice of both the Chief Justices, that conference should presently be had with these sectaries which do forsake our Church and be for the same committed prisoners; for that it is intended if by our

---

[1] They were together when the conferences began.

good and learned persuasions they will not be reduced to conform themselves to their dutiful obedience, then they shall be proceeded withal according to the course of the common law." A list is appended of the prisoners, and of the prisons where they are confined. Two or three prisoners are assigned to each preacher, and what he has to do is "to repair" to these "twice every week (at the least)" and "by all learned and discreet demeanour to reduce them from their errors." Further, with a view to evidence of "conformity or disobedience" at their trial, each preacher is "to set down in writing the particular days" of his "going to confer with" the prisoners; and to set down likewise his "censure" or judgment of them, so that, if "occasion" should demand, he will swear to it. Aylmer anticipated that the preachers would not be eager to undertake such work; and, therefore (in the absence from the city of his chancellor, Dr. Stanhope), he requires Mr. Mollins to send for them and lay "the charge upon them"; and, in case any of them should refuse, to summon him or them to Fulham, having previously sent an exact account of his or their answers. Moreover, for his assistance each preacher is to be supplied with "a brief of the positions holden by the new sect of recusants."

There are 52 prisoners named—10 in the Gatehouse, 5 in the Counter (Poultry), 14 in the Counter (Wood Street), 8 in Newgate, 10 in the Clink, 5 in the Fleet. All are men except one—Edith Burroughe, in Newgate. The three in the Fleet besides Barrow and Greenwood are Robert Badkin, Walter Lane, Daniel Studley. In addition to Studley there are other well-known names. There is Thomas Settle, in the Gatehouse, who "offered prayer" in Penry's house when Christopher Bowman, more than two years later, was married there. There is Roger Rippon, in the Counter, Wood Street, who died a prisoner in 1592—"the last of sixteen or seventeen which that great enemy of God, the Archbishop of Canterbury, with his High Commissioners, have murdered in Newgate within these five years," according to the gruesome epitaph inscribed upon his coffin. There is Christopher Bowman, in the Counter, Wood Street, who, after four years of imprisonment, was released; was married in Penry's house; was chosen deacon of the Church; was again arrested; but lived to fulfil his diaconal office in the exiled Church at Amsterdam. There is George Kniveton, in the Counter (Poultry), who also regained his freedom; was made elder of the Church with Studley at the same time as Bowman was made deacon; renewed his acquaintance with prison life; and escaped with the "remnant" to Holland. There are other names whose only record is, so to speak, a streak of blood. Thus we compare the list with another of earlier date—May or June, 1588—and we find that some names are common to both. There is John Francis, in Newgate, committed (says the earlier list) by the Archbishop of Canterbury prisoner ten months (eighteen months at the date of the second), having a wife and children. There is Robert Badkin, said by the earlier list to be in Newgate and "bailed by Master Yonge," but at the date of the second still a prisoner in the Fleet. There is George Collier, committed by the Bishop of London for hearing a portion of Scripture in a friend's house read by Greenwood on a Lord's day, and has remained a prisoner, in the Clink, nineteen months—twenty-seven at the date of the second list—" without being brought to his answer." There is Christopher Roper, "committed close prisoner" to the Counter in the Poultry "by the Bishop of London," but now, eight months later, in the Clink. There is Quintin Smyth, "taken from his labours, cast into the dungeon (at Newgate) in irons, his Bible taken from him by (Dr. Richard) Stanhoop (Stanhope)," now transferred to the Clink. There is William Denford, "committed (to Newgate) upon the Statute (of Recusancy) close prisoner." There is George Smels (or Smalles) still in the Counter, Wood Street, where "he hath remained" (now twenty-seven months) "unbrought forth," for hearing Greenwood. There is William Clarke, committed to the Counter, Wood Street, by the constable, " for saying they did evil to enforce Master Legate " (out of his bed in the night-time) " without a warrant." There are one or two more, also, whose names emit a gleam of light. There is, *e.g.*, Roger Waterer in Newgate, who, in April, 1593, deposed before his judges that he had been a prisoner three years and three months, never examined, " and confessed that he " was once at an assembly in a Garden House near Bedlam, where James Forrester did expound the Scriptures. There is Thomas Canadine, in the Gatehouse, whom at a later time we meet in Amsterdam as an occasion of scandal; and who, later still, appears in the company of John Smyth's adherents. There is James Forrester, a physician and Master of Arts, who shared the examination of Barrow in March, 1592, and gave way before the ordeal, saying he once " began to incline that way " (the way of the Separatists), " but hath since seen, he thanketh God, their great error." But, after all, the identity extends to comparatively few of the names. Of the 25 in the earlier list only 8 reappear in the later list of 52. In the intervening eight months some have been released; some have died; others have been recently taken. For spies were continually on the watch, doing their best to track the little company as it migrated from house to house, from place to place; and there were few of its members, I imagine, who did not, sooner or later, come to know what it was to lie in a London gaol.

Returning to our list, it is remarkable that as many as forty-two preachers were nominated to confer with the fifty-two prisoners. Most of them, so far as one can judge, belonged to the section of the clergy whose tendencies were Puritan—a circumstance which gives point to what is said by the Editor of the " Conferences," that " the Reformed Preachers are now become the Bishops' trusty actors in their most cunning and cruel enterprises " . . . and that this publication is designed to " give them to understand how *they* have behaved themselves in this business." But there are exceptions. There is, for example, Dr. Bancroft, Dean of St. Paul's, future Bishop of London, and successor to Whitgift in the See of Canterbury, known already as preacher of a famous sermon at St. Paul's Cross.[1] There is Saravia, champion this very year of the existing ecclesiastical order in his "de diversis gradibus ministrorum Evangelij."[2] And there is Dr. (Lawrence) Andrews: at this time incumbent of St. Giles's, Cripplegate; afterwards Bishop and saint of the Church.[3] He was one of three to whom Barrow and Greenwood were assigned. The other two were Mr. Mollins[4] and Mr. Hutchinson. In earlier days the former had been a "zealous man for reformation;" an "exile" who settled at Zurich in Queen Mary's time; and "Greek Reader" among the exiles at Frankfort. He is now Archdeacon of London and a Canon of St. Paul's—"much reverenced for his great learning and frequent preaching." The latter is Vicar of Charlbury, in Oxfordshire; is about to be made President of St. John's College, Oxford;[5] and will die there before he can take his part as one of King James's translators of the Bible. At present he also is among the preachers in or about London.

The order given was that the Conferences should be held twice a week at least. As to the other fifty prisoners, there is no proof that the preachers visited them at all. Nor was the order obeyed strictly in the case of Barrow and Greenwood. Mr. Archdeacon Mollins, who was commissioned to supervise the rest, and whom we look for along with Hutchinson and Andrews, does not appear on the scene once. His colleagues also were irregular. There were two sets of Conferences—proceeding side by side. The first was held on March 9th; the seventh and last on April 13th.[6] Mr. Hutchinson figures in

---

[1] February 9, 1588-9; famous for asserting the Divine right of Bishops.
[2] For which he received the "D.D." of Oxford on July 9, 1590.
[3] Vicar of St. Giles's (1588), Dean of Westminster (1601), Bishop of Chichester, Ely, Winchester; the last from 1618 to 1626, when he died.

[4] 1541–1591; also spelt Molyns (Molins, Mullins).
[5] June 9, 1590; died January, 1606. What position he held in London I cannot find.
[6] Seven Conferences: (1) March 9, Hutchinson and Greenwood. (2) March 17, Hutchinson and Green-

four of them, Dr. Andrews in two. In the remaining three Mr. Sperin is a leading actor, though he is not nominated among the forty-two. In the second of these, Mr. Egerton—to whom the list assigns George Collier and John Sparowe in the Fleet—is with Sperin. In the third he is accompanied by Mr. Cooper, who was supposed to have in hand Robert Andrews and William Hutton, in the Counter, Wood Street.

First Conference. The first meeting took place on March 9, and to this Mr. Hutchinson came alone. He introduced himself by saying that he "came by virtue of Commission in Her Majesty's name, to confer," &c.

Greenwood at once refused to "answer anything until he might have indifferent witness by, and the matter to be written down"; whereupon he "obtained to have pen and ink, and Mr. Calthorp, a gentleman and prisoner, to be witness." Mr. Hutchinson then wrote down that he came "not to examine or anyway to hurt Greenwood," but "to confer about his 'separating,'" and the possibility of finding means "to reduce," or lead him back. Greenwood wrote down that he did not desire Mr. Hutchinson's coming, but was ready for "any Christian Conference" on equal terms—"the matter on both sides to be recorded in writing," because he had been slandered and misrepresented by Dr. Some. Mr. Hutchinson then produced the Bishops' Articles and Dr. Some's book,[1] wishing Greenwood to say whether he allowed or not what was therein charged. Greenwood would not answer, except to say that the articles were the Bishop's "owne," and that Dr. Some's book was "full of lies and slanders." The argument into which

wood. (3) March 18, Hutchinson and Andrews; Barrow and Greenwood. (4) April 13, Hutchinson, Andrews; Barrow, and Greenwood. These four were printed immediately. (5) March 14, Sperin and Barrow. (6) March 20, Sperin and Egerton; Barrow and Greenwood. (7) April 3, Sperin and Cooper; Barrow and Greenwood. These, though held at the same time, did not reach the Press till later in the year.

[1] This was the "Godly Treatise" of May, 1589, dedicated to Hatton and Cecil.

they presently drifted may have been new to Mr. Hutchinson; it is not to us. As was certain to be the case, it developed heat, and ended in nothing.

A second conference occurred between the same parties eight days later, March 17. Says Greenwood, "I was sent for out of my chamber and brought into the porter's lodge in the Fleet, where I found Mr. Hutchinson and one whose name I after understood to be Dr. Bright. These two were closely locked in that no man might hear our conference; only one of Mr. Warden's men besides my keeper came in. So soon as I was come and willed (*i.e.*, directed) to sit down with them, Mr. Hutchinson began " on John's baptism, a thread dropped in the first conference. The discussion of this topic took up all the time and ended as it began. On the next day Mr. Hutchinson came again, accompanied this time by Dr. Andrews; the " other party " being, not Greenwood but, Barrow. Barrow, like Greenwood, reports what took place. " They being set down in the parlor" (the parlour was to accommodate the visitors; they had no mind to breathe the air of the prisoner's chamber; even the porter's lodge may have been too much for them), " with one gentleman whom they brought with them and three of their own servants, I being entered and come unto them, they desired me to sit down with them, and that we might all be covered."

Mr. Hutchinson presumes that his " chamber-fellow," Mr. Greenwood, has told Barrow the " cause of our coming," and Barrow admits that Greenwood had told him how " some had been with him yesternight, but not the cause of your coming to me this day."

Hutchinson. We come to the same end, to confer brotherly with you concerning certain positions that you are said to hold.

Barrow. I desire nothing more than Christian conference, but having been two years and well-nigh a half kept by the bishops in close prison, could never as yet obtain any such conference where the Book of God might peaceably decide all our controversy.

Andrews takes up the words "Book of God," and a conversation ensues which I quote elsewhere.

Hutchinson then refers to his having been at the High Commission which examined Barrow "a year ago," and Barrow complains to the effect already stated.

Hutchinson. We will not hear your complaints because we cannot redress them.

Andrews. For close imprisonment you are most happy. The solitary and contemplative life I hold the most blessed life. It is the life I would choose.

Was the speaker indulging himself in an unctuous sneer? Perhaps not. His life shows that he set high value on contemplation and solitude. But on this occasion he—to say the least—forgot the circumstances.

Barrow. You speak philosophically, but not Christianly. So sweet is the harmony of God's graces unto me in the congregation, and the conversation of the saints at all times, as I think myself as a sparrow on the housetop when I am exiled from them. But could you be content also, Mr. Andrews, to be kept from exercise so long together? These are also necessary to a natural body.

Andrews answers (rather ashamed, it seems to me): "I say not that I would want air." Then, abruptly changing the subject, "But who be those saints you speak of? Where are they?"

Barrow. They are even those poor Christians whom you so blaspheme and persecute, and now most unjustly hold in your prisons.

Andrews. But where is their congregation?

Barrow. Though I knew I purpose not to tell you.

The question seems to bespeak cunning and a sinister purpose, but I doubt if it really did. It is more charitable, and, perhaps, as probable, to suppose that his curiosity was due to simplicity and some lingering embarrassment. One shrinks from the idea that he hoped to entrap Barrow into an admission which might open a way to the arrest of "more victims." All we know of his character pleads to the contrary.

Then Mr. Hutchinson's contemptuous description of the so-called saints as a company of sectaries, sets going a long dispute as to what is a sectary and what a schismatic. Here it suddenly occurs to Barrow that he is one against two; and that their "testimony" "may the rather be taken" than his. Andrews offers to "go and reason with Mr. Greenwood;" but Barrow would rather he "tarried still." It will suffice if he can have "indifferent notaries and witnesses." Accordingly "ink and paper" are brought, many enter into the parlor; and it is agreed to "set down" and discuss a formal proposition.

"Mr. Hutchinson set down this: The Parish Church of St. Bride's is a true church, to which any Christian may join in their public prayers and sacraments as they are by law now established." To this Barrow, of course, opposes *his* definition of a church; and then Mr. Andrews moved that "the question being agreed upon and the time being now far spent we might depart until another time." But "I," says Barrow, "seeing much company gotten in, and nothing more heard against me than this proposition, desired them to say something unto it in that time that remained." The people's freedom of access, their keen interest in what is going on, and Barrow's eagerness to seize an opportunity which comes nearer to his notion of a public conference than anything he has known, are alike noteworthy.

Barrow is allowed to have his way; and the game of battledore went on with the said proposition for ball till not only the time was far spent, but the combatants also. Then Mr. Hutchinson rose, "putting up the paper wherein these arguments and propositions were written into his bosom." To this Barrow "condescended" (or consented), on the promise to let him have a copy and to let him "keep the paper" "upon the next conference."

Barrow's narrative closes with a good illustration of his scrupulousness. Barrow rebuking Andrews is a picture !

B. I reproved Mr. Andrews for swearing unlawfully (by his honesty), and making his faith an idol. *A.* said I knew not what an oath or an idol meant. Mr. Andrews also used this word Luck. I said there was no Fortune or Luck. He quoted Luke x. 31: "By chance there went down a certain priest that way."

Fourth Conference April 13. After nearly a month the fourth conference was held—April 13, 1590. Besides Hutchinson, Andrews, and Barrow, Greenwood also was present. It was as little satisfactory as the previous ones. Barrow reports as many as twenty-two points which his opponents at this time asserted and maintained. But he can only give a confused account of what happened, he says, because all was "so disorderly handled."

Here Hutchinson and Andrews disappear from the scene. But, meanwhile, the two principals have been engaged in three conferences with three other preachers.

Fifth Conference, March 14. Of these, too, we have the record. There is first "the summe of a conference between Mr. Thomas Sperin and me, Henry Barrow, upon the 14th of the third month, in the Fleet, as near as my ill memory could carry away." Ink and paper were laid on the table by the keeper. "There were many in the windows." After a time, "many being gotten into the parlour and more into the windows, we thought it meet to remove up to the chamber where I lie." Aylmer (Bishop of London) is the first topic. Then bishops generally; but Sperin, dreading to admit something which will compromise him with the listeners, presently "declines to say more of bishops' offices." Next, Sperin tries to show that his congregation, though a "parish assembly," is a true church; and that he does his best to keep it pure. Barrow's skilful cross-questioning (in which the lawyer is very manifest) entangles him in more than one "dangerous position."

Six days later he returns with Mr. Egerton. On this occasion Greenwood also was present. Barrow opens the debate by a reference " to that compelling of all the nation into the Church," which took place at the beginning of the Queen's reign. Sperin remarks that the point is not one he need " meddle with," since he was only three years old at the time. But Greenwood holds him to it. He deems it necessary, before proceeding, that Mr. Sperin should distinctly say whether he disavows or justifies that compulsory " gathering of the Church." Sperin answers that he does not justify it. Greenwood replies, yet " you have them (the people gathered) on your side." No, says Sperin, for to my knowledge " once in twelve years the most part of the parish changeth." " But," rejoins Greenwood, " none come but such as then were received, or their seed. For they go but from one parish to another, all the parishes being one body and the Church one." At length they move on to other topics—the maintenance of the ministry, and especially excommunication. Egerton takes his full share of the speaking, but is rather more cautious than Sperin. Both affirm, *e.g.*, that the bishops' ex-communication is but a civil act. Then under Barrow's questioning, Sperin distinguishes : — " The bishops' power is civil, but their action ecclesiastical."

Barrow. And may a civil person execute any ecclesiastical office or action ?

Greenwood. Do you hold the bishops, their commissaries and substitutes *merely* civil, and not ecclesiastical ?

Sperin says " Yes." Then Barrow instantly, " Write that and set it down under your hand."

Sperin. So I will ; and took unto him pen and ink.

Egerton. Why so ? what need it to be written ?

Barrow said " that we may the better know whereof we reason and hold to the point ; " and Greenwood urged that the concession was very material. But Barrow had to write it down himself : " Sperin delaying because of Mr. Egerton."

4

Most of what follows circles round the same point—viz., the unlawfulness of uniting the civil and ecclesiastical in one office. Exclaims Greenwood: "This mixture is the mystery of iniquity and the power of the beast." If anything, Greenwood's tone, on the whole, is sharper even than Barrow's. Certainly, he is generally quite as acute in question and answer; and by no means leaves on one's mind the impression of playing second to his companion. The notion that he was but a "simple fellow" is a mistake.

Egerton's part began and ended with this one Conference. But he had impressed the two prisoners more favourably and hopefully than their other visitors. So they wrote to him, enclosing a copy of the Conference; and seeking to "stir him up not to leave the matter" as it was, "considering the seriousness thereof, but" either to "yield," "or to procure some free and large place and time to make our minds plain, and faith open to one another." They subscribed themselves "most desirous of your fellowship in the faith of Christ," Henry Barrow, John Greenwood.

Correspondence with Mr. Egerton: seven letters between April 12 and May 11 (1590).

(2) April 12, 1590.

Mr. Egerton had no mind to reciprocate their friendliness. In "girding against vain philosophy," in other words, against logic, they "do but as Browne hath done in his ‘brainless reasons’"; and as to the copy of the Conference, he finds it "wanting in some things that were spoken"; he finds "many things expressed that were never spoken"; he finds "most things that were spoken perverted"; and "finally," he finds it "so full of partiality, so void of upright and true dealing, and so far out of order, that" he has "neither leisure, much less any lust, to deal with it." Further, he tells them that "if they give out copies," he will "disclaim" them wheresoever he goes, not only for men void of piety, but even of civil honesty also.[1]

The prisoners were sadly disappointed. "We have read

---

[1] Yet he is willing to write and send an answer—at his leisure—to any "6 or 7 chief reasons" they may have for refusing "to come to our public assemblies" if they will put them "briefly and plainly."

your letter," they say in their reply, "with little comfort"; and our "small spark of hope" is "extinct." But on two things (*inter alia*) they insist—first, that "as for the opinions and name (3) May 2 of Browne," he is "a man with whom" they "had never anything to do, neither may have in this estate of his apostasy"; next, that their report of the Conference is correct—taken down, as it was, "from your mouths, even before your eyes, and read in your presence, and in the hearing of sundry honest witnesses." To ensure accuracy, they had actually sent the copy ("not trusting much to our own memories") to the witnesses for correction before sending it to Mr. Egerton. And, instead of applying general terms of denunciation, it would have been "better for his credit if he had set down some particulars in which the report was false." Signed, "with unfeigned desire of your salvation," Henry Barrow and John Greenwood, "close prisoners in the Fleet for the testimony of the truth of the Gospel of our Lord Jesus Christ, to whom be glory for ever." This came to Egerton's hands on May the 2nd; on the 4th he (4) May 4 wrote a curt rejoinder, in which he simply states and denies their three "arguments," that his ministry (1) as derived from Antichrist, is unlawful; (2) is held in "a false office"; (3) is exercised among "a confused people." And, adds he, "my affirmation is as good as yours. Valete et estote sani. He that wisheth your conversion, J. Egerton." As we might expect, the prisoners, in their next—written the following day —go eagerly and lengthily into these points. Between the date of Egerton's first letter (April 14) and the date on which he received Barrow and Greenwood's second (May 2), there is an interval of more than a fortnight. They refer to this in a (5) May 5 P.S. to their third. "In that you received our second letter no sooner, you are to impute it to your own absence, that could no sooner be spoken withal by our messenger who was at your house to deliver it you upon April 18th, and at sundry times since." In fact, it was Easter-time; and Egerton, had he remained at home, would have been legally bound to "administer the Communion" in his church according to the Prayer Book. They hint that this was not agreeable to his conscience, and he had slipped out of the way. Henry Barrow and John Greenwood, "prisoners for the truth of the Gospel, and witnesses against all Antichrist's marked soldiers and proceedings." Egerton is now thoroughly roused.

"To Mr. Barrow and Mr. Greenwood. More truth and love to you, &c. Because your letter received the 6 of the 5 month hath in it as many lies as mine to you (to my remembrance) hath lines, I think it the best course to set them before you, to move in you some remorse, except it be with you as the prophet saith—*nescit impius erubescere.*" The four last items are these :—" (12) That I hid myself at Easter; (13) that I am bound to minister the Lord's Supper at Easter; (14) that I have the mark of the Beast; (15) that I worship the Image. ' What shall be thy reward, O thou lying tongue?' ' Without shall be dogs, enchanters, . . . and all that loveth and maketh lies.' If Barrow and Greenwood be so void of grace, what should we think of that pitiful band of seduced schismatics ?

"The Lord give you repentance. Amen. 5 May, 1590.

"I. EGERTON."

The prisoners received this on the 10th, and found it so full of "vanitie, vituperie, and blasphemie as it deserveth none answer or speaking of." Nevertheless they answered it next day, point by point, " for the satisfying of others to whom these our controversies may come." But unless their correspondent can " hereafter " season his letters " with more gravity and grace " they will be unwilling to receive any more, or at the least will forbear to answer them. Egerton[1] did not write again. They

Marginal notes:

(6) May 6 By an obvious inversion B. and G.'s letter is said to have been received on May 6, and Egerton dates his answer on the 5th.

(7) May 11.

---

[1] Egerton (1553 ?–1621 ?) was of Peterhouse, Cambridge; was a distinguished scholar; a leader in the formation of the Wandsworth Pres-

went their several ways, and met no more until they came to
the " world of light," and saw that the things which save are
not the things about which they wrangled on earth.

In the meantime Mr. Sperin brought another champion on
the scene, and what Barrow truly calls " a confuse conference,"
the last and perhaps the least edifying of the series, took place. Last Conference,
April 3.
This was on April 3, and the new-comer was Mr. Cooper. The
prisoners seem to have known him, Greenwood especially.
Thus the latter says, " You were made minister by the bishop
before you came to your (present) parish by Powles " (i.e., St.
Paul's); and again: " Before you had a flock (here) Mrs.
Lawson got a licence for you from the Archbishop to preach in
the parish." [1] He reminds him—after Cooper has just denied
his belief in the article about Christ's descent into hell—that
he had " of late (as I hear) subscribed to this article " among
the rest. " Here Mr. C. was smitten with muteness; " and a
gentleman who was standing by said, " Have you done so ? "

Cooper. He careth not what he saith of me.

Greenwood. Will you deny it ? I will bring witness to
prove it unto you before to-morrow at eight of the clock if you
deny it.

The conference opened unpleasantly, for Sperin took upon
himself to use " certain speech openly in way of prayer."
Greenwood resented this. It was " too Pharisaical " if done
for his own sake; and " as for us you know we would not join
unto it." " Your prayers," indeed, " and all your actions are
accursed in this popish ministry you execute." The old charge
of Brownism is made, and is indignantly repelled.

---

bytery, 1572; one of those who presented the " Millenary " Petition to
James I. in 1603—"a man of great
learning and godliness."

[1] Has this anything to do with a
passage in Martin Marprelate—" concerning Mistresse Lawson—profane
T. C.—is it not lawfull for her to go
to Lambeth by water to accompany a
preacher's wife (Cooper?)? Going
also (as, commonly, godly matrons in
London do) with her man? No, saith
T. C., I doe not like this in women.
Tushe, man! Thomas Lawson is not
Thomas Cooper. He has no such
cause to doubt of Dame Lawson's
going without her husband, as the
Bishop of Winchester hath had of
Dame Cooper's gadding. But more
worke for Cooper. Will say more for
Mistresse Lawson."—Hay any worke
for Cooper, p. 37.

Barrow. We are no Brownists. We hold not our faith in respect of any mortal man, neither were we instructed by him, or baptized into his name until by such as you we were so termed.

Greenwood. Browne is an apostate, now one of [your Church. You receive all such apostates from Christ. We never had anything to do with Browne, neither are we members of your Church.

Sperin. You were sometime a member of our Church, were you not ? And now are gone back ?

Greenwood. Yes; but I by repentance left it, finding my ministry wholly unlawful in the very office, entrance, and administration. . . . I was first made a deacon by London to no peculiar congregation, after made full priest by the Bishop of Lincoln.

Several topics are debated—the ministry, the right or wrong of submitting to hear unlawful ministers, the propriety of using the Lord's Prayer in worship. On the second topic some of Greenwood's words, illustrating the bigotry due to his position, may be quoted.

Cooper. If one come into a congregation and hear one preach, he ought not to make question of the minister's calling or refuse his doctrine.

Greenwood. If one come so and before knew that that preacher hath a false outward calling—yea, that he hath no office in a true Church, but is a false prophet, he offendeth in hearing of him, especially in a false church ; for there is no false teacher but teacheth some truth. . . .

Bancroft and some other High Churchmen of the Establishment might have said the same; but, whereas they have many modern descendants, Greenwood has none. We have learnt how to combine respect for his principle with loyalty to the spirit of love.

On the whole, these conferences serve to bring Barrow and his companion nearer to us, and to render them more life-like than anything else that has been handed down. For this reason it may have been worth while to notice them in some detail. But as to any good result, they were worse than useless. On the surface their intention was conciliatory. Their real purpose, however, was inquisitorial—to provide definite evidence for a civil trial. It might seem to indicate no small amount of Christian forbearance and consideration on the part of the bishops to appoint forty-two preachers to "persuade" some fifty poor prisoners; but it was hardly an accident that the other prisoners, after all, were left alone, and attention concentrated on the two leaders—so much so that five of the preachers had them in hand during the same few weeks, with orders, or, at least, permission, to question them, write down their answers, and report to headquarters. It was a subtle way of pursuing judgment under a mask of mercy. And the prisoners knew this well enough. They spoke freely—much more freely than was consistent with prudence—and they did so because, with people "in the windows" and the room listening, they would not even for dear life miss a chance of propagating the "truth." But they were none the less conscious that it was a "contrived new Spanish conference" in which they were taking part; and no slight degree of the bitterness of their tone was due to this fact.[1] Under such conditions nothing good could come out of it; nothing but vanity and vexation of spirit. A similar issue, no doubt, would have waited on that public conference for which the Separatists so longed, had it ever been held. The very confidence, admitting of no possible mistake, with which they would have entered upon it, must have defeated their end. Two sides equally certain and dogmatic can never come within sight of the truth, much less reason about it calmly and impartially. They can only choke themselves with the smoke and

---

[1] They have "contrived this new Spanish Conference sending unto them in their prisons certain of their select souldiers . . . to fish from them some matter whereupon they might accuse them unto their holy father) the B.B.'s, who thereupon might deliver them as convicts of heresy unto the secular powers."—Preface (to first series).

fire of their own passions. But still the demand of the Separatists for "a free and open conference" constrains our sympathy. For at bottom it was the struggling cry of men, as it were, suffocated. They had a word of God in their heart, urging, compelling them to speak; and all means of utterance was denied! They were forbidden to preach, to print, to speak together in private assemblies, while their opinions and characters might be caricatured and blackened to any extent by adversaries. They had no legal way to the public ear at all. They were not suffered even to state their case. Their suffocating sense of wrong had to find an outlet as best it could through secret and obstructed channels. In such a case their entreaty for a free public conference is felt to be a truly modest and pathetic request. Not an unlicensed press, not an unbridled pulpit, not an open platform—nothing of that sort was in their mind; but simply leave, once for all, to meet the gainsayer in a fair field, and to set forth their true position in the light of day. But no; the utmost they could get was the miserable subterfuge of a conference with two or three bishops' messengers! How the fact appeared to them is well seen in the following extract from the editor's preface[1] to the first part of the conferences:—He says he expects "to be blamed at all hands" for publishing them, "but I see not why any should greatly be offended with this my doing, seeing thereby no wrong is done to any man. . . . As for these prisoners that are named, and had to do in this business, there is no cause why they should be offended, seeing they, under their own hands, have made relation hereof unto the Church, and have (for so doing) the practice of the Apostles (Acts iv. 23), as also of our late martyrs in Queen Mary's days in the like cases. . . . As for the other side, if nothing should be published until their consent were had, there should never any of these things come to light. But if they think themselves injured, let them set down the particulars wherein; or, for the further satisfying of

[1] First Series.

all men, let them yet at length condescend to some Christian
and free Conference, where both sides may have liberty to
produce their reasons, a true record of them be kept by
faithful and indifferent notaries, each side be allowed to have a
copy thereof, and time to consider of what is passed accordingly. Thus might the truth soon and peaceably be known,
where the Word of God may be judge betwixt them; from
which whoso departeth, and will not be reduced, let him to
his own peril undergo such censures and judgments as are due
to his error and sin. Only this is sure—wisdom is justified by
all her children."

After the excitement of the Conferences, the days wore
on as before. There was little of external incident to
break the monotony. Barrow had a room " upstairs," with
light enough perhaps, but small; and " wanting air." He
had a companion whose heart answered to his own. He had
his Bible for continual study, and also writing materials
for occasional use. We have heard him resent the diligent
watch held over him by his keepers, and of the frequent
incursions of those sent to rifle him of all his papers and
writings. But his keepers cannot have been always strict.
They must, indeed, have connived at a good deal, else how had
it been possible to find time and means to write anything?
We need not suppose that his keepers were careless or
unusually kind. Barrow had money; and, under the hardest
conditions, money can buy indulgences. We know from other
examples that a prisoner's degree of comfort was regulated by
what he could buy or pay.[1] We have no reason to doubt that
the same rule applied to Barrow. He would have just as
many privileges as he was in a position to purchase. And
these, it is evident, were considerable. He had permission to
receive friends from time to time; and the alert keeper
managed not to notice that they brought him books, and pens
and ink and paper, and desirable information; nor did he

---

[1] Cf the case of Bishop Hooper.

detect the sheets of MS. which they bore away with them. Sometimes quite a number of friends would come, including one or more couples bent on matrimony; and something like a religious service would take place with Barrow and Greenwood among the witnesses. That this is no mere fancy is certain. For, when answering the charge that the Separatists "will not marry amongst us in our churches, but resort to the Fleet to be married by one Greenwood and Barrow," the latter do not deny that "parties" had come to be married in the Fleet, but only that the parties had been married by them. They have not "taken upon them to marry any, or executed that office otherwise than to gather with other faithful, to witness the same, and to praise God for it." Of course, such an event must have passed under the eyes of the keeper, but he was discreetly blind. Nay, although it is doubtless true that, as a rule, Barrow was confined to his room "from the aire and from exercise," it seems as if he may have been allowed once and again to steal even outside the prison, and betake himself to a meeting of the Church. At least—bearing in mind his declaration in the early part of 1591, that he had been closely imprisoned for more than three years—I find no other way of explaining John Clerke's evidence in 1593, that three years before he was "taken in an assembly with Barrow, and not examined till this time."[1] Neither statement can be open to question; and if both be true, Clerke must have met Barrow on some occasion when the keeper had connived at his release for a few hours, perhaps, on his word of honour. Clerke's words imply that when he was taken Barrow was re-taken; and one probable result would be a curtailment of "indulgencies." But not, apparently, indulgence of the pen. For the last months of 1590 witnessed the finishing touches to his "Brief Discovery" and his "Plain Refutation of Mr. Gifford." They witnessed, also, the writing of his "Platform,"[2] and of a "Supplication

[1] Harleian MS., 7,042, 59 (35).   [2] See Appendix iii.

to the Queen." Neal[1] says the latter was intercepted; Strype says it "was conveyed to the Queen's hands."[2] A letter to a Mr. Fisher, which was intercepted, seems to bear out Strype; and to show that Whitgift had been busy counteracting its possible effect on the Queen's mind. The Archbishop, says Barrow, "wants not his intelligences in all places; and belike, being stung in his guilty conscience, and fearing his barbarous and lawless proceedings should now be brought to light, seeks to suppress the same by all secret and subtle means; making and winning the gaolers—by extraordinary favour and entertainment—to give a favourable, if not a partial, certificate of the prisoners living and dead; and so thinking to disprove the said supplication unto Her Majesty." To make good his charges he enclosed a schedule of inquiries and instructions issued to the gaolers, presumably by the Archbishop. He goes on to say that the Archbishop is "still in rage, and has set a day of Pur, if God by their noble Hester prevent him not." He has—e.g., "destined his brother Greenwood and himself to death against the Holy Feast (meaning that of Christmas); and all the others, both at Liberty, and elsewhere, to close prison—their poor wives and children to be cast out of the city, and their few goods to be confiscate." . . . "Is not this a Christian bishop? Are these the virtues of him that taketh upon him the care and government of all the Churches of the land, thus to tear and devour God's poor sheep, to rend off the flesh, and to break their bones and chop them in pieces, as flesh to the cauldron? . . . Yet for our parts our lives are not dear unto us, so we may finish up our testimony with joy. We are always ready, through God's grace, to be offered up upon the testimony of our faith." If they die, their death will be found to "embrace the chief pillars of that Church, and to carry them to their graves."

Things continued as they were. If Whitgift intended to

---

[1] History of Puritans, Vol. i., 479.   [2] Life of Whitgift, Book iv. cap. xi.

act the part of Haman before Christmas, his hand was stayed. Barrow had yet to endure more than two years of misery ere his release came.

1591 was a cruel year for the Puritans generally. In March, the stir about Udall came to a head when he was condemned in death for "zeal" on behalf of the discipline, and alleged connection with Marprelate. Cartwright, with other leading Puritans, had been in the Fleet since the previous September on a like charge, and vainly "petitioned for his liberty" even "upon bond," although "afflicted with excessive pains of the gout and sciatica, which were much increased by lying in a cold prison."[1] Many commoners were interested on his account, including Sir Francis Knollys, a Privy Councillor, who wrote strongly against the "superiority" to law unjustly claimed by the Bishops.[2] Even King James of Scotland felt moved to intercede;[3] and in a letter to the Queen (June 12, 1591), "requests Her Majesty to show favour to Mr. Cartwright and his brethren, because of their great learning and faithful travails in the Gospel." But resistance had its usual result of only hardening Whitgift. He did not need the mad enterprise of Hacket[4] (hung July 18) and his two prophets to confirm him in his course, although, as Fuller says, "this business of Hacket happened unseasonably for the Presbyterians." He needed nothing more than the conviction, which never failed him, that he was absolutely in the right. And the Queen, as always, was there to back him up. At the opening of the new Parliament, February 19, she told the Commons that they "should leave all matters of State to herself and the Council; and all matters relating to the Church to herself and the Bishops." Mr. Attorney Morrice, who moved the House

[1] Neal i., 457. In May, 1591, Aylmer charged Cartwright—before the High Commission—"in abusing the Privy Council by informing them of his diseases, wherewith, indeed, he was never troubled."—Strype's Aylmer, p. 160.
[2] Strype's Whitgift, pp. 350, &c.
[3] Neal i., 457.
[4] Neal i., 462. Hacket, "a blasphemous, ignorant wretch who could not so much as read," "pretended to be King Jesus, and to set up his empire in the room of the Queen's, &c." Arthington and Coppinger were his two prophets.

" to inquire into the proceedings of the Bishops in their spiritual courts, and how far they could justify their inquisition, their subscriptions, their binding the Queen's subjects to their good behaviour, contrary to the laws of God and of the realm; their compelling men to take oaths to accuse themselves; and upon their refusal to degrade, deprive, and imprison them at pleasure, and not to release them till they had complied "—paid dearly for his temerity. " He was discharged from his office in the Court of the Duchy of Lancaster, disabled from any practice in his profession as a barrister-at-law, and kept for some years prisoner in Tutbury Castle."[1] Morrice had influential seconders, Sir Francis Knollys among them; but Parliament, as a whole, bowed to the Queen, and crowned her policy with one of its severest measures—viz., "an Act for the punishment of persons obstinately refusing to come to Church, and persuading others to impugn the Queen's authority in ecclesiastical causes."[2]

Whitgift, therefore, had it all his own way with the Puritans. He might even congratulate himself on seeming to enjoy the special favour of Heaven—if success be the test. For his good fortune did not fail him when he turned to the Separatists. As we know, his emissaries captured the 3,000 copies of Barrow's two last treatises as they were being "conveyed" over from Holland in the early part of the year. We know, indeed, what he did not learn till too late, that some copies of the Treatises came to the light this year all the same —possibly through the persistency of Robert Stokes. But he had another stroke of success in the autumn, when Stokes declared himself a convert to the Church; and so deprived the Separatist authors of the chief agent on whom they could depend for publication. As a matter of fact, nothing else of theirs was printed for years. Greenwood wrote a "few observations" for "the further refutation of Mr. Gifford," but it remained in MS. till 1605; so also did Barrow's

---

[1] Neal i., 465. [2] Neal i., 465-6.

"Few observations of Mr. Gifford's last reply"; and the "Platform," though written somewhat earlier, did not see the light till 1611.[1] They managed to write petitions, letters, &c., and faithful hands were ready to receive and forward them, if skill and secrecy could do it, to their destination. But, so far as the general ear was concerned, they had fallen absolutely dumb—dumb and virtually dead. There is a legend, started by Sir Walter Raleigh in a Parliamentary speech,[2] that the Separatists grew rapidly during the last years of Elizabeth until they numbered some 20,000. Of course, such a statement could only be a guess; and it was a very bad guess. The fact, alas! was far different. Probably Lord Bacon came nearer the mark when he referred to the Separatist sect as almost extinct.[3] Browne, no doubt, had disciples in the Eastern Counties. Individuals of Separatist views may be traced in the West of England. Here and there in other places "feeble lights," kindled by the new doctrine, are dimly discernible. It is not unlikely, however, that London held the only Separatist congregation of any size, and, though able to hold its own, even this could do little more. It had additions, but it also had defections; and the two may have balanced each other.

In fact, the Church went through a long and terrible struggle for existence under Aylmer and Whitgift; and nothing so brings this home to one as a sympathetic reading of its lamentable petitions. They sound like the desperate cry of tortured helplessness. We have seen one of them "delivered to the Queen's Majesty the 13th March, 1588." There were at least three between the end of 1591 and Barrow's death.

[1] See Appendix iv.
[2] Spoken April 4, 1593, post meridiem, on occasion of the second reading of 35 Eliz. He said: "In my conceit the Brownists are worthy to be rooted out of a commonwealth. . . . But if 2,000 or 3,000 Brownists meet at the sea, at whose charges shall they be transported, or whither will you send them? I am sorry for it, I am afraid there is near 20,000 of them in England, and when they be gone who shall maintain their wives and children?"—Dr. Ewes' Journals, p. 516.
[3] Observations on a Libel.—Spedding's Bacon, Vol. I., p. 165 (1861 edition).

The first belongs to the early spring of 1592, and is addressed to the Lord Treasurer (Burghley).[1] It pleads for one or other of four things—a speedy trial, or a free Christian conference, bail "according to law," or removal to "some other convenient place," say Bridewell, "where we may be together for mutual help and comfort, . . . where, moreover, we may provide such relief by our diligence and labours as might preserve life, to the comfort of our souls and bodies." As it is "we, her Majesty's loyal, dutiful, and true-hearted subjects, to the number of threescore persons and upwards, have, contrary to all law and equity, been imprisoned, separate from our trades, wives and children, and families; . . . we are debarred from all lawful audience before our honourable governors and magistrates, and from all benefit and help of the laws." Seeing it is "for conscience only " we are made to suffer, why not at least admit us to " bail " until called upon to stand legal trial; and meanwhile let us be free "to do her Majesty service, and 'walk in ' our 'callings,' to provide things needful for ourselves and those dependent on us ? " But even this is denied. Yet we are " Christ's servants : members of Christ : His anointed ones." Will not Burghley intercede for us ? He can if he will. " You may open your mouth," they cry to him, "and judge righteously, and judge the cause of the afflicted." And if he is not willing to act alone, " yet we most humbly entreat your honour will make the rest of her Majesty's most honourable Privy Council acquainted with our distressed estate, and together grant us some present redress." The style, and especially the insistence on the legal rights of the case, betray Barrow's hand. Very characteristic, too, is the ascription of an ideal worth to these few " poor suppliants," and the prediction that unless justice speedily be done " God's wrath will be so kindled that though Noah, Daniel, and Job should pray for this people yet should they not deliver them " ! The petition has 69 names attached to it: 59 the names of

[1] Strype's Annals, Vol. IV., pp. 127, &c.

living prisoners, and 10 of prisoners who have " ended their
lives, never called to trial."

[1] There is reason to think that during 1590 and 1591 fresh
arrests were comparatively few, and that during the last few
months the condition of prisoners had undergone some relief.
There is also reason to think that a number of the prisoners,
perhaps as a result of Burghley's influence in response to
their petition, were during the next few months liberated
on bail. But the bishops' pursuivants were not inactive.
Possibly the Treasurer's interference was the sign for a
secret order to be still more active. Anyhow, the places
where Separatists had been known to meet, or might be
expected to meet, were closely watched, with a speedy and
gratifying result to themselves. For " on the third of the
fourth month, 1592,[2] about some fifty-six persons, hearing the
Word of God truly taught, praying and praising God for
His favours showed unto us, unto Her Majesty, your honours,
and this whole land ; and desiring our God to be merciful to
us, unto our gracious prince and country "—these fifty-six
persons " being employed in these holy exercises and no other
(as the parties who disturbed them can testify), were taken at
the very place where the persecuted Church and martyrs were
enforced to use the like exercises in Queen Mary's days." So
we learn from a petition drawn up for presentation " to the
High Courts of Parliament within a few days of the Sunday
on which the surprise and capture took place." The petition
is expressly said to have been written by Barrow,[3] and internal
evidence would of itself suggest this. It has all his eloquent
redundance of word and phrase raised to a white-heat of passion.
Who but Barrow was capable of the opening sentences ? " The

---

[1] The evidence is derived from a
comparison of the list of names attached to the petition with the earlier
list of 1589-90. (See Note II., p. 85.)
[2] This date is usually given as
March 4, 1593. But the statement in
the Petition is quite clear.

[3] See Barrow's Platform, by Miles
Micklebound. Says Desiderius : " Was
this Petition of Mr. Barrowe's own
writing ?"—Miles : " The draught of
it was, and some copies also."

Most High God, possessor of heaven and earth, bringeth at this present before your lordships and wisdoms (Right Honourable) His own cause, His own people, His own sworn and most treacherous enemies, together with the most shameful usage of His truth and servants, that ever hath been heard of in the days of Zion's professed peace and tranquillity. His cause and people He offereth unto your consideration and defence in our profession and persons : His enemies and their outrages against His truth and servants, in the persons and bloody proceedings of the Prelates of this land and their complices." The close, though not so audacious, is a rich specimen of his invective. "These godless men have put the blood of war about them in the day of the peace and truce which this whole land professeth to hold with Jesus Christ and His servants. Bishop Bonner, Story, Weston dealt not after this sort. For those whom *they* committed close they would also either feed or permit to be fed by others ; and they brought them in short space openly unto Smithfield to end their misery, and to begin their never-ending joy. Whereas Bishop Elmar, Dr. Stanhope, and Mr. Justice Young, with the rest of that persecuting and blood-thirsty faculty, will do neither of these. No felons, no murderers, no traitors in this land are thus dealt with. There are many of us, by the mercies of God, still out of their hands. The former holy exercise and profession we purpose not to leave by the assistance of God. We have as good warrant to reject the ordinances of Antichrist and labour for the recovery of Christ's holy institutions as our fathers and brethren in Queen Mary's days had to do the like. And we doubt not if our cause were truly known unto Her Majesty and your wisdoms, but we should find greater favour than they did, whereas our estate now is far more lamentable. And, therefore, we humbly and earnestly crave of Her Majesty and your Lordships—both for ourselves abroad and for our brethren now in miserable captivity—*but just and equal trial according unto Her Majesty's laws. If we prove not*

5

our adversaries to be in a most pestilent and godless course, both in regard of their offices and their proceedings in them, and ourselves to be in the right way, we desire not to have the benefit of Her Majesty's true and faithful subjects, which of all earthly favours we account to be one of the greatest.[1] Are we malefactors? Are we anywise undutiful unto our Prince? Maintain we any errors? Let us then be judicially convicted thereof and delivered to the civil authority. But let not these bloody men both accuse, condemn, and closely murther after this sort, contrary to all law, equity, and conscience, where they alone are the plaintiffs, the accusers, the judges, and the executioners of their most fearful and barbarous tyranny. They should not by the laws of this land go any further in cases of religion than their own ecclesiastical censure; and then refer us to the civil power. Their forefathers, Gardiner, Bonner, Story, dealt thus equally. *And we crave but this equity.*[1] Oh, let her excellent Majesty, our sovereign, and your wisdoms consider and accord unto this our just petition. For streams of innocent blood are likely to be spilt in secret by these blood-thirsty men, except Her Majesty and your Lordships do take order with their most cruel and inhuman proceedings. We crave for all of us but the liberty either to die openly or to live openly in the land of our nativity. If we deserve death, it beseemeth the majesty of Justice not to see us closely murdered, yea, starved to death with hunger and cold; and stifled in loathsome dungeons. If we be guiltless, we crave but the benefit of our innocency, viz.: That we may have peace to serve our God and our Prince in the place of the sepulchres of our fathers. Thus protesting our innocency, complaining of violence and wrong, and crying for justice on the behalf and in the name of that Righteous Judge, the God of equity and justice, we continue our prayers unto Him for Her Majesty and your Honours, whose hearts we beseech Him to incline

[1] These words are italicised in the petition.

towards this our most equal and just suit through Christ Jesus our Lord."

It is said in this "Supplication" that the number of persons "in the prisons about London" is "about three score and twelve," including the lately arrested fifty-six. The words are—"the fore-named enemies of God detain in their hands within the prisons about London (not to speak of other gaols throughout the land) about three score and twelve persons, men, women, young and old, lying in cold, in hunger, in dungeons and in irons, *of which number* they have taken the Lord's day last, being the third of this fourth month 1592, about some fifty-six persons." This makes a difficulty. There ought to be one hundred and fifteen—adding the fifty-six to the fifty-nine specified in the earlier "petition" of this year, already dealt with—so that either a number had been quite recently discharged, or a majority of the fifty-six had not been detained, or the number seventy-two is a very rough estimate. Perhaps something may be said for each of these hypotheses. But the first explains most. Thus in the examination of Barrowists, which took place on April 5, 1593, I find the names of at least six[1] old offenders, whose names are in the petition of 1592, who had been out on bail, and had been retaken since the previous December. This does not include Greenwood, Studley, and Thomas Settell, the last of whom had been "out" much longer. Most likely there were others also who escaped recapture, and the fact is proof that some influence, whether Burghley's or not, had been favourably at work.

Again, the "Supplication" says that "within these six years" seventeen or eighteen have died in the noisome gaols. The list of ten deaths, then, in the earlier petition was incomplete, or else—what is much more likely in such a case—that during the last few weeks or months (perhaps a period of wintry weather) death had been uncommonly busy.

[1] Viz., Roger Waterer, George Kniveton, Christopher Bowman, William Denford, Quintin Smith, George Collier.—Harleian MSS. 7,042, f. 85.

We have seen reason to infer that Burghley, who stood so high in the petitioners' esteem, as the one "whom Almighty God" had "preserved to these honourable years in so high service to our sovereign prince and to the unspeakable comfort of this whole land," did bring to them some degree of comfort. As to the High Court of Parliament, whether Barrow's "Supplication" reached its "honourable presence" we do not know, but if it did the House had not yet developed that fine sense of justice which would make it, in our own day, rush to the rescue of the meanest subject in whom the rights of justice were violated; and so the petition went unnoticed. We must say the same of a third petition,[1] in which, at the end of this same year, "the faithful servants of the Church of Christ" supplicated the lords of the Privy Council "on behalf of their ministers and preachers imprisoned." The occasion of this was another outrage. Pursuivants were wont to break into suspected houses "at all hours of the night, there to break up, ransack, rifle, and make havock at their pleasure under pretence of searching for seditious and unlawful books." On December 5, 1592, accordingly, "late in the night they entered in the Queen's name into an honest citizen's house upon Ludgate Hill, where, after they had at their pleasure searched and ransacked all places, chests, &c., of the house, they there apprehended two of our ministers, Francis Johnson (without any warrant at all) and John Greenwood; both whom, between one and two of the clock after midnight, they with bills and staves led to the Counter of Wood Street; taking assurance of Edward Boys, the owner of the house, to be true prisoner in his own house until the next day that he were sent for; at which time the Archbishop, with certain Doctors his associates, committed them all three to close prison—two unto the Clink, the *third* (*i.e.*, Greenwood) again to the Fleet, where they remain in great distress." We learn from Johnson's examination in the following April (5th),[2] that he was *first* "taken in an assembly

---

[1] Strype's Annals, Vol. IV., pp. 181, &c.   [2] Harleian MSS. 7,042, ff. 33, 34.

in St. Nicholas Lane" and "committed to the Counter"; then he was "taken" a second time "in Mr. Boys's house in *Fleet Street*" (or Ludgate Hill). This would imply that he was out on bail in December, like Greenwood. We meet with both of them in the previous September, when, at the house of Fox in Nicholas Lane, the Church met and elected officers. Johnson was made pastor, Greenwood teacher, Daniel Studley and George Kniveton ruling elders, Christopher Bowman and Nicholas Lee deacons. These were all "out" on bail at the time. Nicholas Lee appears to have eluded the pursuivants. Kniveton and Bowman[1] were retaken, and were brought up for examination on April 5, 1593. Studley was taken with Thomas Settell a little later than Johnson and Greenwood. The latter were arrested on December 4, and "since this," says the petition, "they have cast into prison Thomas Settell[2] and Daniel Studley, lately taken in Nicholas Lane upon a Lord's day in our assembly by Mr. Richard Young." At first they were "bailed by the Sheriff of London, but have 'now' (at the date of the petition) been again called for and committed close prisoner to the Gatehouse." We note that Edward Boys has gone to the Clink, and not for the first time. He was a young man—about thirty-three—but an old sufferer in the cause. His name is in the list of 1588, and the entry is suggestive of long fidelity—"Edward Boyes, in Bridewell nineteen months,[3] now close prisoner in the Clink." He disappears from the lists

---

[1] Kniveton was an apothecary of Newgate Market. In his examination, on April 5, he wavered, "was content to have conference." He had been in "assemblies" at Barnes' house, Bilson's house, Lee's house, at the Woods, at Rippon's house, at Deptford Woods. Bowman was a goldsmith of West Smithfield, aged thirty-two; was imprisoned five years since "for putting up a petition to the Queen"—that of March 13, 1588. He had lately been married in Penry's house. —Harleian MSS. 7,042, f. 35.

[2] In his examination on April 5,

Settell says he had been in prison "fifteen weeks past." This would be since the date of his committal, *i.e.*, about December 21. His arrest would be a little earlier. He and Studley were taken in "an assembly at a schoolroom in St. Nicholas Lane." He had been a minister of the Church of England, but "renounced his ministry."—Harleian MSS. 7,042, f. 35.

[3] Boyes may have been, therefore, one of those taken in the house where Greenwood was reading the Scriptures.

of 1590 and 1592, discharged on bail, perhaps; but he has continued to be a true friend to the "saints," opening his house for their assemblies, entertaining and sheltering their ministers, giving freely to their wants. Now, at length, he is in the Clink again—for the last time. He will not be able to stand its noisomeness very long. A few months hence he will be dead, and some twelve months later still Francis Johnson will have married his young widow.

Another interesting fact which we must note is that Penry has returned to London, and has realised at last that his true "brothers of the spirit" are the Separatists. By the light of what a certain John Edwardes has deposed, we can follow some of his movements. Edwardes had been in Scotland. He came thence with Penry the previous November.[1] They halted at Mr. Ireton's house "beside Darby six miles," and dined there. Then they went to Northampton to the "house of Henry Godly, where Penry lodged." Next day they went to St. Alban's, and "lodged at the sign of the Christopher." The day following they journeyed to "Stratford-at-Bowe[2] to the sign of the Cross Keys, where Penry's wife was, and had a chamber." Here Edwardes left him, but they met again "a little before Christmas at a Garden-house at the Duke's Place, near Aldgate, where Penry did preach, and (as he doth remember) Greenwood did preach there also." Then Edwardes "went down into the country." He returned to London "Saturday was seven night." It was a week or two before the end. Edwardes heard that Penry had been "taken"; had been brought "to the constable's house"; had "escaped away on Monday night"; and had named himself "John Harries." "Upon Wednesday or Thursday morning"— after his return—Penry came to Edwardes's "chamber before he was up," and came "booted," ready for riding.

---

[1] Penry himself says "September," but Edwardes is more circumstantial. —Harleian MSS. 7,042, f. 19 (b. 60th).

[2] Penry says we "lighted (first?) at the Cock at Long Lane end," and then to Stratford-at-Bowe.

"On Saturday night," witness "walked with Penry along Cheapside through Newgate; and they went to Nicholas Lee's house, and there he left Penry and his wife about eight of the clock." A service was to be held. But he could not say "who should have exercised that day, nor did he hear of any purpose that they had to go into the country." He understood at the time that Penry "was lodged at Mr. Settle's house." We may supplement from Penry's own evidence.[1] He was in or about London on March 19, and went that night with Edward Grave to Hogsden, where they lay at the Antelope. He may have gone thence, but is not sure, "to one John Millet's house in Hertfordshire." On the 22nd, however, he was at Ratcliffe, and, with Arthur Billot and others, was taken.[2]

It is a bare recital, but is a recital which has all the elements of a tragedy. It rends the veil. We see a hunted man stealing disguised from place to place under the shadow of night, or riding away in the cold grey of the early morning. We see faithful comrades eager to shelter him and alert to watch; we see brief meetings of husband and wife, father and young children; we imagine the wasting anguish of heart which filled the intervals; we see informers never far off, and pursuers never giving up the chase. We see him run down at last.

Meanwhile, what of Barrow? We find no hint of a meeting between him and Penry. Penry did not, so far as appears, visit the prison. Barrow could not, like Greenwood, be present at any of the "assemblies" outside. His situation remained as hard as ever. He was denied both bail and conference. Failing the former he became, during the last weeks of his life, increasingly urgent for the latter. First, he tried to move Egerton,[3] the Attorney-General; and, then, when this

[1] Harleian MSS. 7,042, f. 19.
[2] Harleian MSS. f. 85, a "fortnigh past," says Billot—i.e., March 22nd.

[3] Thomas Egerton, 1556–1616, natural son of Sir Richard Egerton, Ridley, Cheshire. Made Attorney-

came to nothing, turned once more to the Council. His appeal to the Attorney-General is brief enough to quote.

"My most humble and submissive desire unto your Worship was, and is, that forasmuch as there remain sundry ecclesiastical differences of no small weight between me, with sundry other Her Highness's faithful subjects, now imprisoned for the same on the one side; and this present ministry, now by authority established in the land, on the other, undecided and as yet undiscussed, your Worship would vouchsafe to be a means to Her Most Excellent Majesty, that a Christian and peaceable disputation by the Scriptures might be vouchsafed unto some few of us, with whom, or how many of our adversaries herein shall in wisdom be thought meet, for the ready and happy deciding or composing the same : protesting to your Worship, in the sight of God, at whose final judgment I look hourly to stand, that I hold not anything in these differences of any singularity or pride of spirit. And, as I am hitherto certainly persuaded, by the undoubted grounds of God's Word, the profession and practice of other reformed Churches, and learned of other countries. Whereof if we, Her Majesty's said few imprisoned subjects, shall fail to make evident and assured proof, and that those learned shall show any other thing by the Word of God, in the said Christian conference desired, that then I, for my part, vow unto your Worship, through God's grace (as also I am persuaded, my said imprisoned brethren, permitted this conference, will do the like), that I will utterly forsake any error I shall be so proved to hold, and in all humbly consent to submit to our now dissenting adversaries in all these matters, wherein now we differ, if they shall approve them unto us by the Word of God.

"By which charitable act your Worship may put an end to

General on June 2, 1592—hence date of petition was at least later than this—afterwards Lord Keeper of the Great Seal and Lord Chancellor; died as Lord Ellesmere.

these present controversies, reduce all wherein we err, and appease many Christian souls.

" Your Worship's humble suppliant,

" HENRY BARROWE."[1]

Alas! Egerton thought it a case for the bishops. He handed the letter to Whitgift, who with other bishops, &c., "considered of it," and decided as Egerton knew they would. "It is not equally fit," said their lordships, " to grant a disputation to sectaries." For these among other reasons:—The erroneous opinions of these men have been already condemned by just treatises of the most famous learned men that have lived since restitution of religion; it is no reason that religion and the controversies thereof, the same being already established by Parliament, should be examined by any inferior authority by way of disputation; it hath ever been the manner of heretics to require the same by great importunities and continual exclamations; they that require disputation of the civil magistrate will not stand to the judgment of the civil magistrate; if the Church should satisfy every sect that ariseth there were no end of disputations. Nothing could well be more contemptuous or infallible! He replied by an address to the Council, entitled, " A Motion Tending to Unity." In this he entreats that there may be a conference granted such as was granted to Campion or Hart, the papists, " or else that there may be some conference between two or three of each side, before a good number of your Honours and Worships in some private chamber, the main questions agreed upon (with preparation of fasting and prayer). And when the time comes, omitting all taunts and by-matters, only searching the truth in love: to the touchstone, to the law, and to testimony." He assures the Council that they could produce three or four men

[1] Strype's Annals, Vol. IV., pp. 239, &c.

from London alone[1] well qualified to take part in such an argument—men who have been "zealous preachers in the parish assemblies, not ignorant of the Latin, Greek, and Hebrew tongues, nor otherwise unlearned, and generally confessed to be of honest conversation." He reminds the Council that there are right honourable and godly personages, not by any means of his own way of thinking, who, he believes, would welcome such a conference—men like gentle and learned Mr. Reynolds,[2] of Oxford, and Sir Francis Knollys. He then rises into a noble strain. "If these motions take effect we are verily persuaded that the controversy will soon end (with all or most of us). For by these means shall we poor wretches (which only make this separation, as knoweth the Lord, for love we have to keep His commandments, and for fear to disobey Him) perceive more plainly whether as men and simple souls we be deceived by any false light, or else, as His dear children (for so we hope), honoured and trusted with the first view of, and faithful standing in, a cause of holiness and righteousness. Where(fore), in most humble and earnest manner, and even as you fear God and love righteousness, and as you strive to resemble Him in liking better of them that are hot than of those which are lukewarm, we entreat your Honours and Worships to labour these, or some better motions for procuring unity and mercy; and for that the blessings promised to faithful men and peacemakers may light upon you and yours; and that the curses threatened for the contrary may be far from them. You reverend magistrates and noble guides of this most flourishing commonwealth, we beseech you again and again, in the Lord Jesus, search yourselves narrowly when you seek Him whom your soul loveth, and think how you would desire to be dealt with if you were in our

---

[1] We know of at least four who had been "ministers" of the English Church, viz., Greenwood, F. Johnson, Thomas Settell, William Smith (of Bradford, Wilts—ordained by Bishop of Coventry and Lichfield).—See Harleian MSS. 7,042, f. 35.

[2] Dr. John Reynolds (1549–1607), "the pillar of Puritanism, and the grand favourer of Nonconformity "—so Wood, Athenæ Oxonienses—President of Corpus Christi, Oxford, champion of the Puritans in the Hampton Court Conference. Declined a bishopric.

case, and so deal with us and our teachers. If you suppose them and us to be in grievous error, for common humanity sake (were there no further cause) let us not perish, either secretly in prisons or openly by execution, for want of that uttermost help which lies in your power to afford them that are not obstinate men. . . ."[1] Of course, the appeal was vain. Instead of a conference came a trial. For by this time the case against him had been completed, and justified the hope that his conviction and execution might be secured by means of the civil court. It was drawn from his writings. One after another these had fallen into the Archbishop's hands, and he had no doubt that there was more than enough in them to condemn their author by virtue of the statute (23 Eliz., cap. 2) against seditious books. On March 11, 1593, he was summoned before Judges Popham and Anderson.[3] A copy of the pamphlet, "Certain Letters and Conferences," was shown him. Did he acknowledge it as his? Yes, he and Greenwood had compiled it. And "A Collection of Slanderous Articles"? Yes. Greenwood, questioned separately on the same day, answered to the same effect. On the 20th Barrow was examined with regard to "A Brief Discovery of the False Church" and "A Plain Refutation of Mr. Gifford," and owned to *them*. The same day Greenwood owned, for his part, to what he had written against Mr. Gifford. All this was preliminary. Its purpose was to establish the fact of authorship—as the examination of Studley and Forester (on the 20th), Bowles[3] and Stokes (on the 19th) was to establish connection with the authors. The decisive day was March 23. Mr. Attorney Egerton thus reports[4] the result to the Lord Keeper of the Great Seal:—

    "This day—23rd March, 1592-93—the Court hath proceeded against Barrow and Greenwood for devising, and against

Trial March 11, 1593.

Conviction March 23, 1592-93.

---

[1] Strype's Annals, Vol. IV., pp. 241, &c.
[2] Egerton Papers, pp. 166-179.

[3] Otherwise Bowle, Bull.
[4] Harleian MSS. 7,042, f. 34.

Scipio Bellotte,[1] Robert Bowlle, and Daniel Studley for publishing and dispersing seditious books." All have been "atteynted by verdict and judgment, and direction (has been) given for execution to be done to-morrow as in cases of like quality. Bellott,[2] with tears, affirmed that he had been misled. The others endeavour to draw all that they have most maliciously written and published against Her Majesty's Government to the bishops and ministers of the Church only." . . . He adds that "if execution is to be deferred" let it "be known this night." Execution was deferred; and on the 26th Egerton writes again : "I have spent this whole afternoon at a fruitless, idle conference, and am but now returned both weary and weak." On the 28th he writes, once more, to say that yesterday, immediately after his return from the Parliament House he did write to the Lord Treasurer "the manner and success of his conference with Barrow." We will now turn the shield and listen to Barrow himself.[3] He is writing to "an honourable lady and countess of his kindred" . . . "in the time between his condemnation and execution." "For books," he says, "written more than three years since (after well near six years' imprisonment sustained at their hands) have these Prelates by their vehement suggestions and accusations, caused us to be indicted, arraigned, condemned . . . upon the statute made the twenty-third year of Her Majesty's reign. Their accusations were drawn up into these heads :—(1) That I should write and publish the Queen's Majesty to be unbaptized; (2) that the State is wholly corrupted from the crown of the head to the sole of the foot—in the laws, judgment, judges, customs, &c., so that none that feared God could live in peace therein; (3) that all the people in the land are infidels.

---

[1] There are two of this name mentioned in the Egerton Papers : one, Arthur, who was examiner (reader) of the MS. of " A Collection of Certain Letters, &c."; another—to whom Barrow gave drafts of two letters to write. Perhaps " Scipio " is the latter.

[2] Bellot and Bowle "died awhile after in prison in Newgate." See "An Apologie or Defence of such true Christians as are commonly (but unjustly) called Brownists" (1604), p. 95.

[3] Apologie, pp. 89–94.

As to the first it is an utter mistake, "both contrary to my meaning and to my express words . . . I (have) purposely defended Her Majesty's baptism against such as held the baptism given in Popery to be no baptism at all." As to the second, what I wrote "was drawn from Isaiah i. and Rev. xiii." I had "no evil mind toward the State, laws, or judges; but only showed that when the ministry—the salt, the light—is corrupt, the body and all the parts must needs be unsound." As to the third, "I answered that I gladly embraced and believed the common faith received and professed in this land as most holy and sound; that I had reverend estimation of sundry, and good hope of many hundred thousands in the land, though I utterly disliked the present constitution of this Church in the present communion, ministry, ministration, worship, government, and ordinances ecclesiastical of these cathedral and parishional assemblies." " Some other few things such as they thought might most make against me were called out of my writings and urged: as, that 1 should hold Her Majesty to be auti-Christian, and her Government anti-Christian." "A great and manifest injury." But all I said in self-defence was of no avail, "no doubt through the Prelates' former instigations and malicious accusations." And so "I, with my four other brethren, were the 23rd of the third month condemned and adjudged to suffer death as felons upon these indictments aforesaid. Upon the 24th, early in the morning, was preparation made for our execution. "We"—"brought out of the Limbo, our irons smitten off"·—were "ready to be bound to the cart, when Her Majesty's most gracious pardon came for our reprieve. After that the bishops sent unto us certain doctors and deans to exhort and confer with us." But it was too late. "Our time was now too short in the world." We had need to bestow it not "unto controversies so much as unto more profitable and comfortable considerations." Yet we said that if they would "get our lives respited" and join with us two of our brethren . . . whom we named," then would

Execution "stayed,' March 24.

we " gladly condescend to any Christian and orderly conference by the Scriptures." This offer was ignored. And " upon the last day of the third month. my brother Greenwood and I were very early and secretly conveyed to the place of execution, where being tied by the necks to the tree, we were permitted to speak a few words . . . And having both of us almost

Execution stayed a second time, March 31.
finished our last words, behold! one was even at that instant come with a reprieve for our lives from Her Majesty, which was not only very thankfully received by us, but with exceeding rejoicing and applause by all the people—both at the place of execution, and in the ways, streets, and houses as we returned . . . And sure we have no doubt but the same our gracious God that hath wrought this marvellous work in Her Majesty's most princely heart—to cause her of her own accord and singular wisdom, even before she knew our inno-cency, twice to stay the execution of that rigorous sentence, will now much more—after so assured and wonderful demon-stration of our innocency—move her gracious Majesty freely and fully to pardon the execution thereof, as she hath never desired, and always loathly shed, the blood of her greatest enemies, much less will she now of her loyal, Christian, and innocent subjects, especially if Her Majesty might be truly informed both of the things that are passed and of our lamentable estate and great misery, wherein we now continue in a miserable place and case, in the loathsome gaol of Newgate, under this heavy judgment, every day expecting execution." Your ladyship, then, will do a right Christian and gracious act " to inform Her Majesty of our entire faith unto God, unstained loyalty to Her Majesty, innocency and good conscience toward all men ; and so to procure our pardon," or else removal of " our poor worn bodies out of this miserable gaol (the horror whereof is not to be spoken to your Honour) to some more honest and meet place, if she vouchsafe us longer to live. Let not . . . right dear and elect lady, any worldly or politic impediments or unlikeli-hoods, no fleshly fears, diffidence, or delays stop or hinder you

from speaking to Her Majesty on our behalf before she go out of this city." The letter is dated the 4th or 5th day (the writer does not quite know which) of the fourth month, 1593, and is signed,

Your Honour's humbly at commandment during life, condemned of men, but received of God, HENRY BARROW.

One can hardly doubt that the lady[1] was moved by so piteous an appeal to do her best. But if she did she failed. "On the 6th day of the same month presently following was he and Mr. Greenwood conveyed again to the place of execution and there put to death. And this so early and secretly as well they could in such a case." Thomas Philippes, *alias* Morice, in a letter to William Sterrell,[2] tells us that "there was a Bill preferred against the Barrowists and Brownists, making it felony to maintain any opinions against the ecclesiastical Government. This Bill, truly described as the murderous Act to retain the Queen's subjects in obedience, passed the Upper House "by the Bishops' means," but when it came to the Lower House (on April 5[3]), "it was found so captious" that it ran great risk of being thrown out altogether. Finally, however, "by the earnest labouring of those that sought to satisfy the Bishops' humours," it passed. But, says Philippes, "they have minced it as is thought, so as it will not reach to any man that shall deserve favour." And "the day after the Lower House had showed their dislike of this Bill," Barrow and Greenwood "were, early in the morning, hanged." He adds: "It is plainly said that their execution proceeded of (the) malice of the Bishops, to spite the Nether House, which

Execution takes place, April 6.

---

[1] Was she his cousin Agnes, wife of the Lord Keeper's eldest son, Sir Nicholas Bacon?

[2] April, 1593. S. P. Dom: Eliz. Vol. 244, No. 124 (quoted by Arber in 'Story of the Pilgrim Fathers," p. 83).

[3] This is Arber's date. D'Ewes, in his "Journals" (p. 516), gives the 4th. It was then that Sir Walter Raleigh expressed his opinion about the

· Brownists. With reference to the "Bill," he said: "It is to be feared that men not guilty will be included in it. And that Law is hard that takes life and sendeth into banishment where men's intentions shall be judged by a jury, and they shall be judged what another means. But that Law that is against the fact is but just, and punish the fact as severely as you will."

hath procured them much hatred of the common people affected that way." He also declares in the same letter that "the (first?) reprieval proceeded of a supplication made to the Lord Treasurer, complaining "That in a land where no Papist was touched for religion by death," the blood of men who concurred " in opinion, touching faith, with that (which) was professed in the country, should be first shed: desiring, therefore, conference to be removed from their errors by reason, or else further satisfaction of the world touching their opinions." This " supplication " came to the hands of Whitgift, "who, nevertheless, was very peremptory, so as the Lord Treasurer gave him and (Richard Fletcher) Bishop of Worcester some sound taxing words." Burghley also " used some speech to the Queen, but was not seconded by any (of the Privy Council)," and is supposed, consequently, to have become "more remiss," which, from what we know of his character, is not unlikely.

We may add the following story which is told by Governor Bradford.[1] It sounds rather apocryphal, but the editor of Barrow's "Platform," who calls himself Miles Micklebound, also relates it as something *told to himself* by " a gentleman of a good house." Micklebound, perhaps, was the first to set it going in Separatist circles. The story is that "Queen Elizabeth asked the learned Doctor Raynolds what he thought of those two men—Master Barrow and Master Greenwood? And he answered Her Majesty that it could not avail anything to show his judgment concerning them, seeing they were put to death. And being loath to speak his mind further, Her Majesty charged him, upon his allegiance, to speak. Whereupon he answered, That he was persuaded, if they had lived, they would have been two as worthy instruments for the Church of God as have been raised up in this age. Her Majesty sighed and said no more.

[1] In his " Dialogue, or the sum of a conference between some young men born in New England and sundry ancient men that came out of Holland and old England—1648."— Young's Chronicles (1844), pp. 431-2.

And afterwards riding to a park by the place where they were executed, and being willing to take further information concerning them, demanded of the Right Honourable Earl of Cumberland (that was present when they suffered), what end they made? He answered, " A very godly end, and prayed for your Majesty and the State."

Bradford gives the story almost word for word as Micklebound does, and doubtless got it from him.[1] Micklebound adds what Bradford also repeats, that "Mr. Philips,[2] a preacher famous, having heard and seen Master Barrow, his holy speeches, and preparations for death, said, 'Barrow, Barrow, my soul be with thine.' For thus have I been credibly informed." Still less likely, perhaps, is the following, which yet scarcely ought to be omitted:—"That the Queen demanded of the Archbishop 'what he thought of them in his conscience.' He answered, 'He thought they were servants of God, but dangerous to the State.' 'Alas!' said she, 'shall we put the servants of God to death?' And this was the true cause why no more of them were put to death in her days."[3] We cannot do better than conclude with a further quotation from Bradford :—

" *Young Men.* Did any of you know Mr. Barrow? if we may be so bold to ask ; for we would willingly know what (was) his life and conversation ; because some, we perceive, have him in precious esteem, and others can scarce name him without some note of obloquy and dislike.

" *Ancient Men.* We have not seen his person, but some of us have been well acquainted with those that knew him

---

[1] Micklebound wrote in 1611 ; Bradford in 1648. Bradford quotes him repeatedly, but simply as something "in print." I follow Miles.

[2] Here Bradford has it : " First from Mr. Philips, a famous and godly preacher, &c.," making Philips reporter only. This, no doubt, was Edward Philips, M.A. (of Pembroke College, Oxford), who became a preacher at St. Saviour's, Southwark, and attracted a large auditory, mostly of zealous Puritans. He was committed to the Gatehouse by Whitgift in 1596. We find him among the preachers appointed to confer with the prisoners in 1590. Francis Johnson often mentions him.

[3] Bradford is sole authority for this "Dialogue," pp. 432–3. But he gives it as " What some of us have heard by credible information."

6

familiarly both before and after his conversion ; and one of us hath had conference with one that was his domestic servant and tended upon him both before and some while after the same.   He was a gentleman of good worth, and a flourishing courtier in his time, . . . and accomplished with strong parts.[1] . . . And thus much we can further affirm, from those that well knew him, that he was very comfortable to the poor and those in distress in their sufferings ; and when he saw he must die, he gave a stock for the relief of the poor of the Church, which was a good help to them in their banished condition afterwards.   Yea, and that which some will hardly believe, he did much persuade them to peace, and composed many differences that were grown amongst them whilst he lived, and would have, it is like, prevented more that after fell out if he had continued."[2]

NOTE I.

WAS BARROW MARPRELATE ?

DR. DEXTER, in claiming the Marprelate Tracts for Barrow,[3] lays stress on similarity of style, and especially the occurrence of legal phrases, which suggest a lawyer rather than a minister.   Tests of style are largely subjective.   My own impression, e.g., quite differs from Dr. Dexter's on this point ; and I should say that Barrow's style is, on the whole, very unlike that of Marprelate.   But this may go for little, though I have compared the two with some care.   As to the legal phrases, they may go for even less.   Such phrases as "mend your answer," a "scandalum magnatum," "called in Coram," "freeholder," "Court of Requests," a "suit," the "cause," "without testimony," "by hearsay," "plain theft," &c., can hardly be said necessarily to presuppose a legal training.   Some of them are not legal at all, in the special sense ; and all are commonplace.

The points, however, to be emphasized are such as these :—

1. *Barrow was a Separatist, whereas the "Tracts" are merely Puritan.*

Of course the two terms are, to a great extent, identical.

Thus Barrow might well have written the following :—"The Puritans (falsely so-called) show it to be unlawful for the magistrate to go about to

---

[1] Then comes the story of his conversion.

[2] Young's Chronicles, pp. 433-35.

[3] "Congregationalism, as seen in its Literature," pp. 196-202.

make any members for the body of Christ; they hold all officers of the Church to be members of the body; and, therefore, they hold the altering or the abolishing of the offices of Church government to be the altering and abolishing of the members of the Church; the altering and abolishing of which members they hold to be unlawful because it must needs be a maim unto the body. They hold Christ Jesus to have set down as exact and as unchangeable a Church government as ever Moses did."[1]

But he could not possibly have written this :—" The minister's maintenance by tithe no *Puritan* denieth to be unlawful. For Martin (good Mr. Parson), you must understand, doth account no Brownist to be a Puritan."[2] Martin is indignant that Bishop Cooper[3] should have confounded Brownists and Puritans by ascribing to the latter so many " inventions of his own brain " : " as that, *e.g.*, it is not lawful for Her Majesty to allot any lands unto the maintenance of the minister, or the minister to live upon lands for this purpose allotted unto him ; but is to content himself with a final pension, and so small as he have nothing to leave for his wife and children after him (for whom he is not to be careful, but to rest on God's Providence), and is to require no more but food and raiment that in poverty he might be answerable unto our Saviour and His Apostles." This may be, says Martin, the doctrine of Brownists ; but the Bishop is guilty of " a most notorious, wicked " slander " in fathering these things upon those whom they call Puritans, which never any, enjoying common sense, would affirm." Nay, " bring me *him* " . . . " who holdeth " any such doctrine, and " I will prove him to be utterly bereaved of his wits." But this was just what Barrow did hold. Witness, *e.g.*, his declarations before the Council already quoted, and witness especially his " Platform " which has this entirely for its drift. So clear a contradiction may be deemed decisive.

2. *But we note a second point.*

Dexter admits that Barrow must have worked, if at all, " in co-operation with Penry " ; and that, if Barrow were Martin, Penry was " nearly the only man then outside the Fleet Prison who was master of the secret." This, of course, would mean mutual intimacy and sympathy. And says Dexter, " it is clear[4] that a close intimacy soon afterwards existed between him and John Penry, with no evidence that it did not date back far enough to cover all the needs of the case." *There is evidence, however, that at least so late as the date of the " Brief Discovery of the False Church," 1590–91, the intimacy did*

---

[1] Quoted from " Hay any Worke for Cooper."
[2] " Hay any Worke for Cooper."
[3] In his " Admonition to the People of England."
[4] How clear ? If " soon afterwards " means subsequent to 1589, it is clear, on the contrary, that Penry went to Scotland; that he did not return till the late autumn of 1592; that he spent the next few months of his life in evading " pursuivants "; and that there is nothing to indicate that he saw Barrow again. It is questionable, indeed, whether they had any *personal* acquaintance at all. See infra.

not exist; or, if it did, was by no means sympathetic. For in that book are several references to Penry which Dexter appears to have overlooked. Before citing them let me explain their origin. We have had occasion already to mention Dr. Some's "Godly Treatise" against Barrow and Greenwood. It is dedicated to Hatton and Burghley, Chancellors respectively of Oxford and Cambridge; and, in reminding them that these two men, "as yet very wilful and ignorant," are "the Masters" of the Anabaptist "College," the author urges severe measures. "The way to cure" such men, "if God will, is to teach and punish them." So were heretics dealt with in the Primitive Church; so were the Arians in Constantine's time; so were the Donatists in Augustine's day. And this is God's order. These men have given out that the Bishops and clergy only are against them; let the Chancellors, as heads of the civil power, show that they are against them no less, and "are able to repress them." But he assails Penry as well as Barrow and Greenwood. He had done so a year before in his first "Godly Treatise," adducing there a "Table of (sixteen) gross errors and Anabaptistical fancies." In his present treatise he brings forward two charges :—(1) That Penry comes very "near" to the Anabaptistical Recusants, Barrow and Greenwood, in their assertion that the "Discipline" is an essential part of the Church; (2) that "Mr. Penry jumps with them in their argument that baptism administered and received in the Popish Church is not God's, but the devil's Baptism." Penry prepared "An Answer," which (on January 29, 1590) was seized[1] in his study at Northampton. This led a "friend" to take up the matter. The friend, it appears, was Job Throckmorton,[2] and his defence of Penry took the title, "Master Some laid open in his colours, wherein the indifferent reader may easily see how wretchedly and loosely he hath handled the cause against Mr. Penry. Done by an Oxford man to his friend in Cambridge." With respect to Some's two charges particularly he denies any leaning on Penry's part to the Brownism of Barrow and Greenwood, and represents him as holding Some's own view of Romish baptism—viz., that it *may* be invalid, and yet that its subjects need not be rebaptized. Her Majesty—*e.g.*, though she had received baptism at the hands of a Popish priest, need not "be brought back again to the Sacrament of her entrance and engrafting into the Body." Now Barrow's view of baptism was peculiar. He thought that even if "falsely administered," it had the character of an indelible seal, like circumcision, and was incapable of repetition. He thus evidenced his own deep reverence for the rite as such. But Penry's Oxford friend, and Penry, too, seemed to play fast and loose with baptism. It might be worthless as done by a Popish priest, and yet need not be done again. Especially must there be no question about the Queen's baptism! So, when the treatise came somehow under his eye at the time he was engaged on the "Brief Discovery," we find him exclaiming: "If Mr. Penry pro-

[1] Arber's Introductory Sketch to the Marprelate Controversy, p. 173.

[2] Arber's Introductory Sketch to the Marprelate Controversy, p. 179.

vide not better stuff for his own defence than his friend of Oxenford (Oxford) hath as yet brought, I can tell him this—that both he and his companion must become Brownists (as they, to the dishonour of Christ, term us), or else this Popish Doctor (Some) will prevail against them—for that most odious and unChristian flattery of Her Majesty will neither cover nor cure this sore." Such an outburst scarcely favours the notion that Barrow and Penry were friends, or of one mind. But he is yet more severe. He includes the scholar of Oxford, whom he calls "Mr. Penry's Proctor," and even Penry himself apparently, in the class of "scoffing divines," one of his names for the forward Preachers, Reformists, Puritans, who (among other faults) place their reliance rather on "Authentic Authors" like Dr. Fulke (with his "doughty Sir John of Beverley")[1] than on the simple Scriptures. In short, although he is one of those "poor persecuted Christians" whom Penry's friend (in Penry's name) "despises and blasphemes," "baptizing" them "into the name of Browne," yet he can afford to pity them; and does, indeed, "grieve and blush for shame" at their evil handling of "so glorious a cause."[2]

Surely the conclusion is unavoidable that, if Barrow could not have been "Martin" unless he had the constant assistance of Penry, then "Martin" he was not. To this may be added—as an offset to Dr. Dexter's assurance that when Barrow refers to Martin in his "Brief Discovery" he never does so "in such a manner as to imply hostility, or even to intimate dislike"—the fact that once he calls him the "Libeller"[3]; and the more decisive fact that, in his "Plain Refutation of Mr. Gifford,"[4] he speaks of the "preachers which make show as though they sought a sincere reformation of all things according to the Gospel of Christ," adding, "and these are hereupon called Precisians, or Puritans, and now lately "Martinists."[5] Finally, whereas Dr. Dexter appeals to the "elaborate defence of Martin" in a "Petition directed to Her Majesty" (1590)—as still "more to the point"—it is certain that the "Petition" is a Puritan document, and so not of Barrow's writing.[6]

NOTE II.

Comparing the list of names subjoined to Barrow's Petition (early spring of 1592) with the earlier list of 1589-90 (February), it is interesting to note:—

(1) That all the names reappear except three—those of Thomas Settle, William Clark, and Richard Wheeler. The prisoners, therefore, of February, 1590, are in prison still with these exceptions.

[1] Referred to in the Treatise.

[2] Barrow argues the case against the Clerk (the great Clerk, the scholar) of Oxford—whom evidently he does not know—in a long parenthesis (pp. 104-122) of his "Discovery." From these the quotations are made.

[3] Brief Discovery, p. 195.

[4] p. 136.

[5] He says these resemble, or rather exceed, that ancient sect of the Pharisees "in preciseness, outward show of holiness, hypocrisy, vain glory, covetousness."—Ditto.

[6] Appendix iii.

(2) That twelve are common to the list of 1590 and the still earlier list of 1588 (May or June), so that these have been prisoners at least from this latter date, and some, of course, considerably longer—*e.g.*, George Collier in 1588 had been imprisoned 19 months, John Frances 10 months, William Bromall 12 months.

(3) That of the ten reported dead in the latest list, nine had been breathing the "infected" air of the prisons since before May (or June) of 1588. They are Henry Tomson, a prisoner since the autumn of 1586; Jerome Studley (was he Daniel's brother?) committed since the early months of 1587, "for not swearing before the Bishop of London . . . having a wife and six children, and nothing but his labours in his calling to sustain them"; John Chaundler, having a wife and eight children; George Bryghte (*or Dinghtie*), "committed from Newgate by the Recorder of London for commending a faithful Christian which was there indicted"; Richard (or Roger) Jackson; Widow Row; Nicholas Crane, a man of sixty-six (at the date of his arrest), having a wife and children; Widow Meynard (Mainard); John Purdy, committed to Bridewell "by Canterbury"—there "cast into 'Little Ease,' the 'Mill,' and beaten with cudgels in that prison for refusing to hear the priest of that house." He is the Purdy (or Padry) by whom Barrow "sent out" the sheets of his "Discovery of the False Church" to Daniel Studley.

(4) Most of these must have died before February, 1590. Otherwise their names would be in the list then issued by those to be conferred with; but they are not. This, indeed, is not quite conclusive, as Purdy must have been still alive towards the end of 1590, if he did for Barrow the service just mentioned. It is clear, however, that the cases of death had nearly all occurred long previous to 1591, and were not increasing.

(5) This would seem to indicate that the treatment of prisoners had become more lenient to some extent; an inference which another fact may be taken to confirm, viz., the extensive removals from other prisons to Bridewell. Two only of the twenty-five in the list of 1588 are assigned to Bridewell. In the list of 1590 (containing fifty-two) there are none. But between the latter date and the early months of 1592 no fewer than seventeen have been transferred to Bridewell from Newgate and the Counter in Wood Street—chiefly the latter. One, indeed—William Broomal—has been there for nearly five years, although unnamed in the Bishop's list. Was he passed over (like John Purdy, perhaps, and Thomas Legate, also unnamed) as a person too insignificant? Bridewell was bad enough as a residence, but that it was a more "convenient place" than the other London prisons is proved by the prayer of the prisoners to be all sent there, if they cannot obtain bail. We may consider it, then, as implying some softening of rigour on the Archbishop's part that so many had been sent there already. At any rate, there was no increase of severity toward the rank and file of the prisoners. But Barrow and Greenwood were not among the fortunate seventeen. There was no relief for them.

(6) It is also noticeable that from February, 1590, to the beginning of

1592 (perhaps later)—a period of nearly two years—there seems to have been scarcely any new arrests. For the list of 1591 (or 1592) is professedly complete, and yet it shows but nine prisoners in addition to those of 1590. One of these, Thomas Stephens, is among the deceased. A few weeks or months of prison-life have been too much for him. The others are : John Gualter and Thomas Reeve in the Gatehouse; Luke Hayes and Richard Umberfield in Bridewell; Edmund Marsh, Anthony Johnes, — Cook, — Anger, in the White Lion. Many of the rest (some thirty-nine), as is said in the petition, have endured the " great penury and noisomeness of the prisons " for the " space of two years and a half." Twelve, we know, have endured these miseries four years or five. Three only—all found in the Bishop's list, and one of them, William Clark, in the earlier list—have regained their liberty. Three out of sixty released in the course of several years is not a large proportion. It illustrates, in a striking way, the tenacity with which the bishops gripped their prey. Death was more merciful.

-

Barrow's Doctrine of the Church.

Desiderius : Wherefore are the chief defenders of this cause called Brownists ?

Miles : Because one Mr. Brown, minister of a church, heretofore professed their cause, published it in print, and for a time continued the practice of it. . . .

Desiderius : Was there none that did write for this cause before Brown ?

Miles : Yes, verily. The Prophets, Apostles, and Evangelists have in their authentic writings laid down the grounds thereof, and upon that ground is all their building reared up, and surely settled. Moreover, many of the martyrs, both former and latter, have maintained it, as is to be seen in the acts and monuments of the Church. Also, in the days of Queen Elizabeth there was a separated Church, whereof Mr. Fitz was pastor, that professed and practised that cause before Mr. Brown wrote for it.

BARROW'S "PLATFORM,"
BY MILES MICKLEBOUND (1611).

BARROW'S DOCTRINE OF THE CHURCH.

BARROW gave a supreme authority to the Scriptures. He would receive, and he aimed to teach, nothing which they did not sanction. He wished his own words and those of others to be tested only by this rule. Here, said he, is "the golden reed" for measuring "our temple, our altar, and our worship." Here is the "light that shineth in dark places whilst we travel in the dangerous wilderness of this world." Here "the whole wisdom and counsels of God for their direction and instruction in all things are fully revealed unto us; . . . neither hath any angel in heaven, any mortal man, no, nor the whole Church, power or prerogative to alter or neglect the least iota or tittle thereof." And, therefore, "unto all the power, learning, deceit, rage of the false Church we oppose that little book of God's Word which (as the light) shall reveal her, as the fire shall consume her, as an heavy millstone shall press her and all her children, lovers, partakers, and abettors down to hell; which book we willingly receive as the judge of all our controversy, knowing that all men shall one day (and that ere long) be judged by the same. By this book whoso is found in error or transgression let them have sentence accordingly." [1] And, indeed, the question as to what should be held finally decisive of matters ecclesiastical was of critical importance. The whole issue of the argument between Barrow and his opponents turned upon it. Was reason to any extent an authority, or the early fathers, or traditions of any sort? Barrow said "No," and said it with absolute assurance. He is not un-

The Scriptures are the golden measuring reed.

[1] See opening pages of the "Discovery of the False Church."

willing to profit by the " examples and practice of those faithful
(men) that first came out of the Popish Church and enterprised
the erection and practice of Christ's ministry and ordinances
amongst themselves, according to that measure of knowledge
God gave them." [1]   He is willing to learn from the faithful of
every age in the same way.   But all these may err; all must
be confirmed or corrected by the written Word.   This alone
is "our warrant of all those things we do or refuse to do."
By this alone we stand—" gladly submitting ourselves, all our
actions and whole faith " unto the "proof and trial thereof." [2]
In this respect he was a Protestant of the Protestants.

Still, Barrow did not think he could rightly interpret the
Word by his own private judgment.   He needed guidance,
and found it in the illuminating presence of Christ's Spirit.
This belief is finely expressed in one of the " Prison " Conferences.   Barrow had just complained that he "could never
as yet obtain any such conference where the Book of God
might peaceably decide all our controversies."

The Word is interpreted by the Spirit.

Dr. Andrews (his opponent). Why, the Book of God cannot
speak ; which way should it decide our controversies ?

Barrow. But the Spirit of God can speak, and which way
is that Spirit tried or discerned but by the Word of God ?

Andrews. But the spirits of men must be subject unto
men.   Will you not subject your spirit to the judgment of
men ?

B. The spirit of the prophets must be subject to the
prophets, yet must the prophets judge by the Word of God.
And for me I willingly submit my whole faith to be tried and
judged by the Word of God, of all men.

A. All men cannot judge ; who, then, shall judge of the
Word ?

B. The Word—and let every one as judgeth take heed that
he judge aright thereby ; Wisdom is justified of her children.

[1] Plain Refutation of Mr. Gifford, p. 196.   [2] Plain Refutation of Mr. Gifford, p. 196.

A. This savoureth of a private spirit.

B. This is the Spirit of Christ and His Apostles, and most publicly they submitted their doctrines to the trial of all men. So do I.

A. What! Are you an Apostle?

B. No; but I have the spirit of the Apostles.

A. What! the spirit of the Apostles?

B. Yes; the spirit of the Apostles.

A. What! in that measure?

B. In that measure that God hath imparted unto me, though not in that measure that the Apostles had, by any comparison. Yet the same spirit. There is but one Spirit.[1]

Thus holding by the written Word as interpreted by the Spirit, he deemed himself safe, neither striking against the rocks of Popery, nor falling upon the shelves and quicksands of Anabaptistry.[2] He did not, like the former, add tradition to Scripture; nor, like the latter (as he supposed), make Scripture subordinate to the inner light.

Consulting, then, the New Testament alone, what is the Church?

I. "A faithful . . . people gathered by the Word unto Christ, and submitting themselves" to Him "in all things is a Church."[3] More particularly, "The true planted and rightly established Church of Christ is a company of faithful people—separated from the unbelievers and heathen of the land—gathered in the name of Christ, whom they truly worship and readily obey as their only King, Priest, and Prophet, and joined together as members of one body, ordered and governed by such officers and laws as Christ, in His last will and testament, hath thereunto ordained—all and each one of them standing in and for their Christian liberty to practise whatsoever God hath commanded and revealed unto them in His holy

Definition of a Church.

---

[1] Compare Discovery of False Church, p. 196.

[2] Compare Discovery of False Church, p. 32.

[3] Discovery, &c., p. 34.

Word within the limits of their callings, executing the Lord's judgments against all transgression and disobedience which ariseth among them, and cutting it off accordingly by the power which their Lord and King Christ Jesus hath committed unto them." [1]

Such a congregation, though consisting but of two or three, is complete in itself. It owns no Lord but Christ. In Him "all the members . . . have a like interest—in His Word, in the faith. They altogether make one body unto Him. All the affairs of the Church belong to that body together. All the actions of the Church . . . be the actions of them all jointly and of every one of them severally . . . as the members are jointly bound unto edification, and unto all other helps or service they may do unto the whole. All are charged to watch, exhort, admonish, stir up, reprove, &c., and hereunto have the power of our Lord Jesus, the keys of the kingdom of heaven, even the Word of the Most High." [2] . . .

Thus the Church is a brotherhood : a communion of saints. But "though there be a communion in the Church yet there is no equality. The Church knoweth how to give honour and reverence unto their elders, especially to them that labour in the word and doctrine. The Church of Christ is taught to obey and submit unto their leaders, to acknowledge them that labour amongst them, and that are set over them in the Lord and admonish them; and to hold those in superabundant love for their work's sake. The elders also amongst themselves know how to give honour one unto another by going before; yet all this without prejudice to themselves that give, or detriment to him that receiveth it; without the loss of the least jot of their own liberty, or puffing him up or setting him in any unlawful authority. They give it to his labour, diligence, virtue, and desert, which ceasing, they straight withdraw their praise, and

---

[1] Letter to Cartwright, Travers, &c. (1588). [2] Discovery of False Church, p. 85.

in the stead thereof use exhortation, admonition, yea (if need be) censure. . . . All the gifts God hath given any member are to the service of the whole body: he that will be greatest must be as the least; he must wash the feet, and not have his feet kissed, of the least; all superiority is here comprised within the bounds of Christian order and modesty. Humility goeth before and is the companion of honour; honour is not here conferred to lift up the hearts of the greatest above the least, but rather for the counsel, care, love, service unto all; it is willingly given unto such by all; ambition and vain glory are here carefully avoided both by the givers and receivers. . . . The greatest elder of the Church, the Pastor, is but a servant and steward of the House, not Lord of the Heritage; but (*i.e.*, only) a member, not lord, of the body—to be honoured for his excellent place in the body and gifts of God; to be reverenced for his faithfulness, labour, and diligence. Yet this must ever be remembered, his honour, consisteth in his service, his service belongeth unto all; so that the least member of the body hath like interest in him as he in the least member; the least member hath like liberty and freedom with him in Christ, though not like gifts or function of Christ."[1]

So far, however, the description is general, and may have left no very clear impression. To come, then, to something more definite. Barrow claims that the exact pattern of a true Church is given us in the New Testament. For is it to be supposed that

(1) God could be less careful " for the structure, instruments, forms, order, and ordinances " of the Christian Church than of the Jewish Temple?[2]

(2) " With what extreme desire have all the prophets longed after and (with what) great delight written of the excellent beauty, heavenly government, inviolable order of the Church? " . . . " Faithful Jews " had indeed " the inward government

Reasons for expecting an exact pattern of the Church in the New Testament.

---

[1] Discovery of the False Church, pp. 224-5.

[2] Discovery of the False Church, p. 195.

and sanctification of the Spirit before Christ came in our flesh "
. . . but "because they wanted the heavenly practise and
ministry of the Gospel, the heavenly orders, exercises, and
communion of His Church, they were called from those ritual
types and figurative shadows, whereby in their infancy and
nonage they were trained and shut up, unto the open sight and
clear beholding of the glory of the Lord with open face—all
vails being taken away; and unto the free and orderly practice
of the same Gospel according to Christ's New Testament—all
trumpery traditions being abolished."

(3) There are "sundry places in the New Testament "
which indicate "that the ordinances left for the building,
administration, and government of the Church are the commandments of God perpetual, inviolable."

Such passages as 1 Tim. v. 21; vi. 13; 1 Cor. xiv. 37,
imply that in the Church "nothing" is to be "according to
inclination, but all by commandment." And such a chapter as
1 Cor. iii. is meant to prove that "the Church of Christ ought to
be built in all things according to the will of Christ as He hath
set down in His Testament. Otherwise it cannot either be said
(to be) His house nor the builders thereof (or the builded
therein) His faithful servants." Similarly, the teaching of
Romans xii. is to the effect that "as no mortal man can make,
fashion, dispose, or knit together these human members of a
natural body, so much less can he make any other members
serve in the places of the true natural members, or by any
means place, fasten, and knit those—as by joints and sinews—
unto and in a man's body." But it is objected, "If that
outward form of discipline were of the essence of the Church,
then where that form of discipline either was or is not, there
was and is no Church—which is a gross absurdity." Barrow
answers, "Our question here is not whether the Church may
not sometime upon some necessities be without this order, or
some part thereof; but whether the Church may receive any
other form of government instead of this." There are, as

Cp. also
1 Cor. xi.
12; iv. 17;
2 Cor. i. 13;
2 Thess. ii.
15; Coloss.
ii. 5.

The
Church
may some-
times come
short of
the true
order;

matter of fact, times when "some necessities" enforce the Church "to be without this holy order for a season—as in the first gathering of the saints, especially *now* when we are not to expect any such miraculous or extraordinary giving of God's Spirit as was in the primitive times . . . also, in time of persecution, when the Church cannot peaceably meet either to choose or exercise any ministry, or that their chief and principal members be held from them in prisons, or at such time as the chief elders are taken away, either by death or otherwise fall away. In these and such like times the Church may for a season, upon necessity so enforcing, do without this established order; but this is neither willingly to neglect it nor presumptuously to reject it. Here hence it followeth not that this holy order is not always necessary, because it is not nor cannot be always executed; so (*i.e.*, else) they might conclude all God's laws not always necessary, perpetual and expedient, because they are not, or cannot be, always practised by us. Should our infirmity, sin, or default take away the stability or truth of God's ordinances?" In fine, "nothing is more sure than this, the true Church can be established into no other order, it can receive none other officers or laws than are in Christ's Testament prescribed."[1]

But may never change the order.

What is this order? First, as regards the ministry. It "consists of two sorts": elders and deacons. Of the elders, some "give attendance unto the public ministry of the Word and Sacraments." These are the pastor and teacher. Others "give attendance to the public order and government of the Church." These are the "governing" elders. As to deacons, they are "to attend the gathering and distributing the goods of the Church."[2] Barrow also names the elders ἐπίσκοποι, or overseers, and specifies their functions as follows:—The pastor exhorts, and none but he can "deliver" the sacraments; the teacher expounds "doctrine"; the elder,

The Ministry

---

[1] Discovery of the False Church, pp. 197 to 215. [2] Discovery of the False Church, p. 46.

so-called in the narrower sense, assists the pastor and teacher to govern. Further, the deacons are divisible into deacons proper, who collect and distribute the benevolence and contributions of the saints; the relievers, who attend to the sick and impotent, &c.[1]

Is derived from the whole Church; These " permanent officers "—" so few in number, easily recited," and sufficient—the Church, as a whole, must appoin and control. This is its inalienable right and solemn obligation. Every minister of a true Church, says Barrow, is first duly proved . . . by rules of the New Testament, apparent graces, manifestation of the Spirit, unreproveable conversation. Next he is " chosen and ordained with prayer and fasting in and by the congregation." Finally, he is always " responsible to the Church, and liable to its censure if in anything " he should " transgress or offend."[2]

This being so, some points seem clear :—

Hence the Church prior and superior; (a) One is that the Church is prior and superior to its institutions. The Church is a company of faithful people. This is its essential quality. If, therefore, by "no default or negligence in them," they have "as yet attained to have neither a ministry nor sacraments among them" they are none the less a Church, for even sacraments "are not a perpetual mark of the Church." And as to ministers, Barrow puts the case clearly enough in his conversation with Dr. Andrews :—

Barrow. There must be sheep before there be a flock, a flock before there be a shepherd.

Andrews. A flock and a shepherd are relatives.

Barrow. There must be a flock before there can be a shepherd, because the people must choose the pastor.

Andrews. That is a device of yours.

Barrow. Will you call the commandment of Christ my device ?[3]

---

[1] Plain Refutation, &c., p. 106.
[2] Discovery of the False Church, p. 46.
[3] Conference, March 17, 1590.

(b) Another plain inference is that there can be no quali- **And all its members are spiritually, though not officially, equal.** tative difference between the people and the ministers. They are only parts of a larger whole, and the "whole lump" is holy. They receive grace as the humblest member of the Church receives grace—from immediate relation to Christ. Therefore "we hold all true believers ecclesiastical and spiritual." "We know not what you mean by your old popish terms of laymen."[1]

(c) A third conclusion is that ministers always presup- **A church of mere "officers" impossible.** pose a Church, and apart from the Church are an impossibility. No Church, no ministers. No true Church, no true ministers. And so "if the Church, consisting of private men" (that is to say, the true Church), "may not in this estate meet and ordain Christ's true ministry amongst them, then is there no true ministry upon earth, neither ever can be until God raise up new apostles and evangelists, and buildeth a new Church upon a new foundation, which shall be when we have a new Christ."[2]

(d) Accordingly, no one whom the Church itself has not **Ministers cannot be imposed on a church; or be lawfully called apart from it.** called has any right to be its minister. A ministry exercised merely by authorisation of bishop, patron, or prince is utterly unlawful. Not lawful even is a ministry grounded on the consciousness of an inward call. About this Barrow is very explicit. "Gifts do help to make men fit for a ministry, but do not make them ministers, much less *true* ministers. For every true minister must not only be qualified with gifts fitting for the same, but must also be lawfully called thereunto."[3]

Barrow.[4] How can you approve your own ministry by the Testament of Christ?

Sperin. My ministry is from God, with the approbation of the assembly of the Church where I am. . . .

Barrow. Your entrance was by the patron and bishop, your office to a town priest or parish parson, your administra-

[1] Certain Slanderous Articles, No. IV.
[2] Plain Refutation of Mr. Gifford, p. 197.
[3] Miles Micklebound in Barrow's Platform.
[4] Conference, March 14, 1590.

tion according to the prescription and limitation of your lord the bishop, to whom you have sworn your canonical obedience.

Sperin. The patron doth elect by consent of the people, who have yielded their right unto him as unto the wisest and worthiest among them.

Barrow. The patron got his power rather from the Pope; he exercises it without privitie and maugre the will of the people; he may be a child, woman, or a hundred miles off.

Sperin. I make less matter of my ordination than of my ministry.

Barrow. Yet without a true calling you cannot exercise any true office.

Sperin. The calling is not the substance of the ministry.

Barrow. He which wanteth the calling of Christ unto the ministry cannot have or exercise any ministry in the Church; but you want the calling of Christ unto your ministry: therefore the ministry you exercise is not of Christ.

Sperin. I have the true calling of Christ unto my ministry in my conscience. . . . I stand more upon this and the consent of the people than upon my outward calling by the bishop. . . .

Barrow. But what, then, think you of the calling by these bishops?

Sperin. I confess it to be unlawful.

Barrow. Set down that under your hand.

Sperin. To what end? That were to bring myself into danger.

Barrow. Are you afraid to witness unto the truth? Well, but being unlawful, how chances you were not afraid to receive it and still to retain it?

Sperin. I did it in ignorance. I have since repented it.

Barrow. How can that be, seeing you still retain, still administer by the same bishop's licence, and still stand under his yoke and obedience?

Sperin. I attribute much to the civil magistrate. I do it because of the civil magistrate that authoriseth the bishop; . . . and when you affirm that the Queen and the Parliament do wickedly in giving this power and authority unto the bishops, will you write *that* ?

Barrow. Yes, that I will, by the grace of God, whilst I have breath, and seal it with my blood also, if so God will. . . .

Sperin (returning to his earlier plea). I thank God I have *His* calling unto my ministry, which is the inward calling, being approved by my gifts unto my flock; so that though there were error in my outward calling, which I have repented, yet my ministry is not disannulled.

Barrow. With what conscience can you now call that an error in a true calling, which even now you confessed to be a false calling ? . . . make it either good or evil, lawful or unlawful, by the Word of God . . . it is too anabaptistical to justify open transgression by the inward conscience or gifts. Might not any thus usurp the civil magistrate's office also by their inward gifts, wisdom, knowledge, fitness, &c. . . . ?[1]

Barrow is inexorably consistent. If, *e.g.*, a true calling is necessary to the making of a true minister, and a true calling comes only through the voice of a true Church, then is it not vain to quote the fruits of a ministry in proof of its validity ? Certainly, says Barrow; even the Priesthood of Rome might stand by this test; for not seldom its preaching may be a means of salvation to individual souls. For such a fact proves only how God may choose any man's lips " to beget faith " in His elect. It can avail nothing to establish what is contrary to the Word of God. So he says to those who remain in the Church of England (though disposed to admit that its constitution is anti-Christian), because of the comfort received from some of its ministers, " as for the comfort

[1] Cf. Conference with Cooper, April 3, 1590.

received by their preaching, it having no promise of blessing in the Word of God (your Church and whole ministry being accursed), is rather a fearful sign of the effectual working of their delusions, than any reason whereby you may assure yourselves, or justify them, in their ungodly proceedings. . . ."[1]

Stringent logic.

We have here the logical outcome of a determination to assert, at all costs, what was held to be the Divine order of the Church. A like logical stringency, combined with a quite different conception of the Church, has driven the High Anglican of our own day to a like result.

This is not the place to attempt criticism. My purpose just now is simply to expound. And having seen how strict Barrow could be, it is desirable to show something of his

Prophecy.

breadth. This may be illustrated by his view of Prophecy. Elders and Deacons represent the permanent, unchangeable functions of the Church. But the Church, besides these, has in prophecy an abiding gift of the Spirit. Its presence is significant of an inspired community. Its end is "the edification, exhortation, and comfort of the whole body." Its means is some spontaneous declaration of the Divine will "according to the Scriptures." Its subject may be any true believer. It is the Spirit's own voice, and therefore may by no means be "quenched." But it is proved to be of the Spirit by its moderation and self-control.

The Presbyterians regarded the gift with suspicion, and tried to explain it away, so far as private members of the Church were concerned.

(a) They said it was to be "understood only of such ministers as have the gift of preaching (as they call it), holding it unlawful for any one else to speak of the Scriptures by way of interpretation and prophecy, especially to expound them in the church or congregation."[2]

[1] Discovery of the False Church, p. 154.　　[2] Discovery of the False Church p. 169.

(b) But although "the Pastor and Teacher are the only offices that I now know appointed to the ministry of the Word,"[1] yet *this* gift is not confined to them. It is dispensed to others also, and may be freely exercised, so far as they exercise it "according to the proportion of faith, speaking as the words of God always, keeping themselves within the bound of sobriety and truth."[2] It is the "first ordinance that the Lord commanded and commended in His Church, under the Gospel, exhorting *all* His saints to the same, as the most special and excellent gift, yea, and most needful at all times, but especially when the pastor and teacher are either taken away by death, imprisoned, or exiled."[3]

(c) And therefore, "it is pride, insolence, yea, cruelty to assume unto themselves only this bountiful grace of God," alleging, perhaps, that otherwise one might expect to see "women" claiming "to speak"; "the offences of Corah and Uzziah" repeated; even the "council chamber" invaded.[4] Again he says, "Prophets (I mean such as are known to have the gift of interpretation of Scriptures) have all of them liberty to speak what God revealeth unto them besides that which hath been delivered, so that they neither hinder, disturb, or interrupt the public ministry of the Church, but use their liberty opportunely and holily to edification. They have liberty also, yea, their especial duty it is, to observe and publicly to reprove any false interpretation, or false doctrine, delivered publicly in the Church by whomsoever; yea, this power hath the least member of the Church, in due order and place, if the prophets and elders should oversee, omit, neglect, or refuse. The whole Church also, even every peculiar Christian congregation, hath power in itself to censure not only any doctrine delivered, but the person of any member or minister of the same con-

[1] Discovery of the False Church, p. 170.
[2] Discovery of the False Church, p. 170.
[3] True Description of the Visible Congregation of the Saints, &c., p. 6.

[4] Discovery of the False Church, p. 173. Cf. Greenwood (conference with Egerton), "Gifts of interpretation are sufficient calling to speak of the Word in the congregation in due order and place."

gregation."[1] Hence to forbid prophesying would be "to stop up the conduits and springs of the Church, or rather of God's graces, whereby the Church should be watered and refreshed."[2]

Discipline. Some of the words last quoted—"the whole Church, even every peculiar congregation, hath power in itself to censure "— point to what Barrow emphasizes as almost the clearest note of a true Church, viz., its right and power to discipline itself. His chief complaint against the Church of England, and main argument for separation, is that it lacks and has even deliberately renounced this high privilege. He is dissatisfied, also, with the Presbyterian scheme, because it transfers such privilege from the Church as a whole to some of its members, or to some outside authority.

"The poor parish or congregation where these priests serve may not meddle or have to do with the election, adminis- tration, or deposing of these their ministers. For why? They are laymen and have no skill, neither ought to intermeddle with ecclesiastical affairs, or with the Word of God. Be their minister never so blind, insufficient, or vile a wretch, detected of never so horrible sins, yet may not they remove him. Their only help is to complain to their lord. Yea, all the priests of the law, both pontifical and reformists, agree in this point, and conclude that the lay people (as they term them) ought not to intermeddle either with the deposing their minister or reproof of his doctrine." If they have ground of offence the one sort (*i.e.*, the pontifical) sendeth them to their lords the bishops; the other (*i.e.*, the reformists) referreth them . . . to a provincial or classical synod or permanent council of priests, &c., . . . whose "oracles" must be received "as most holy and canonical." But in truth every true Church consists of a Christian congregation, and "every Christian congregation hath power in themselves, and of duty ought, presently and

---

[1] Plain Refutation, &c., p. 139. [2] Discovery of the False Church, p. 174.

publicly to censure any false or unsound doctrine that is publicly delivered or maintained amongst them, if it be known and discerned unto them; yea, any one member in the Church hath this power whatsoever *he* be, pastor or prophet, that uttereth it; as also to show how far this their pulpit preaching differeth from that heavenly, blessed exercise of expounding Scripture or prophecy in the Church of Christ."[1]

Barrow, then, was not a Presbyterian. This should be carefully noted. On the one hand, while granting to "Synods or councils" some good uses, he says, "they can neither add to nor diminish from the power of the Church, or execute and alter any part of the Church's duty."[2] He has no relish for what he calls the "Geneva consistory." He considers that it means "advancing and erecting one particular congregation as a judge and a mother over other their sisters." The result of this may be "the erecting in the same consistory one particular pastor as judge, &c.," and thence to something like a Pope is an easy step. But "every particular congregation hath the power of our Lord Jesus Christ against all sin and transgression to censure the sin, and excommunicate the obstinate offenders."[3] On the other hand, he has just as little sympathy with the view which would commit the government of a Church to its officers only. We have seen that he divides the regular officers into elders and deacons. Both these are ministers, not masters of the Church. Deacons, he says, are no "governing officers" at all. One who so described them seemed to him guilty of "gross error and ignorance." "This he never learned in Christ's Testament," although it may well be "the practice of the Church of Rome and England, where are such jolly archdeacons and ruffling deans. The deacon's office in the Church is to gather and distribute, not to govern."[4] Elders, too, are appointed "to see the government and order of Christ observed,

[1] Discovery of the False Church, p. 165.
[2] Discovery of the False Church, p. 166.
[3] Plain Refutation, &c., pp. 79–80.
[4] Discovery of the False Church, p. 223.

not to take all into their hands." [1] On this point Barrow has been misrepresented. It has been said that Barrow differed from Browne in the fact that, "while Browne vested all the power of discipline in the whole body of the members of each local church, Barrow and Greenwood thought it would be wiser and more Scriptural for this to be delegated to the elders." [2] But Barrow's statements, and Greenwood's no less, are quite explicit. " I never," says Barrow, " thought that the practice of Christ's government belonged only to those officers. I rather thought it had been their duty and office to have seen this government faithfully and orderly practised by all the members of the Church . . . so that if these officers or any of them transgress, the Church reserveth power to every member freely (according to the quality of the offence and the rules of the Word) to admonish and reprove the whole, to censure and excommunicate such officers so offending." Among the doctrines held by Mr. Egerton [3] was this: "The true Church may be without the power of Christ to censure or redress." To which Greenwood answered, "Christ has given to every Church His power to censure and redress." Also this—we abstain (in the English Church) to excommunicate, because we have no elders as yet. To which Greenwood answered, "The Church is never without the power to excommunicate." And this—"Our pastors only now want some censurers." To which Barrow answered, "The least member of the Church that is a communicant hath as much interest in all the censures of the Church as the pastor, and have equal power according to the rules of the Word to censure the pastor for error or transgression as the pastor hath to censure them." It was Barrow and Greenwood together who said, "The true officers of Christ usurp no tyrannical jurisdiction over the least member, neither do any public thing without the consent of the whole con-

---

[1] Discovery of the False Church, p. 223.

[2] Adeney: "The Church in the Prisons," p. 18.

[3] In Conference.

gregation, much less may the presbytery (or eldership) excommunicate any person by their sole power, seeing Christ hath given this power to the whole Church and not solely to the presbytery. . . . The prince also, if he will be held a member of Christ or of the Church, must be subject to Christ's censure in the Church."

As no true Church can dispense with its right to self-control, so must it be *ruled* entirely by the Word. The whole process of discipline is laid down there, or clearly implied.[1] Great stress is laid on Matt. xviii. 15-20, as expressing the spirit which should animate each member of a Church, and the Church collectively, in dealing with an offending brother. The same passage shows, too, what, and how solemn, an act is excommunication, the last penalty which a Church may inflict. But there are other passages having a like significance. Thus, says Barrow :— The process of discipline must be Scriptural.

(a) We read in 1 Cor. v.; Titus iii. 10; 1 Tim. i. 20: excommunication to be an utter disfranchising and public cutting off of all convinced obstinate offenders from all interest in Christ, and all communion with His Church in the open congregation.

(b) We read in the said 1 Cor. v., as also in Matt. xviii. 17; xxviii. 20; Rom. xvi. 17; 2 Thes. iii. 6, 14: the power and execution of this censure to be committed to the whole Church.

(c) We see also (from these places) the pastor and all the teachers and other members of the Church (to be) subject unto this censure—yea, and the Church where these members make such offence is to proceed against them, to avoid them, to excommunicate them. Read for further proof—Gal. i. 8, 9; 1 Tim. vi. 3, 5; 2 Tim. ii. 17; iii. 5; 2 John 9, &c.; Col. iv. 17; Philipp. iii. 2, 17, 18, 19.

(d) We see again, especially from 1 Cor. v., that excommunication must be public. This is the only legitimate

[1] Discovery of the False Church, pp. 242-3.

manner of it. It must be done in the "congregation where the whole Church is assembled." It must be done in "the usual (not the Roman) tongue." It must be done after, and only after, "the fault is publicly known, either in the first committing of it, or else by process of contemning admonition." . . .

(e) Finally, the Church may not hesitate to excommunicate the prince if necessary—in the same terms as any one else—he still retaining his "civil estate and dignity wherein God hath placed him," and still being "reverenced and obeyed of the whole Church as such a magistrate whom God hath set over them."

"Suspension" not lawful. There was a practice of "suspension," called by Barrow "a new-found censure brought by the Reformists [1]—as it were a shutting out of the holiest of all, out of the chancel, where the priest by sole authority reigneth." In plain words, persons guilty of certain milder offences were withheld from the Sacrament of the Supper: "such, e.g., as were not in love and charity with their neighbours." Barrow pronounces the practice unlawful, not because he was averse to a compassionate dealing with offenders, but because the practice was left to the sole discretion and will of the priest; because it had no sanction in the New Testament; and because if a sin deserves suspension from the Lord's Supper it deserves excommunication. This last reason is explained by Barrow's conception of what the Lord's Supper is and involves.[2] It is somewhat mystical and difficult to grasp. Certainly the Lord's table meant more to Barrow than a table of remembrance. He is fond of the words, "The cup of blessing which we bless, is it not a communion of the blood of Christ? The bread which we break, is it not a communion of the body of Christ?" He says:—

The Lord's Supper.

1. The bread and wine are a "lively and most comfortable symbol of our communion with Christ, as also each with other

---

[1] Discovery of the False Church, p. 233.					[2] Discovery of the False Church, pp. 234-7.

in Christ, . . . public, free, open, and alike common to all saints."

2. The whole Church (much less any one of it, *i.e.*, a priest) cannot separate the least of His members from the Lord's Table so long as "they remain members of Christ and are not cut off from His Body." Here, as generally, "His Body" means the visible Church. To belong to a true visible Church was to be a member of Christ's Body, and carried with it all the blessings of such a relation, particularly that of fellowship in the Church's highest act. You cannot justly be cut off from that unless for reasons which justify your expulsion from the Church altogether. If you are esteemed a "withered branch" it is the Church's solemn duty to cast you out entirely. If, notwithstanding some open sins, you are judged to be still spiritually alive, then

3. To debar you from the Lord's Table is "to deprive" you "of the communion of Christ and of the Church, and so of life"; for "except ye eat the flesh of the Son of Man and drink His blood ye can have no life in you." He goes on: "I acknowledge that many thousands that never attained the symbol of the Supper, yet do feed of the body and blood of Christ unto eternal life; yet this I say, that such as by censure are put back from the Table of the Lord are cut from the communion of Christ and of His Church, and so from life; for if he have not communion with Christ and His Church he can have no life; he cannot be both thus separate from their communion and have it together. They that pluck away the seal cancel the deed." Here the high place assigned to the Lord's Supper is obvious. It is far more than a commemorative act. It is a special means of grace. Christ can impart His life to a believing soul under any circumstances, but the ordinary channel of its communication is the bread and wine of the Supper. It is, therefore, a very grave thing to exclude a person from it. It is like destroying the seal by which the soul's deed of covenant with Christ is made sure. Only those should be

excluded who by open and obstinate sin have already given
strong ground for believing that they have no part in Christ.
Exclusion in this case would be merely declarative of an evident
fact.   But any one who might deserve such a penalty deserves
not only to be suspended from Church-fellowship in one
respect and for a time.   He deserves to be excluded in every
respect and for good.

4. "How," he asks, "can a member that is publicly
convicted of, and remaineth obstinate in, open sin be shut out
from the Table of the Lord, and yet be received and admitted
as a member unto the other ministry of the Church, e.g., the
prayers, contributions, &c. ?   Belike, the other ministry and
prayers of the Church are not so holy as this Supper ? . . ."
But they are.   One of Barrow's favourite positions is that
there is nothing "indifferent," nothing unsanctified so far as it
belongs to the Church.   The Church is an organic unity.   All
its parts have their own function, but all conduce to one end.
You can, then, enjoy the good of all, or of none.   If you are
unworthy to partake of the Lord's Table you are *ipso facto*
unworthy to communicate with the Church's prayers or
ministry.   You must be allowed neither to give nor receive.
You are to be as "a heathen man and a publican."

Baptism.   Barrow's view of baptism may here be stated.   He says,
"None can be a member of a planted Church but such as are
baptized."   Baptism is like circumcision—the common seal to
all that are within the covenant, to the Church and their seed.
This appears from the practice of Christ and His apostles.   "They
that were baptized were added and numbered to the Church, and
not until then received into the fellowship; how friendly and
well affected soever they were unto the Church." [1]   And more
emphatically still[2]—"one inch can we not stir in this building
and business of the Church until we be baptized."   Of course
it follows that under no circumstances can a company of un

[1] Discovery of the False Church,   [2] Discovery of the False Church
p. 105.   p. 105.

baptized persons make a Church, or rightfully discharge any Church function such as "to choose or execute any ministry, deliver or receive the other Sacrament." According to Barrow the congregations of the English Establishment were in this case. For "we find in Christ's Testament three things required" unto every true Sacrament: (a) "A lawful minister of the Gospel to deliver them"; (b) "A faithful people, or their seed, to receive them"; (c) "The outward elements and form of words which our Saviour Christ ordained" . . . "where any of these wanteth" the Sacraments are "adulterate and false."[1] But the Church of England fails under each of these heads. Its ministry, as derived from Rome, is anti-Christian; its assemblies are "a profane and confuse people"; its form of administration is corrupted by "fond trifling ceremonies." As to baptism in particular, the fact that the "baptism of the Church of England is no true baptism," and that this was the only baptism known "at the change of religion," in the first days of Elizabeth, shows "all the people" *then* to have been "unbaptized": and the further fact that the English clergy owes its ordination to Rome shows "all the people" since then to have remained unbaptized. For "where there is no Church there is no calling; but all the ministers of the Church of England were made either in the Church of Rome or by virtue of that ministry fetched from the Church of Rome, and that within the memory, yea, within half the age of a man. Therefore we may by his own (Dr. Some's) reason conclude all this ministry, both bishops and priests, to be Romish, anti-Christian, and false; and so the Sacraments by them delivered are no true Sacraments. . . ."[2] In connection with this matter a curious case is discussed. Some friend[3] of Mr. Penry, whom Barrow names the scholar of Oxenford—a Puritan— had taken up much the same position. In his eyes,

---

[1] Discovery of the False Church, pp. 99, 100.
[2] Discovery of the False Church, p. 104.
[3] Job Throckmorton (see chap. i., Excursus I.)

therefore, baptism generally in the English Church was false. But he had made, at least, one great exception. On some occasion when the Queen had publicly received the communion, the scholar, with Penry and other Puritans, had approved her act. Barrow calls this approval a piece of " most odious and un-Christian flattery." Why? Because Her Majesty was an unbaptized person—so were the presiding priests; hence, according to the scholar's own principles, they had no right to give, nor she to receive, the Sacrament. It seems strangely narrow on Barrow's part—as narrow as what we are wont to hear from the High Anglican nowadays. He claimed, however, to be simply consistent, and charges the scholar with implicitly " yielding the whole cause in open field."

It is startling, after this, to find Barrow practically stultifying himself. For so he does, it seems to me, when he turns to consider his own baptism and that of the other Separatists. He had said, " The baptism of the English Church is false ; our own baptism, therefore, having been received in that Church, is of no account "; yet " not one inch can we stir in the building and business of the Church until we be baptized." This looks like a deadlock. You must be baptized ere you can even begin to build the Church ; you cannot be baptized without a true minister ; there cannot be a true minister unless there is first a true Church to call and ordain him. What is to be done? Re-baptism in some way would seem to be inevitable. But Barrow shrank from this. *Re*-baptism was *Ana*-baptism, the *horribile nomen* of the time. His detestation of the poor Anabaptists was as great as any man's. He seldom mentions them without adding some abusive epithet. They are the "wicked Anabaptists " — the damnable, execrable, blasphemous Anabaptists. They are an embodiment of the worst heresies. They are representative of all schism in the Church and sedition in the State. To be compared with them in any point, as he and his fellows often were, was the least endurable of insults. This inveterate prejudice hindered him from see-ing, lover of truth as he was, that Anabaptism expressed the logic of his position. He was forced into an untenable com-promise. During his examination before the High Commission —March 24, 1586-7—one of the questions which Whitgift commanded to be put was: "Whether he (Barrow) thinketh that such as have been baptized in the Church of England since Queen Elizabeth's reign have been rightly baptized or ought to be baptized again?" Answer: "I think as before of your sacraments, that they have not been rightly baptized according to the institution of Christ; yet that they need not, neither ought to be, baptized again." In drawing up a report of the examination Barrow adds here a parenthesis which clearly betrays what was in his mind:—"I doubt lest the Archbishop, hearing my answer of re-baptizing, caused it to be left out of the question; and my answer, taking that which might best serve their own turn, to bring us into suspicion of error and hatred." What, then, is his compromise? It turns on a dis-tinction between false baptism and baptism adulterate. Baptism is false when "it has been delivered by an infidel who never had knowledge of God in Christ." In such a case it is absolutely invalid. Adulterate baptism is that received in a false Church which holds true Christian doctrine. In such a case it is "never a cancelled record." Undoubtedly "such baptism as is delivered in the false Church is no true seal of God's covenant (commonly called a true sacrament)," and yet it is the fact "that such outward washing or baptism delivered after their superstitious manner in that idolatrous place ought not unto such to be repeated as afterward forsake the false Church and join unto the Church of God." "Thus is this hard knot (even with a trise) undone." It looks as if the knot were more tangled than ever. For if a false Church makes a false ministry, and a false ministry makes a false sacrament, as Barrow has said, what can make the Romish baptism true? Can it be that Barrow, so loftily spiritual in the general strain

8

of his thought, means to attach a magical force to the mere
baptismal formula? There seems no other explanation. But
he himself appeals to Scripture. He finds it written how in
Hezekiah's days (2 Chron. xxx. 11, 18; xxxv. 17) and in Ezra's
days (Ezra vi. 21, 22) certain "schismatical Israelites" were
permitted to "return to the true Temple and be received to the
Passover" at Jerusalem "without re-circumcision," although
their circumcision, undergone in a schismatic Church, was not
a true one. Even so, he argues, the Church of Rome (or
England) may be false, its ministry false, its baptism false; yet
the latter may pass muster and open the door to the Lord's
Supper. The two cases are analogical; the one intended, as it
were, to anticipate and illuminate the other. "We need not
say with Dr. Some that the baptism delivered in the false
Church is a *true* seal of the covenant; nor, with his adversary
(Mr. Penry's Proctor), that such as there received their
baptism are not (touching the outward action) baptized." This
may be light, but it has all the appearance of darkness, and
Barrow confesses that it is not the light of reason. Certainly
we cannot understand how something clean should thus come
out of something unclean; but we must "with reverence rest in
the practice of the Holy Ghost, though neither they nor I be
able to arrive to the wisdom thereof."[1]

It is a curious instance of the sophisms into which even a
true man may run when clear sense has for once yielded the
reins to blind fear. For, as we have seen, the fear of anabaptism was upon him.

Most of the chief features in Barrow's doctrine of
the Church have now been mentioned. It has in pastor,
elder, and deacon its permanent officers. It has in the prophets
its free pupils of the Spirit. It has in its unquestioning
loyalty to the law of Christ a sure guide to thorough self-
discipline. It has in the consciousness of His immediate
presence, power to exercise the same without respect of persons.

[1] Discovery of the False Church, pp. 116, 117.

It has in the two Sacraments the "seal" of entrance into His covenant and fellowship. All the stones necessary to the building of a true Church are here.

But, picturing the Church to ourselves as thus organised, there are still some questions we naturally ask.

As regards the ministry, *e.g.*, did Barrow believe in men who should be ministers and nothing more, *i.e.*, living entirely for the work of the Church apart from secular business? His answer is not clear. We may infer, however, its affirmative character from the fact, *inter alia*, that he expects ministers to need maintenance; and is only singular in his view of the means. State-pay in any form he repudiated. "As for the *true* ministry . . . they depend upon the providence and blessing of God, upon that flock unto which they administer. They are content, in the greatest plenty, with sufficiency of necessary food and raiment for them and their families. . . . And of this also they are neither their own carvers nor judges, but it is administered unto them from time to time by the Church to which they serve and attend as need requireth and their present ability affordeth."[1] But the maintenance, no less than the government of a Church, should be in the hands of "members" only.

Sperin. Why is it not lawful for a minister to be maintained with the goods of unbelievers?

B. Unbelievers have nothing to do, neither are bound to the maintenance of the ministry. This contribution is called in the New Testament a duty and communication of the saints, an offering and sweet odoure unto God. But unbelievers may have no spiritual communion with the saints, neither may offer with them in the Church, neither have interest or anything to do with the ministry. Therefore may not be bound, nor received, to contribute unto the maintenance of the ministry."[2]

Stronger still is the following: It is "odious and unmeet

(margin: A Minister may live for and by his work.)

(margin: But must decline the gifts of the profane.)

---

[1] Discovery of the False Church, pp. 189, 140.   [2] Conference, March 20, 1590.

for any Christian ministers, who are not to stand hired (pastors) to such dogs and swine, to minister to them the Gospel and Sacraments for their goods and hire. It was not lawful for the priest under the law to receive the offering of any stranger from the faith. Such might not enter into, or offer in, the temple. Neither now under the Gospel may the unbelieving have any fellowship with the Church, or communicate in, or intermeddle with, any action of the Church. But this contribution *is* an action of the Church, a communion and duty of the saints." How execrable, then, is the "sacrilege and covetousness" of such as owe their "set stipends" to the tithes and "goods of the profane"![1]

Of course the ministers here thought of are those who give themselves continually to the Word; not deacons nor ruling elders, but pastors and teachers. Every Church has need of such for its due edification, and such a minister needs the use of all his time for due and effectual service. For Barrow was not content with unprepared or rhapsodical utterances in the Church. Robinson's sober words on this point might have been his own.

John Robinson on the need of ministerial "industry and care" in preparation.

"In some works of the Spirit . . . in which the Lord useth our industry and care, He is infinitely more to be magnified than in any whatsoever the immediate and miraculous work of the same Spirit wherein he useth it not." . . . Nay, "compare we even extraordinary gifts with extraordinary, we see that God used the industry and pains of the extraordinary prophets for the reading and meditating in, and of, the law: and of the latter prophets of the former prophets' writings. As also of the Apostles in the reading, knowledge, and memory of them both; yea, even of the very heathen authors, whose sayings they sometimes quote in their prophecies or sermons;[2] the like industry or care not being required for the gift, or use, of strange tongues; and

---

[1] Plain Refutation, p. 147.

[2] Acts. xvii. 28, Rom. iv. 3–10, 1 Cor. xv. 33, Tit. i. 12, 2 Tim. iv. 13.

yet did the Holy Ghost much more excellently utter itself in their prophesies and sermons than in their tongues." [1] Even so, Barrow expected every preacher to be "painful"—*i.e.*, to use all care and thoroughness in his work. He did not, accordingly, despise learning. He only demanded that it be of the right sort—such as properly belongs to the man of God. Biblical study should take the first place, but in due subordination to this he by no means disparaged other studies. On the contrary, he would have them brought within everyone's reach. "As for schools to teach the tongues, or any laudable or necessary art, I wish them in abundance; that if it were possible, not only the youth, but even the whole Church might be trained therein; I with my whole heart wish that all the Lord's people were prophets. Such an enemy am I to true knowledge and learning, that I would not have it any longer kept secret in a mystery, but even proclaimed upon the housetop in every city and in every street; yet still and ever with this caution that these schools be in an established Church (I mean in such places where the saints live together in the faith, order, obedience, and communion of Christ)." [2] He objected therefore to the Universities. They seemed to him no fit place for young men, still less for ministers.

Barrow agreed with him.

Gave first place to Biblical study.

Depreciates the Universities.

"The Churches of Christ have no such colleges, societies, fellowships; they have no such profane arts, education, and literature; they have no such degrees and ostentation of learning; neither are there found either Bachelors or Doctors of Divinity. Their pastors and teachers are chosen for their knowledge, gravity, godliness of life; they have no such fashions and blasphemous titles, but are called to a labour and a charge; for the faithful performance whereof they rather desire to be commended than to be greeted in the market-place. As they are by the Church wherein they serve called to this

---

[1] The People's Plea for the Exercise of Prophecy—Works, iii. pp. 296-7.

[2] Discovery of the False Church, p. 178.

office, so are they orderly and reverently ordained by and in
the same congregation, with fasting and prayer, &c.; and
not arrayed in scarlet, with the habit, hood, tippet, cornered
hat, with their maces and beadles proclaiming before them, and
such a train of the pope's clerks, young and old, following them
through the streets till they march to the place where they
play their prizes; neither are they in this manner dubbed
Doctors by the delivering a book unto them—sworn upon a book
to their father's fidelity and their mother's mysteries—adopted
their son by a ring and a kiss, or enthronised in a chair with
many other ceremonies, and (so) made Doctors of Divinity:
Doctors in name and title only, without any certain office or
Church, wherein and whereunto to administer. For this title of
Divinity I know not how to give it unto any mortal man
without blasphemy, Christ only excepted . . . who is the
only universal Doctor of all His disciples and of all true
religion."[1] Barrow anticipated George Fox in some points,
e.g., in his refusal to take an oath on the Bible; in his objection
to naming the days of the week Sunday, Monday, &c.; and
here in his dislike of titles, at least, so far as the Christian
minister was concerned. He was, indeed, suspicious of anything not distinctly sanctioned by Scripture, especially if
sanctioned by the "false" Church. But where they railed at
him as utterly ignorant, and as labouring "to bring in
barbarism," they were in error. He was a scholar, and a lover
of scholars, and a minister could not be too well educated.
Only let him know his Bible thoroughly, and judge all other
seeming knowledge in its light. Though this might be narrow,
it was not barbarous. As a matter of fact the first leaders of
the Separation were all scholars—mostly trained and distinguished in the Universities. Barrow, Greenwood, Francis
Johnson, Clifton, Ainsworth, Penry, Robinson are not names
suggestive of ignorance. It was, indeed, their richer mental
no less than spiritual culture which commended them as much

But not a "barbarian."

[1] Discovery of the False Church, p. 176, 177.

as anything else for leadership in a community where all alike were "saints"; nor has the preference for an educated ministry which is characteristic of Congregational Churches in our own day any real reason to fear that it is departing from the tradition of their earliest time.

The position of regular minister as conceived by Barrow was one of singular dignity. He was had in all reverence for his work's sake. If a teacher, it was his to expound the Scriptures; if a pastor, it was his to exhort, to baptize, to administer the Lord's Supper, to pronounce the "censures" of the Church.

There was no confusion of office, and no interference. Supposing, e.g., that the Church had not yet ordained a pastor, or had been temporarily bereft of him, no one else could be allowed to usurp his special functions. The London Church went without the Lord's Supper for months because it had no pastor or because its pastor was in prison. Greenwood excused himself for letting his boy—a year and a-half old—remain unbaptized by saying, "I have been in prison and cannot tell where to go to a reformed Church where I might have him baptized according to God's ordinance." [1]

But, notwithstanding such high respect for the minister's office, he was himself still a "layman." In other words, ordination did not endue him with any peculiar grace which severed him from the rest of his brethren. It gave him a higher office, but he continued one of themselves, accountable to them, under Christ, for the way his office was discharged, capable of being degraded from it in case of unworthiness, liable, thus, to lose entirely the ministerial character. He even ceased to be a minister if he forsook the people by whom he had been ordained, and went away to another Church, unless the latter ordained him again for themselves. The point is not quite clear, for there is no case in the earliest days of the Separation by which it can be tested. Johnson, e.g., was pastor of the

_____
[1] Examination before the High Commission.

same people in London and Amsterdam; Robinson of the same
people in Scrooby and Leyden. But the general language of
Barrow entirely favours the statement that a true ordination
differed from false as well in scope as in origin and nature—
the false bestowing a right to seek and accept a " charge "
anywhere, the true bestowing the right to minister only to a
particular congregation. The distinction, therefore, between
" ordination " and " recognition " services has grown up later,
naturally enough in view of the confidence which one Church
would learn to put in the previous choice of another; and also
harmlessly enough, save so far as it may have tended to
encourage the essentially sacerdotal notion of " once a minister
always a minister." There is no room for " indefectible "
grace in the Congregational idea.

Marrying
and bury-
ing not
incident
to the
Minister's
office.Among the duties proper to a ministerial office it is strange
to find that Barrow did *not* place marrying and burying. As to
marriage he says, " I have always found it the parents' office to
provide marriages for their children while they remain in their
charge and government; and that the parties themselves
affianced and betrothed each other in the fear of God and in
the presence of such witnesses as were present, and that in
their parents' or other private houses, without running to
church to the priest. . . . I ever took marriage for an
ordinance and action of the second table, and see not why they
might not as well set up the tables of the money-changers or
bring in any other civil business or chaffaire as this into the
Church."[1]

So, too, of burial he asks, " Where in all the Book of God
have they (the priests of the English Church) learned to say
prayers or preach over (I will not though I might truly say *for*)
the dead? Where may I find in the Book of God that it
belonged to the minister's office to bury the dead? Why (of

---

[1] Discovery of the False Church,
p. 123. Cf. Certain Slanderous Articles
—No. 12 ; also " Platform," where

Miles Micklebound argues the matter
at length. So Robinson, &c.

all other places) must men be buried in the church or churchyard, else they have not Christian men's burial ? "[1]

No play could be allowed to pious sentiment. The rule
or example of the Word must decide. So likewise in relation
to the public services of the Church. Everything done or
omitted had to ground itself on the plain authority of Scripture. Its commands extended to every detail, and its silence
was as much a command as its speech. "All God's outward
worship and public or Divine service must, in every part and
ceremony or gesture thereof, be so pure and free from all kind
of mixture of any human invention as all things of the very
least moment whatsoever, being directly ordered according to
the pattern showed in the mount of God's holy Word, every
believing heart may rejoice at the most comely order and holy
beauty of God's own ordinances, and adjudge it high presumption to tender any innovation by far-fetched devices and
novelties, or some old tradition or worm-eaten ceremony. . . ."
These are not the words of Barrow himself, but of a disciple[2]
true to his spirit.[3] Could it be thought that God legislated
for the very pins and tassels of the Jewish sanctuary,
and did not do likewise for His spiritual house? That
the question carried with it a strong *a fortiori* argument seemed to Barrow self-evident. It did not occur
to him that the Church, because spiritual, was free; that
its freedom was positive as well as negative—freedom not only
from the Levitical law, but freedom also to shape the forms of
its own life. He called this "Anabaptistical." Hence he did
not consider it possible that to the Apostles externals of worship

Public
worship
must be
shaped by
apostolic
precedent

---

[1] Discovery of the False Church,
p. 126. Cf. Certain Slanderous Articles
—No. 12 ; also "Platform," where
Miles Micklebound argues the matter
at length. So Robinson, &c.
[2] Certain reasons of a private Christian against conformity to kneeling
in the act of receiving the Lord's
Supper. By Thomas Dighton, Gent.,
1618. Preface, p. 4.

[3] Cf. the close of Discovery of the
False Church—the whole Church and
all its proceedings must be built upon
Christ's Testament—every soul and
every action shall be judged by Christ's
Testament—nothing is pleasing to
God, or will stand before the face of
Christ, that is found disagreeing to
Christ's Testament. Cf. especially pp.
195-7 of the "Discovery."

were something indifferent. No, the unalterable pattern is there in the few externals which they practised or can be shown to have countenanced. The many about which nothing is said or hinted were done away.[1]

An ordinary service of the Church, then, consisted of prayer, reading and exposition of the Scriptures, exhortation—with space reserved for prophesying, discipline, and the Sacraments, if necessary. There was also singing, but only of the Psalms. In one of Gifford's "defamatory articles," he says, " ye speak so profanely of the singing of the Psalms." "No," answers Barrow, "not against that most comfortable and heavenly harmony of singing Psalms; but against the rhyming and paraphrasing of the Psalms as in your Church. Nor yet so much against *that* as against the apocryphal erroneous ballads in time-song (hymns?) used commonly in your Church instead of the Psalms and holy songs of the canonical Scriptures."[2] The Psalms, then, as they stand—not paraphrases, still less man-made hymns—were all that should be sung in the Church, no regard being had to "time" or probably to tune; but yet making "a most comfortable and heavenly harmony," as doubtless they did for men whose "harmony" was mainly the peace of God in their own souls. For however dreary Barrow's type of "service" might seem to us, with our modern passion for brevity, for variety, for choirs and "organs and curious prick song," it was not dreary to him, to Greenwood, to Robinson, and those who gathered with them.

---

[1] Yet he urges the principle of "spiritual" freedom with great force in such a passage as the following, where his object was to expose the bondage of a "stinted" liturgy :— " Is the Church of God still in wardship and such infancy? Shut up as under a garrison : that it must have such tutors and rudiments? Is not Christ now dead, risen, and ascended? And hath freed His Church from such tutelship? He Himself now becoming their lawgiver and minister in person ; and hath now given them His Holy Word and Spirit, to administer wisdom unto them, in all freedom to use the same, His Word, according to His will, and their own occasions, unto His glory and their comforts."—(Discovery of False Church, pp. 67-8.) Thus those who claim a reverent liberty in modes of worship are only more true to Barrow's own principle than he himself (fettered by the dogma of verbal inspiration) was able to be.

[2] Observations of Mr. Gifford's last reply, Article XI.

"The glory of the Lord filled the house." Said Barrow in prison, with a pathos which touches the heart, "So sweet is the harmony of God's graces unto me in the congregation, and the conversation of the saints at all times, as I think myself a sparrow upon the house-top when I am exiled from them." Vivid experience of spiritual things—the Lord's presence in the midst, the power of the Word, the love of the brethren— absorbed and satisfied him. He had little patience with "that which draweth down the mind from meditation and heavenly contemplation to sensual and carnal delight." He assumed too readily that of this kind are all "church music and songs as they be now used in cathedral (and other) churches." He did not believe that such "music and songs" could ever be a means of grace, a means of uplifting the affections toward God. We do not wonder. But neither can we wonder if such severe spirituality entailed the penalties of a reaction. For it meant a strain on the average Christian—unsustained by Barrow's enthusiasm—which became, and is, too hard to bear.

As a rule,[1] the "Separatist" meetings were open to all. *Relation of the Church to the World.* No questions were asked, though the stranger might haply turn out a traitor. This was courageous if not wise. Probably they had in mind the example of the Corinthian Church; how "it kept a place for him that is without," and how, sometimes, the effect of the Word was to "convict" him and make manifest the secrets of his heart, and constrain him "to fall down on his face and worship God."[2] The chief purpose, however, of the Church in its gatherings was not conversion but edification. Preaching was directed not to the unsaved but to the saints. There is not a word in Barrow, so far as I know, which indicates that he thought of the Church as *an evangelising agency.* There is much about the necessity of separating from the world, but nothing about the necessity of saving it. Of course, this was quite consistent with earnest desire and effort, on the part

---

[1] The exception was in a time of active persecution.

[2] An illustration may be seen in the story of Barrow's own conversion.

of individual members of the Church, to win souls for Christ. Such desire and effort did exist, undoubtedly, and may often have resulted from the Church's teaching and influence.   But, as a community, the Church was self-centred; its aim being, on the one hand, to put away out of its practice everything unclean, everything with the least taint of Antichrist, and, on the other, to help one another "to walk in the way of the Lord," to apprehend truly and apply faithfully His whole will.

As things were this was natural, not to say inevitable.   In the first place, the Church had no scope for preaching to men at large, watched and persecuted as it was.

In the second, its root conviction, its *raison d'être*, was that the Church must be made pure if the Gospel was to have its due, its saving effect.   For of what use to turn men to Christ if at the same time you joined them with a corrupt Church wherein they could not possibly obey Him, and were continually tempted to slight or break His commands.   In fact, a twofold conversion was needed—one from the world, another from the Church.   The Separatists found their peculiar calling in the latter.

In the third place, one may trace a certain fatalism in Barrow's way of regarding men's relation to saving faith. His Calvinism, and that of the Separatists generally, was of a high and unflinching type.   The number of the elect was eternally fixed; the calling and justifying of them all was a work of mere grace.   No human act, done or undone, could alter the fact.   Preaching might "mediate" the call of God to an elect soul; but the call would assuredly reach it, whether there was preaching or not.   Hence, Barrow could feel certain that God had "many thousands" in the world, in the Church of England, "yea, even in the Popish Churches" of His "dear elect," whom He in "His due time by His appointed means will call."   Why, then, take *any* trouble concerning men—why, in particular, make such a fuss about establishing them in a true Church?   The logic of the position is hard to defend, unless we say that the act of faith is necessarily so hidden and mysterious as to lie plainly beyond man's province, whereas human agency in the sphere of Church polity does count for something. Anyhow, it was not till Calvinism had been virtually abandoned that the Churches which followed in the footsteps of Barrow came to an adequate sense of their responsibility for "outsiders."

Lastly, there were few Separatist communities when Barrow wrote, and what there were had little, if any, means of intercourse with one another. Perhaps he had experience of only one ; and so the question of their mutual relations scarcely pressed for discussion. But how he would have dealt with the matter it is not difficult to see. Each Church, of course, was to be, as a rule, independent. Still, occasions might arise when it would be fitting to accept or render help. He mentions one in his account of ordination. When a congregation has chosen its pastor the next step is to ordain him. If the congregation have an eldership of its own then "the most meet instruments" to ordain him are these. If not, then it should have recourse "to the elders of some other faithful congregation, one Church being to help and assist another in these affairs."[1]

Under the Presbyterian discipline a large place was given to synods and councils. There is a passage in his "Plain Refutation of Mr. Gifford" which shows that Barrow did not think such bodies unlawful in themselves, or without their use, if they could be had without prejudice to the ultimate rights of the Church. "Synods and councils were not instituted to pluck away the power, or to execute the public duties of the Church, but to instruct, stir up, and confirm them in their duties; to show them the rules of God's Word, and not to break them or to make new. . . ." Moreover, "in a Christian synod no Christian ought to be shut out, but with equal power and freedom to speak in assent or

Relation of Churches to one another.

---

[1] Plain Refutation of Mr. Gifford, p. 130.

dissent of anything there handled as occasion requireth. Yet ought every Christian to use this power and liberty aright, not disturbing the holy order of the Church, presuming to speak before their ancients, or against anything by them said, without showing just cause, and always keeping themselves within the compass of faith and sobriety."[1] A synod which has no right to make laws for the Churches, and only exists to help them to perform their duties, in which, too, not elders merely but every private Christian may equally claim to express his mind, might as well be called a Congregational Union. Nor is there a hint that Barrow would have wished to organise the Churches for other than deliberative and administrative ends.

As to one thing, viz., discipline, Barrow was specially peremptory in his demand that there should be no external interference. Cartwright's "Directory of Church Government," which Barrow seems to have known, lays it down, e.g., that "when there is question concerning a heretic" complaint shall be made first to the consistory (now called session), then that two or three neighbour ministers shall be called—men godly and learned, and free from that suspicion, by whose opinion he may be suspended till such time as the Conference (Presbytery) may take knowledge of his cause— then, if obstinate, the Conference (or in the last resort the Synod) may excommunicate him. Barrow, as if with this ordinance in mind, says : "The excommunication of a heretic after he is duly convinced and found obstinate, belongeth not to any bishops or *elders of other Churches*, but unto that congregation whereof this heretic stood a joined member."[2] For "every particular congregation hath the power of our Lord Jesus against all sin and transgression to censure the sin and excommunicate the obstinate offender." "Neither hath Christ given unto any one Church more power or prerogative than unto all

[1] Plain Refutation of Mr. Gifford, p. 81.

[2] Plain Refutation of Mr. Gifford, pp. 80, 81.

other; or set one Church above and over another, otherwise than to wish and seek the good each of other and of all, to admonish, exhort, stir up each other as occasion requireth. . . . As to pastors and elders their office extendeth but unto those flocks whereof the Holy Ghost hath set them overseers. . . . Again, excommunication is no part of their ministry, neither hath God tied it unto the office of any, but left it a public duty of the whole congregation to be done of all with one consent."[1]

Words more explicit could not be found wherein to assert and accentuate the indefeasible rights of "each several Church" and of each several member of the Church as the kernel of all.

The upshot, said the scoffing objector, will be chaos. And his amiable forecast has too often, as in the case of Amsterdam, largely come true. But Barrow had ample faith. He was an idealist always; and it was an ideal (likewise often verified) which floated before his inward eye when he said :—

"As for the order of their assembly it is not tumultuous or contentious, but rather an heavenly school of all order, sobriety, and modesty, which the angels with great delight behold— every one there knowing his calling, place, and bounds, which he without present blame may not break; as free, but not having that liberty as a cloak of wickedness, but as the servants of God, whose law is here purely and sincerely taught, every estate and degree instructed how they ought to walk and behave themselves towards God and men in all manner of conversation; nothing more, or more often, inculcate, than to yield due honour, obedience, submission unto all magistrates, parents, superiors; and that not for fashion sake or ignorantly, but as of knowledge, faith, and conscience toward God."[2]

[1] Plain Refutation of Mr. Gifford, p. 79.

[2] Discovery of the False Church, p. 219-220.

NOTE I.

BARROW'S VIEWS AS TO THE ECCLESIASTICAL POWERS OF THE PRINCE.

Plausibly enough Barrow was charged with advocating and fomenting disloyalty. He resented the charge as tending to identify him with the Anabaptists. "There is not a sentence in our writings," he says, which hints at absolute independence of "the Superior Powers that God hath set over us."

His views in this respect, briefly stated, are as follows :—

1. It is "the office and duty of Princes and Rulers. . . . to suppress and root out of their dominions all religions, worship and ministries"[1] other than the true. Hence the Church of England ought to be instantly disestablished, and its clergy as the maintainers of "heinous abuses and intolerable enormities" ought to go. It should, at the same time, be disendowed; and its revenues be confiscated to the use, not of so-called Patrons but, of the Queen—who "may of her royal authority assume not only *them*, but even what part of her subjects' goods it shall please her in way of tribute." Nay, if the Queen did her duty thoroughly she would have even the Church-buildings destroyed—considering that they were first founded by Pagans or Papists; that their "first faith" was Popish, and that "they are built altogether to the form of the old Temple of the Jews."

2. It is the Prince's duty to enforce attendance on the services of the true Church. "We acknowledge that the Prince ought to compel all their subjects to the hearing of God's Word in the public exercises of the Church."[2]

3. He is bound to suppress evils contrary to the law of God as well within the Church as without. Here, by the law of God is meant what Barrow calls the "judicial law of Moses" which has never been repealed. "God hath in His book made most perfect and necessary laws both for Church and commonwealth. He requireth of the king and magistrate to see these laws executed and not to make new. He that maketh any new laws taketh unto himself the office of God, who is the only lawmaker."[3] . . . Were this law allowed its due place and force, such evils as incest and adultery would not be passed over or punished lightly; and evils like blasphemy, open idolatry, disobedience to parents would be punished by death.[4]

---

[1] See "Platform."
[2] Plain Refutation of Mr. Gifford, Preface.
[3] Discovery of the False Church, pp. 218-9.
[4] Discovery of the False Church, p. 220.

4. As to that part of the Divine law which relates exclusively to the Church, its constitution, doctrine, and discipline, the Prince must see it obeyed, but must do so indirectly. "It is not the Prince's office" to rule the Church in person, but "to command the Church to do it by such instruments as God hath thereunto ordained."[1]

5. If the Prince fails to do this, if he forbids the Church to reform itself by the true pattern, or if he attempts to impress upon it his own laws, resistance is not merely justified—it is obligatory.

It is "beastly and hellish doctrine" which declares that the Church, in correcting its own "faults," "refuseth the peace of the Prince and provoketh him to strike."[2]

And "when the Prince shall in anything be found contrary to God, God is then to be obeyed rather than man."

"The Prince demandeth my goods—I am readily and willingly to depart with them all unto him without inquiry. But if the Prince command me" to do what is to me unlawful—e.g., "pay tithes" or a "pension to an anti-Christian minister"—I may not obey, but rather suffer, his indignation, yea, death.[3]

6. The Prince's personal standing in a Church is that of any other individual. He cannot, e.g., "compel any to be a member of a Church, or the Church to receive any without assurance by the public profession of their own faith, or to retain any longer than they continue to walk orderly in the faith."[4]

He cannot enter the Church or exercise any office or discharge any function whatever except by consent of the Church accorded in the usual way.

"He entereth by the same door of faith" as others do. He is bound "to the strict observation and defence of God's laws in his calling as wel as any other; and is for any transgression thereof liable and subject to the censures and judgments of Christ in His Church—which are without partiality or respect of persons."[5]

NOTE II.

BARROW'S ARGUMENT FOR THE DESTRUCTION OF CHURCHES.

Reference is made in the preceding note (I.) to Barrow's belief that the "church-buildings" ought to be destroyed. The passage in which he maintains this is a literary curiosity :—

"These synagogues are built together to the form of the old Temple

---

[1] Plain Refutation of Mr. Gifford, p. 202.
[2] Plain Refutation of Mr. Gifford, p. 204.
[3] Discovery of the False Church, p. 90.
[4] Plain Refutation of Mr. Gifford, Preface.
[5] Discovery of the False Church, p. 14.

of the Jews in a long square east and west, with their holy court walled
round about, commonly called the churchyard, which is holy ground and
serveth for Christian burial, being altogether exempt from civil use; yet is
it lawful for the young men and maids to play there together upon their
Sundays and holy-days.   But whoso smiteth any in that holy ground, by
statute is to have his hand cut off therefor.

"These synagogues have also their battlements ; another porch adjoining to their church—not here to speak of the solemn laying the foundation, where the first stone must be laid by the hands of the Bishop or his
suffragans, with certain magical prayers and holy water, and many other
idolatrous rites.

"They have . . . their folding-doors, and an especial Levite, the
parish clerk, to keep the key.

"They have, at the west end, their hallowed bells, which are also
baptized, sprinkled, &c.

"They have their aisles and their body of the church.

"They have also their cells to the sides of the walls ; their vestry to
keep the priest's ministerial garments, where they are to attire and dress
themselves before they go to their service.

"They have their treasury.

"All the cathedral or mother churches also have their cloisters for
their Dean, Prebendaries, Canons, petty Canons, singing men and singing
boys, &c., within their precincts and walls to abide and dwell, that they
may keep the watch of the Temple and their hours of orisons.

"Again, they have in the body of their church their hallowed font to
keep the holy water wherewith they baptize, all other vessels and waters
to the use of baptism being by express law forbidden.

"They have also their holiest of all, or chancel, which peculiarly
belongeth to the priest and choir, which help the priest to pray and sing
his service.

"They have their rood-loft as a partition between their holy and
holiest of all.

"The priest also hath a peculiar door into his chancel, through which
none might pass but himself.

"Now the church thus reared up is also thoroughly hallowed with their
sprinkling water, and dedicate and baptized into the name of some especial
saint or angel, as to the patron and defender thereof against all enemies,
spirits, storms, tempests, &c.

"Yet hath it within also all the holy army of saints and angels in
their windows and walls to keep it.

"Thus, I think, can be no doubt made but that the very erections of
these synagogues (whether they were by the heathens or Papists) were
idolatrous."[1]

Consequently, "so far is it that God will be worshipped in them that
He will not have them so much as reserved lest they defile the land and

---

[1] "Discovery of the False Church," pp. 130-131.

draw us to idolatry, as by experience they lately have seen in Queen Mary's time, and we now with grief behold amongst ourselves."[1]

It may be pleaded[2] that "the use of many things whose original is impure may be pure"; and so that "these old places and temples may be used to the worship of God." But this is "flat contrary to the laws of God"—*e.g.*, Deut. vii. 15, 16; xiii. 17. And "one of these laws of God and places of Scripture" is more than "all the authority of Calvin, Augustine," and the rest.[3]

According to Paget of Amsterdam (" An Arrow Against the Separation of the Brownists," p. 28), Barrow afterwards came to see somewhat differently, and "recorded" his "doubting" "in that piece of paper which is pasted upon the margin of his book over against the place (p. 133) where he had maintained such a vehement detestation of them," *i.e.*, the church buildings.

Henry Ainsworth, against whom Paget wrote, seems never to have doubted that Barrow's first view was right. But Francis Johnson, who, at the time of his "Answer to Henry Jacob" (1600), p. 65, was of Barrow's earlier mind, also came to see differently, and it is one of the "Retractations" which he announced in his "Christian Plea" of 1617 (pp. 25–6).

---

[1] "Discovery of the False Church," p. 133.
[2] Barrow mentions Dr. Some as pleading to this effect and citing Calvin on his side. *Cf.* Hooker's Ecclesiastical Polity, Book V., §§ xii.-xvii., written with express reference to Barrow.
[3] Page 134.

BARROW AND THE REFORMISTS.

BARROW AND THE REFORMISTS.

THE Elizabethan settlement of the Church was a compromise which satisfied very few. All the old bishops, with one exception, scouted it; and if all save some 200 of the clergy submitted to it they did so merely to keep their livings. Could they have preserved the Church as it was they would have been glad. They felt no need for change, nor did the people generally. The ancient order was much more to their taste than the new. Even its corruptions and superstitions had become picturesque and venerable.

"The politicians were the only class of the community heartily attached to the (new) Church system, and they were attached to it, not for the religion which it taught but for the social order which it maintained and the assistance which it lent to the Government."[1]

To the men who had come directly under the influence of the Reformed Churches abroad, and under that of Calvin particularly, Elizabeth's "doubting and hesitating" policy was a keen disappointment. These men were comparatively few in number, but, by their learning, character, and earnestness, they were the inevitable leaders of the Church. Its chief positions came to them as a matter of necessity. They were the only class from whom the bishops and other dignitaries, or from whom professors at the Universities, could be selected. This ascendancy of the Reformist element should be borne in mind. Elizabeth's compromise was embodied in the Prayer-book; but it is doubtful if any one, including the Queen herself, felt about

[1] Wakeman's "Church and the Puritan," p. 15.

the Prayer-book as later Churchmen have done—felt that it
was a happy, almost an inspired, compendium of "old and
new"; not too much of either; enough of the old to retain the
Church in unbroken union with Catholic Christianity, enough
of the new to content every reasonable demand for adaptation
and progress.[1] Not at all. When the Queen insisted on a
return to the use of the old clerical vestments and the blending
of Calvinian (or Zwinglian) and Catholic formulas in the Communion service, she really obeyed no higher inspiration than
personal liking and political expediency; while it would be
difficult to mention one among the bishops at the beginning of
her reign who thought the shape then given to the worship and
discipline of the Church something perfect and final. They
might agree with the politicians that it was desirable or
necessary, for the sake of social order, to promote general
uniformity; but always with a margin of liberty in things indifferent, and with full reservation of the right to point out
defects, and bring to pass, if possible, changes for the better.
The Queen, however, took a firm stand. She was not prepared
for further change of any sort or degree. And the result of
her stubborn persistence was a natural one. It led an increasing number of the clergy to persuade themselves that their
scruples were baseless; that the prescribed rubrics were all
they should be; that, at any rate, the legally established was
the morally binding and ought to be enforced on recalcitrants.
A conspicuous instance was Whitgift, who had "scruples" and
expressed them during his early University days, but (conscientiously, of course) found his way out of them when their
actual effect on the Queen's mind, and probable effect on his
career, became apparent. Most of the bishops and higher
clergy took the same line. Their predilection was for a system
more elastic and more distinctly Protestant. But their position
called for acquiescence. So they acquiesced; and they went on
to defend the established order by verbal subtleties and legal

[1] See Wakeman—The History of the English Church.

severities which cannot but have involved an ugly twist to many a conscience.

Barrow had these before his eyes when, in his vehement and rather intemperate way, he speaks of the "Pseudo-Martyrs" and "runaway Professors" (*i.e.*, those who had fled under Mary and returned under Elizabeth), who, as soon as they "were once warm in their nests, *then* forgot they all their former peregrinations, and disowned the vows they then made, seeking now to fortify and establish their own, and not Christ's kingdom. And to this end they invented, obtained, and erected their blasphemous High Commission, instead of the Spanish Inquisition, where they got power over all causes . and persons ecclesiastical, to make or abrogate what laws they list, and to impose them upon the whole Church, which is the whole land." Of course the statement that the bishops invented the Court of High Commission is incorrect; but they were among its chief members and ministers, and, to be this willingly, they had to undergo a mental process in which circumstances certainly proved too strong for conviction.

There was another class which was both the occasion of the name Puritan, and to which at first it was restricted, though getting afterwards a much wider extension. We may describe them in general terms as those who, "using a ceremonial for the most part contrary to the law of the Church, nevertheless claimed to be faithful members and true representatives of the Church, not for what she was, but for what they fully believed she was intended, and was going to be . . ." and who "were willing to tolerate an Episcopal and sacerdotal system as long, and as long only, as it abstained from asserting its principles, and was capable of being worked in their own interests." They increased rapidly in the early years of Elizabeth. They could claim many of the clergy and many more of the laity, especially in London, Northampton, Lancashire, and the Eastern Counties. They were strong in Parliament, and were not absent from the Privy Council.

Men like Humphreys and Sampson, the Earl of Leicester, Sir Francis Knollys, Burghley, and Spenser the poet, are representative of the type. At a later time they are the majority of those who signed the Millenary Petition. Reynolds and Knewstubbs spoke for them at the Hampton Court conference. Pym and others acted for them when at last their time came. They were as little in favour of full-blown Presbyterianism as of an absolute Episcopacy. They did not wish to overthrow the constitution of the Church, but to uproot its abuses. A curtailment of clerical power, and a removal of Popish ceremonies, such as kneeling at communion, signing of the cross at baptism, the ring in marriage, the wearing of certain vestments—this would have contented them. For the rest they were conformists, and were resolved to remain so.

There was, however, a third party, consisting of men " who carried their Calvinistic principles a little farther, and added to the negations of their Protestant creed either a belief in Presbyterianism as the Divinely-ordered system of Church government, or such a conscientious abhorrence of Episcopacy and Church order as made them consider obedience to it a positive sin." Illustrious examples of this class were Cartwright, Travers, Dering, Udall, and, till near the end of his life, Penry. Their cause was set forth in the first and second Remonstrance, in Cartwright's replies to Whitgift, in Travers's " Holy Discipline of the Church," in Udall's " Demonstration of Discipline," &c. " Marprelate " was their popular advocate, and his diatribes against the Church as it was show both the bitterness and the utterness of their " nonconformity." But they, too, had no thought of Separation. Their policy was to remodel and take over the Church from within. " They sought to establish a separate disciplinary machinery of their own, which should supersede that of the Church." They attempted " to revolutionise—or rather, as it would appear to them—to develop the Reformation of the Church by a subtle

and underhand policy, instead of attempting to do it through
the ordinary machinery of Convocation or Parliament. It was
all the more dangerous from the strong sympathy which the
attempt met with from the neighbouring Presbyterianism just
established in Scotland, and the dominant Calvinism of Protestant Europe." "In 1572 . . . the first English Presbytery was set up at Wandsworth, in Surrey, where elders were
chosen and a system of rules agreed upon. We find the same
efforts gradually spreading into other parts of the country.
Under Whitgift's primacy, in 1586, Presbyterian classes were
established in Warwick and Northampton, where the Geneva
Book of Discipline was subscribed, and a mutual engagement
entered into to observe its Articles. Cartwright . . . was
the first subscriber to the Warwick classis. It seems probable
that similar associations were very early introduced into
Cheshire and the adjoining county of Lancaster." [1] "In
this way a complete Church system on a Presbyterial
model was formed, which was to work in obedience to the
Church system already established by treating it as a mere
legal appendage, until the time came when, undermined from
below, it might be successfully and entirely overthrown."

Regular conformists, nonconformists of a mild type, Presbyterians, these then were the parties comprehended within the
Church. Naturally, resistance was drawn most to the Presbyterians. As long as Grindal was Archbishop the treatment
of them was comparatively lenient. But when Whitgift
succeeded in 1583 the storm burst. He came to power
charged by the Queen "to restore the discipline of the
Church, and the uniformity established by law which"
(said she), "through the connivance of some prelates, the
obstinacy of the Puritans, and the power of some noblemen, is run out of square." Matters had, indeed, reached
a crisis. The issue was clear. Should there be a rule of
the bishops or of the presbytery? Neither Whitgift, on the

[1] Tayler's Religious Life of England, p. 102.

one hand, nor the " Disciplinarians," on the other, had any mind to conciliation or a *via media*. Read only, for example, John Udall's address " To the supposed Gouvernours of the Church of England, the Archbishops, Lord Byshops, Arch-deacons, and the rest of that order." It is a challenge to accept the discipline on pain of hell fire :—" Repent, repent ! Be not ashamed to amend, though others have found you out the way. Judge yourselves while you have time, lest you be made firebrands of hell beyond all time. . . . The Lord open your eyes, that you may see the confusions whereof you are the cause, and give you true repentance or confounde you in all your purposes that be against Him and the regi-ment " (*i.e.*, discipline) " of His Son Jesus Christ." [1] There is no compromise here. Nor was there in Whitgift's action. He struck right at the root of the tree when, a few days after his elevation, he sent out to all bishops a strict injunction to admit none to preach " unless he be ordained according to the manner of the Church of England or unless he subscribe to the three following articles :—

" 1st. To the Queen's supremacy over all persons and in all causes ecclesiastical and civil within her Majesty's dominions.

" 2nd. To the Book of Common Prayer and of the ordina-tion of priests and deacons, as containing nothing contrary to the Word of God ; and that they will use it in all their public ministrations and no other.

" 3rd. To the Thirty-nine Articles of the Church of England, agreed upon in the Synod of 1562, and afterwards confirmed by Parliament."

Till now Presbyterian orders had been allowed—so late as April 6, 1582, Grindal had licensed one John Morrison, a Scotch divine, who had been " admitted and ordained to sacred orders and the holy ministry by the imposition of hands, according to the laudable form and rite of the Reformed

[1] Introduction to the "Demonstration of Discipline" (1588).

Church of Scotland," to preach "in any convenient places in
and throughout the whole province of Canterbury." Till now,
too, submission to the Prayer-book and the Queen's supremacy
had been of a more or less general and indefinite character,
with many degrees of tolerated dissent. But now Presbyterian
varieties (or vagaries) of worship were to be utterly excluded,
and the validity of Presbyterian orders utterly denied.
Nothing could be more drastic. One hears without surprise
that an immediate result was the suspension of several hundred
ministers—some of them "dignitaries in the Church" and
many of them "graduates in the University." Nor is one surprised to find that "many good and pious men strained their
consciences on this occasion—some subscribing the articles
with protestation in open court, as far as they are agreeable to
the Word of God; and others *dempto secundo, i.e.,* taking away
the second."[1] But one *is* surprised to mark how few of the
advanced Presbyterians seemed to realise the situation.
Moderate Puritans, whose scruples went no farther than a few
ceremonies, who would have asked no more if certain rubrics in
the Prayer-book had been expunged or modified, might well be
tempted to debate the question whether, for the sake of such
things, they ought to disregard the needs of their "poor
families" and the "cries" of their "poor people," who without
them would have been "as sheep having no shepherd." Men,
however, who suddenly found themselves confronted with the
demand to declare the Church in all respects divine, while they
believed, and had proclaimed, it to be anti-Christian, could
surely not hesitate what course to take. Their position in the
Church was untenable—Whitgift meant to make it so legally,
conscience should have made it so morally. It looks like
solemn trifling when, on the one part, men such as Travers
and Sparkes—ardent defenders of the Holy Discipline—with
Whitgift and the Bishop of Winchester on the other part, hold
a conference at Lambeth,[2] in the presence of the Earl of

[1] Neal's Puritans, Vol. I., p. 354.   [2] 1584. Neal's Puritans, Vol. I., p. 374.

Leicester, Lord Gray, and Sir Francis Walsingham, "concerning things needful to be reformed in the Book of Common Prayer." They discourse about the Apocryphal writings, about baptism, about the sign of the cross, about clerical "apparel." "The noblemen request some favour for the ministers." "My Lord of Leicester thinks it a pitiful thing that so many of the best ministers, and painful in their preaching, should be deprived for these things." But Travers and Sparkes knew quite well that "these things" were the least of all in their eyes. Whitgift knew the same. The difference between them was fundamental. Suppose they had yielded as to "these things," would it have rendered the position of Travers and Sparkes in the Church any the less anomalous? To remain there, would they not still have had to swear that its whole constitution and administration was Scriptural? The marvel is how men so sincere, and above five hundred more "who had subscribed the Holy Discipline," ever "made a shift" to keep their benefices. It is not a sufficient apology to say, with Neal, that Whitgift's action in decreeing the three articles was illegal. This fact may condemn Whitgift; it cannot possibly exculpate the five hundred. It rather increases one's wonder. For it was surely worse to subscribe, as they must have done, articles which seemed to them illegal as well as intrinsically wrong than to subscribe articles which, however wrong in themselves, might be confessedly legal. The Presbyterians, to say the least, were inconsistent. We can sympathise with them, remembering how passionately they clung to the hope of a speedy turn in their favour, and how intensely repugnant to them was the thought of separation. But their conduct was a misfortune to themselves and their cause. For it undermined their own integrity, and greatly weakened their influence.

Barrow's attitude to these men, whom he calls Reformists, forward ministers, Martinists, &c., will now be more intelligible. Speaking generally, it was one of unmitigated resentment and contempt. For him they are "these Pharisees," "these sectorie teachers," "these stipendarie roving predicantes," "these wandering stars," "these sighers for reformation," "these conscience botchers." Let us set down the main heads of his indictment:—

I. For one thing, Barrow beheld in the Reformists men who were bent on erecting a system no whit less tyrannical than the Episcopal.

Its advocates said that once established everywhere all evils everywhere would cease. Barrow thought not. The discipline would effect a change rather of names than things. For the old "parsons and questmen" each parish would have "its pastors and elders"; for the "Commissaries' Courts" there would be the "Synods"; for the "High Commission" there would be the "High Councils." It would, in fact, find itself very much at home, and the people would not find it "half so strange as it seems." True it would be "troublesome to the Lord Bishops, their courts and attendants, and to the dumb ministers." It would clear *them* out of the way. But the people would arrive at no larger spiritual freedom. The former despotism and exclusiveness would continue. "Their permanent Synods"—what are they? Their "power is absolute over all churches," yet they "consist only of priests or ministers." "The people of the churches be shut out." "Their most holy decrees" are "without controlment unless it be by the Prince or the High Court of Parliament." Great importance is attached to degrees of rank, to rules and orders. The office of President especially is one to be coveted. It is the office about which "their predecessors had no small stir" long ago, "until Holy Father the Pope put an end to the strife by getting the chair." [1] As for these "new officers"—these ruling elders who seem to share power with the ministers—"they shall be but of the wealthiest; honest, simple men of the parish shall sit for ciphers dumb by their pastor and meddle with nothing; neither—poor souls—

[1] Discovery of the False Church, pp. 190-91.

shall they know more than they say.   As for the ordering
of all things, it shall be in the pastor's hands only, especially in
some chief men who shall be their Presidents and rulers of
Synods and Councils, and so the people kept as far from the
knowledge and performance of their duties as ever they were."

II. Barrow, then, was no friend to the "discipline." To
him, as to Milton, Presbyter was but Old Priest "writ large."
He had no wish to see the one make way for the other.   He is
glad to see that so far, "through the mercy of God," the
Pontificals (i.e., the Bishop's friends) have been able "to stop
and make head against" the Reformists' "new devised
forgeries." He hopes the time will never come when the
Reformists will have succeeded in bringing over the civil
power to their side.   For this would simply mean a repetition,
in the Presbyterian interest, of what took place in the beginning of the Queen's reign—an attempt to convert the nation
"by virtue of one Parliament in one day."   "The whole land"
would still be "the Church, and every parish therein" would
still be "a particular congregation of the same." [1]   Moreover,
"the fat livings and lordly revenues of these Bishops, Deans,
&c.," [2] would still be retained only with a change of hands.
For they have not the least intention to rely for their temporal
support on Christ's way—the "dutiful contributions of their
flock."   No; it is not endowments they condemn, but the
present owners of them.   Their "corrupt covetous mind" is no
less set upon them than is that of the Pontificals.   Barrow
could discern nothing attractive in such a programme.   He
says it merely "seeks to bring Christ in by the arm of flesh."
But have we not seen that Barrow himself invoked the aid of
civil power?   What difference was there between his action
and that of the Reformists?   This, at least, that Barrow did
not ask to have the Church established, but only the false disestablished.   The Reformist asked both one and the other.
Barrow said, "Clear the ground, and let the Free Church

[1] Discovery of the False Church, pp. 189-90.   [2] "Platform," no paging.

establish and develop itself." The Reformist said, "Set up and do for the true Church all that you have done for the false." Barrow's conception of what the civil power might rightly do was defective, but it was considerably nearer the truth than the Puritan.

III. Meanwhile, the Reformists are in the Church, playing, in Barrow's eyes, a pitiful part. He is hard enough—too hard—on the Pontificals, but his wrath burns like a furnace against the conforming Reformists, and the evident reason is that he deems them faithless to "known truth." Thus, they are as sure as himself that bishops, being anti-Christian, cannot make true ministers. Further, they contend that right ordination is essential to a right calling, and that "of necessity ordination must always be done by a Christian presbytery or eldership." This is their avowed doctrine (though the whole of it is not his). But how does their practice square with it? How have many of them been made ministers? Whose hands have ordained them? The bishops' and the bishops' only. Whatever virtue, then, belongs to their "orders" is episcopal; and is, therefore, on their own showing, nothing at all. Yet they go on officiating in the Church. Practically without ministerial standing, they stand by their livings. Their own theory makes their ministerial acts and claims null and void; yet they desist from neither. To Barrow such duplicity was detestable. He had sacrificed everthing himself in order to be true, and had no patience with those who played with conscience, as he thought, for a piece of bread.

He was equally hard on the preachers,[1] i.e., those who, being without benefice, had received the bishop's licence to preach. The number of these was considerable, though it grew less towards the end of Elizabeth's reign. Their occasion lay in the urgent needs of the Church. For, besides the fact that many parishes had no minister at all, those which had were very fortunate if he could preach. When Archbishop Parker

---

[1] Their usual name is "Lecturers."

made a visitation of his diocese in 1590[1] he found many
churches shut up; he found others where there was no preaching, not even a homily read, for many months together; he
found counties in which there was no sermon within a compass
of twenty miles.   In Cornwall[2] there were 140 clergymen, not
one of whom could preach a sermon; and most of whom were
pluralists and non-residents.   London—"accounted as the
morning star"—was also in evil case.   "One-half at least" of
its parishes was said to be "utterly unfurnished of preaching
ministers and pestered with candlesticks not of gold but of
clay, unworthy to have the Lord's light set in them"; while
of the other half, "scarcely the tenth man" made "conscience
to wait upon his charge."[3]   At first the dearth of preaching
could be accounted for by the simple incompetence of the
clergy.   Most of the old mass-priests who retained their livings
were illiterate—so were the "sundry artificers and men of base
occupation" whom the bishops, for want of better men,
admitted to the ministry.   Not a few of them could scarcely
read, much less preach; and the lives of many made them unfit
to preach had they been able.   Then, in 1560, an admonition,
issued by Archbishop Parker, forbad all persons under the
degree of M.A. to preach or expound the Scriptures—which
was likely to render sermons still more scarce.   And the fact
that the M.A.'s were apt to be "suspended" for nonconformity—the younger men from Oxford and Cambridge being
much inclined that way—brought the number of churches
served with preaching ministers yet lower.   To meet this great
deficiency, at least in part, was the purpose of the licensed
preachers.   "Under the character of curates or lecturers" they
engaged themselves to some "idle drone" of an incumbent,
and "for a small recompense from" him, together with "the
voluntary contributions of the parish," they did his work of
preaching; and did it in so "warm and affectionate" a way as
generally to gain "the hearts of the people."   Sometimes they

[1] Neal, Vol. I., p. 157.   [2] Neal, Vol. I., p. 320.   [3] Referring to 1577.

resided upon their curacies and went from house to house visiting their parishioners and instructing the children. Sometimes they were itinerant. " They travelled up and down the
counties from church to church, preaching where they got
leave, as if they were apostles." There can be no doubt that
they were, for the most part, excellent men, that the people
heard them gladly, and that their labours were often " greatly
blessed." But, strange to say, they were offensive to the
bishops. The bishops " continually persecuted " them. One
after another they caused them to be made " close prisoners in
the Gatehouse," or " well laden with irons in the White Lion
or in the Clinke." They were resolved " never to cease   .   .   .
until they had rooted them out of the Church." [1]   This
hostility showed itself most vigorously under Whitgift; but
existed, more or less, from the days of Parker. And the reason
was, that these preachers were among the most aggressive and
influential of the nonconformists. They used the bishop's
licence to cry down the bishops. Becoming aware of this, the
bishops once and again cancelled all existing licences; and
ordered new ones to be taken out, on terms, of course, which
made the oath of obedience to themselves more strict. But
either the preachers disregarded the order, and went on in
virtue of their old licence; or took out a new one under a promise of obedience which they did not mean to keep. Their
motives, no doubt, seemed to themselves excellent; the action
of the bishops, no doubt, was tyrannical and adverse to the
spiritual interests of the people. Nevertheless, it is difficult to
justify the preachers except on the principle of doing evil that
good might come. And it is easy to understand why the
bishops should be especially irate with them. But Barrow
outdid the bishops. Whenever he speaks of the " preachers,"
his language is scathing. They seem to him alike dishonour-
able and dangerous. As men who expect payment for preaching, they are " stipendary, mercenary men, making merchandise

[1] The State of the Church of England—"Deotrophes," by John Udall (1588), p. 5.

of the Word and open port sale of the Gospel;" as men who usually take up their abode in "some great or nobleman's house," they are "sycophants," "trencher priests, knowing well how to insinuate themselves," "where they are sure to be well fed and safe from all storms;" as itinerants they are "stellæ erraticæ," "wandering stars," "roving predicantes," "always ready upon the hearing of a better bargain to remove;" as masters of "ambiguous and doubtful terms," in order to reconcile their "reformist" tendencies with their acceptance of the Prayer-book, they are pernicious deceivers, hypocrites; as railers, with the bishops, at "Christ's most faithful servants—slanderously called Brownists," they are the greatest "hinderers of Christ's Kingdom."

"These preachers," he says, "are bound hand and foot by the oath of canonical obedience to the bishops, from whom they have received their licence and authority to preach, with condition not to preach against anything by public authority established, how ungodly and enormous soever it be; and also have submitted their whole doctrines and persons to these their ordinances not to teach any truth, or against any error that they inhibite—to preach or cease to preach, to administer or cease to administer, at their discretion and inhibition, and for their private estate, by them (the bishops) to be enjoined what kind of apparel to wear when they ride, walk abroad, or administer; not to marry without their knowledge, consent, and licence even, to this or that particular woman, &c. Must not this needs be an excellent ministry and ministration of the Gospel that is thus mancipate to, and by, these slaves, that is thus bought and sold, limited, prescribed, restrained?" [1] This, according to Barrow, is what their oath of obedience involved. If they do not so act they are disloyal to their word; if they do act so they are disloyal to their "reformist" conscience.

One of his charges against them is that they are centres in

[1] Plain Refutation, p. 136.

a parish not of union and peace, but of disturbance and schism. They settle there usually by invitation of some who "dislike and loathe" the "ministry set over them." "To such people being" (*i.e.*, if they are) "rich and able to pay them well these sectorie, precise preachers run for their hire and wage, but chiefly for vainglory and worldly estimation." They do not withdraw the people openly from their "dumb and plurified pastor." That were too perilous a course, however clearly it may be God's will. No; "yet for their own estimation, advantage, and entertainment they will, by all subtle means underhand, seek to alienate the hearts and minds of this forward and best-inclined people" from him, "and slily to draw them unto themselves. . . . Here hence ariseth those schisms and sects in the Church of England, some holding with these preachers which make show, as though they sought a sincere reformation of all things according to the Gospel of Christ . . . and these are hereupon called Precisians or Puritans, and now lately Martinists. The other side are the Pontificals, that in all things hold and jump with the time, and are ready to justify whatsoever is, or shall be, by public authority established." [1]

But their most glaring offence he takes to be menpleasing. The following is surely a reminiscence, however exaggerated, of what had come before his own observation:—
"Well, now, if these noble or rich men be given to riot and gluttony, with all manner of delicate fare pampering up the flesh, &c., *that* in them (say these preachers) is but good housekeeping. If they and their retinue exceed in monstrous and vain apparel, *that* is but raiment fit to their degree, age, or sex. If they keep and nourish troops of idle serving-men and followers, *this* still belongeth unto their degree. If they and their whole household spend all their lifetime in fleshly and vain sports and gaming, so that numbers of men have no other trade, and be wholly

[1] Plain Refutation, p. 135-6.

employed to the keeping of hawks and dogs to serve the lusts of these men, all this is covered under Christian recreation and pastime, and is tolerable enough so he (the rich man) will hear a sermon and call his family to a lecture—yea, the priest will not then stick to stay and look on until the games at tables or set at cards be done; yea, or at some odd times to make their exercise give place to an interlude. As for their common table talk, they may there be as profane as Esau, and use there what merriments, scoffs, jesting, and vain speech they list; all is in the way of mirth and good fellowship, is wrapped up in the cloth, and sanctified with Mr. Preacher's short grace. As for their (the rich man's) most insatiable and greedy covetousness in purchasing and joining not field unto field, but town unto town, until they be lords of a whole country " (county), " *that* is but good husbandry, wise foresight, and allowable providence for them and their posterity." " Be the sin never so odious and apparent, if it be in a man of authority these prophets, these preachers, dare not reprove it, for *that* were both to transgress their commission and forfeit their letters patent. But now, on the other hand, for such sins as either these chief of their auditory are not apparently (manifestly) affected with, or else can endure to be weaned of . . . let their preachers alone. They will rouse and handle *them* to the quick. If, *e.g.*, they whom they seek to please be rather given to prodigality, profusion, &c., O, so they will *then* be-bait the covetous, scraping drudge out of the church. And so of the contrary, where the chief of their auditory are more parsimonious and covetous, *then* will they as much cry out of waste, excess, riot, apparel, diet, &c. ; *then* may not a great ruff look into the church lest they will do penance that wear it." [1]

Moreover, the preachers are those of the Puritan party who have and use most influence in arresting the reformation which they ought to promote. For they are " the Church's chamber-

[1] Discovery of the False Church, pp. 148-9.

lains or tapsters that stand at the door of her house, . . . of every high place in the land, and invite, and toll in their guests which flow in unto them at the sound of their bell." Instead of carrying their revolt from the Church to the issue demanded by its first principles, and seeking to carry the people with them, they summon them to stay inside, and stay inside themselves at any cost. All that pass on unheeding "hinder the discipline," they cry; "and, therefore, they assay by all means to turn them out of their way; which, if it will not be, then they denounce them, and proclaim them as most bitter enemies—Brownists, schismatics, proud and ignorant persons, disobedient to magistrates. Whom (i.e., the magistrates) they stir up in their pulpits to send out their horsemen and chariots after them to bring them by force back again into Egypt, and to hold their bodies in most noisome, vile, and strait prisons, except they will come to these fowlers' nets their high places" (i.e., the churches).

Thus, "with all their preaching they have not led their hearers one step toward perfection, but as they stood thirty years ago in the self-same state are they still—in the self-same confusion, idolatry, disorder."

In a word, his quarrel with men of the Cartwright and the Gifford type is that they are afraid themselves to be consistent, and are the bitterest foes of men like himself whose courage is greater. He wants Christ to be an absolute King; so do the Reformists. He says—pointing to the Church of England— Christ is not, and never can be, King in a Church derived, constituted, and administered as this is; they agree. He asks, Ought we not then to obey Christ in any case? They agree. And if obedience, except of a most imperfect sort, has been made impossible to us within the Church of England, may we not, ought we not, to come outside? They answer, "The logic may be sound, but the course suggested is unlawful, is dangerous, is, in short, out of the question; and if you take it we shall join against you." And they did. An example is ready to hand.[1] Some time in 1586 Barrow and Greenwood "delivered to Mr. Cartwright, Mr. Travers, Mr. Charke, and Mr. Floyde" a list of arguments for instant separation. Beginning with a definition of the true Church, they go over the points in which the "Parish Assemblies" come short—*e.g.,* how they consist *not* of a company of faithful people but of the multitude of the profane; how they make *no* separation from the heathen of the land; how they are *not* gathered in the name of Christ but of Antichrist; how they worship God not truly but after a false and idolatrous manner; how they receive not, nor obey, Christ as their Prophet, Priest, and King; how they are *not* ruled by the Old and New Testaments, but by the canon law; how they have not the power which Christ hath given unto His Church unto the world's end to bind or loose, to reform things that are amiss—and conclude: "Infinite were the reasons which from these several heads, as, likewise, from their particular transgressions and defaults, might be drawn. But the best argument to confute and cut down this trumpery at once is, according to the commandments of God, to preserve our bodies and souls free from abominations by a speedy separation and withdrawing ourselves from amongst them; and to confute their last and only argument" (*i.e.,* persecution), "whereby they uphold their ruinous kingdom—namely, their penal law—by Christian patience and an upright and godly life."

The four Reformist leaders kept a disdainful silence. But they were appalled. They and their followers were driven by the spectre of "Separation" to side more and more with the bishops. There is a great difference in their tone towards the latter after the consequences of their earlier language and attitude had been realised. If the story be true of Cartwright's friendliness with Whitgift in his last days, and of his accepting a licence to preach from the Archbishop "upon

[1] Another conspicuous example is George Gifford, of Maldon, died 1620, the occasion of Barrow and Greenwood's chief controversy.

promise not to meddle with controversies," [1] which promise he kept during the rest of his life, it need not surprise us. Thousands were virtually doing much the same. The editor of the " Conferences " spoke the truth when he declared " to the Reader " that " the Reformist preachers are now become the bishops' trusty actors in their most cunning and cruel enterprises. . . ." They have the popular ear in their pulpits, and it is "upon these men's words" that the people are " sufficiently satisfied " that the Bishops do well " to persecute these poor afflicted prisoners, who love not their lives unto death, that the truth may come to light to thy salvation." Had not Barrow, then, some excuse for exclaiming: " How great the perfidy and apostasy of these Reformists, that knew and pronounced in open Parliament that they (the bishops) were not of God, and sought to have them utterly removed, yet now, for filthy lucre, and for fear of persecution, subscribe, swear, and submit to their anti-Christian hierarchy." [2]

The question whether Nonconformist premisses issued logically in separation was much and hotly debated in the years immediately following Barrow's death. The defenders of the Establishment saw, and said from the first, that they did. Whitgift urged this as a strong point against Cartwright. Hooker, too, reminded the Presbyterians of those " who, concurring with you in judgment about the necessity of that discipline, have adventured without more ado to separate themselves from the rest of the Church, and to put your speculations in execution. These men's hastiness the warier of you do not commend ; ye wish they had held themselves longer in, and not so dangerously flown abroad before the feathers of the cause had been grown ; their error with merciful terms ye reprove, naming them, in great commiseration of mind, your poor brethren." " They, on the contrary aside, more bitterly accuse you as their false brethren, and against you they plead, saying, 'From your breasts it is that we have sucked those things,

---

[1] Walton's Life of Hooker, pp. 37-8.   [2] Plain Refutation, p. 176.

which, when ye delivered unto us, ye termed that heavenly, sincere, and wholesome milk of God's Word—howsoever ye now abhor as poison that which the virtue thereof hath wrought and brought forth in us.' "[1]   Hooker had no doubt that the "foolish Barrowists" were right in their inference.   But it became the main concern of the Presbyterians to prove them wrong, and to do so by no means "with merciful terms." "Vile calumniations and bitter scoffs, proclaiming us to the world to be Schismatics, Brownists, Donatists, &c., and matching us many times with the most notorious heretics and blasphemers that they can think upon, of purpose to make our purpose and profession odious to all men"—these were the sort of weapons employed.   You could not frame a more stinging insult against a Puritan than to call him a Brownist.   In "a true, modest, and just defence of the " (Millenary) "petition against the Oxford confutation of it," we read, for example, "Our brethren needed not to have cast the Brownists in our nose, seeing it is well known that the ministers which desire reformation have, most of all other, opposed themselves by writing to that faction."   More indignant still is the following:—"Now it grieved me not at this time a little that Satan should be so impudent as to fling the dung of that sect into my face, which with all my power I had so vehemently resisted during the whole course of my ministry in England. . . . Hannibal said once, there was not so much as one in all the enemies' camp that was called Gisco ; so may it truly be said how not so much as one of the godly ministers that suffer in England about the discipline that may deservedly be called Brownist."[2] But the fact could not be gainsaid that the Puritan logic both fairly might and actually did lead to separation.   "I know what I say, and have good experience of this thing," declared John Canne,[3] "for there is not ten of a hundred which separate

[1] Preface to Ecclesiastical Polity, pp. 125-6.
[2] Robert Parker, quoted by Lawne in the "Profane Schism," p. 68.
[3] Necessitie of Separation (1634). To the Reader.

from the Church of England but are moved first thereto (I speak of outward means) by the doctrine of the nonconformists, either in word or writing taught to the people." Barrow himself is a case in point. Other cases abound. Thus, in the "examination of Barrowists" which took place in April, 1593, we find the confession again and again that the impulse to leave the Church came from Puritan preachers. "Edward Grove" said he "was led this way (six months ago) by the sermons of Mr. Gardiner and Mr. Philips." Christopher Bowman said that "the forward ministers caused him to fall into these assemblies"—particularly Mr. Chadderton on Romans xii. Thomas Micklefield said "he was persuaded by hearing the sermons of Mr. Sparkes, Mr. Cooper, and others." Again, there appeared in 1606 the Recantation of a Brownist, written by Peter Fairlambe, who deplores that he should have been enslaved for so "many years together" to such "erroneous opinions," but pleads, by way of excuse for himself and warning for others, that he was "led into the schism of the Brownists or Donatists of England by following and believing certain of our preachers who drew many into a course—under pretence of extraordinary zeal—the grounds whereof drove us into another far worse (God knows), namely, to that of separation from the Church of England; being taught by the first sort (commonly called Puritans) that the ministry and discipline of our Church is anti-Christian, which whosoever believeth (having a good conscience) cannot choose but fall into that separation as I did." He quotes Cartwright and others who have written that "the Discipline is a part of the Gospel"—is an inseparable mark of the true Church; or, that "we stand not for trifles as for cap and surplice, but for the true worship and the true sacraments of Jesus Christ," inasmuch as "our public worship (as it is now) was raked or culled out of the Pope's dunghill," and "our ministry is come as out of the Trojan horse's belly"—and is sure that if this be true then "the Brownists were in the right, for then could not our Church be the Church of God."

We must not judge too severely. It is not easy to be consistent. It takes a clear head to see all the consequences which depend on one's cherished principles; and it needs a moral hero to be guided by them practically, whithersoever they may lead. We should not forget, moreover, that consistency became more and more difficult to the Puritan. His trust was in the civil power. He had some reason at first to hope that the civil power could be won over to his side. He did his utmost to bring this about, and was countenanced by many in high place. But, as time went on, he beheld with dismay the civil power subjected to men who were determined to stamp him out. It was one thing to be bold and aggressive while the Government was comparatively lax in opposing him; it was quite another thing to maintain the same attitude after the reins of authority had passed into Whitgift's hands, or after the passing (in 1593) of " the Act to retain the Queen's subjects in obedience "; or after the Canons of 1604 had made even a questioning of the Church in any point "excommunication de facto." In fact, however numerous the Puritan ministers and their following might be, they had come nearly to the end of their political influence before the death of Elizabeth; and, after the accession of James, they became for a period mere cyphers. And so a choice was presented to them which could not but sift the chaff from the wheat. They had either virtually to retract their former denunciations of the Church, to be silent, to conform, or else to separate and dare all. For the most part they chose the first course, and avenged an uneasy conscience by turning more fiercely than ever upon the " Brownists." Says Henry Ainsworth at this time, 1608: "The Reformists' cause called Puritanism . . . as all men see . . . decreaseth daily. The Prelates are the men that prevail, their Canons are confirmed, their ceremonies flourish, and their horns are exalted," and " worthy is it to be observed how the ministers of England are come to contradict and depart from their own grounds for to maintain their corrupt estate." As to the doctrine of Separation especially, "the ministers will neither teach nor suffer it to be taught, but block up the Kingdom of Heaven as much as they can, that men may not enter. They blame us for nothing so much as for separation when nothing is so needful to be done, if we will keep the covenant of our God." Perhaps we might have done the same ourselves. It is well to realise the force of their trial, and to remember that martyrs are not found like pebbles in every place. But the greater honour surely to those who "followed the gleam" into exile and unto death; the greater charity for the vehemence and bitterness of their speech against such as halted and drew back!

THE BISHOPS OF BARROW'S DAY.

THE BISHOPS OF BARROW'S DAY.

In considering the treatment of Puritans and Separatists by the bishops under Elizabeth, fairness demands that some facts should be kept clearly in mind :—

(1) The bishops were in a state of dependence on the Crown—a state which seemed to them natural and inevitable.

(2) They were, as Ministers of the Queen, pledged to enforce uniformity. On this point the Act of 1559 is clear. While the duty of executing its provisions is at the same time laid upon " the judges and other lay officials," it is entrusted especially to the bishops and their subordinates.

(3) The reluctance of the former to put forth the vigour of the law against Protestants led to the result that " the campaign against the Protestant Nonconformists was left to be carried on by the bishops, the ecclesiastical courts, and the clerical officials."[1] Act 1 Eli: sections 6, 11

(4) The bishops, on the whole, were not very eager to play the part assigned to them. Active persecution of Nonconformists was practically limited to a few dioceses. Even when most severe it went on mainly under the auspices of two men— Aylmer and Whitgift. Not seldom the bishops were of Parkhurst's mind : " I find by good proof that the rough and austere manner of ruling doth the least good; and, on the other part, the contrary hath and doth daily reclaim and win others."[2]

(5) This attitude of the bishops (generally) is manifest from the fact that the Queen was repeatedly urging them to

[1] Prothero, " Select Statutes," p. 83, Introduction.　　[2] Strype's Annals, Vol. II. part i., p. 510.

greater zeal. Thus, in her proclamation of 1573 (against Non-conformists, *i.e.*, "despisers" or "breakers" of the order prescribed in the Book of Common Prayer), she "giveth a most special and earnest charge to all archbishops, bishops, archdeacons, and deans, and all such as have ordinary jurisdiction in such cases, to have a vigilant eye and care to the observance of the orders and rites in the said book prescribed, throughout their cures and diocese, . . . upon pain of her Majesty's high displeasure for their negligence, and deprivation from their dignities and benefices, or other censures to follow, according to their demerits." Again, in her speech to Parliament at its prorogation (March 29) 1585, she was peremptory in declaring herself "over-ruler" of the Church ; and that her "negligence" could not "be excused if any schisms or errors heretical were suffered." Then, turning to the bishops, "all which (faults, &c.) if you, my lords of the clergy, do not amend I mean to depose you." She would by no means "tolerate new-fangledness." For some make "too many subtle scarrings of God's blessed will as lawyers do with human testaments" ; . . . a course "dangerous to a kingly rule" ; . . . nay, "according to their own censure" they "make a doom (judgment) of the validity and privity of their Prince's government, with a common veil and cover of God's Word." To this the bishops must endeavour to put an end.

Barrow (though not more so than some of the Puritan writers, notably Marprelate) denounced bishops indiscriminately. His strong objection to their office created a strong prejudice against them personally. He seems almost to have reached the point of believing that a bishop must needs be not only a false minister of the Church, but a bad man. This, of course, on the face of it, is unlikely ; and, as a matter of fact, is untrue. There were estimable men among them. Thomas Cooper—*e.g.*, whom Barrow calls "that old Pharisee, T. C." —was such a man. He was Bishop of Lincoln from 1570 to 1584, and then Bishop of Winchester till his death, ten years later. In the latter diocese, says Anthony Wood, "as in most parts of the nation, he became much noted for his learning and sanctity of life." Wood may be hardly an impartial witness, but his testimony does not stand alone. An intimate friend speaks of him as "A man from whose praises I can hardly temper my pen." The tone of his "Admonition to the People of England"—the authorised answer to Marprelate—tends to confirm this judgment. It has sharp and bitter passages, as might be expected, but, in the main, it is restrained, dignified, and Christian. Martin makes some scurrilous and unfeeling references to the great trouble of Cooper's life. If, however, the following be true, his nobleness needs no other proof. His wife was, we are told, "utterly profligate." [1] But he condoned her unfaithfulness again and again, refusing to be divorced when the heads of the University offered to arrange it for him, and declaring that he would not charge his conscience with so great a scandal. On one occasion his wife, in a paroxysm of fury, tore up half his "Thesaurus," [2] and threw it into the fire. He patiently set to work and rewrote it.

Besides Cooper, one might mention Thomas Bickley [3] (Bishop of Chichester, 1585-96), of whom it is said that he was "diligent in discharging the duties of his office, and was much respected and beloved in his diocese"; and John Piers, or Peirse (successively Bishop of Rochester [1576-7], of Salisbury [1577-1589], and Archbishop of York [1589-94]). In his early days he was Rector of Quainton, Bucks, and "in this country cure, having only the companionship of rustics, he fell into the habit of tippling with them in ale-houses, and was in great hazard of losing all those excellent gifts that came after to be well-esteemed and rewarded in him." He was weaned

---

[1] This was "the great trouble of his life."

[2] Published 1565: "Thesaurus linguæ Romanæ et Brittanicæ accessit Dictionarium Historicum et Poeti-cum," 2nd edition 1573, 3rd edition 1578, 4th edition 1589.

[3] The instances are mostly taken from the years following 1580—Barrow's period.

from the habit by the exhortation of a clerical friend, and so
strictly abstemious did he become, that even in his last sickness
his physician was unable to persuade him to take a little wine.
In later years he is known among the Puritans as one of the
" relentless prelates," on account of his stern dealings with
Edward Gallebrand, a ringleader of the Presbyterian party in
Oxford.   But, as we have just seen, he could be stern also with
himself ; and there can be no doubt that he was a good man.
" At York, as in all his previous episcopates, Piers left behind
him   a high character as ' a primitive bishop,' ' one of the
most grave and reverend prelates of the age, winning the love
of all by his generosity, kindliness of disposition, and Christian
meekness.' "   " Malice itself spared him," says the preacher [1] of
his funeral sermon, " even that malice which blotted and
blemished the names of most of the lights of this land never
accused him.   But I call this the least credit of a thousand.
From the first hour that he came into this province, you know
his behaviour among you at all seasons ; how he kept nothing
back that was profitable, but taught you openly, and through
every church ; witnessing both to Jews and Gentiles, Protestants and Papists, repentance towards God and faith towards
Jesus Christ."   Such instances do not show, of course, and are
not meant even to suggest that the bishops were saints.
There were no saints among them, if the test be spiritual
enthusiasm.   Perhaps the most characteristic description of an
Elizabethan bishop would be to the effect that (as in the case
1579-1609.   of William Overton, Bishop of Coventry and Lichfield), he was
" genial, hospitable, and kind to the poor " ; or (as in the case
1584-90.   of Thomas Godwin, Bishop of Bath and Wells), that he was
" hospitable, mild, and judicious " ; or (as in the case of Park-
1560-74.   hurst, Bishop of Norwich), that he was " a genial, scholarly,
pliant, hospitable gentleman, but little more."   This, however,
though far enough from saintliness, is also far from downright
wickedness.   No doubt there were cases even of downright

[1] Dr. King, his chaplain (Strype's Annals, Vol. IV., p. 288-9).

wickedness. But, if so, they were very rare; and Martin's alliterative denunciation of all the bishops as " proud, Popish, presumptuous, profane, paultrie, pestilent, and pernicious prelates " is absurd. Of the bishops living when Martin wrote, there was perhaps only one whose character was really bad. I do not mean Aylmer, for the charges hurled at him by Martin —so far as they affect his personal character—can neither be said to have been proved, nor to have been of much account, if they were. I refer to Marmaduke Middleton (Bishop of St. 1582-90 David's), whose record was bad from first to last, and who was at length degraded by the High Commission at Lambeth Palace, and formally divested both of his " episcopal robes and priestly vestments." [1]

It may further be admitted that, speaking generally, the bishops were learned men. Martin had the audacity to reproach Cooper with " want of learning." To which, with the "Thesaurus " in his hands, he did not need to reply by referring to his distinguished Oxford career, and to the fact that since he was a young man in Magdalen College " he hath been brought up in the love of the Gospel," and has made himself familiar with " the writings of the ancient fathers and the best authors of this age since the renewing of the Gospel." [2] In fact, nearly all the men who became bishops between 1580 and 1600 were more or less distinguished scholars. Their career at Oxford or Cambridge is usually the same— B.A., M.A., B.D., D.D. with a Fellowship of some college, or a mastership, on the way. It is said of Bullingham (Bishop of 1581-98. Gloucester and Bristol) that he was " conspicuous neither for learning nor refinement." But we read even of him that he was " admitted to the B.D. degree at Oxford after twelve years' studying." And as to others, Thomas Godwin (Bishop of Bath and Wells), e.g., was an " eminent scholar "; Edmund

---

[1] He was charged with having two wives, with contriving and publishing a forged will, with simonical practices, &c.

[2] Admonition to the People of England (1589), pp. 59, 60 (Arber's Reprint in the English Scholars' Library).

Keake (Bishop of Rochester, Norwich, and Worcester) was—
according to Archbishop Parker—" a serious, pious, and *learned*
man ".; Piers had been Master of Balliol, then Dean of Christ
Church, where he was "a great instrument of the progress of
good learning," and is called by Camden " theologus magnus,"
as well as " modertus." Aylmer, too—tutor in his early days
of Lady Jane Grey, and co-worker with Foxe, at a later date,
in his Latin translation of the " Acts and Monuments of the
Martyrs "—had learning enough, whatever else he lacked. So
certainly had Whitgift. He was Margaret Professor of Divinity
at Cambridge in 1566, Regius Professor in 1567, and Master
of Trinity the same year, a post which, by admission of friends
and foes alike, he greatly adorned. He is said to have been
ignorant of Greek, so much so that he could not read his
Greek Testament, a statement which Mullinger, who ought to
know, says he " has seen nothing to contravene." [1] But in his
" Defence of the Answer to the Admonition " (especially in the
third portion) the quotations abound from Greek as well as
Latin writers, and are translated in the text; so that unless the
translating was done for him, he must have been able to read
the originals.   There was a plentiful lack of learning among
the inferior clergy, though less and less towards the end of
Elizabeth's reign, as the universities became more efficient; but
there was no great lack among the bishops, however " vain and
useless " it may have seemed to Martin, and also to Barrow.

Still there is another side to the picture. With due allowance under the heads of character and learning, we cannot be
surprised that the bishops, as a class, excited contempt and
indignation.

(1) In the first place, their subserviency was manifest to
all. This, indeed, was their recommendation in the eyes of
Elizabeth. It was the condition, implied or expressed, on which
they received their appointment. Good looks might turn the
scale with her, other things being equal. She was attracted,

[1] History of Cambridge University, p. 420.

we are told, by the "handsome person, courtly manners, and ability as a preacher" of Richard Fletcher, Bishop of Worcester and London. And she was "so pleased with the 'good parts' and 'goodly person' of Thomas Godwin (Bishop of Bath and Wells), that she made him one of her Lent Preachers." But nothing of this sort availed unless there was, at the same time, a disposition to fall in absolutely with her wishes. We know how she suspended Archbishop Grindal, and embittered his last days, when he crossed her decision in the matter of the prophesyings. We know that her sustained regard for Whitgift had its ground in the fact that the imperiousness of her "little black husband"[1] never thwarted her own, but took pleasure in carrying out its behests. Men, therefore, by becoming bishops signed away their independence for good and all. As a rule, no doubt, they did so willingly; they had no independence to begin with, but if they had it met a speedy death. Richard Cox, Bishop of Ely—one of Elizabeth's oldest prelates—took up a stiff attitude at first. He "refused to minister in the Queen's chapel because of the crucifix and lights there, and justified himself in a letter to her Majesty."[2] But when we read his letter[3] to her, years later, expatiating on her benefits to the Church, we see that the old spirit which once encountered John Knox at Frankfort has succumbed. What he would fain have cured he has learned to endure and excuse. Much more in the case of other prelates whom we have mentioned. The Bishop of Peterborough—Howland—in his earlier years was an adherent of Cartwright, and signed the petition to Burghley in his behalf; but he settles down into "a man of gravity and moderation—of neither party or faction." The Bishop of Chichester (Bickley) acquired considerable reputation as a reformer and preacher of reformed doctrines. He was one of Edward VI.'s chaplains, and there is a story that he once "broke the Host in pieces in the

[1] The Queen's name for him, according to Isaac Walton, in his Life of Hooker.
[2] July 28, 1559.
[3] 1574.

college chapel at Windsor and trampled it under his feet."
Here, surely, was the making of a fervent Puritan, but the
royal breath subdued him to a moderate heat. The Bishop of
Bath and Wells (Thos. Godwin) was, likewise, a "zealous
reformer" in Edward's days, and even so late as 1562 is said to
have signed a "petition for discipline of the Church"; but
Elizabeth took him by the hand and his reforming zeal soon
died away. As for Bullingham (Bishop of Gloucester and
Bristol), his subserviency proceeded from the opposite direction. He began in the old faith, and was very slow in
embracing the tenets of the Reformers. In Edward VI.'s
days he went into voluntary exile, taking refuge at Rouen. On
the accession of Mary he returned, and became domestic chaplain to Gardiner, Bishop of Winchester, and rector of Boxwell
and Witherington in Gloucestershire (his native county).
Elizabeth arrived, and, at first, Bullingham was "quite and
clean despatched from all his livings for his obstinacy." But
not for long. In 1565 we find him a prebend of St. Paul's, and
well on the way to preferment. Archbishop Parker called him
"an honest, true-meaning man." Marprelate called him "a
Mass-monger, an old papist priest," one whom "beef and
brewis had made a priest." We may be content to say that he
honestly persuaded himself, as Burghley advised his son to do,
that he could best "serve God by serving the Queen." The
bishops wore the Queen's livery like the rest of her servants.
They were her creatures, made by, and for, obedience. The
result was bound to be a featureless, passionless uniformity.
Their one rule was to "keep in step." A striking example of
subserviency at its worst is presented in Fletcher, Bishop of
Bristol, Worcester, London. He was Dean of Peterborough at
the time of Mary Queen of Scots' trial.[1] He preached before
the Commissioners for her trial in the chapel of Fotheringay
Castle ; drew up a detailed report of their examination of
Mary ; officiated as chaplain at her execution.[2] His was the

---

[1] Oct. 12, 1586.   [2] Feb. 8, 1587.

solitary voice which echoed with a stern and loud " Amen "
the Earl of Kent's imprecation, " So perish all the Queen's
enemies." The answer to this evident bid for preferment was
the Bishopric of Bristol. Three years later, he moved a step
higher into the See of Worcester. But he was in the habit of
" spending much more of his time at Court than in his
diocese ; " and in 1594 he managed to succeed Aylmer. In his
letter[1] to Burghley—the usual mediator—" beseeching " him to
plead his cause with Her Majesty, he gives several reasons for
desiring a " remove " to London above all places in the realm,
except the real one, which was that there was a lady, widow of
Sir Richard Baker, " very fine and handsome," whom he had
a mind to take for his second wife; and that the lady was bent
on remaining near the Court. As soon as he came to London
he married her; and as soon as the Queen heard of it, she not
only forbade him the Court, but suspended him " from the
exercise of all episcopal functions." Then he wrote to the
Lord Treasurer, declaring that rather than have lost the
Queen's favour, " he could have wished to have been sequestered
from his life itself," and intreating his intercession. After
six months the suspension was taken off, and then he wrote
again that " to hear of the least her Highness gracious inclination towards him, in her princely clemency, he could not
sufficiently express to his good Lordship how greatly it had
comforted him—having these six months thought himself (as
the prophet spake) free among the dead, and like unto him
that is in the grave, made unprofitable unto God and Her
Majesty's service."[2] A little later he wrote to try and enlist
Burghley among the " divers friends that have of late moved
Her Majesty, according to my most humble desire, that it
would please Her Highness to give me access unto her presence." For " 'tis now a year within a week or two since I have
seen Her Majesty "—time which " hath seemed longer " " than a

---

[1] Strype's Annals, vol. iv., p. 288.   [2] Strype's Whitgift, Bk. iv., cap.
xiii., p. 429.

whole age " (seculum).[1] Of course, Fletcher's extreme " courtli-
ness " may have been peculiar to himself; but his case throws
vivid light on both sides of the relation between the bishops
and Elizabeth : her despotic rule and their abject dependence.
In truth, "no one of them was strong enough to rise superior
to the spirit of his time. The mastery of the Queen over
Church and State, and the energy of her Ministers, on whose
extraordinary ability and unscrupulous loyalty she could rely,
made her supremacy in ecclesiastical matters hardly less real or
less galling than that of her father. The ecclesiastics of her
time, and especially during the latter half of her reign "—when
her power had consolidated itself—"truckled and obeyed."
Remembering this, it is easy to understand the scorn of men
like Barrow who believed—and were ready to die for their
belief—that the office of a true bishop is purely spiritual; that
he ought to subject himself to the will of Christ alone as
supreme Teacher and Ruler of His own Church; and that, if
need be, His will ought to be enforced as impartially and strictly
against the Queen as against the Church's meanest member.

(2) It must be admitted, too, that their scorn could find
ample fuel for itself in the bishops' unblushing worldliness.
For the Queen, of course, a bishopric meant its emoluments.[2]
She had no scruple in keeping a see vacant so as to enjoy its
revenues. She kept Durham vacant for two years, Salisbury
for three, Colchester for four, Bath and Wells for five, Bristol
and Gloucester each for six, Ely for eighteen, &c. Neither did
she hesitate to move a bishop from one see to another merely
in order to secure for herself the " first-fruits " which a new
bishop always had to pay. The material aspect of the matter
was all she saw. And the same was true of courtiers and
nobles, who regarded a bishopric as an estate of which the

[1] Strype, Life of Whitgift. Bk. iv.,
App. xx., p. 183.
[2] See this illustrated by Sir John
Puckting's "petition to the Queen for
a lease of part of the possessions of
the Bishopric of Ely : a motion to fill
that vacant see," "showing how Her
Majesty might clear £2,000 odd by
the transaction" (Strype's Annals,
Vol. IV., pp. 343-6).

lands or palace might be leased to them on easy terms or
handed over to them altogether. But the bishops, so far as
one can see, were like-minded. For them also the material and
secular seemed to overshadow the spiritual. They were not
worse than others in this respect, but they were no better.
Martin said,[1] with more truth than usual, "they be carnally
disposed and not evangelically, and this their affection and corruption they show to the world by hoarding of great sums of
money, by purchasing lands for their wives and children, by
marrying their sons and daughters with thousands, by increasing their livings with flocks and herds of grazed cattle, by
furnishing their tables with plate and gilded cups, by filling
their purses with unreasonable fines and incomes." And
Bishop Cooper made a lame reply when he said:[2] "That those
which now be, or of late have been, bishops in this Church,
should be so carnally and grossly given over to the world and
the cares thereof . . . my heart abhorreth to think; nor
will the fear of God suffer me to judge it to be true." It is
not a question of "thinking" but of fact; and the fact that
the bishops, as Cooper declared, did "earnestly and zealously
teach and defend"[3] true doctrine "in their preachings" and
did "carefully beat down the gross superstition of Antichrist
and his ministers" is irrelevant. Three facts especially have
impressed me:—First, how seldom a would-be bishop, or a
bishop desirous of some richer see, waited till he was *called.*
Whenever details relating to an appointment have been
recorded, we generally find that the successful candidate,
among others, has employed "influence"; and that the man
whose influence he has been most anxious to employ, either
directly or indirectly, is Burghley. Cooper said,[4] "The best
sort of ecclesiastical livings are in the disposition of the
Prince's authority. And those honourable that have to do
therein and are counsellors to Her Majesty, be not so unwise

[1] The "Epistle."
[2] "Admonition," &c., p. 112.
[3] Ditto.
[4] "Admonition," pp. 109, 110.

but they can espy ambition in him that sueth and laboureth for them. And if they do perceive it they are very greatly to blame if they suffer it to escape without open shame or other notable punishment, and thereby bring suspicion either upon themselves or upon those that be about them." In this he shows more innocence than knowledge. Burghley could have enlightened him. He must have received scores, probably hundreds, of letters, to say nothing of personal applications, with reference to episcopal elections alone. He did not mind, for he was a man of the time. But we may be sure he was not deceived. He saw well enough what lay behind the decorous veil of pious phrases, and was not the less disposed to speak for a man because he more than suspected him of ambition. Let me cite one or two illustrations. Howland was discontented with his see of Peterborough, and wrote himself to Burghley, after the death of Piers, in 1594, earnestly begging " a removal to a better support." Matthew Hutton, Bishop of Durham, succeeded Piers in the Archbishopric of York, and might have done so in any case ; but no sooner does he hear " that Her Majesty hath set down a full resolution to remove me to York," than he is eager to clinch the matter.[1] He is " aged and decayed," as he says, and it were " more fit for me to think of my grave than any honours in this world." Yet he writes post-haste to Burghley, and at the same time to his son, Sir Robert Cecil : " Because I would be loath either to seem too forward in hasty sending, or, in protracting the time, to be thought undutifully careless of so gracious a resolution " ; and, when the promotion has been assured to him, he writes again : [2] " I think myself most bound to the Queen's most excellent Majesty . . . and I account the blessing to be the greater because the same God, who of His undeserved goodness inclined the royal heart of so gracious a Sovereign to my good, hath also moved your lordship from time to time to further me." Perhaps the ambition

[1] Strype's Annals, Vol. IV., p. 276-7.   [2] Ditto.

here was rather for honour than wealth, but it would be absurd to deny the ambition. Again, Bullingham wanted a remove from the Bishopric of Gloucester, and when the See of Oxford fell vacant, in 1592, he got Aylmer to obtain it for him, if possible;[1] and Aylmer did his best, pleading that "it was very fit for him, from the weariness of the place, and to make some addition to his poor portion." Bullingham was not a favourite with the Queen, perhaps not with Burghley, and the suit did not prosper. Probably Cooper never heard that it had been made, as he may never have heard of a hundred similar ones. Once more, Bilson, who wrote on "The Perpetual Government of Christ His Church" (1593) is better understood when we read what he wrote to Burghley. The Lord Treasurer, at first of his own accord, had, it seems, "set" him "down to the Deanery of Windsor," which Bilson had "never refused," although supposed to have done so. Now, with due gratitude for this favour, he becomes "a humble suitor to" his lordship for "his assistance to obtain Worcester." The rest of the letter gives us a clear glimpse behind the scenes: "My Lord of Canterbury's favour by friends I have sought; but he is besieged by some about him, that he is not suffered to follow his own inclination." Whitgift he is sure would prefer him, but has been led to "move Her Majesty for Dr. James. If my lord Archbishop were not overcarried by others, this court would desire no better judge, whether of us twain hath taken more pains in the Church" (Dr. James had not written "The Perpetual Government") "and served Her Majesty with greater charge. But my facility being surprised by others, I am forced to appeal to your honourable and indifferent wisdom and favour, since Her Majesty useth the advice of more than one in these matters; and am willing by your lordship's censure to stand or fall, as never meaning to molest friends for anything that your grave and worthy judgment shall think

---

[1] He asked that "it might be joined in commendam to his own poor one" (Strype's "Aylmer," p. 168).

unfit."[1] He won his suit, and soon afterwards was advanced to Winchester. These cases, by no means the worst, are samples of many. They do not prove what Marprelate and Barrow asserted, and Cooper denied, that the Elizabethan bishops were more "corrupt" than those of any previous age. But they do show that "heaving and shoving," "canvassing and working for bishoprics," to quote Cooper's words,[2] did prevail.[3]

Another fact pointing to the same conclusion is that the bishops were in almost every case pluralists. Sometimes they were so to an extent which shocked the conscience of the authorities even in those lax days. Thus a commission of inquiry was issued into the administration of Hughes, Bishop of St. Asaph; and the report,[4] endorsed by the Lord Treasurer's own hand, described the bishop as holding in commendam (besides the archdeaconry and the rectory of Llysvaen) fifteen livings, thus having in his hands "nine livings *cum curâ* and seven *sine curâ*"; and though six had been resigned by him, it was only "upon having of better." Of course, this was an extreme case. But the case of Overton, Bishop of Coventry and Lichfield, reads almost as bad. Thus I find the following :—1553, rector of Balcombe, Sussex, and vicar of Eccleshall, Staffordshire ; 1555, rector of Swinnerton, Staffordshire ; 1559, prebendary of Winchester ; 1560, receives "livings of Upham and Nurstling"; 1561, is given "living of Exton"; 1562, adds that of Cotton ; 1569, also the living of Buriton. In 1563 he was made canon of Chichester, in 1567 he is treasurer of Chichester Cathedral, in 1570 he obtains a canonry at Salisbury, and, in the same year, the rectory of Stoke-upon-Trent and of Hanbury. He may not have held all

---

[1] October 31, 1595, Strype's Annals, Vol. IV., p. 318.
[2] "Admonition," p. 107.
[3] Aylmer's example has not been mentioned. But it was perhaps the worst of all. Read the story of his appeals to Burghley to get a "remove" from London—first to Winchester, then to Ely : appeals which extended over three years (1579–82) ; and landed him in what he calls his "low lingering hope." He made interest for Ely before old Bishop Cox was dead ; and two days after his death was instant with Burghley, to "promote" his interest. Strype's Life of Aylmer, pp. 109–112.
[4] Dated February 24, 1587.

these together—probably did not ; but some of them at least—
perhaps most—must have been held simultaneously, and we do
not hear of any remonstrance. Again, we read of Fletcher
(Bishop of Bristol, Worcester, and London) that in 1585-6 he
was prebendary of Lincoln Cathedral and rector of Barnack,
Northamptonshire, and, in addition, had " the rich living of
Algarkirk, in South Lincolnshire, which, together with his
stall, he was allowed to retain in commendam when he became
Bishop of Bristol." We read of Leake (Bishop of Rochester,
Norwich, and Worcester) that, at his elevation to the see of
Rochester he was empowered " to retain the Archdeaconry of 1571.
Canterbury (which he had held since 1564, with various other
livings and offices), and the receiving of Purleigh in commendam." We read of Blethyn (Bishop of Llandaff, 1575-90),
that he held at the same time as his bishopric " several livings,
in order to add to the scanty endowments of the see."
Scambler was at once vicar of Rye, chaplain to Parker, Prebendary of York, Canon of Westminster, before he became
Bishop of Peterborough. Howland, who succeeded Scambler,
" held the living of Sibson (Leicestershire) in commendam,
and laboured under imputations of having impoverished his
bishopric to gratify his patron Burghley." Young, Bishop of
Rochester, being taken to task by Burghley for his com- 1578-1605.
mendams, admitted that out of these he got—with the addition
of what he calls " casualties "[1] —£120 annually.; and thought it
enough to answer that he could not live without them, as " the
clear yearly value " of his bishopric did " not amount to above
£220."[2] I set down these instances almost at random, and should
expect to find—though I have not had time to make sure—that
the evil they exhibit attached more or less to every bishop
on the bench.

Of course, an inevitable result of pluralism was non-
residence. Neither a bishop, nor any of the lower clergy,
who held several livings, could *live* in all the parishes for which

---

[1] Perquisites ?   [2] Strype's Annals, Vol. IV., p. 315.

he was responsible, and often he did not live in any of them, and did not even provide, as according to the Queen's injunctions[1] he was bound to do, that there should be a curate able not merely to " read," but " to teach the principles of religion." What is described as something fairly typical of the general state throughout the country at the end of Elizabeth's reign may here be quoted. The writer[2] is a Church historian, and the reference is to a diocese which Barrow may be presumed to have had before his eye in more than one place of his writings. Dr. Montgomery was a Dean of Norwich. In 1604 he came into possession of three Irish bishoprics, and " forthwith took up his residence in Ireland, though still retaining his deanery, and rarely, if ever, showed himself in Norwich, except upon audit days to receive his dividends. This went on for ten years, until at last—having in the meantime resigned Derry and Raphoe, and taken to himself the Bishopric of Meath in their stead—he was induced to resign his Deanery of Norwich on being indemnified for his loss of income." The writer adds —speaking still of Norwich—that " Dr. Suckling seems actually to have been the only member of the chapter who ever pretended to reside, and the cathedral-close was a vast heap of ruins." This surely was " a means to keep the country in ignorance, at a time when there were only 3,000 preachers to supply 9,000 parishes,"[3] even had all been resident, the rest being quite neglected, or given over to the ignorant and incompetent. Yet when the House of Commons petitioned[4] the Lords spiritual and temporal, to redress this evil—among others—archbishop, bishops, and clergy all took fire. They presented " a very pathetical " address to the Queen[5] . . . intituled " a petition . . . that the Bill against Pluralities pass not." " In most humble

---

[1] Issued 1559, see Nos. 3, 4, 5, 33, 44.
[2] Dr. Jessopp in *Diocesan Histories*, " Norwich," pp. 179–180.
[3] Sir Francis Knollys' words— Strype's Whitgift, p. 194. This fact was urged as an excuse for non-resi-dence. But the Puritans replied: (1) You eject or reject many of the best preachers; (2) you allow a few to monopolise the best livings, and so discourage candidates for the ministry.
[4] December, 1584.
[5] Strype's Whitgift, p. 194-5.

wise," as "poor, distressed supplicants," they complained of it, in that it "impeacheth your Majesty's prerogative royal; impaireth the revenue of the Crown; overthroweth the study of Divinity in both Universities; depriveth men of the livings they do lawfully possess; beggareth the clergy; bringeth in a base, unlearned ministry; taketh away all hope of a succession in learning; will breed great discontent in the younger sort of students, and make them fly to other seminaries where they may hope for more encouragement, &c. . . . all which we are ready with your Highness's favour and licence to justify before any competent judge, if we be permitted an indifferent hearing. In the meantime and always, most humbly committing our poor state to your Majesty's most gracious and princely clemency—on which, next under the goodness of Almighty God, it doth wholly depend—we do in all submission, both in respect of ourselves, and especially in regard of our successors, most instantly pray such speedy remedy in this behalf, as to your most excellent Majesty, and wonted godly care of religion, shall seem fit." Whitgift's hand is visible here, the reasons adduced for the petition being much the same as the nine which he is expressly said to have drawn up.[1] It was a melancholy display. Bishops and clergy often had need of the spur where matters spiritual were concerned, but touch their "temporalities," or threaten to do so, and they were instantly alert, anxious, angry. With the bishops thus proving themselves by speech and example men who—in Sir Francis Knollys' words[2]—seemed less desirous "to feede theyre flocke than to regarde the wolle, or the milke of their flocke," it is easy to excuse the vehemence of men like Barrow.

Equally significant of the same worldly temper were the disputes which so often occurred about Church estates and revenues. Years of Cox's life (Bishop of Ely) were worried and wasted by a dispute of this kind, in which he and his wife

[1] Strype's Whitgift, p. 193.   [2] Strype's Whitgift, p. 193.

were accused of covetous and corrupt practices.[1] Here, certainly, the covetousness, at least, was rather on the side of his
accuser Lord North.[2] But it is pitiful to observe the eager
clutch of the old bishop on what he holds to be his own, and
the passion he expends on a cause so alien to the spirit of his
calling. It may be said that Cox was not animated by selfish
motives, but simply by a desire to guard his bishopric from the
"voracious maw" of greedy nobles—as it may be said of
Sandys that the impassioned letter[3] he wrote to the Queen about
her wish to lease two great manors, Southwell and Scrooby,
with all their members and appurtenances, was the dictate of a
conscience which did "not seek" himself, "but the good of
the" Church. Read, however, the letter written by Sandys to
Burghley four years later.[4] What a sordid picture it suggests!
The Dean of York has accused him of giving "divers leases
unto his children in reversion, and no fine reserved thereof
unto the use of the Church"; and, further, of granting
"the patent of the chancellorship to a boy (of his own) of
nine years of age. The Archbishop retorts that the dean's
complaints "smell of mere malice"; that the dean is a man
"that hath no great regard what he saith nor what he
sweareth"; that the dean "will not remember how that my
predecessor,[5] within two months that he was translated to Canterbury, gave unto his kinsmen and servants, and for round
sums of money to himself, sixscore leases and patents; and
even then when they were thought not to be good in law; and
the dean and chapter confirmed fourscore of them, and that
without stop or dislike; and that, I suppose, gratis." *He*
might do anything. . . I may do nothing. . . Yet he had
but given to his "six sons every one two leases in reversion,"
being "bound in conscience to take care of his family," and

[1] Strype's Annals, Book I., chap.
xxxiv.
[2] And also Sir Christopher Hatton,
the vice-Chamberlain, who wanted the
bishop's house in Holborn by lease.

North wanted the manor and lands of
Somersham.
[3] November 24, 1582.
[4] May 22, 1586.   Strype's Annals,
Vol. IV., 595-8.
[5] Grindall.

paying dean and chapter "for the confirmation thereof £4 for every lease; in the whole £48." He had, too, bestowed the chancellorship upon his son—not a boy of nine, but a man of twenty-five, a Master of Arts of three or four years' standing, and "a great deal elder in discretion, sobriety, and learning." He had, besides, conjoined in a registership two younger sons —"the one, being at Cambridge, of nineteen years of age, a good student; the other, a scholar in the grammar-school at York, of thirteen years of age." This is all! And for this "the dean spitteth out his venom still, and hath used means to infect the very courts."[1] Similar in spirit was the quarrel between Sandys and Aylmer, who succeeded him in the see of London.[2] Similar, again, were the complaints of Scambler, Bishop of Norwich, against his predecessor (Freake), although, as Strype remarks, "the same complaints might be made of his own conduct at Peterborough"; a statement confirmed by another witness, who says that Scambler was notorious as a shameless spoiler in a generation of shameless spoilers; that his pillage of Peterborough was outrageous; and that his complaint of the wrongs done him by the greed of Freake was "impudent." This case, as connected with Norwich, can hardly have failed to attract the special notice of Barrow no less than that of Aylmer, and the earlier case of Parkhurst.[3] If, indeed, Barrow took his impression of the episcopal character mainly from the three bishops of his native diocese who belonged to his time (always with the addition of Aylmer), its unfavourableness needs no other explanation. Of Scambler we have just spoken. The disorders of Freake's household were a notorious scandal, and it became a common saying that "if any one came to the bishop without a present his shrew of a

---

[1] Strype's Annals, Vol. IV., 595–ff.
[2] Aylmer got the see at Sandys' recommendation 1576. Aylmer required as his due the whole incomes and benefits of the bishopric for the last half-year. Both appealed to the Lord Treasurer. Sandys charged Aylmer with ingratitude, envy, "coloured covetousness," "dissimulation." Aylmer persisted, and brought on "a greater and longer difference" by claiming for "dilapidations."—Strype's Aylmer, pp. 25–28.
[3] Bishop of Norwich, 1560–1574.

wife will look upon him as the Devil looks over Lincoln."
And even Parkhurst, certainly the best of the three—whom
Neal[1] (following Strype) describes as " a zealous Protestant,
. . . a learned divine, a faithful pastor, a diligent and constant preacher, and an example to his flock in righteousness, in
faith, in love, in peace, and in purity "—even he presented a
worldly side which must greatly have lowered his spiritual
influence. Strype says[2] " he was exceeding · hospitable, and
kept a table for the poor." Another less partial account
says:—" He was a popular and amusing person, clearly a man
of expensive habits, and not too high-minded. Money he must
have, and while the hideous venality of the times needed to be
resisted by a prelate at once frugal and austere, Bishop Parkhurst showed a bad example in making merchandise of the
Church of God." " The condition of his diocese when he
came to it was deplorable beyond description." This was due
partly to the prevalence of a " vile system, whereby lay patrons
not only sold their patronage openly, but as openly exacted
from the incumbents an annual pension from the benefice,
which was a first charge upon the income, and, in many
instances, the bargain was a ruinous one to the wretched
parson. The result was that in 1562 more than half the parish
churches in the diocese were found to be vacant, and everywhere a serious decline in the number of candidates for Holy
Orders was observable." This evil Parkhurst, it would seem,
did little or nothing to remedy. But while " clergy and laity
were left to do almost as they pleased, the bishop kept open
house in a lavish way, sometimes at the palace of Norwich,
and, latterly, at his house at Ludham." Of course he was
popular. One who keeps open house, be he bishop or not,
is sure to be popular, while the careful man will be
accounted mean. Young, Bishop of Rochester, for example,
was reported[3] to be " extremely covetous," the reason being

---

[1] History of Puritans, Vol. I., p. 289.   [2] See his letter to Burghley, Strype's
[2] Annals, Vol. II., p. 343.   Annals, Vol. IV., pp. 315–17.

that he "appeared" to keep "a near and miserable house." His defence was that his "whole income reached but to £340 a year," and that of this £250 went, on the average, "in meat and drink only." He submitted that such a sum was as much as, or more than, he ought to spend for "mere maintenance," considering that with the remainder he had to provide for "reparations of houses and farms, and chancels, removing of house-stuff and furniture, apparelling" himself and "wife," maintaining his "son at London at school, and liveries, stable charges, expenses in law and physic, gifts, rewards, and toward the serving of the realm when it is required." But then he is not one of those "prodigal clergymen," who, "to spoil of Christ's patrimony or their own, in epicurism and belly-cheer, and other vaunting and bravery, do pour out they care not what, and would absume Crœsus' and Solomon's treasury if they had it," and, therefore, he is called covetous!

In conclusion, we have admitted that the bishops were not bad men on the whole. But they were creatures of their time. Current opinion, as well as tradition, tended to inspire them with secular views of their office. It raised them to the rank of nobles; it called upon them to live like nobles. Some of them did so; many tried to do so; all regarded their lordly estate as essential to the credit of their spiritual functions. As Whitgift declared—"Religion is the foundation and cement of human society, and when they that serve at God's altar shall be exposed to poverty, then religion itself will be exposed to scorn and become contemptible."[1] Barrow, with his eye turned on Christ and the apostles, thought this strange doctrine; and he would fain have done what, according to Whitgift, Julianus the Apostate did "in derision"—he would fain have made bishops and clergy poor as bringing them to a state "which was most meet and profitable for Christians," and that they "might sooner come to the kingdom of heaven."[2]

[1] Strype's Whitgift, p. 87.   [2] Strype's Whitgift, p. 215.

ARCHBISHOP WHITGIFT AND HIS
"ECCLESIASTIAL POLITY."

ARCHBISHOP WHITGIFT AND HIS "ECCLESIASTIAL POLITY."

" JOHN WHITGIFT was born (at Grimsby, 1530 or 1533) in the county of Lincoln, of a family that was ancient, and noted to be both prudent and affable and gentle by nature; he was educated in Cambridge (first at Queen's College, 1548-9); much of his learning was acquired in Pembroke Hall (where Mr. Bradford the martyr was his tutor); from thence he was removed to Peterhouse (made Fellow 1555); from thence to be Master of Pembroke Hall; from thence to the Mastership of Trinity College (July, 1567); about which time the Queen made him her chaplain, and not long after Prebend of Ely (December, 1568) and the Dean of Lincoln (1572); and, having for many years past looked upon him with much reverence and favour, gave him a fair testimony of both by giving him the bishopric of Worcester (1577), and—which was not with her a usual favour—forgiving him his firstfruits; then by constituting him Vice-President of the Principality of Wales (1578). And, having experienced his wisdom, his justice and moderation in the menage of her affairs in both these places, she, in the twenty-sixth of her reign, made him Archbishop of Canterbury (1583), and trusted him to manage all her ecclesiastical affairs and preferments." Such, in Isaac Walton's words,[1] is the outline of Whitgift's life. He owed to an uncle, it is said, his first insight into " the rottenness of the popish system." During the perilous times of Mary he had " resolved to retire to the continent," but was induced by the master of his college

---

[1] Life of Hooker, p. 30. But the particulars within brackets are added.

(Dr. Perne) to remain and, apparently, to trim his sail to the
wind.   In after days the master figured among Puritans as the
type of a turncoat ("the old turner" is Martin Marprelate's
name for him); and the pupil was made to share in his discredit.   Towards the end of 1565 Whitgift joined with others of
the University "in an urgent letter to Cecil, their chancellor,
deprecating the orders made for the stricter use of the apparel."
The letter was ill taken, and the severe rebuke it drew forth
had the effect on Whitgift of routing his Puritan scruples for
ever.   When Thomas Cartwright, as Lady Margaret's Professor
of Divinity, "ventured in some of his lectures to show the
defects of the discipline of the Church," Whitgift was his foremost assailant.   Mainly at his instance, Cartwright was
"refused the degree of D.D., suspended from lecturing, and
finally—having appeared, December 11, 1570, before Whitgift
(now vice-chancellor) and other heads—he was, as he would
make no concession, deprived of his professorship and inhibited
from preaching within the jurisdiction of the University."
Whitgift went further.   On the alleged ground that at the
time of his election to a fellowship of Trinity Cartwright was
only a deacon, although the statutes required him to swear that
he was "in priest's orders," Whitgift accused him of "flat
perjury" and got him expelled from the college in September,
1572.   In the same year appeared the two famous admonitions
to Parliament; the first written probably by John Field and
Thomas Willcocks, the second certainly by Cartwright.   This
Puritan manifesto became so popular, and was held to be so
injurious to the Church, that an answer seemed necessary.
Whitgift was chosen to make it.   He had it ready before
January, 1573.   Cartwright immediately produced a "Reply."
Whitgift met the "Reply" by a "Defence of his Answer" in
1574.   To this Cartwright rejoined in his "Second Reply" in
1575, with a sequel in 1577.   Of these Whitgift took no notice—
because he was silenced, said his opponents.   Cartwright was
a Puritan idol; and Whitgift's prominence as his persecutor,

and then as champion of the Church, drew upon him intense hatred. The effect was to exasperate a naturally "choleric" temper. He took it for his mission in life to suppress the Puritans. His means were comparatively limited until he rose to the highest office of the Church. Then he had a free hand. The "three articles" of 1583; a revived and extended High Commission; the "twenty-four articles" of 1584, made up a terrible instrument of attack. Having constructed it carefully, he employed it relentlessly. Suspensions, ejectments, fines, imprisonments were the order of the day. So far as these went, Puritans of every shade were sufferers. The extreme penalty, marking the extreme outcome of the Archbishop's policy, was reserved for the "Separatists."

He could not fail to arouse fierce enmity. By the more violent of the Puritans he came to be styled "Beelzebub of Canterbury, the chief of the devils," an "ambitious wretch," "sitting upon his cogging stool, which may truly be called the chair of pestilence." To Barrow, as we have seen, he was "a monster, a miserable compound . . . the second Beast that is spoken of in the Revelation." Many others less coarse in their language were not less severe in their judgment. He still stands beside Laud as an incarnation of ecclesiastical narrowness and vindictiveness. But he was not this entirely. He was more and better than he seemed to the Puritan, as the Puritan was more and better than he seemed to Whitgift. In such cases men seldom seek, or care to see, the good points in each other. It is certain, however, that Whitgift had his good points. He was widely esteemed at Cambridge. His departure, we are told, drew forth an extraordinary display of "goodwill and regard." For not only had his career, particularly his mastership of Trinity, been conspicuously successful, but "even among the Puritan party, severely as he had dealt with Cartwright, there were not a few whom Whitgift had won over, by his *conciliatory demeanour* and *persuasion*, to more moderate views." [1]   Again, Sir Henry Wotton, who "knew him well in his youth, and had studied him in his age," cannot have been altogether mistaken when he gave him this character—"That he was a man of reverend and sacred memory, and of the primitive temper; a man of such a temper, as when by lowliness of spirit did flourish in highest examples of virtue." Hooker, too, the "judicious," though a friend of Whitgift, was never a flatterer; and must have had some warrant for speaking of his "accustomed clemency," and for the statement that "the errors which we seek to reform in this kind of men (i.e., the Puritans) are such as both received at your hands their first wound, and from that time to this present have been proceeded in with that *moderation* which useth by patience to suppress boldness, and to make *them* conquer that suffer." [2]

In fine, Whitgift turned his worst side to the Puritans—a consequence of the fact that they so often turned their worst side to him; and also of the fact that his ecclesiastical views, held with a tenacity equal to their own, appeared so immeasurably more reasonable and safe.

We cannot, then, expect to be in a position to do him justice unless we try to understand what his views were. There is the more call to do this as his views were not a merely private interpretation of the Episcopal case, but expressive of the general mind, and in close agreement with those of Hooker. Perhaps the best way will be to let him state them briefly in his own words. The main points are the following :—

The Church.

(1) There are "only two essential notes of the Church." These are, "the true preaching of the Word of God, and the right administration of the sacraments." [3]

Its Government.

(2) There is "no one certain and perfect kind of govern-

---

[1] Mullinger's Cambridge, p. 274.
[2] Dedication of Book V. of the Ecclesiastical Polity. Whitgift's

"Posy or Motto," was *vincit qui patitur.*
[3] Works, Vol. I., p. 185 (Parker Society's edition).

ment prescribed and commanded in the Scriptures to the Church of Christ."[1] "It is true that nothing in ceremonies, order, discipline, or government in the Church is to be suffered, being against the Word of God.[2] . . . But that no ceremony, order, discipline, or kind of government may be in the Church, except the same be expressed in the Word of God, is a great absurdity, and breedeth many inconveniences."[3] For example, "The Scripture hath not prescribed any place or time wherein, or when, the Lord's Supper should be celebrated, neither yet in what manner. The Scripture hath not appointed what time or where the congregation shall meet for common prayer, and for the hearing of the Word of God, neither yet any discipline for the correcting of such as shall contemn the same. The Scripture hath not appointed what day in the week should be most meet for the Sabbath-day, whether Saturday, which is the Jews' Sabbath, or the day now observed, which was appointed by the Church. The Scripture hath not determined what form is to be used in matrimony, what words, what prayers, what exhortations. The Scripture speaketh not one word of standing, sitting, or kneeling at the communion ; of meeting in churches, fields, or houses to hear the Word of God ; of preaching in pulpits, chairs, or otherwise ; of baptizing in fonts, in basons, or rivers, openly or privately, at home, or in the church, every day in the week, or on the Sabbath-day only. And yet no man (as I suppose) is so simple to think that the Church hath no authority to take order in these matters."[4] Similarly there is no unchangeable rule as to officers of the church and their appointment. Here also considerations of "time, place, person, and other circumstances" must decide. When Paul said to Timothy, "Lay thy hands rashly on no man," the apostle approves the "ordering and electing of ministers" by a bishop. But not by a bishop only. "For sometime one alone did choose and ordain, sometimes many, sometimes ministers only, and sometime the people also." It

[1] Page 184.   [2] Page 180.   [3] Page 190.   [4] Pages 200-1.

is a question of expediency. "The election of the minister by the Church is fittest for the time of persecution . . . when there was no Christian magistrate." But another mode may be meet "for the time of prosperity and under a Christian magistrate."[1] The one general rule by which the Church is to guide itself is that of Paul—"Let all things be done decently and in order."[2]

The Church of England.

(3) In this respect the Church of England is for England the best possible. For "the state of this Church of England at this day, God be thanked, is not heathenish, Turkish, or Papistical, in which condition many things might be done that otherwise are not to be attempted; but it is the state of a Church reformed, and by authority and consent settled, not only in truth of doctrine, but also in order of things external, touching the government of the Church and administration of the sacraments. Wherefore the controversy is not, whether many of the things mentioned by the Platformers were fitly used in the apostles' time, or may now be well used in some places, yea, or be conveniently used in sundry reformed churches at this day; for none of these branches are denied, neither do we take upon us (as we are slandered) either to blame or to condemn other churches, for such orders as they have received most fit for their estates; but this is the whole state of our controversy, when we of this Church, in these perilous days, do see that we have a great number of hollow hearts within this realm that daily gape for alteration of religion, and many mighty and great enemies abroad, busily devising and working to bring the same to pass, and to overthrow the state both of religion and of the realm—whether seeing we have a settled order in doctrine and government received and confirmed by law, it may stand with godly and Christian wisdom, with disobedience to the Prince and law, and with the unquietness of the Church and offence of many consciences to attempt so great alteration as this platform must

[1] Pages 425-429.   [2] Page 212.

needs bring, and that for matters external only, and with such eagerness and bitterness, that they deface and discredit the whole state of this Church, with all the preachers and ecclesiastical governors of the same, as remaining in horrible corruptions and antichristian deformities, and thereby fill the mouths of the adversaries with greater matter of obloquy to deface the Gospel than ever of themselves they had been able to devise."[1]

(4) The keystone of the fabric is the Prince. "The continual practice of Christian Churches (in the time of Christian magistrates), before the usurpation of the Bishop of Rome, hath been to give to Christian princes supreme authority in making ecclesiastical orders and laws, yea, and that which is more, in deciding of matters of religion, even in the chief and principal points."[2] Christ, indeed, is the only Head of the Church, if by the Head you understand "that which giveth the body life, sense, and motion ; for Christ only by His Spirit doth give life and nutrition to His body; He only doth pour spiritual blessings into it and doth inwardly direct and govern it. Likewise He is only the Head of the whole Church, for that title cannot agree to any other. But if by the head you understand an " external ruler and governor of any particular nation or church (in which signification head is usually taken) then I do not perceive why the magistrate may not as well be called the head of the Church, i.e., the chief governor of it in the external policy, as he is called the head of the people and of the commonwealth." [3]

Position of the Prince.

(5) The unique position and powers of the Prince are due to the fact that Church and commonwealth are virtually identical. " For I perceive no such distinction of the commonwealth and the Church that they should be counted, as it were, two several bodies, governed with divers laws and divers magistrates, except the Church be linked with an heathenish and idolatrous commonwealth. The civil magistrate may not take

Church and Commonwealth are Identical.

---

[1] Vol. I., pp. 4, 5.　　[2] Works, III., p. 306.　　[3] Vol. II., p. 85.

upon him such ecclesiastical functions as are only proper to the
minister of the Church, as preaching of the Word, administering of the sacraments, excommunicating, and such like; but
that he hath no authority in the Church to make and execute
laws for the Church, and in things pertaining to the Church,
as discipline, ceremonies, &c. (so that he do nothing against
the Word of God), though the papists affirm it never so stoutly,
yet is the contrary most true."[1]   Again, "your distinction," he
says to Cartwright, "betwixt the Church and the commonwealth, if it were in Nero's or Diocletian's time, might be
admitted without exception; but in my opinion it is not so fit
in this time, and especially in this kingdom."   Nay, "it cannot yet sink into my head that he should be a member of a
Christian commonwealth that is not also a member of the
Church of Christ, concerning the outward society."[2]   Whitgift
was thus a pure Erastian, and this fact explains several things.

Rule of the   Thus, first, the character of the (visible) Church and its re-
People.   lation to the Sovereign yields the strongest reason against a rule
of the people.   For the Church now includes men who are
drunkards, superstitious, or infected with errors in doctrine,
&c., and, therefore, is unfit to govern itself, especially in "the
election of ministers."[3]   Moreover, "if such elections should be
committed to the people the civil magistrate (who hath the
chief government of the Church, and to whom the especial care
of religion doth appertain) should not be able to procure such
reformation, nor such consent and agreement in matters of
religion as he is when he hath himself the placing of bishops
and such as be the chief of the clergy; for the people . . .
would usually elect such as would feed their humours, so that
the Prince neither should have quiet government, neither could
be able to preserve the Church, nor yet to plant that religion
that he in conscience is persuaded to be sincere."[4]   In short,
the Prince only has the right to ordain laws for the Church.   No
doubt "he may if he will depart from his right and abridge

[1] Vol. I., p. 22.   [2] Vol. I., p. 388.   [3] Vol. I., p. 384.   [4] Vol. I., p. 466.

himself of the authority committed unto him by God." In some realms he does so. "But he need not so do except he list . . . and this I am well assured of, that in a monarchy and in a kingdom such as this realm of England is, it cannot be practised" (not even to the extent of letting elders rule in the Church) "without intolerable contention and extreme confusion."[1]

Secondly, it was in consequence of this doctrine that Whitgift regarded himself as acting quite legally when the things he did were done with the authority or consent of the Queen. As in things civil the Queen was above Parliament, "because the judgment, confirmation, and determination" of all laws rested in her, so in things spiritual. It was enough for him if he had, or could win, her acquiescence in his proceedings. Thus: "In the month of September (1583) divers good articles were drawn up and agreed upon by himself and the rest of the bishops of his province, and signed by them. Which the Queen also allowed of, and gave her Royal assent unto, to give them the greater authority." Consent of Parliament did not seem at all necessary—although these "good articles" exposed every nonconforming Puritan preacher to deposition. So with the famous (or infamous) twenty-four articles which Burghley found "so curiously penned, so full of branches and circumstances, as I think the inquisitors of Spain use not so many questions to comprehend and to trap their preys." It is a mistake to suppose that the Archbishop was to any extent conscious of acting illegally. The articles were agreed upon in the Court of High Commission,[2] and accordingly lacked nothing to make them good law. The Queen was the fount of law. Attempts on the part of Parliament to regulate the Church (his secret thought may have been—even to regulate the State) were an impertinence.

Law—the Queen.

---

[1] Vol. III., p. 165.

[2] Coram . . . delegatis Regiæ Majestatis ad causas ecclesiasticas per literas Patentis magno Sigillo Angliæ rite et legitime fultis.

Thirdly, dissent from the "Establishment" involved not merely heresy and schism, but treason.

"If you will have the Queen of England rule as monarch over all her dominions, then must you also give her leave to use one kind and form of government in all and every part of the same, and so to govern the Church in ecclesiastical affairs as she doth the commonwealth in civil." But the effect of Nonconformity is "to divide one realm into two, and to spoil the Prince of the one half of her jurisdiction and authority." It can, therefore, as little be tolerated as a felony. It is a crime of the same nature. And if the civil judge is bound in the Queen's name to punish the one, so must a bishop the other. To bear this in mind is very necessary. It was the prevalent view. Whitgift spoke truth when he said, "There is no reformed church that I can hear tell of but it hath a certain prescript and determinate order, as well touching ceremonies and discipline as doctrine, to the which all those are constrained to give their consent that will live under the protection of it; and why then may not this Church of England have so in like manner? Is it meet that every man should have his own fancy, or live as him list?" Scarcely any one would have been found to say "yes," least of all the Puritans. The idea of a Church-State was universal—outside the small circle of Separatists, and carried with it as a self-evident corollary the idea that the Church like the State must be uniform; that its laws must be uniformly enforced; and that the State is the authority which must enforce them. Where Whitgift differed from men like Cartwright was not in regarding heresy and schism as a form of treason, but in identifying the State with the Queen, and the law of the Church (practically) with her declared will.

(6) A circumstance not so commonly and clearly recognised as it needs to be if Whitgift's increasingly severe treatment, first of the Puritans and then of the Separatists, is to be understood, is this—his horror of Anabaptism and his con-

viction that their novel proposals and unruly behaviour were hurrying Church and commonwealth into calamities similar to those for which he held Anabaptism accountable on the Continent. This is put in the forefront of his " Answer . . . to Thomas Cartwright," and he was haunted by it all his life. He prints " certain notes and properties of Anabaptists and other perturbers of the Church collected out of Zuinglius and others,"[1] in order that he may lay them before " such as be in authority, and have the government of the Church committed unto them," with an " exhortation " to beware.

" Considering the strangeness of the time, the variety of men's minds, and the marvellous inclinations in the common sort of persons (especially where the Gospel is most preached) to embrace new-invented doctrines and opinions, though they tend to the disturbing of the quiet state of the Church, the discrediting and defacing of such as be in authority, and the maintaining of licentiousness and lewd liberty; I thought it good to set before your eyes the practices of the Anabaptists, their conditions and qualities, the kind and manner of their beginnings and proceedings, before the broaching of their manifold and horrible heresies, to the intent, that you, understanding the same, may the rather in time take heed to such as proceed in like manner, lest they, being suffered too long, burst out to work the same effect."[2]

Cartwright bitterly resented the imputation. " It is more than I thought could have happened unto you, once to admit into your mind this opinion of Anabaptism of your brethren, which have always had it in as great detestation as yourself, preached against it as much as yourself, hated of the followers and favourers of it as much as yourself."

But Whitgift held his ground. He would not accuse anyone. He was looking to principles and tendencies. Those which he saw in the " admonition " to Parliament, those which he saw also in the writings of Cartwright and his sympathisers,

---

[1] Vol. I., pp. 125-139.   [2] Whitgift, Vol. I., p. 77.

were of just such a sort as would lead, unless instantly checked, to all Anabaptist excesses. Cartwright might protest as he liked; the event would show. And, doubtless, when the stir arose first about Browne, and then about Barrow, Whitgift felt that he had been a true prophet. Whitgift's logic or instinct was sound. The principles of Anabaptism were revolutionary. They could not but work against the existing state of things in the Church, though the first intention was to let them work in a peaceful way. There was, too, a much closer kinship between them and English Nonconformity, especially in its developed form of Separatism, than the latter dared to confess even to itself. It could not possibly go on growing without detriment to what in Whitgift's eyes was a Divinely constituted order. This was to become manifest to the world ere many years were past. His intolerance, then, was directed by a true insight. Believing as he did, the spirit embodied in Cartwright and Barrow was indeed a spirit of evil which, at any cost, must be cast out. We may deplore the fact that one with an ecclesiastical creed so essentially wrong should have had so much power, but we cannot deny him the credit of sincerity and consistency.

(7) Our quotations have been taken from the work he wrote while still master of Trinity College—ten years before his elevation to the archbishopric. They enable us to see that he had already, in 1578, matured the views on which, after 1583, he so resolutely acted.

He knew his own mind. He had a policy of which he was sure. "Convenient discipline, joined with doctrine, being duly executed, will soon remedy all." He longed to see it enforced by those in authority. He would fain be in authority himself, because he was conscious of a will to enforce it which could not be shaken.

Such is our impression of the man as derived from his own words. He is not amiable. But is he simply a narrow-minded, mean, and tyrannical priest, who gained power by servility and adulation? I think not. I think justice, no less than charity, may incline us to believe what he says in self-defence. "I neither esteem the honour of the place (which is to me gravissimum onus) nor the largeness of the revenues (for the which I am not as yet one penny the richer) nor any other worldly thing, I thank God, in the respect of doing my duty." [1] "I have taken upon me the defence of the religion and rites of this Church, the execution of the laws concerning the same, the appeasing of the sects and schisms therein, the reducing of the ministers thereof to uniformity and due obedience. Herein I intend to be constant; which also my place, my person, my duty, the laws, her Majesty, and the goodness of the cause, requireth of me . . . vincit qui patitur. And, if my friends herein forsake me, I trust God will not, nor her Majesty, who have laid the charge on me, and are able to protect me; upon whom only I will depend." [2]

He did cruel wrong to our ecclesiastical forefathers, and it is hard to think of him without indignation. But he is to be respected for that which may redeem from moral blame-worthiness even one who does the most injurious things. He was sincere. He thought "he was offering service unto God."

[1] To Burghley, July 3, 1584 (Whit-gift's Works, Vol. III., pp. 602-7).

[2] To Burghley, July 15, 1584 (Whit-gift's Works, Vol. III., pp. 607-9).

BARROW AND THE ANABAPTISTS.

BARROW AND THE ANABAPTISTS.

WE have seen that Barrow cherished all the prevalent feelings of horror with which, in his day, the Anabaptists were regarded. Nothing worse was conceivable than to be an Anabaptist. He was a being, not to reason with, but to revile and repudiate. The charge, or even hint, of agreeing and sympathising with him in any point was a bit of the vilest mud one could fling at an opponent, and evoked on his part a feverish anxiety to clear himself. We have seen this anxiety in the case of Barrow during one of his examinations when the question of baptism was mooted. He felt it always.

Nor was the feeling unnatural. The facts about Anabaptism, so far as known, were of a character to alarm and offend; and they were made to appear at their worst through being reported by enemies. Perhaps the general impression, even yet, is that Anabaptism was a simply monstrous phenomenon; a blood-red spectre which swept across Germany, inspiring riot and rebellion. If we consult an authority like Herzog, for example, we read that "Anabaptists" is the name of a violent, mystical sect which, representing the deepest-going radicalism, broke away from the general reformatory movement of the sixteenth century, and soon became lost in fanaticism and excess. . . . Starting with "the rejection of infant baptism" . . . it became the watchword of "one of the wildest and fiercest sects ever bred within the pale of the Christian Church."

But we must distinguish. Thus, it is not correct to speak of the Peasants' War, as is generally done, which culminated in the Massacre of Frankenhausen (1525), as due to

Anabaptism. Rather, that war was the outcome of a general social revolt on the part of the "common man," though this revolt drew a " very decisive impetus " from a renewed popular acquaintance with the Bible. For[1] "here in what the reformers called God's Word " he "found the bearers of it at all times animating the courage of the down-trodden and the oppressed; and even God Himself was there revealed as suffering with man and bent on his deliverance. 'I have seen, I have surely seen the affliction of My people, and have heard their cry by reason of their task-masters, for I *know their sorrows.*' " Little else is needed to explain the enthusiasm, the intoxication of hope with which the peasants armed themselves to cast down the " mighty from their seats," and so prepare the way for a better time. Their leader, Thomas Münzer (1490–1525), was not an Anabaptist. He had some correspondence with the Anabaptists, and this fact may have occasioned the mistake which identifies them with his cause. He was not, however, one of them, nor did they approve of him, so far, at least, as his methods were concerned. " The Gospel must not be protected by the sword, as they understand he thinks and holds. *True* Christian believers are sheep for the slaughter, and must, in anguish and need and trouble, suffer persecution, and be baptized into death. Thus are they proved and arrive at eternal peace, not through the slaughter of their earthly, but through the destruction of their spiritual foes." Nor was he sound on the particular question of baptism. For they need to tell him that "baptism signifies that through faith, and by the blood of Christ our sins are washed away, that we should die to sin, and walk in newness of life and spirit." He needed to be told also that children can do without baptism, since they " know not the difference between good and evil," and "will be saved through the sufferings of Christ, the new Adam."

[1] All the quotations in what follows are from Mr. Richard Heath's " Rise of Anabaptism "; perhaps the only safe English authority on the subject

No doubt the "cause" of the common man was that of the Anabaptist too. He abhorred the evils of the time he longed and expected to behold the "reign of righteousness" established; but his spirit was predominantly religious, and the weapons of his warfare were not carnal.

Hence it follows that the true temper of Anabaptism is not to be judged by the state of things in the city of Münster (1534), which more than anything else have made the name odious. When the new movement organised itself in Zürich, its first centre, it took the form of an unworldly brotherhood. One thought alone was its animating motive,—to restore the spirit of apostolic days. "The New Testament knew nothing, the Brothers said, of interest and usury, tithes, livings, and prebends; but the Christians it spoke of considered their earthly goods as belonging to the whole body. Nor did they read of any among them assuming offices of authority in the world, or using the sword; their only weapon was suffering, their only means of reforming offenders brotherly admonition, and, as a final resort, excommunication." To this was added a denial of infant baptism, and a demand that the baptized should consist alone of those who could "exercise faith or understanding." Certainly such a movement had a revolutionary tendency. For "if the brothers were right, the Christendom then existing must cease to be." But, left to itself, it would have found its true level, and dropped its merely visionary elements amid the hard facts of experience. To leave the new movement alone, however, was not the way of the time. Zwingli, who himself so needed tolerance, took the lead in devising measures of resistance. Ere long "inhibitions, arrests, examinations, imprisonments, penalties"—and finally death, were in full swing. The Brothers were scattered, and, like the first Christians, kindled their light wherever they went. Switzerland and the Tyrol became strongholds for them. "On one side of the Bremin alone" (a river in the Tyrol) "fifty places are mentioned where, in the course of 1529, Baptists were known to be." At the same time persecution waxed hotter. "The burning piles everywhere darkened the sky. The gaols were filled with miserable prisoners, the country was full of forsaken houses, and hungry, weeping children, and there was not a ray of hope that the trouble would come to an end." Many found an asylum in Moravia, where for a time the ideal of a "common life" was successfully carried out. But persecution made an end here also. Said King Ferdinand, in an edict of 1535, "neither Lutherans nor Zwinglians, nor, in fact, any sect will suffer among them these heretics, it is, therefore, the will and intention of His Majesty not to suffer them any more in Moravia." Soon, therefore, the quiet community was broken up into bands of wanderers, not knowing whither to go. Their miseries may be imagined. In other parts of Germany the case of the Anabaptists was even worse. Thus, in Southern Germany "some two thousand or more Baptists are estimated to have been put to death in a few years. In some places the slaughter amounted to wholesale massacre. Up to the year 1531 there were killed in Ensisheim 600 Baptists; in Linz 73; in the Palatinate 350. It was much the same in the Netherlands. Here all persons suspected of Anabaptism, or of sympathy with it, were liable to forfeit their lives and goods. "Prophets, apostles, bishops, baptizers were —said the Emperor's decree—' to be burnt to death.'" Others, even if they renounced their evil opinions, and sincerely repented, were to suffer—the men with the sword, the women in a sunken pit, *i.e.*, they were to be buried alive. There were during 1535, executions for Anabaptism in twenty-three towns in Holland, "and little trouble was taken as to whether those who suffered were insurrectionists or not."

For by this time, 1535, the spirit of insurrection had become strong and widespread. Persecution had driven wild "a people outwardly calm, but of intense inward feeling." When the movement began its motto may be said to have been, the meek shall inherit the earth. If they renounced the ways of the world, if they gave themselves up to follow the Lamb whithersoever He might lead, if they were content to obey and suffer in all quietness and patience, the "Brothers" were sure that the kingdom would be theirs. One of the grievances against them was that they refused to bear arms, to pay the war-tax, or to acknowledge, except passively, any king other than King Jesus. In 1529, however, Melchior Hoffmann[1]— already famous as a preacher and leader of the people—threw in his lot with the Baptists; and with him a new leaven was introduced which began to work mightily. To him was due the strange notion—so often cited as the distinctive theological heresy of the Anabaptists—that Christ did not take His flesh from Mary, but that the Word itself without any human intervention became flesh. "The Saviour," he said, "passed through the Virgin Mary as sunshine through a pane of glass." He too, was responsible for that doctrine of the last things which so rapidly infected the movement, "and rendered it more and more visionary." It was Hoffmann, especially, who taught the Anabaptists to believe that a saint might justly wield the sword against his enemies, might serve and defend the kingdom of Christ by force. There were those who strongly opposed him. But the natural man in the Anabaptist made it sweet doctrine. The Melchiorites—the name given to Hoffmann's followers— became dominant, and all the excesses into which the Anabaptists plunged were the result.

The fall of Münster, however, had a sifting effect. Such utter failure of the fleshly arm to bring in the kingdom proclaimed God's judgment against the upholders of it, and recalled the Baptists to their earlier principles. In August, 1536, a great gathering took place near Buckholt, in Westphalia, to consider their position. The violent party had its representatives, but found little support—"the power of the unruly Anabaptists was completely destroyed." On the other hand, the great idea of the entire distinction

[1] He died in prison, 1542, and was in favour with Luther for a time.

between the province of the Church and that of the State
came clearly to light, and was enthusiastically welcomed.
The man who gave it prominence and brought it home with
convincing power, Menno Simons, rose henceforth to a place of
commanding influence.[1] Nevermore had the doctrine of force a
chance among the Anabaptists. They settled down into communities, often called Mennonites, of pure-living, spiritual-
minded Christians. But they could not escape from the past.
An evil name clung to them. It was still believed that they
were secret traitors as well as scandalous heretics. Wherever
the secular arm could reach them they were hurled to prison
and the flames. Alva made the furnace seven times hotter for
them than for any other sect in the Netherlands. Thousands
went to deaths of every imaginable cruelty. Their "martyrology"[2] is a more affecting monument of triumphant
patience and faith than even that of the Protestants whom
Foxe has extolled. There was no eye to pity, no arm to save,
not even in England. Many fled for refuge to London and the
Eastern counties, wishing only to live and die in peace. But as
soon as their presence was known steps were taken to root
them out. On May 25, 1535, for example, nineteen men and six
women, born in Holland, were examined in St. Paul's Church,
London. Fourteen of them were condemned; a man and a
woman were burnt at Smithfield; the remaining twelve were
distributed among other towns, there to be burnt. Latimer,
for whom the same fate was in store, refers to this occurrence
simply to show how Anabaptists, like "another kind of
poisoned heretics that were called Donatists," "went to their
death intrepide," "cheerfully."[3]   Under 1538, "I read,"
says Fuller,[4] "that four Anabaptists (who for the main are

[1] Barclay's "Inner Life of the Religious Societies of the Commonwealth,
pp. 76, 77.
[2] A Martyrology of the Churches of
Christ commonly called Baptists (by
Van   Braght),   Hanserd   Knollys
Society's Publications, 2 vols.

[3] Froude's England, II., 257.
[4] Church History, lib. iv., 229. Nov.
6, 1539, has an "injunction" against
the Anabaptists. In the same year
sixteen men and fifteen women were
banished for Anabaptism. See Crosby's
History of the Baptists, I., 38-42.

but Donatists new dipt), three men and one woman, all Dutch, bare faggots at Paul's Cross, and three days after a man and a woman of their sect were burnt in Smithfield." Under Elizabeth, again—in May, 1575—" twenty-seven Anabaptists were arrested in Aldgate and brought to trial. . . . Four of them carried faggots at St. Paul's Cross, recanted, and were pardoned. Eleven who were obstinate were condemned in the Bishop of London's court and delivered over to the secular arm. One yielded, the rest were banished, except two. These were burnt on the 22nd of July, " in great horror, crying and roaring," although John Foxe had written to Elizabeth to remonstrate, and actually obtained a month's reprieve.

In the case of such Anabaptists as came before the English authorities there is this excuse for severity that, besides being supposed to favour the overthrow of all governments, they held what were deemed damnable theological errors. Thus the opinions of the persons examined in 1535 were :—

(1) That in Christ is not two natures—God and man.

(2) That Christ took neither flesh nor blood of the Virgin Mary.

(3) That children born of infidels may be saved.

(4) That baptism of children is of none effect.

(5) That the sacrament of Christ's body is but bread only.

(6) That he who after baptism sinneth wittingly, sinneth deadly, and cannot be saved.

The fifth opinion was, of course, a " heresy " common to all the more extreme Protestants. The second—and also the first which is its corollary—prove that the Refugees agreed so far with Melchior Hoffmann. The third resulted from the Anabaptist belief that children could not be punished for Adam's sin, and were embraced within the saving grace of Christ's atonement. The fourth was what attached to the Baptists their distinctive name. The last was a perversion of

their view, based on 1 John iii. 9, that the new birth issues
necessarily in " a new life and a walking in true repentance,
and are the Christian virtues, according to the example of our
Lord."   All this was unspeakably dreadful to the orthodoxy of
the time.   Indeed, every element of their teaching was dreadful
to someone.   Nevertheless, the spirit of the Anabaptists was
profoundly Christian, and the most essential elements of their
teaching reveal a depth of insight far greater than that
attained by many of the Reformers, not excluding Luther.
Let me mention two :—

(1) Their doctrine of the Word.   One of the men whose
influence penetrated far and wide among them was Hans
Denck,[1] "a remarkable young man " of "gentle, unassuming
character."   His brief life soon came to a violent end, after
years of continual flight from city to city.   He was a mystic in
the strain of his thought.   For " the human conscience," said
he, " contains a spark of the Divine nature, so that God Himself
may be said to be present in every man."   To the urgings of this
inner Word, Denck affirmed, a man could be obedient; and that
such an act of obedience was an act of faith.   For to Denck this
Inner Voice, prompting to righteousness, was no other than
the Word of God, which in Christ became man, and which will
to all eternity, as the spirit of love, work in man.   Thus to him
Christ had always lived in man, and ever will live in man, not
merely figuratively, but in reality."   As to Holy Scripture, it contains the " written Word of God," it is the " standard of faith ;
but the ground of faith must lie in the truths taught by experience."   Faith thus arising found in Holy Scripture an educa-
tive and formative influence of the highest value.   But " Holy
Scripture was not to be understood except by the help of the
Holy Spirit, and faithful obedience to the commands of Christ."
This doctrine, involving a conception of human nature so
alien from the ordinary, yet so accordant with the thought of
John and Paul, became general among the Anabaptists.   It is

[1] Died of the plague at Basle, 1527.

asserted strongly by Menno Simons, and reappears in the " Inner Light " of George Foxe. Barrow, as we have seen, considered the doctrine dangerous, and so it was if it meant what he fancied—an opposing " of the inward spirit against the revealed Word of God." In some cases, no doubt, it did come to mean this. Every doctrine is open to abuse. But as understood by Denck and Menno Simons it expressed a truth with which Barrow himself agreed. The difference between them lay rather in the fact that he grasped it less clearly, and was less consistently true to it than they.

(2) Their doctrine of spiritual freedom flowed directly from their doctrine of the Word within. Men who had received an unction from the Holy One, and might come to know all things pertaining to life and godliness if they but followed faithfully His interpretation of the written Word, felt it to be a sacrilege to admit interference on the part of the secular power in matters of conscience. Hence it was that the Baptists arrived at a clearer and broader idea of toleration than any of their contemporaries. Let the State keep to its own sphere. Its sphere was the relations of men in civil society. Its function was to order these relations with a view to safety and quietness of life. Christians, therefore, were to obey all laws of the State so far as such laws did not contravene what they knew to be the laws of Christ. But the relations of the soul to God were outside its province. Here every man must stand alone; must realise his own responsibility; must bear his own burden. Here the only Master is Christ. Those who heard and obeyed His voice—His true sheep—might, and indeed were under obligation to, proclaim the fact by submitting to the seal of Baptism, and by forming themselves into visible communities. Thus they became known to one another as brethren, and as brethren it became their duty and privilege to edify and admonish one another. But, even so, the unity was spiritual and free. There should be no compulsion—not so much as that which lay in the imposition

14

of a common creed. "The agreement of their membership," says Barclay,[1] with reference to the Waterlander Mennonites, "did not rest upon a purely doctrinal basis in the shape of any creed, but on the general sense of the Church or Churches of the plain meaning of the New Testament Scripture. The Mennonite confessions of faith were, as in the case of the early Baptist churches in this country, generally used for the purpose of avoiding misapprehension, and to prevent the ignorant abuse with which they were loaded from misleading the public.[2] So far it may be said that Barrow and the Baptists occupied much the same ground, for there is no reason to think that he or his followers regarded a creed as anything more than a free and spontaneous declaration of faith. But a firmer hold on the spiritual principle which necessitates freedom made the Baptist quicker to see that freedom and the prescriptive claim of the State to rule the Church in any manner or degree, could not hold together.

Barrow esteemed it a proof of their ignorance and barbarism to deny that it belongs to "the office and dutie of the Prince to see abuses reformed as well in the Church as in the commonwealth." In this point, at least, he had everybody with him. The Baptist stood alone. It has been said that Barrow's forerunner in the Separatist campaign, Robert Browne, went as far as the Baptist. But he did not. To say that Browne denied the right of the Prince to step inside the Church and reform or direct it is quite to misapprehend his position.

Thus his "treatise of Reformation without tarrying for any, and of the wickedness of those which will not reform till the magistrate command or compel them," suggests by its very title what Browne really taught, viz., that the magistrate ought to see that the Church is well "builded" and reformed; that if the magistrate fails to do his duty in this respect the Church need not "tarry for him, but ought to reform itself according to the will of its Master, Christ; moreover, that the magistrate

[1] Inner Life of the Religious Societies of the Commonwealth, p. 83.   [2] Page 83.

may only enforce Christ's will on the Church, never his own; and that the Church is required to obey at all times and at all risks, the former in preference to the latter." Certainly a limit is here put to the magistrate's authority, and one which implied a claim to act without it in some cases, or against it in others. But the right of interference is not denied—the complaint rather is that its exercise may be wrongly applied or too long delayed. Far more radical was the position of the Anabaptist. He shut the Prince out of the holy place of conscience altogether. His right to enter, if he entered at all, was neither greater nor less than that of a private person. As a Christian brother, if he had previously joined himself to a Christian brotherhood, he might share in its discipline. But otherwise he might not do even that. For "the magistrate is not by virtue of his office to meddle with religion or matters of conscience, to force and compel men to this or that form of religion or doctrine; but to leave Christian religion free to every man's conscience, and to handle only civil transgressions (Rom. xiii.), injuries and wrongs of man, in murder, adultery, theft, &c., for Christ only is the King and Lawgiver of the Church and conscience (James iv. 12)." These are John Smyth's words, and were written after 1600. But John Smyth drew his inspiration from the Mennonites, and did no more than express their view—a view which finds as clear utterance in the earliest Baptists as in the latest. In fine, the true spirit of Anabaptism was one of tender regard for the conscience as the dwelling-place of God. . . . "Without in the least derogating from the honour due to the noble army of martyrs who, in all lands and ages, and of all creeds and religions, have practically died for this holy cause, we may claim a leading and definite place for the Anabaptists, since it was they who first of all Christian people claimed liberty of conscience as a Divine right which no power on earth may deny. And when we think that from liberty of conscience naturally flowed liberty of thought and liberty of worship, free speech and a free Press, we may form some faint idea of the debt of gratitude mankind owes the Anabaptists."

Perhaps, however, their distinction lies not so much in a clear recognition of the principle as in the wish to see it broadly and practically applied.

It is a fact that Luther, for example, at one time asserted the principle in words which leave scarcely anything to be desired on the score of comprehensiveness.

"It is," said he, "at a man's own risk what he believes, and he must see for himself that he believes rightly. Belief is a free work; thereto can no man be compelled. . . . Thoughts are toll-free. . . . Heresy can never be kept off by force. Heresy is a spiritual thing, which no iron can hew down, no fire burn, no water drown." [1]

Such expressions "cover almost the whole theoretical ground of religious liberty," and seem to promise tolerance for all opinions avowed in the name of conscience. Nor was Luther by any means the most intolerant of the Reformers. He had no desire to put any man to death for heresy; and in this showed himself superior to Zwingli or Melanchthon. He did not think it right—yea, he thought it a great pity that "such wretched people (as the Anabaptists) should be so miserably slain, burned, cruelly put to death." "Every one should be allowed to believe what he will." But questions arose in his mind—largely suggested by the views and doings of these same Anabaptists— which made him pause, doubtful and afraid. He fell, along with the Reformers generally, "into the trap which lies in wait for all earnestly believing men, in the distinction set up between heresy and blasphemy. Is there not a point at which the expression of unbelief becomes an insult to the majesty of God, and so an offence against the laws of man? . . . Then, again, granting that difference of belief is to be tolerated, to what lengths ought toleration to go? Does it

[1] Beard's Hibbert Lecture, pp. 171-2.

include full right of citizenship, with liberty to preach and print? Or are heretics to be allowed to live side by side with orthodox believers only on condition that they hold their tongues? Is it, in any case, right to co-operate with them for political or religious purposes?"[1] Luther's answer to such questions led to limitations of his principle, which made it practically of little effect. Religious communion must be refused to Zwingli because his conception of the Eucharist was akin to blasphemy as well as heresy. Toler- ance must be denied to any who avowed dissent from the "con- fession of faith" adopted by the political State to which he belonged, because such dissent was incipient political treason. The opinions of Anabaptists must be rigorously put down, because the free expression of them would prompt to action subversive of the grounds of all existing institutions. Timidity of this kind was natural enough under the circumstances. Nothing is rarer than a courage thoroughly inspired by the conviction that what is true is safe. Most of us think so in the abstract, but are continually coming across reasons which induce us to think otherwise in the concrete. In this par- ticular case, indeed, it is the foresight or experience of consequences which has again and again raised the doubt whether what claims to be a true principle is really true; is not rather a pestilent error. How can that be a true principle which would forbid you to restrain even the man who, in the name of conscience, might break, or advocate the breach of, every commandment of the decalogue? And of course the objection is sound *if conscience is to mean the mere persuasion of being right, however it may have originated.* Then certainly excesses born of whim, prejudice, passion, but pleading the sanction of conscience, will often need to be checked, and checked forcibly—at least when they reach the point of action—if social order is not to relapse into social chaos. But conscience is not whim, prejudice, passion; it is

[1] Beard's Hibbert Lecture, p. 173.

the power latent in man's spiritual nature of discerning the genuine character of right and wrong. This is true, and may be accepted even by those who differ among themselves as to how man's nature has become possessed of such a power. And, since right and wrong—or moral truth—is that which underlies our whole life as social beings; is that which yields to all human relations their stability; is that which determines all the real duties growing out of them; is that which secures all human progress—it is plain that loyalty to conscience can never conflict with any really human interest. One might as well say that the power to calculate numbers, motions, and distances can conflict with the interests of astronomy. What, however, one may say is that conscience, like other human powers, attains its full development gradually; that its insight cannot be perfect all at once; that its judgments, therefore, may sometimes be wrong, or only partially right; that it needs discipline; that the surest means of discipline are furnished by experience; that on this account it ought to be free even to make mistakes, as the very condition of learning how to correct them. History confirms this view. The upward march has taken place most surely, not in the case of those people that have had right and wrong dictated to them by some extraneous authority, but in the case of those that have believed in conscience, have asserted for themselves the right to interpret its voice; have gone far wrong sometimes in the desire to go right; have wrestled their own slow and painful way out of the evils into which moral error has led them. It is thus that they have become taught of God, and have learnt to perceive what is the good and acceptable and perfect will of God. There is no other way. Men must be free to err if they are ever to reach an intelligent and widening grasp of the truth. And the deepest motive for claiming and granting such freedom is the old Anabaptist faith that conscience is the organ of an inner light which comes from God, which is ever battling with the darkness of man's sin and ignorance, which will triumph over both in the end.

How far the Anabaptists would have remained faithful to their own principle had they chanced to come to supreme power, it is hard to say. Quite possibly they, like so many more, might have become persecutors in their turn, and found good excuses for it. But fortunately they were not put to the test—they were always a " miserable minority "—and so the glory of their witness has come down undimmed: this, namely, that they were among the first to see, the boldest to preach, and the foremost to suffer for, the duty of a human soul to guide itself freely by the light of God.

On the whole, it may be said that Barrow was far nearer to the Anabaptists than he knew. Had he by any chance taken a place without knowing it in one of their ordinary assemblies, he would have felt very much at home. The plain walls of the meeting-house, the absence of a pulpit, the conduct of worship by "elders," the simple appeal to the authority of Scripture, the prominence given to "exposition," the "liberty of prophesying," the collection by deacons for the necessities of the poor, would all have been to his mind. And when cases of discipline came on at the close, perhaps, of the service, still there would be nothing to excite a suspicion that he was not among his own people.

He had said, as we know, that he did not, like the Anabaptists, expect an absolutely pure Church on earth, and that it was a libel on the part of Gifford and others to say he did. But he would have found that the Anabaptists were just as little or as much open to the charge as himself. They held the same idea of the Church; they took the same way to keep it pure. They did not, however, any more than he, conceive it possible to exclude all false brethren, nor were they specially severe in their judgment or treatment of those whose falseness was made clear.

Indeed, apart from a number of comparatively superficial

differences—due partly to circumstances and partly to a more scrupulous fidelity to their common principle of reverence for Scripture, there was nothing in the sphere of church-practice which need have held Barrow and the Baptists apart, except the doctrine of baptism. This certainly seemed to be a difference of vital import. And, so far as Barrow is concerned, we have already seen the reason why. No doubt he maintained infant baptism conscientiously, no doubt he maintained it on what he thought strong Scriptural grounds; but his real reason for maintaining it was the fact that he loathed the people whose name identified them with its denial. On the contrary, to the Baptist the difference was vital, because here, again, Scripture seemed to be with him, and reverence for Scripture was a primary duty. And one cannot help feeling that in this respect the Baptist had the best of the argument. Infant baptism may be, and, I think, is defensible as a thoroughly Christian ordinance; but not on the ground of strict adherence to the letter and precedent of the New Testament. Barrow virtually admitted as much by not attempting to occupy this ground, and by appealing to the extremely precarious analogies of the old covenant. In other words, Scripture taken literally, as he and the Baptist believed it ought to be taken, gave him little or no positive support, and had he been free from the fear which made it so difficult to see this, his logical bent would have led him into the Baptist camp. The Baptist—from the point of view, be it remembered, of unflinching literalism—was the Separatist fully developed.

But this refers only to his ecclesiastical position. As to theological difference the case is not the same. Here what meets us is diametrical opposition rather than development. Barrow was a Calvinist, and accepted all the implications of his creed with full consent. We turn to John Smyth, for example, whose creed came to him mainly from Menno, even as his had its roots for the most part in the teaching of men like Denck, and we find ourselves in another world. " God created man with freedom of will, so that he had ability to choose the good and eschew the evil, or to choose the evil and refuse the good; and this freedom of will was a natural faculty or power, created by God in the soul of man."

"Original sin is an idle term, and there is no such thing as men intend by the word, because God threatened death only to Adam, not to his posterity, and because God created the soul."

"Infants are conceived and born in innocency without sin, and so dying are undoubtedly saved; and this is to be understood of all infants under heaven, for where there is no law there is no transgression; sin is not imputed while there is no law, but the law was not given to infants, but to them that could understand."

"Adam being fallen, God did not hate him, but loved him still, and sought his good, neither doth he hate any man that falleth with Adam; but He loveth mankind, and from His love sent His only begotten Son into the world, to save that which was lost, and to seek the sheep that went astray."

"God never forsaketh the creature till there be no remedy, neither doth He cast away His innocent creature from all eternity; but casteth away men irrecoverable in sin."

"As no man begetteth his child to the gallows, nor no potter maketh a pot to break it; so God doth not create or predestinate any man to destruction."

"Although the sacrifice of Christ's body and blood offered up unto God His Father upon the Cross be a sacrifice of a sweet-smelling savour, and God in Him is well pleased, yet it doth not reconcile God unto us, which did never hate us, nor was our enemy, but reconcileth us unto God and slayeth the enmity and hatred which is in us against God."

"The efficacy of Christ's death is only derived to them which do mortify their sins, which are grafted with Him to the similitude of His death, which are circumcised with circumcision made without hands, by putting off the sinful body of the flesh, through the circumcision which Christ worketh who is the minister of the circumcision for the truth of God, to confirm the promises made to the fathers." At the time of their utterance there was no welcome for the warm evangelical spirit which breathes through these statements. On the contrary, remembering the detestation with which what came to be called Arminianism was regarded, we understand that the fact of the Anabaptist being an Arminian as well, and something worse, would render him doubly offensive. But the Anabaptist's theology was not an accident, or an arbitrary product. It was, I think, a result of his two first principles working in combination : his faith in the Inner Light and his reverence for the written Word. For, faith in the Inner Light, at least, in the case of the more deeply thoughtful and devout of its disciples, really meant *faith in the highest intuitions of the spiritual reason ;* and this, when brought to a study of the written Word, could not fail to operate selectively, fastening on what was agreeable to the most worthy conception of God and man, and tacitly ignoring all else. And thus the Anabaptist may be said to have anticipated long ago the method which theologians have come frankly to adopt as a guiding light in all their best constructive efforts.

PART II.

THE AMSTERDAM CHURCH.

THE EXILED CHURCH.

The " little flock " that made up the London Church is an object of pathetic interest to one who cares to trace its fortunes after the Spring of 1593. Its natural leaders—Barrow, Greenwood, and Penry—are dead. Some of its members are still at large; many are in prison. No more public executions take place—these are found to excite too much attention and sympathy; but the work of death goes on. Three years later, it is recorded that "twenty-four souls (including aged men and women) have perished in the prisons within the City of London only (besides other places of the land), and that of late years." [1] No wonder, when we read how the prisons are "most vile and noisome," how many of the prisoners lie there " laden with irons," and have been " detained many years." [2] No wonder, too, that the effect of such "inhumanity" has been to cause not a few " to blaspheme and forsake the faith of our glorious Lord Jesus Christ." [3] The year, however, which witnessed the death of Barrow, Greenwood, and Penry brought a change of policy. Those who stood firm were offered an alternative. Instead of death they might choose exile. On April 10, 1593, " heavy decrees," say the exiles, " came forth that we should foreswear our country and depart, or else be slain therein."

[1] Preface to the Confession of Faith of certain English people living in exile, &c., 1596. Norwich, Gloucester, Bury (St. Edmunds) are mentioned. Coppin and Thacker were executed at Bury. William Denys at Thetford in Norfolk. These (with Barrow, Greenwood, and Penry) exhaust what claims to be a complete list of those who " witnessed unto death "—according to Miles Micklebound in Barrow's " Platform."

[2] Ditto.

[3] Ditto.

Of course, the reference is to "an act to retain the Queen's subjects in obedience," which passed its second reading on April 4, and became law before Parliament was dissolved on the 12th. It purported to be a "Bill for explanation" of 23 Elizabeth 2, but was much more "captious;" and, on this account, met with warm resistance and some amendment in the Lower House. For, though it aimed directly at Brownists or Barrowists, there were those who feared that it might enmesh others as well, or even instead.[1]

Its main clauses were as follows:—"If any person above the age of sixteen years shall obstinately refuse" to go to some authorised church, or shall "by printing, writing, express words, &c., go about to persuade" anyone to deny Her Majesty's authority in ecclesiastical matters, and to abstain from coming to church, and to be present at unlawful assemblies, he, "being lawfully" "convicted," shall be committed to prison "without bail or mainprize." If he repent within three months, he shall "repair to some parish church on some Sunday or other festival day, and then and there hear Divine Service; and at service-time, before the sermon, or reading of the Gospel," shall read a prescribed form, solemnly confessing his grievous sin, and his resolve never again to offend. If, on the contrary, he still be found obstinate, he shall then "upon his corporal oath" abjure the realm and all the Queen's dominions "for ever." And if, having so sworn, he "shall not go to such haven and within such time as is appointed," or shall "return into any of Her Majesty's dominions without Her Majesty's special license," he shall "be adjudged a felon," and die a felon's death. Moreover, "all his goods and chattels" shall be "forfeit to Her Majesty for ever,"

[1] Cf the speech (on April 4th) of Mr. Finch:—The Bill "pretendeth a punishment only to the Brownists and Sectaries, but throughout the whole Bill there is not one thing that concerneth a Brownist, and if we make a law against Barrowists and Brownists let us set down a note of them who they are."—D'Ewe's Journals, p. 516. Note how "Barrowist" has become a familiar appellation.

and "all his lands" during his own life. Finally, to leave no loophole for escape or pity, a fine of £10 a month is threatened to any one who shall, after due notice, "relieve" the offender,[1] or shall "maintain, retain, or keep him" in his house or otherwise. This Act was "to continue no longer than to the end of the next Session of Parliament." But in reality, by successive renewals, it continued operative into the reign of Charles I.[2] Penry was hung on May 29, and doubtless it was with the thought of this Act in his mind that he wrote the last words of tender counsel to his brethren, which have been so often quoted: "Seeing banishment, with loss of goods, is likely to betide you all, prepare yourselves for this hard entreaty . . . and I beseech you . . . that none of you in this case look upon his particular estate, but regard the general estate of the Church of God; that the same may go and be kept together whithersoever it shall please God to send you. . . . Let not the poor and friendless be forced to stay behind here, and to break a good conscience for want of your support and kindness unto them. . . . And . . . I humbly beseech you . . . that you would take my poor and desolate widow, and my mess of fatherless and friendless orphans with you into exile withersoever you go . . . let them not continue after you in this land, where they must be forced to go again into Egypt; and my God will bless you with a joyful return into your own country for it." Further: "I would wish you earnestly to write, yea, to send, if you may, to comfort the brethren in the West and North countries, that they faint not in these troubles; and that also you may have of their advice, and they of yours, what to do in these desolate times. And if you think it anything for their further comfort and direction, send them, conveniently, a copy of this

---

[1] Except the person so relieved, &c., "be wife, father, mother, child, ward, brother, or sister, or wife's father or mother, or the husbands or wives of any of them—not having any certain place of habitation of their own."

[2] It was continued by 39 Eliz. 18; 43 Eliz. 9; 1 Jas. i. 25; 21 Jas. i. 28. Prothero's "Select Statutes," pp. 89-92. It was to come into force forty days after the end of the Session, i.e., after April 12th—after May 22nd.

my letter, and of the declaration of my faith and allegiance, wishing them, before whomsoever they be called, that their own mouths be not had in witness against them in anything. Yea, I would wish you and them to be together, if you may, whithersoever you shall be banished; and to this purpose, to bethink you beforehand where to be, yea, to send some one who may be meet to prepare you some resting-place."[1]   As occasion served, the advice was acted upon.   Some of the "distressed congregation left for Holland[2] in the summer or autumn of the year."   We hear of them at Campen, "a little Dutch town, situated on the Yssel, near its entrance into the Zuider Zee, and some fifty miles along the curve of the shore of that sea, a little north-east of Amsterdam; and at Naarden, a small village on the same shore, perhaps thirty-eight miles nearer that city." We are told that they were supported partly by a legacy of Barrow's,[3] partly by contributions from London and Middleburg,[4] partly by the gifts of a church of English merchants at Barbary,[5] and partly, of course, by their own labour, so far as possible.   There is reason to believe that once, at any rate, if not oftener, they were aided by the magistrates during their stay at Naarden; and similar aid may have been extended to them at Amsterdam.[6]   This was in the earlier years of exile, when they were "embarrassed by general obloquy,

[1] Quoted from volume (in Dr. Williams's Library) which contains also Penry's examination and declaration of faith, and the examinations of Barrow and Greenwood. Penry's letter is addressed to the distressed congregation in London . . . whether in bonds or at liberty; and its members (or the chief of them) are indicated by letters, except the pastor's. "My beloved brethren—Mr. F. Johnson, Mr. D. M. S., Mr. S., Mr. G. J., Mr. J., Mr. H., Mr. B., Mr. S. R. B., Mr. R., Mr. K. N. B., Mr. B. J., Mr. N. P., Mr. W. C., Mr. P. A.; My brethren—Mr. J. C., Mr. W. B., Mr. A. P., Mr. M. M., Mr. E. C., Mr. C. D., Mr. G. M., Mr. A. B. = 22.

[2] "After the introduction of the reformed religion into the Low Countries in 1573, the utmost religious freedom was allowed, all sects were tolerated, and an asylum was opened for fugitives from persecution from every land."

[3] Bradford's Dialogue, Young's Chronicles:—"When he saw he must die he gave a stock for the relief of the poor of the church, which was a good help to them in their banished condition afterwards," p. 434.

[4] Robert Harrison's church still survived.

[5] "The Recantation of a Brownist," by Peter Fairlambe (1606), implies the existence of "Brownists" in Barbary.

[6] Dexter.

almost consumed by deep poverty. . . ." It was a hard lot for all, but especially for such as had been gently brought up. "Some who had been students were content to card, and spin, or to learn trades, thereby to maintain themselves." George Johnson says of himself that "many weeks he had not above sixpence, or eightpence the week to live upon." And the story told of Ainsworth is familiar —how on "his first coming to Amsterdam he lived on nine-pence a week . . . with roots boiled."[1] Moreover, "the frowns and sharp invectives" which they had to endure in England surrounded them also in their place of exile. The ministers of Amsterdam, at least, were not friendly. As Bradford reports,[2] and Ainsworth shows,[3] "they did look awry at *them* when they would give help and countenance to" the mere Puritan.

But let us return to London. On April 5, the day before Barrow and Greenwood's execution, "the Dean of Westminster (*Dr. Goodman*) and others" spent some hours examining thirty-two Separatists.[4] Penry and F. Johnson were among them. Eight others were old prisoners retaken. Arthur Billot, "a scholar and a soldier," whose connection with the printing of Barrow's books is evidently known to his judges, was taken at the same time and place as Penry. Katherine Onyon is a prisoner for the first time, but is doubtless the widow Onyon, who is described (in 1588)[5] as "one of their chief conventiclers," and who ran away for fear of punishment because her child, then twelve years old, had not been baptized. Now alas! she gives way and "is willing to go to Church." John Clerke, too, is under examination for the first time, though he has been

---

[1] Bradford's Dialogue, p. 440.
[2] Dialogue, p. 440.
[3] See "Paget's Arrow Against the Separation of the Brownists," 1618.
[4] Harleian MSS., 7,042, f. 35. Goodman (Gabriel), 1529(?)–1601, had been Dean of Westminster since 1561, holding at the same time much other preferment. He was Burghley's chaplain and very intimate with him. He is often found on the Commission for Ecclesiastical Causes. Even Archbishop Parker thought him "too severe."
[5] Harleian MSS., 7,042, f. 16, "Certain wicked sects and opinions."

in prison three years.   The rest are new names—mostly young
men of the artisan or labouring class[1] who have been "taken"
at assemblies during the last six weeks.   Several of them
"submitted" outright or consented to have conference, and
were probably enlarged upon bond.   We are near the mark if
we say that of the thirty-two some twenty-four were found
obstinate and remitted to prison.   John Clerke is noted as
particularly stiff-necked, and "it was thought good that he
should be sent to Bridewell to grind the mill."   Perhaps at this
time sixty at the utmost were in the several London prisons.
Two years later the number was much less.   This is made clear
by a list[2] of "Prisoners for Religion" . . . which was
"sent up from the ecclesiastical commission."   It enumerates
eighty-nine altogether (inclusive of ten "enlarged upon bond"),
of whom three only are said to be "Brownists"—one in the
Clink (Johnson?), another in Newgate (Studley?), a third in the
Fleet (George Johnson?).   There may have been a few more;
for in the case of five prisons the class is not specified.   One
more, at any rate, there was—John Clerke, in Bridewell.   But
the great majority were Popish recusants.   In the course,
therefore, of these two years most of the Separatists had been
discharged; and, if the terms of the Act were enforced, they
had no choice but to go abroad, unless they had made promise
to conform.   In the meantime, doubtless, others came and
went, that is to say, were arrested, imprisoned for three
months, then compelled to forswear themselves or their native
land.   And in this way, as well as by the secret migration of
"uncaptured" brethren, the London church would gradually
transfer its main body to Amsterdam.   But it did not dissolve
away.   As late as 1624 it was holding together.   For in that
year John Robinson wrote[3] to it as "the Congregational

[1] The age of the majority is between twenty and thirty. One is a fishmonger, another a weaver, a third a pursemaker, five or six are shipwrights. There is a joiner, a coppersmith, a clothworker, a shoemaker or two, a feltmaker, two or three tailors, &c.
[2] Strype's Annals, Vol. IV., p. 808.
[3] Ashton's edition of his works, Vol. III., pp. 381-5.

Church in London," and answered (in the affirmative) one of its questions—viz., whether a neighbouring congregation which had recently been gathered at Southwark by Henry Jacob, "be a true church or no." Of its history in the meantime we have only hints. Slanderer Lawne's[1] statement that "the Brownists' company remaining in London have oft laid upon one another, one half devouring another at once," tells us that the London company did not enjoy unbroken peace. Lawne's own letter[2] to the same "company," retailing "divers slanders of the (Amsterdam) elders and brethren," tells us that he once hoped to further his ends in Amsterdam by enlisting support in London. Daniel Studley's letter[3] to one of the London brethren, which brought the recipient over to Amsterdam post haste in order to expose the writer before the whole congregation, reminds us that local severance was not supposed to touch the integral unity of the Church.

Its two sections, indeed, were still one body though land and water came between. Pastor, elders, and deacons were the same for both.[4] When Johnson, Studley, Kniveton, Bowman reached Amsterdam there was no thought of re-electing them to their several offices. They had been elected in September, 1592, once for all.[5] The only vacant office was that of teacher—by Greenwood's death; and this was the only vacancy needing to be filled. Both sides looked to Johnson and the elders for guidance. Cases of discipline, as far as practicable, were, by both sides, submitted to them for judgment, if not for decision. In the absence of the pastor neither side had the ordinances of baptism or the Lord's

---

[1] "Profane Schism," p. 63.
[2] "Profane Schism," p. 7.
[3] Richard Clyfton's "Advertisement," pp. 115-125.
[4] *Roger Waterer* (a long-sufferer in the "cause," whose name, as a prisoner, appears in 1590, 1592, 1593) was the "chosen and appointed" messenger between them.

[5] The church at Amsterdam for five or six years practised as the pastor, elders, and brethren in prison at London wrote unto them, and refused to choose officers on the spot.—"A Discourse of Some Troubles . . . at Amsterdam," by George Johnson (1603), p. 10.

Supper. Each was content simply to meet for exhortation and prayer. After Johnson and Studley had settled permanently at Amsterdam, it lay within the right of the London branch to organise itself independently of the other. But we do not find that it did. We hear nothing of a new pastor or new elders.[1] Probably its recognition, at least of Johnson as pastor,[2] lasted till his death ; and this, perhaps, may explain why afterwards it turned for counsel rather to Robinson than to Ainsworth. Significant of the same fact is what we notice in Robinson's letter that he mentions the " teacher "[3] of the Church, but is silent about pastor and elders. Our conclusion is that there were none. At the time (1624) the congregation was practically destitute even of a teacher, for he and some brethren had lately seceded. Without pastor, elders, and teacher it might seem not to be a church at all. It feared this itself. But Robinson says it is a church still, since the " visible and ministerial church is the whole body and every member thereof."[4] And a church it remained until, one by one, its members were drawn (most likely) into Mr. Jacob's congregation, and there had experience of the first real pastoral care[5] they had ever enjoyed.

We may now give our attention to the exiles. The pastor joined them at Amsterdam in September, 1597. He had been a prisoner for nearly five years.[6] He had been in great danger and his sufferings had been great.[7] For a time, at any rate, he was confined to " a noisome chamber " in the Clink. He was not granted any " liberty of the prison." His books and

---

[1] George Johnson (p. 44 of the above) says the pastor, &c., at Amsterdam " like not to hear that a church should be established at London, and discouraged the appointment of Mr. C—r as teacher there."

[2] So the " Pilgrim Church " recognised Robinson till his death.

[3] Works, Vol. III., p. 384.

[4] Works, Vol. III., p. 385.

[5] Jacob went to America in 1624, and was succeeded by John Lath-

rop, " a man of earnest but humble spirit."

[6] Since December 5, 1592.

[7] See his letter, &c., to Burghley, Strype's Annals," Vol. IV., pp. 187-194. F. Johnson (1562-1618), Fellow of Christ's College, Cambridge. 1588— imprisoned for an ultra-Puritan sermon in St. Mary's. 1589 (December)—pastor of a Puritan church at Middelburg. 1592—becomes Separatist.

writings were taken away. He expected to be arraigned under the Act 35 Eliz., and wrote to Burghley ably maintaining that this statute—much less 23 Eliz. 2—did not fairly touch his case. After this—January 8, 1593-4—we lose sight of him. He does not appear to have been brought up again for trial. But on April 4, 1597, he, his brother George[1] (whose imprisonment in the Fleet had been almost as long as his own), Daniel Studley (who had been sentenced to death with Barrow), and John Clerke (of whom we have heard) were handed over, by order of the Privy Council, to some merchant adventurers who were fitting out an expedition to Rainea.[2] Francis and Studley were together on the *Hopewell*; George and Clerke were put on board the *Chancewell*. The venture came to grief. "The *Chancewell* was wrecked on July 3; the *Hopewell* was back in the Bristol Channel on September 11." All four Separatists then escaped to Holland.

Before we follow them, one interesting episode in the pastor's prison life invites notice. I mean his acquaintance and encounter with Henry Jacob. It began about 1596, and its occasion has been found in certain attempts made by Puritan Churchmen—using Jacob as their agent—to win Johnson back to the National Church.[3] But Johnson's own account suggests something more accidental. About three years since, says he, writing late in 1599,[4] "Master Jacob having some speech with certain of the Separation . . . concerning their peremptory and utter separation from the churches of England, was requested by them briefly to set

---

[1] 1564-1605. At Christ's College, Cambridge, from 1580-88. "Then taught in a school at the house of Fox, in Nicholas-lane." 1593 (February)—in Fleet.

[2] The Magdalen Isles, in the Gulf of St. Lawrence. Arber's Story of Pilgrim Fathers, p. 107. For purpose and particulars of the voyage see Mackennal's "Story of the Separatists," pp. 110-112.

[3] Article on Johnson in National Dictionary of Biography.

[4] "An Answer to Master Jacob, His Defence of the Churches and Ministry of England," by Francis Johnson, an exile of Jesus Christ—1600. Preface. This controversy disproves the statement that Jacob "so far identified himself with the Separatists that he shared their banishment in 1593."—Mackennal's "Story of the Separatists," p. 100.

down in writing his reasons for a defence of the said churches, and they would either yield unto him his proofs or procure an answer unto the same." "Whereupon," Mr. Jacob set down his argument, "which the said parties did send to Master Fr. Johnson, being then prisoner in the Clink in Southwark, who made an answer unto the same, containing three exceptions and nine reasons in denial of the assumption, whereunto Master Jacob replied. Afterward Master Johnson defended his said exceptions and reasons. And, finally, Master Jacob replied again," which brings us to Johnson's "answer to Master H. Jacob, his defence of the churches and ministry in England . . . printed in 1600." They encountered each other face to face as well as by writing. Thus, in answer to Jacob's denial that "when and where the Word is preached among" them—in the Church of England—"it is done by virtue of a false office and calling . . ." Johnson says,[1] "Often have I heard you say so, but never could I hear you prove it." Again, he refers to what passed at a conference between them "in the presence of others that can witness it."[2] It took place on April 3, 1597, the very day before Johnson sailed from Gravesend. On this occasion Jacob wrote down the following, "word for word":—"A power borrowed from Antichrist to excommunicate may externally be committed unto a people, and used by *them* who have power to excommunicate from Christ." "When you had set it down," adds Johnson, "I desired your proof of it from the Scriptures. But none could be had; I could not obtain *that* at your hand. Thereupon I took the paper and wrote underneath your assertion thus:—This is against the Scriptures: 1 Cor. v. 4, 5, compared with 2 Cor. vi. 14, 15, 16, 17; Ezek. xliii. 8; Matt. xviii. 7, 18, 19, 20; and 1 Kings xviii. 21. Fran. Johnson."

It is a flash of light on the two men. Not less so, as illustrating Jacob's then state of mind, is the following[3]:—"Of yourself, among other things, once I asked this, whether you

[1] Answer, &c., p. 23.   [2] Answer, &c., p. 172.   [3] Answer, &c., p. 182.

were so minded, for the ministry which Christ had appointed
in His Church, as (that) you thought you ought and would
die for it, God assisting you. To which you answered yea.
Whereupon presently I asked again, Whether you were so
minded for the ministry of the Church of England, as you
thought you ought and would also die for it? To which
you answered, No." Johnson was hardly the man to deal
successfully with Jacob. He could not understand one who
was feeling his way; who shrank from the falsehood of
extremes; who longed to reconcile the claims of love and
truth. The main point in dispute, says Jacob, is "that
our public book of Articles of Religion (so far forth as it
erreth not fundamentally, as it doth not) containeth sufficient
to make a true Christian."[1] He says it does, and that, therefore, " you ought not wholly to separate from us, neither to
condemn us wholly as abolished from Christ." Johnson holds,
on the contrary, that the differences between them are
irreconcilable ; and that so long as Jacob, or anyone else,
abides where he is, he cannot belong to the household
of faith, cannot even look to be saved. And it is in
defence of this position that he and others have submitted to
" bonds, exile, and death." Jacob's rejoinder is that if such be
the witness for which they suffer he knows of none who can
pity them. " You suffer more than you need if that you would
but acknowledge the grace of God with us so far as it is. It is,
therefore, not Christ's cross in that regard but your own that
ye bear."[2] " Touching which bloody mind and speech of
yours," says Johnson, " I leave you and it unto God, who seeth
and will judge. Only let the reader note here again that not
the prelates alone, but you also (the forward preachers and
professors) have wittingly and willingly your hand in our
blood."[3] Both were right. The points of difference were
radical, as Johnson said, and as Jacob himself came afterwards
to see. But they were radical only in respect of the constitu-

[1] Answer, &c., p. 166.   [2] Answer, &c., p. 112.   [3] Answer, &c., p. 177.

tion of a church. They were not of a kind, as Johnson also at a later time confessed, to prevent necessarily that personal loyalty to Christ which alone saves. At this stage, however—owing largely to Johnson's narrowness—the two men recoiled from each other. It needed the influence of John Robinson's gentler hand and broader mind to draw Jacob into the right way.[1]

As already said, the next day after the conference with Jacob, Johnson started on the voyage which, for him and his companions, ended not at Rainea but at Amsterdam. A somewhat earlier[2] arrival was Henry Ainsworth. "He was newly come out of Ireland with others poor" as himself—a single young man, very studious, and content with little. If he lived some time on ninepence a week it was not the fault of the people, "for he was a modest and bashful man, and concealed his wants from others, until some suspected how it was with him, and pressed him to see how it was; and after it was known, such as were able mended his condition, and when he was married afterwards (1607) he and his family were comfortably provided for." We may as well add at once what else Governor Bradford has said of him. "A very learned man he was, and a close student, which much impaired his health. We have heard some, eminent in the knowledge of the tongues, of the University of Leyden, say that they thought he had not his better for the Hebrew tongue in the University nor scarce in Europe. He was a man very modest, amiable, and sociable in his ordinary course and carriage, of an innocent and unblameable life and conversation, of a meek spirit and a calm

[1] Some time after 1604 he sojourned for a time in Leyden, and boarded with Mr. Parkes and Dr. Ames. Here he came under Robinson's influence. This, of course, was later than 1609 (Young's Chronicles, p. 439).

[2] Paget, in his "Arrow Against the Separation of the Brownists" (written 1617), says to Ainsworth, "How comes it that you have lived more than twenty years as a neighbour, &c.," p. 119. H. Ainsworth (1570-1622), born at Swanton Morley, Norfolk; studied at St. John's, at Gonville and Caius Colleges, Cambridge; about 1598 entered service of a bookseller at Amsterdam as a porter. See Axon's "Henry Ainsworth, the Puritan Commentator." But 1593 is too early.

temper, void of passion and not easily provoked. And yet he
would be something smart in his style to his opposers in his
public writings; at which we that have seen his constant
carriage, both in public disputes and the managing of all
church affairs, and such-like occurrences, have sometimes mar-
velled. He had an excellent gift of teaching and opening the
Scriptures, and things did flow from him with that facility,
plainness, and sweetness as did much affect the hearers. He
was powerful and profound in doctrine, although his voice was
not strong; and had this excellency above many, that he was
ready and pregnant in the Scriptures, as if the Book of God
had been written in his heart: being as ready in his quotations,
without tossing and turning his book, as if they had laid open
before his eyes, and seldom missing a word in the citing of any
place, teaching not only the word and doctrine of God, but in
the words of God, and for the most part in a continued phrase
and words of Scripture. He used great dexterity, and was
ready in comparing Scripture with Scripture, one with another.
In a word, the times and place in which he lived were not
worthy of such a man."[1]

With Ainsworth's election to the vacant office of teacher
the constitution of the Church was complete. For the
first time since 1592 (September)—and then only for a month
or two—the Church could enjoy all its privileges, all its
"means of grace." What these were in the ordinary service a
few years later—and doubtless from the beginning—is told us
by Richard Clyfton.[2]

First, there was prayer and giving thanks by the pastor or
teacher, next the Scriptures were read, two or three chapters,
as time served, with a brief explanation of their meaning.

---

[1] Bradford's Dialogue in Young's
Chronicles, p. 448-9. In Axon's Life
a list of twenty-seven writings by
Ainsworth is given. The first is "A
True Confession of Faith of Certayne
English people living in Exile," &c.,
1596. Johnson is usually said to have
had a hand in this—and very likely
had. It was republished with the
"Apology" in 1604 (with a quite
different preface).

[2] An "advertisement" concerning a
book, &c., 1612.

Then the pastor or teacher took some passage of Scripture and expounded and enforced it.

After this the sacraments were administered (by the pastor). Lastly, a collection was made,[1] as each one was able, for the support of the officers and the poor.

In Clyfton's time, moreover, "some of the Psalms of David were sung by the whole congregation both before and after the exercise of the Word." Perhaps this was the established custom. But, after a time, the practice was introduced of singing the Psalms "done up" in rhyme and metre, an innovation which gave offence to some. Thus one of *Christopher Lawne's* complaints was against "their corrupt manner of worship in singing their new . . . rhymes"; "their naughty order in singing Psalms in such a metre and such a rhyme—of so harsh and hard a phrase—that they knew not what they meant, neither could they sing with understanding." He says, further, that "copies" of the new Psalms "were kept from the people," that each Psalm was "read after a broken manner in public" (line by line?), and that by "the uncouth and strange translation" they made the congregation "a laughing-stock to strangers."[2] Possibly the innovation was due to Ainsworth. At least, in his annotations on Exodus xv., he gives a rhymed version of the Song of Moses, and also a tune to which it may be sung. The first verse runs :—

> Unto Jehovah sing will I,
> For He excelleth gloriously;
> The horse, and him that rode thereon,
> Into the sea thrown down hath He.
> Jah is my strength and melody,
> And hath been my salvation.

He says, "this (meaning his version and time) may be sung also as Psalm cxiii." Moreover, his "Book of Psalms, Englished both in prose and metre," was printed by 1612, and

---

[1] William Mason, shipwright, aged 21 . . . deposed, in 1593, that " he gave 6d. a week which the deacons received " (Harleian MSS., 7,042. f. 35.)

6d. then equalled much more than 6d. now.

[2] Profane Schism, p. 9.

This may be sung also as the 113th Psalm.]

Un - to Je - ho - vah sing will I, for he ex - cel - leth

glo - rious - ly ; the horse and him that rode

there - on, in - to the sea thrown down hath hee,

Jah, is my strength and me - lo - dee; and

hath been my sal - va - tion.

TUNE ADAPTED TO THE SONG OF MOSES (EX. XV.) AND SUNG (PROBABLY) IN THE AMSTERDAM MEETING HOUSE.

if specimens of these—as yet unpublished—were "lined out" from time to time for the congregation to sing, this would account for what Lawne says about the absence of "copies." It must be owned that Ainsworth did not excel in rhyme, and that Lawne might well speak of "uncouth and strange translation." Take this, *e.g.* : —

> Thou doest wonders ! Hast outspread
> Thy right-hand ; them, the earth swallowed.
> Thou in Thy mercy leadest-on
> This people which Thou didst redeem :
> And in Thy strength Thou guidest them
> Unto Thine holy mansion.

Who would not sooner hear or sing the smooth, unrhymed verses ?—

> Thou stretchedst out Thy right hand ; the earth swallowed them.
> Thou leadest forth in Thy mercy, this people which Thou hadst redeemed : Thou guidest them in Thy strength, unto the habitation of Thy holiness.

For the rest, we observe that no place in the service is formally assigned to prophecy. We know the Church had its prophets. Jacob Johnson and Thomas Cocky are mentioned as figuring in that capacity. We hear of occasions when they exhorted the congregation; when, alas! they even openly contradicted and quarrelled with each other.[1] But this was when they felt specially "moved." Prophecy was not a regular office. It was not limited to any particular person or time. It might break out at any point of the service. Hence the possibility of confusion; and hence the ordinance which Robinson made, doubtless profiting by experience,[2] "that it be performed after the public ministry by the teachers, and under their direction and moderation, whose duty it is, if anything be obscure, to open it; if doubtful, to clear it; if unsound, to refute it; if unprofitable, to supply what is wanting, as they are able."

[1] Profane Schism, p. 83. But Johnson and Cocky were not the only prophets. On p. 59—*e.g.*, "another" is mentioned.

[2] Robinson's "Cathechism," Q. 32— Works, Vol. III., p. 433.

With regard to the sacraments, as the pastor was the same we may be certain that the manner of their administration was the same as when Daniel Buck[1] saw Johnson administer them in London. In baptism "he took water and washed the faces of them that were baptized, . . . saying only," as he did so, "I do baptize thee in the name of the Father, of the Son, and of the Holy Ghost, without using any other ceremony therein." In the Lord's Supper "five white loaves, or more, were set upon the table." Then "the pastor did take the bread and delivered it to some of them, and the deacons delivered to the rest; some of the . . . congregation sitting and some standing about the table." Next, "the pastor delivered the cup unto one, and he to another, till they had all drunken; using the words at the delivery thereof according as it is set down in the eleventh of the (1) Corinthians, the 24th verse." And "a very grave man he was"—we learn from Bradford—"and an able teacher, and was the most solemn in all his administrations that we have seen any, and especially in dispensing the seals of the covenant, both baptism and the Lord's Supper."[2]

"Truly," adds Bradford, "there were" in the Church at Amsterdam "many worthy men, and if you had seen them in their beauty and order, as we have done, you would have been much affected therewith, we dare say." . . . "Before their division and breach they were about 300 communicants, and," besides pastor, teacher, elders, and deacons, they had "one ancient widow[3] for a deaconess, who did them service many years, though she was sixty years of age when she was chosen.

---

[1] In his examination, March 9, 1592–3—see Strype's Annals, Vol. IV., p. 245. Of Buck Francis Johnson says he was a man that hath turned his coat . . . as often as D. P. (Dr. Perne), the old turncoat, did, if not oftener." "He it was that by divers letters desired of me to answer Mr. Jacob's argument" (1596). Later, "for his revolting from the truth and so persisting" he was "cast out from" the Church "and delivered unto Satan" (Answer to Master Jacob, Preface).

[2] Dialogue, Young's Chronicles, p. 445.

[3] Was this widow (Edith) Burrough, mentioned as a prisoner in 1588, 1590, 1592? There were two other widows, prisoners, but they died before 1588.

She honoured her place, and was an ornament to the congregation. She usually sat in a convenient place in the congregation, with a little birchen rod in her hand, and kept little children in great awe from disturbing the congregation. She did frequently visit the sick and weak, especially women, and, as there was need, called out maids and young women to watch and do them other helps as their necessity did require; and if they were very poor, she would gather relief for them of those that were able, or acquaint the deacons; and she was obeyed as a mother in Israel and an officer of Christ." [1]

The story so far is suggestive mainly of trials patiently borne and of progressive life; [2] but troubles sprang up which cast dark shadows on the scene. Though we fain would, we cannot pass these by, for this, if for no other reason, that they have recently been lifted into such prominence, and so presented, as to leave the impression that their effect was to extinguish the light altogether.

I. There was among the members a strict and a comparatively liberal party. Thus Daniel Buck said, "Some of you hold it utterly and simply unlawful to swear by a book, to prove a will, take an administration, or sue in the ecclesiastical courts; to shut up your shops on holy days and festival days, &c. And (you say) that these are the inventions of Antichrist. Others of you hold these things altogether lawful, and have, and do, put them in practice, with many such like things which I could name, but these shall suffice." [3]

One of the very strict was George Johnson, the pastor's brother. He was shocked at the apparel of the latter's wife—the widow Boyes whom Francis married in the Clink (1594).

---

[1] Dialogue, Young's Chronicles, pp. 455-6.

[2] But not entirely—e.g., Ainsworth's appointment had caused some disturbance and led even to the excommunication of some malcontents (G. Johnson's Discourse, p. 10). There had been troubles about a certain Mr. M., Mr. G., and Mr. S. M. (ditto, p. 25).

Bowman had been deposed for alleged peculation (1595). Slade (the elder) had been excommunicated for "apostasy"—i.e., going to service at a Dutch Church (ditto, p. 53).

[3] Quoted by F. Johnson—without denial—in his "Answer to Master Jacob," preface.

Not only himself but "all sorts of people" were shocked, said George, and he felt it his duty to write to her, voicing their displeasure. She did not amend. "Then he tried to get others to interfere, but they were loath, and would not." Next, he wrote to his brother, telling him that Mrs. Francis and the Bishop of London's wife "for pride and vain apparel were joined together"; and what scandal was abroad, "because Francis Johnson being in prison, and the brethren in great necessity beyond the seas," *she* "wore three, four or five gold rings at once." Moreover, "her busks and her whalebones in her breast" were "so manifest" that "many of the saints were grieved." Let her "pull off her excessive deal of lace"; discontinue the whalebones; exchange "the showish (showy) hat for a sober taffety or felt" . . . quit the "great starched ruffs, the musk and rings"; and "let sobriety and modesty be used." After much ado, in which Daniel Studley is said to have been active on the side of strictness, the "little rift" was healed, and the music of peace returned. The brothers drew together again—George confessing[1] that Francis became very kind and loving to him. This was in London.

But ere three months were passed after arrival at Amsterdam, the quarrel broke out again.[2] Nothing more likely than that the impoverished brethren, struggling in a strange city for bare subsistence, should (apart from the spiritual aspect of the matter) regard anything like luxury in living or dress as rather heartless. George, who might have preserved the peace, was provoked to break it by the fact, which he took for a slight, that his brother did not (with good reason surely) ask him to occupy rooms in his own house. There were stormy church meetings. There was an assiduous kindling of that

---

[1] "Tokens and duties of love passed between us from one prison to another." Studley, and "a letter, broke the peace" (G. Johnson's "Discourse," p. 28.

[2] Again, through Studley. At first Studley, says George J., used "most fair words" to him—yea, "they were bedfellows and in consultation together." But as he "waxed stronger" he "began to blow the bellows" (Discourse, p. 28).

zeal which in God's name does the devil's work. There was much occasion for scoffing and blaspheming given to unsympathetic outsiders. And at length it came to this—the pastor took a firm stand. He said the contentious ones " contributed nothing to his support ; that his wife bought her own clothes ; and that, if she could not wear what she had, he would be gone." But sooner than let *him* go the majority of the Church were of opinion that George deserved to go.[1] So they cast him out, about the year 1599.

Robinson having learnt the facts a few years later, and with Johnson's defence in his hands, approved the step ; for George had become " a disgraceful libeller."[2] Ainsworth also approved it, declaring that he was cast out " for lying and slandering, false accusation and contention." [3] Considering that Ainsworth was on the spot ; that he was thoroughly acquainted with both sides of the case ; and that he was confessedly " a moderate man," his words ought to be decisive as to where most of the blame lay.

The case of John Johnson, the father, is not so clear. Ainsworth does not mention it ; and his silence may be significant. If we had only the evidence of the father's letter Francis would stand without excuse. The letter,[4] in its main heads, is this :—

' 1. Coming in my old age so far, so hard and dangerous a journey to seek and make peace between you, the Church and

[1] He admits that he received " a small weekly allowance " from the Church for a time (Discourse, p. 37), but that in the end " the whole congregation " sided with his brother—persuaded that George had " a cracked brain " (Discourse, p. 184).

[2] A Justification of Separation (Works, Vol. II., p. 59).

[3] Counterpoyson, p. 50. This book should be carefully distinguished from " A Counter-poyson," by Dudley Fenner (1584 ?). The date of A.'s book is 1608. It was he, says George, who " pronounced the sentence against me at the first proceedings " (Discourse, p. 184).

[4] Printed by Lawne in Profane Schism, &c., pp. 64-66.

[5] Arber says—Story of the Pilgrim Fathers, p. 110—" It was probably from," Richmondshire—i.e., the North Riding of Yorkshire, his birthplace, that the old man came to Amsterdam. But more probably it was from London (see Johnson's letter to Burghley, Jan. 8, 1593–4). " Yes, when our poor old father, *this bearer* "—i.e., of the letter. His excommunication *implies* that he was a member of the London branch of the Church.

your brother, I could never see the least inclination in you to peace. . . .

2. Lodging in your house the first week, you were so far from peace and so unkindly used me that you made me weary before the week was ended; so was I forced to shift to my other son's lodging (*i.e.*, to his son Jacob's).

3. You sought to catch and ensnare me in my words; and afterward, as I perceived, also seduced the elders and the people to like dealing.

4. You "let me stand two hours on my feet before you and the people; and yourself sat all the time; and not once bid me sit down yourself, neither spake to the people to bid me.

5. Not once in the space of six weeks did you come to visit me, or ask how I did; being in the same city with you.

6. You did not write to me, "in the space of five years or more," to say "that you were desirous to see my face, or that I should be welcome to you, when I wrote to you of my purpose in coming."

7. You heard me scoffed and gibed by divers in the congregation, and not once rebuked them.

8. You became so hardened that you sat as principal and heard your father excommunicated.

9. Coming afterward to you, and talking to you, you said you might not keep company with me.

This is black enough, nor are we in a position to challenge any of the father's statements. But it is not all the truth. Every statement may be literally accurate, and yet with fuller light from the circumstances it might look very different. If we knew, for example, what had passed in London, we might not wonder in the least that Francis expressed no desire to see his father in Amsterdam. The father says he came "to seek and make peace," but Robinson says[1] he came to "take the part " of George, and speaks as if his "*excommunication*" at least was justified. Jacob Johnson appears like one of the

---

[1] Works, Vol. II., p. 59.

father's supporters, but he really adhered to his brother, and years later (after December, 1610) is met with as an elder in the "Franciscan" Church. And the silence of Ainsworth may mean nothing after all; for Bernard, whom he is refuting, does not mention the father, so that there was no reason why Ainsworth should. Finally, on the whole matter let us hear Governor Bradford, who is "perfectly trustworthy," although he happens to be charitable! In the dialogue so often cited between "some young men and sundry ancient men that came out of Holland and old England," say the former: "But he (F. Johnson) is much spoken against for excommunicating his brother, and his own father, and maintaining his wife's cause, who was by his brother and others reproved for her pride in apparel." *Ancient men:* "Himself hath often made his own defence, and others for him. The Church did, after long patience towards them, and much pains taken with them, excommunicate them for their unreasonable and endless opposition, and such things as did accompany the same, and such was the justice thereof, as he could not not but consent thereto. In our time his wife was a grave matron, and very modest both in her apparel and all her demeanour, ready to do any good works in her place, and helpful to many, especially the poor, and an ornament to his calling. She was a young widow when he married her, and had been a merchant's wife, by whom he had a good estate, and was a godly woman; and because she wore such apparel as she had been formerly used to, which were neither expensive nor immodest, for their chiefest exceptions were against her wearing of some whalebone in the bodice and sleeves of her gown, corked shoes, and other such-like things as the citizens of her rank then used to wear. And although, for offence sake, she and he were willing to reform the fashions of them so far as might be without spoiling of their garments, yet it would not content them except they came full up to their size. Such was the strictness or rigidness (as now the term goes) of some in those times, as we can by experience, and of our own knowledge, show in other instances."[1]

II. Fresh exiles swelled the Church from time to time. Some of them—perhaps most—came from London. We read of four who came in 1604, "enforced to abjure the land for the Gospel's sake . . . after they suffered three months' imprisonment."[2] But not all. Some came from the "West," in consequence, very probably, of those communications which followed on Penry's letter. Among these were Thomas White and twelve or thirteen others. They joined the Amsterdam congregation about 1603, and White, at least, had left within two years. George Johnson gives us to understand that White and Powell—one of his band—were ambitious of " office," and took offence at being neglected. If so, one motive is clear for White's speedy revolt, and for his immediate publication of what professed to be a "Discovery of Brownism; or, a brief declaration of some of the errors and abominations daily practised and increased amongst the English company of the separation remaining for the present at Amsterdam in Holland."[3] Thus arose the Church's second grievous trouble.

The pastor soon had a reply out, entitled, "An Inquiry and answer of Thomas White, his Discovery," &c.[4]; and, before this, two of the persons most implicated, Daniel Studley and Judith Holder, had taken steps to prosecute White " before the magistrates of the city."[5] They had better have left the

[1] Young's Chronicles, 446–7.
[2] See "A Memorandum, Anno Domini 1604," in Miles Micklebound, quoted in appendix. We learn from George Johnson's "Discourse " (pp. 44, 205–6) that there were accessions from a church at Norwich; that this was "the elder sister "; that Mr. Hunt was its pastor; that Studley had had some connection with it. There was a letter (dated March 6, 1600) from Hunt to F. Johnson accusing Studley of an arbitrary act of interference while Hunt, two of the elders, and the deacon were in prison at Norwich.

[3] London, 1605, November, printed by E. A. (Edward Aldee) for Nathaniel Fosbrooke, &c. (26 pp.). (Arber's Story of the Pilgrim Fathers, p. 119.)
[4] 1606. Here (in the Preface) Johnson says that White " was heretofore separated from the Church of England, and a joined member of a church in the West of England, professing same faith with us; then he came to Amsterdam and joined the Church there. He has now revolted, setting himself tooth and nail against us."
[5] Ditto, pp. 28–9.

nasty little book alone, for nasty it is both in spirit and details. What its spirit is like may be judged by the following:—"Master Ainsworth, whom " F. Johnson " terms a man approved in Christ," is one that hath turned his coat as oft as ever D. B.,[1] if not oftener . . . he is a teacher stained with hypocrisy . . . spotted again and again with apostasy . . . a means to bring in false doctrine." Assertions such as these which are *known* to be utterly false, cast discredit on all the accuser may say of anyone or anything else.

Still we are not concerned to deny, or refute, his charges generally. No doubt there were facts solid and unsavoury enough to serve well the purpose[1] of a venomous heart. But suppose we grant this—suppose we grant[2] that the Church contained five or six persons accused or strongly suspected of sins more or less criminal; suppose the Church —perhaps, because the proof of guilt was not convincingly strong, perhaps for some less worthy reason—refused, or was slow, to eject them; suppose the pastor and elders, in one case calculated to create needless scandal, came to a decision without consulting the Church; suppose the elders, or the Church, in another case, contrary to one of their avowed principles, had recourse to "the censure of suspension for months" before proceeding to the act of excommunication; suppose, finally, the Church sometimes and the pastor sometimes (as he himself admits) expelled members too lightly, too rashly, too violently, and in too wholesale a fashion—what then? Well, we reach the conclusion, of course, that the character and discipline of the Church were by no means

---

[1] Daniel Buck. The reference is to Johnson's words about Buck and Ainsworth in his Answer to Jacob (1600). Bradford says, "For his (Ainsworth's) apostasy this was all the matter. When he was a young man, before he came out of England, he, at the persuasion of some of his godly friends, went once or twice to hear a godly minister preach." George Johnson had set the charge going " in a book " which he " writ." (His " Discourse, &c.," 1603.) Dialogue, p. 449.

[2] What follows covers the whole ground of White's indictment.

thoroughly consistent and perfect; far less so, we may even say, than itself deemed them to be. But the important point to observe is that if we go on to conclude that the whole congregation was, or was fast becoming, "a bad lot" we go far beyond the evidence—nay, we go in the teeth of evidence compared with which the word of Thomas White is a mere nothing. For what Governor Bradford thought of the Church we have heard; and yet Bradford made the acquaintance of the Church two years after White had disappeared, and lived in full view of it for a year, and (by the hypothesis) must have witnessed it at a still lower stage in its downward career! Either, then, "errors and abominations were *not* daily practised and increased," as White gave out; or, Bradford was not merely "good natured and optimistic,"[1] but morally blind and insensitive. It should not be difficult to decide between the alternatives—especially when we find that Christopher Lawne, several years[2] later, can do little more than vamp up White's old stories in his own more elaborate endeavour to make the Church odious!

III. The next trouble arose in connection with John Smyth —a remarkable man who merits more than a bare reference. The place and date of his birth are not known. For the latter, probably 1572 is near the mark. He went up to Christ's College, Cambridge, about 1586, and had Francis Johnson as his tutor.[3] He took his M.A. 1598.[4] He was ordained by William Wickham, Bishop of Lincoln. He held no benefice, so far as we know; but is heard of as a preacher or lecturer in the city of Lincoln. "A few years ago, Professor Whitsitt, of Amsterdam, found in the library of Emmanuel College, Cambridge, a little book of his, entitled "The bright morning starre, or the resolution and exposition of the 22 Psalme. Preached

[1] So Arber, "Story," &c., Preface, p. 3.
[2] 1612–1613. See next chapter.
[3] Bradford is the authority for this statement. Dialogue. p. 450.
[4] The date of his graduation has been given as 1575–6, but Francis Johnson did not "matriculate" till April 1, 1579. See Arber's "Story," &c., p. 132.

publicly in foure sermons at Lincoln by John Smith, preacher of the city, 1603."[1] This does not prove that the preacher and our John Smyth were the same. But proof is supplied by the following—"a booke called a Paterne of true Prayer or Exposicon uppon the Lord's Prayer, done by John Smythe, &c., of Lincoln," was entered at Stationers' Hall March 22, 1605; and Richard Bernard, his neighbour, friend, and future opponent, expressly tells us that its writer was John Smyth, the se-Baptist.[2] Moreover, he is spoken of as once "preacher to the city of Lincoln" by John Cotton, the eminent New England Puritan, who had been a vicar in Lincolnshire, at St. Botolph's, Boston, for twenty[3] years.

It has been usual to say that Smyth was pastor of the Gainsborough Church from 1602 to 1606. The facts just mentioned show that the earlier of these dates, at least, must be wrong. We are not bound, indeed, to believe that Smyth was still in Lincoln on March 22, 1605. Not even the words of the Epistle Dedicatory, which say that the writer, "being (then?) the lecturer in the city of Lincoln," "delivered" the treatise "to the ears of a few, not long since."[4] compel us to this. There is nothing to show that the epistle was not written, and the book printed, some little time after he had left the city. But the end of 1604, at any rate, seems to be the earliest possible date of his settling at Gainsborough. And if he removed to Amsterdam in 1606 his English pastorate was very short indeed, or, rather, had no existence.

What is needed, in order to clear away some confusion, is to state the true sequence of events.

1. The common origin of the Separatist Churches at Gainsborough and Scrooby is described by Governor Bradford.[5] "So many, therefore, of these professors" (i.e., those of the

[1] Brown's "Pilgrim Fathers," p. 86 (Popular Edition).
[2] Arber, pp. 133—4.
[3] 1612–1633.
[4] Arber, p. 134.
[5] Chronicles of the Pilgrim Fathers (Young), pp. 19–21.

"north parts" who had become "enlightened by the Word of God" on the subject of the Church, through the "travail and diligence of some godly and zealous preachers ") "as saw the evil of these things" (*i.e.*, "base, beggarly ceremonies," "lordly, tyrannous power of the prelates," &c.) "in these parts, and whose hearts the Lord had touched with heavenly zeal for His truth, they shook off this yoke of Antichristian bondage, and, as the Lord's free people, joined themselves (by a covenant of the Lord) into a church estate, in the fellowship of the Gospel, to walk in all His ways, made known, or to be made known unto them, according to their best endeavours, whatsoever it should cost them." Bradford himself "takes no notice of · the year of this federal incorporation" [1]; the date 1602 is given by his nephew, Mr. Secretary Morton. And it is to be particularly observed that 1602 dates the beginning of "a church estate." *It has nothing to do with John Smyth.*

2. Then, "These people became two distinct bodies or churches, in regard of distance of place, and did congregate severally, for they were of several towns and villages, some in Nottinghamshire, some in Lincolnshire, and some of Yorkshire, where they bordered nearest together." [2] According to date in the margin, which may be Morton's or Bradford's, this local division took place in 1606. This date also has nothing to do with Smyth.

3. But "in one of these churches, besides others of note, was Mr. John Smith, a man of able gifts and a good preacher, who *afterwards* was chosen their pastor." [3] Consequently, it would appear that Smyth became pastor at Gainsborough some time later than 1606, when the church was constituted. But still he may have been on the spot some time earlier; and the way I read the situation is this. John Cotton tells us that "the tyranny of the Ecclesiastical Courts was harsh towards him (*i.e.*, Smyth), and the yokes put upon him in the ministry too grievous

---

[1] Ibid, p. 22, note.   [2] Ibid, p. 22.   [3] Ibid, p. 22.

to be borne." [1]   Here we have a reference to his experience as a (Puritan) preacher in Lincoln, and the external cause of his being moved toward Separatism.   Hearing of the "people" about Gainsborough, eighteen miles away, he came among them near the close of 1604.   Then befell a period of mental distress.   For nine months he doubted what course to take. He had much intercourse with other "forward" ministers, especially with Richard Bernard, who seemed to be in a similar state of mind. [2]   At length the shadows fled away, and so far as the "necessity of Separation" was concerned, he never doubted again—a fact to which "the town of Gainsborough and those there that knew" his "footsteps" could bear testimony. [3]   He now joined the Church as a private member, and for awhile so remained.   Then—perhaps early in 1607—his gifts and character raised him inevitably to the pastorate.   But what is said of the Scrooby Church was true, doubtless, of the Gainsborough—"they could not long continue in any peaceable manner, but were hunted and persecuted on every side, so as their former afflictions were but as mole-hills to mountains in comparison to these which now came upon them." . . . And "seeing themselves thus molested, and that there was no hope of their continuance there, by a joint consent they resolved to go into the Low Countries." [4]   None worked harder to bring about this resolve than Thomas Helwys—a man of "note" in Smyth's church. [5]   John Robinson, glancing back

[1] Bradford's Dialogue (Young), p. 451, note.
[2] He speaks of this time in his "Parallels, Censures, Observations" (1609) pp. 4, 5, 128. He mentions a Conference at Coventry; a walk with Bernard from W (orksop), when "all the journey" B. was casting about to despatch his "estate and get away with safety"; a proposal of B.'s to "call out 100 persons" from different parishes "to enter into covenant together not to hearthe dumb ministers," &c., p. 4.   [3] Ibid, p. 128.
[4] Bradford's Chronicles, p. 23.
[5] I take this to be fairly certain; for (a) Smyth refers to a time when he was

sick in England, at Bashforth's, and when he was "troublesome and chargeable to" Helwys. See his "Retraction." (b) He was of Smyth's company at Amsterdam, and seceded with him (1608). (c) Smyth says, "It is well known to all the company that I have spent as much in helping the poor as Mr. Helwys hath done" (Retraction, p. vi.).—Barclay's "Inner Life of the Religious Societies of the Commonwealth."   When he distinguishes Helwys's company from his own—in a preceding sentence—he is thinking of those who remained with Helwys after he himself had made the second separation of 1609.

at what first led him as well as Smyth to think seriously of emigration, says, " it was Mr. Helwisse, who above all, either guides or others, furthered this passage into strange countries; and if any brought oars, he brought sails."[1] His zeal is explicable when we read that " on July 26, 1607, his wife Joan was brought from York Castle to appear before the Ecclesiastical Court, and sent back thither, along with John Drewe and Thomas Jessop, for refusing to take an oath according to law."[2] But if this gave occasion to Helwys's zeal, its object could scarcely be achieved all at once. Inquiries would need to be set on foot and practical measures concerted, which would take up time. And so it does not surprise us to find Smyth still signing himself, or still addressed, as " Pastor of the Church at Gainsborough," as late as November or December, 1607.[3] We thus seem driven to the conclusion that there was no long interval between the departure of Smyth's company and that of Robinson's—a few months at the most. For " all " the latter had " got over " to Amsterdam by the early summer of 1608.

IV. Assuming, then, that Smyth, Helwys, and the rest reached Amsterdam during the last weeks of 1607, or the early spring of 1608, we see that the special trouble they caused must have begun almost forthwith. For before the year was out—which, on the old style, commonly used by the Pilgrims, might mean before March 25, 1609—Smyth had both joined and left Johnson's church, and had published a pamphlet declaring why—entitled, " The Differences of the Churches of the Separation." [4]

There are two phrases in this writing which have been taken to prove that " the Gainsborough Church on its arrival at Amsterdam " did *not* join " the ancient exiled Church there." These are the phrases in which Smyth

[1] Robinson's Works, iii., p. 159.
[2] Brown's Pilgrim Fathers, p. 97.
[3] Arber, p. 136.
[4] " Containing a description of the Liturgy and ministry of the visible Church, annexed as a correction and supplement to a little treatise lately published bearing title, Principles and Inferences respecting the Visible Church," 1608 (early).

speaks of Johnson's church as the "Ancient Brethren of the Separation," and of his own community as "the brethren of the separation of the second English Church at Amsterdam." Happily, there is clear light on the point. For in the next year Henry Ainsworth wrote what he called a "Defence of Holy Scripture, worship, and ministry used in the Christian Churches separated from Antichrist against the challenges, cavils, and contradictions of Mr. Smyth in his book, entitled 'The Differences of the Churches of the Separation.'" Here Ainsworth expounds [1] the *stages* of difference with Johnson's church through which Smyth had passed. So far, they were three:—First, Smyth objected to the use of the translated written Scriptures in public worship. He thought that the teachers should bring the originals, the Hebrew and Greek, and out of them translate by voice. Next, he objected to something in the "ministry and treasury of the Church." Ainsworth does not distinctly say what. But Smyth's position was this: "We hold, that in contributing to the Church-treasury there ought to be both a separation from them that are without, and a sanctification of the whole action by prayer and thanksgiving." [2] The former was not different from the theory and practice of Johnson's church. Perhaps it omitted the latter. Thirdly, he objected to infant baptism. [3]

The *first* was the only "difference between Mr. Smyth and us (says Ainsworth) when first he began to quarrel"; then, "after much time spent about this controversy," he passed on to the second, while still confessing that we, "the ancient brethren of the Separation (as he calleth us), are to be honoured," as having "reduced the Church to the true primitive and apostolic constitution"; "and now, [4] as a man benumbed in mind," he has come to the third, and protests

[1] In the Introduction.
[2] The Differences of the Church, 6th position.
[3] Ainsworth makes no reference to Smyth's Arminianism, which appears to have been a yet later development,
though Mr. Arber has assumed that he "threw off his Calvinism at once and so made a bottomless gulf between the two Churches" *from the first.* "Story," &c., p. 186.
[4] In 1609.

that we are "a false Church, falsely constituted in the baptizing of infants" and in our "own baptized estate."[1]

Moreover, Ainsworth uses words which are unintelligible save on the supposition that Smyth had been associated with himself in one and the same Church. Such as these:—

"If we would have laid aside our translated Bibles communion would have been kept with us." "The Church out of which he (Smyth) was gone by schism." "We desired"—quoting Smyth—that the practice of using translations "might be refrained *for our sakes that we might keep communion.*"

But, of course, having seceded and set up for himself, it was natural that he should describe the new Church as he did —"the brethren of the separation of the second English Church." Dr. Dexter thinks "as many as seventy-five or eighty must have gone out with Smyth."

(a) "These," says John Robinson,[2] "having utterly dissolved and disclaimed their former church state and ministry, came together to erect a new Church by baptism; unto which they also ascribed so great virtue as that they would not so much as pray together before they had it. And after much straining of courtesy who should begin . . . Mr. Smyth baptized first himself and next Mr. Helwisse, and so the rest, making their particular confessions."

(b) But before March 12, 1609-10, he repented, and with thirty-one others made a further separation. Smyth's explanation was that when he baptized himself "he *then* thought that there was no Church with whom he could join with a good conscience;" but, since then, he had been led to see that the Mennonite Churches were "true Churches," and had true ministers "from whom baptism may orderly be had"; and, this being so, it was not "proper" for private persons to baptize and set up churches without first joining themselves to "true

---

[1] Hence it is evident that Smyth's change of view with respect to baptism also came comparatively late.

[2] Works III., p. 168.

Churches " already existing. He was not, indeed, a believer in " apostolic succession." " I deny," he says, " all succession except in the truth." But " I hold that we are not to violate the order of the Primitive Church except necessity urge a dispensation."[1] If the Mennonite Church was a true Church and the only true Church in Amsterdam, Smyth did but act logically when he sought union with it. A document containing his application has been preserved, and has the names of the thirty-one others who applied with him.[2] Owing to some doctrinal differences the wished-for union did not take place till 1615, three years after Smyth's death. During the " brief remainder " of his life, Smyth gathered his little band in the hinder part of a great cake-house or bakery, belonging to Jan Munter, a friendly Mennonite. Here he held services, " unconnected with any Christian organisation," till the summer of 1612, " when he fell sick with consumption." "After seven weeks of increasing debility, on 1st September of that year he was borne from the cake-house to his burial in the Niewe Kirk."[3]

It may be added that his old comrade, Thomas Helwys, was not among the thirty-one. He continued stoutly to defend the right of self-baptism and of baptism by others than an " elder." " Whosoever," said he, " shall be stirred up by the same Spirit, to preach the same Word ; and men thereby " are " converted, may . . . wash them with water, and who can forbid ? "[4] He contended sharply with Smyth for coming to doubt this, and charged him with sin against the Holy Ghost. He manifested a bitterness which pained Smyth deeply.[5] Helwys returned to England before his friend's death, and they

[1] Barclay's " Inner Life," &c., pp. 70, 71.
[2] Arber, p. 138.
[3] Ditto, p. 140.
[4] See letter (to Smyth?) quoted by Barclay, p. 71.
[5] But why does Mr. Arber say (Story, &c., p. 187) that he and the majority cast out Smyth and the rest? I can find no authority for this statement at all. Besides, the majority seem to have been with Smyth. For when he signed the Mennonite Confession of Faith forty-one signed with him. See Barclay, p. 72.

never met again.   With some followers from Amsterdam for a nucleus, he founded the first "General Arminian Baptist Church in London."

John Smyth, take him all in all, is a beautiful character. Ainsworth, Clyfton, even Robinson, were very hard upon him— not unnaturally, considering the rapidity with which he advanced and the variety of his "heresies."   In fact, "his Arminian and Baptist opinions were regarded by every branch of the Separatists as calculated to bring the separation into still greater contempt. . . . They cannot speak of him with calmness.   His happy and triumphant assurance of salvation, on his death-bed, is characterised as 'sad and woeful'; and he is treated as a brother who is lost."[1]   But we see the heart of the man in his last book, called "The Retraction of His Errors." It is a noble utterance; and one feels sure that if any of his old acquaintance—Robinson, for example—ever chanced to read it, they would realise, with some contrition, how unduly harsh and shallow their judgment of the writer had been.   One who could write such words as these, whatever else he had missed in his short life, had won at length the mind of Christ : " Howsoever, in the days of my blind zeal and preposterous imitation of Christ, I was somewhat lavish in censuring and judging others; and namely, in the way of separation called Brownism, yet since having been instructed in the way of the Lord more perfectly, and finding my error therein, I protest against that my former course of censuring other persons, and especially for all those hard phrases wherewith I have in any of my writings inveighed against England or the separation "—i.e., (a) against the English Church so far as its errors are due to mere ignorance of the truth ; for " if a sin of ignorance make a man an Antichristian then I demand where shall we find a Christian?" or (b) against such of the "separation" as Mr. Bernard, Mr. Ainsworth, Mr. Clyfton; "for I should

---

[1] Barclay, p. 108; who also quotes John Cotton's words—his death " is set as a seal to his gross and damnable Arminianism."

have, with the spirit of meekness, instructed them that are contrary minded, but my words have been stout and mingled with gall." . . . "My desire is to end controversies among Christians rather than to make and maintain them, especially in matters of the outward Church and ceremonies; and it is the grief of my heart that I have so long cumbered myself and spent my time therein, and I profess that differences of judgment for matter of circumstance, as are all things of the outward Church, shall not cause me to refuse the brotherhood of any penitent and faithful Christian whatsoever. And now from this day forward do I put an end to all controversies and questions about the outward Church and ceremonies with all men, and resolve to spend my time in the main matters wherein consisteth salvation. Without repentance, faith, remission of sin, and the new creature, there is no salvation—but there *is* salvation without the truth of all the outward ceremonies of the outward Church."[1]

V. The last and most disastrous trouble of all reached its climax in 1610. It had been growing for a year at least. Ainsworth seceded in December, 1610; and says, "we had, by a twelvemonth's dispute, tried if we could have come to accord; but we are further off it at the end than at the beginning." Before 1609 there is no sign that the relations between pastor and teacher were strained. In 1600 Ainsworth is, for Johnson, "my work-fellow to the Kingdom of Christ, approved in Christ." He probably came with Francis Johnson, and "other his assistants, to make humble suit to the king in 1603,"[2] when they presented (by means of an unnamed "honourable personage") three petitions on behalf of certain his "loving and faithful subjects, some living in foreign lands abroad, some here at home in our native country, imprisoned, and otherwise subject to many great calamities for the truth of the Gospel of our Lord Jesus Christ." He was joint author

---

[1] Barclay, app. to chap. VI. ii.-iv.   [2] Miles Micklebound in "Platform"; and "Apology" (1604).

with Johnson—in 1604—of "An apology or defence of such true Christians as are commonly but unjustly called Brownists." He had stood by Johnson during the trouble with his brother, with his father, with Thomas White. He had written for Johnson and the whole Church in his controversy with John Smyth. He and Johnson were still working together amicably when John Robinson came on the scene, and for some time after— though Robinson perceived already the smouldering fire which was "like to break out" in "flames of contention."[1] The outbreak was due to Johnson. Bradford tells us that the pastor was weary of the "many dissensions" which were traceable, as he thought, to popular government. But probably he had never wholly abandoned his earlier Presbyterianism. If George Johnson can be credited, this had influenced the government of the Church long before 1609. Referring to so early a date as 1598, he says: "The elders end and determine matters, yet they will pretend that the Church doeth it; whereas, in truth, they give the Church the title and name, but they usurp the power." The tendency thus to usurp powers which belonged to the whole congregation might easily have been checked by the pastor, but was rather encouraged. And Daniel Studley, we are told, was his "standard-bearer."[2] Indeed Studley—a "subtle man,"[3] whom the pastor too much regarded—may have been more responsible for the crisis than Johnson. He had reason to fear the people. For, on one occasion "fifteen" members of the Church "joined to propose and request that Studley vacate his office as elder." And if he then declared, as report says: "Here is a beginning to tread the pathway to popular government; the very bane to all good order in Church and commonweal," he would not be slow to work for its suppression; and, at the same time, would be sure to provoke

[1] Bradford's Chronicles, p. 33.
[2] Christopher Lawne's epithet.
[3] Johnson, "by reason of many dissensions that fell out in the church and the subtilty of one of the elders of the same, came after many years to alter his judgment about the government of the Church and his practice thereupon."—Bradford's Dialogue, p. 445.

the more active resistance of those who realised that he was
assailing a vital principle. The months immediately preceding the breach were a miserable time. The Church was
openly divided into two parties—the Franciscans and the
Ainsworthians. Ainsworth, for one, suffered keenly. He
felt bound in conscience to take a firm stand, but he did it
with a heavy heart. He loved peace, and favoured "moderation." He tried hard to find some middle path, some satisfactory compromise. He met the usual fate. At last things
became intolerable. Johnson and his party had the upper
hand in the meetings of the Church, and disturbed them with
perpetual "returns" to the one controverted subject. "Daily,"
says Ainsworth,[1] "in their public doctrines and prayers they
inveighed against the truth they formerly professed; wounded
the conscience of the brethren; and sought occasions to draw
men from the right way and practice of the Gospel." Under
such circumstances "peace and goodwill" were out of the
question, and Ainsworth, with a large proportion—perhaps a
majority—of the congregation withdrew. Johnson treated
the secession as a "schism and rending" of the Church.
Accordingly, he caused Ainsworth to be deposed "from the
office of a teacher," and, with "his company," to be cast
out.[2] Ainsworth, on his part, was content simply to separate.
"He and his company," we are told, "did not excommunicate
Johnson and his party, but only withdrew from them when
they could live no longer peaceably."

At first Ainsworth used a Jews' synagogue[3] for the
place of worship—in the same street as the old meeting-
house, next door but one. Of course this led to frequent
collisions, and did not tend to allay irritation. Before long
steps were taken with a view to deciding to whom the
old meeting-house belonged. Ainsworth is emphatic in his

[1] His Animadversion to Master
Richard Clyfton, &c. (1613), p. 134.
[2] Paget's "Arrow Against the
Separation of the Brownists," p. 94
(1617).
[3] Ditto, p. 304, cf. Profane Schism,
p. 26.

assertion that he and his congregation did not move first.[1] "It was publicly agreed," he says, "in *our Church* that we would rather bear the wrong (of losing the meeting-house) than trouble the magistrate with our controversy; neither have we ever commenced such a suit." But the "chief owners" of the house were "two brethren and a widow" of the congregation. "The estate" of these "was such as they could not bear the loss and damage." They sought to gain their right, first, through "friendly agreement," then through the arbitration of "indifferent citizens." This failing, they "had to seek help of the magistrates." In the process "the Church's right was called in question," and "some certain" were appointed to "answer for the same." At the outset the case was laid before the Burgomasters *privately*, "who laboured by persuasion with our opposites to put the matter to the arbitrament of good men chosen by both sides, but they still peremptorily refused." Consequently, it went to the judges, who "nominated two indifferent men to hear the case." They did this twice, "under penalty the second time"; but "our opposites held out," and "pleaded that they which build on another man's ground are by law to lose their building." The plea could have no force because the so-called owner of the ground was simply "one man (now among *them, i.e.*, the Franciscans), whose name was used but in trust" at the time of purchase. At length, therefore, Johnson with his flock found themselves homeless.

Nor did the troubles of the "ancient Church" end here. There was, for example, the revolt of Christopher Lawne, and his set, who were ejected during the last six months of 1611. There was also the "deposition"[2] of Studley, when his unworthiness could no longer be doubted even by a too considerate pastor. Not unnaturally the scene of so much disaster became hateful, and in 1613 Johnson led his diminished and discouraged people to Emden. How he fared

---

[1] Animadversion, pp. 2–3.   [2] 1612.

there we cannot say. But he did not stay long. For in 1617 Johnson describes himself [1] as " Pastor of the ancient English Church now sojourning at Amsterdam." This was his last stage. He was only fifty-five, but, worn and weary, he died in the January following. Of the people some rejoined Ainsworth. [2] The greater number " prepared for to go to Virginia." They put themselves under the care of their elder, Francis Blackwell, who played them false. Our last glimpse of him and them [3] is in the mid-Atlantic, on a ship, " packed like herrings," with 180 persons. Northwest winds drive the ship out of its course. Dearth and dysentery are on board. The " master of the ship " dies, " some six of the mariners " die, 130 of the passengers also die. Blackwell is among them and most of his company. So ended one remnant of the " ancient " and once flourishing Church.

As to Ainsworth he had yet some five more years in which to go on " teaching " his people in the recovered "old meeting-house." These last years were comparatively free from the disputes which he loathed, and could be devoted to the Biblical study which he loved. The " Book of Psalms—Englished both in prose and metre "—with annotations [4]; annotations on the Five Books of Moses [5]; an edition of " Solomon's Song of Songs in English metre," were all the product of his last ten years. In such " profitable labours " he immersed himself; and, as a consequence, suffered from " continued infirmity " of body. He died at the end of 1622, or the beginning of 1623. The traditional story of his violent end by poison at the hand of Jews has been exploded. [6] The real cause of death was a " fit of gravel," " a disease brought on or aggravated by sedentary work."

[1] Title-page of his last book, " A Christian Plea," 1617.
[2] It may be noted that Richard Clyfton, their own teacher, died in 1616.
[3] Bradford's Chronicles (Young, pp. 70-73).
[4] 1612.
[5] In five vols., 1616, 1617, 1618, 1619.
[6] In Mr. Ernest Axon's " H. Ainsworth: His Birthplace and His Death,"—reprinted, with additions, from the National Dictionary of Biography in a small volume entitled, " Henry Ainsworth, the Puritan commentator " (Manchester, 1889).

John Canne—who became the third pastor of the church founded by Henry Jacob at Southwark, and, subsequently, pastor of the Broadmead Baptist Church at Bristol—succeeded him, and was pastor still in 1634, when he printed his "Necessity of Separation." What befell the Church after he left is not clear. But it kept up some sort of distinct organisation till 1701, and then what remained of it became merged in the Scotch Presbyterian Church, which originated in 1607 and has continued in the city to this day.

John Robinson's stern letter of September, 1624,[1] to the Church at Amsterdam, entitled "An Appeal on Truth's Behalf," was meant for Ainsworth's congregation, and proves that a bad spirit developed itself swiftly as soon as he was gone. The bad spirit must still have held possession, to some extent, in 1630, when there came out "Certain Notes of Mr. Henry Aynsworth his last sermon. Taken by pen in the publique delivery by one of his flock,[2] a little before his death. Anno 1622. Published now at last by the said writer as a love-token of remembrance to his brethren, to inkindle their affections to prayer, that scandalls (of manie years' continuance) may be removed, that are barrs to keep back manie godly, wise, and judicious from us, whereby we might grow to further perfection again." The text is 1 Peter ii. 4—"Unto whom coming, a living stone, rejected indeed of men, but with God elect, precious."

Altogether this record of the first sustained experiment in the application of "Free Church principles" leaves a melan-

---

[1] Works III., p. 387 ff.
[2] The Preface is signed Sabin Starsmore. He and his wife had been members of Mr. Jacob's church at Southwark. They were transferred to Robinson's church, somewhat to the surprise of the old London church. Sabin, the husband, figures as the bearer of letters from Robinson and Brewster to Sir John Wolstenholme, January and February, 1618. When next we come across him he is in the Counter Prison, Wood Street, September, 1618, through the treachery of Blackwell. Then we learn that he and his wife had been received into Ainsworth's church, and as this sermon shows he was alive in 1630 and still in Amsterdam. See Robinson, Works III., p. 384; Arber, pp. 292-5; Bradford, p. 73.

choly impression. Well might Ainsworth exclaim, " We desire the Christian reader not to be offended at the truth because of our infirmities who cannot walk in it as we ought; nor to stumble for the troubles and dissensions which Satan raiseth among God's people."

But let us gather the lessons of it from the wise words of Robinson :—

"As Paul complaineth that sin, taking occasion by the law, wrought in him all manner of concupiscence, so, indeed, hath the malice of Satan and man's corruption taken occasion to work much evil of this kind, by sundry good things specially found in the professors of this truth (*i.e.*, the truth of the Separation); as, by their knowledge, zeal, and liberty of the Gospel.

"Knowledge, saith the apostle, puffeth up, . . . and hence was it that the same church to which he so writes, exceeding other churches in knowledge, are the more in danger of contentions without special knowledge and watchfulness. Ignorant persons and peoples are for the most part easily ruled, as being content to trust other men with their faith and religion; neither was there ever so great peace in the Christian world, as it is called, as in the deepest darkness of popery.

Again, "as the greatest zeal for God is rightly found amongst God's people, so is peace and agreement greatly endangered thereby, if it be not tempered with much wisdom, moderation, and brotherly forbearance; and that they consider not aright that both themselves and others are frail men, and compassed about with much ignorance, and infirmity otherwise; who are therefore to study, not only how to have that which they like, but also how to bear that in other men (if not intolerable) which they like not; otherwise, whilst men think by their zeal to warm the house, they will burn it over their own, and other men's heads.

"And lastly, they only, who enjoy liberty, know how hard

a thing it is to use aright. And when I see them in England wondering at the dissensions in this way, methinks I see two prisoners, being themselves fast chained and manacled together by feet and hands, wondering to see that other men, at liberty, walk not closer together than they do. Their thraldom makes them unequal censurers of the abuse of our liberty. How many thousands are there, whose very hearts are fretted with the chains of their spiritual bondage! Yea, how many several factions of ministers are there, whose differences, if by servile fear they were not nipped in the bud, would bring forth no small both dissensions and divisions; as at this day woeful experience teacheth in the reformed churches, whose dissensions do infinitely exceed all that ever have been amongst us! As ignorance begot, so tyranny maintained the greatest peace and unity when popish iniquity most prevailed." [1]

A way of looking at things which is not out of date even yet!

[1] Works, Vol. III., Preface to Religious Communion, pp. 99–100.

THE QUESTION OF THE ELDERSHIP AT AMSTERDAM AND LEYDEN.

THE QUESTION OF THE ELDERSHIP AT AMSTERDAM AND LEYDEN.

THE Amsterdam Church—humanly speaking—was built on Barrow. In the main it faithfully accepted and practised his views. Its leaders quoted him largely, and always with the deference due to an authoritative teacher. When, for example, Henry Jacob tried[1] to make a point by adducing Barrow (and also Penry) as more charitable than Johnson in his judgment of the English Church, the latter simply declares that Jacob is either ignorant or disingenuous. For Johnson's principle is that the maintenance and teaching of some " excellent truths " is not enough to make members of the English Church true Christians so long as they hold and teach them in a false church estate. This was Barrow's principle.[2] " He testified unto death and sealed with his blood that you all stand in anti-Christian estate "; so too did " Penry in the same year."

It might, indeed, easily be shown that for some years the Amsterdam Church heard little or nothing from their pastor and teacher which Barrow would have repudiated. A clear proof of this is furnished by their Articles and Confessions of Faith, first published in 1596. In 1604, the date of their Apology, the case remained the same—though a certain modification of opinion with regard to the Lord's Prayer is noticeable.[3]

As time went on, however, Johnson drew off from his former strict adherence to Barrow and from some of his own earlier positions.

A list of his aberrations, or, as they are called,

---

[1] A Defence of the Churches and Ministry of England (1599).
[2] Johnson's " Answer," pp. 177-8.
[3] See Article nine, " that the Lord's Prayer and the liturgy of His own Testament might be used, but no other."

" articles of his creed forsaken by Mr. Johnson," is given
by Ainsworth.[1]

The standard to which the latter refers is the Confession of
Faith, compared with " Our Apology."

From this it appears that Johnson now[2] denies that (1)
" Every church or congregation hath power to elect and ordain
their own ministry, and upon desert again to depose—yea, and
excommunicate them "; or (2) " that the power to receive in or
cut off any member is given to the whole body together of
every Christian congregation "; or (3) " that the hierarchy of
archbishops, lord bishops, priests, &c., are a strange and anti-
Christian ministry and officers—not instituted by Christ's Testament nor placed in or over His Church "; or (4) that the
" ecclesiastical assemblies " of the English Church " cannot be
esteemed true visible churches "; or (5) that " all such as have
received any of those false offices (of lord bishops, priests, &c.)
are to give over and leave them " when they come "to our
faith and Church "; or (6) that a church consists of those who
" willingly join together in Christian communion and orderly
covenant "; or (7) " that a people so joined together may proceed to choose and ordain their officers "; or (8) that the
Popish Church being a false Church, its sacraments are likewise false, and so it is necessary for those who leave it to be
rebaptized. We might hence be inclined to say that Johnson
has " recanted " altogether. But this would be hasty. Johnson himself still claimed to be a consistent Separatist. On the
four cardinal points of worship, ministry, discipline, and
membership, he still maintained that the English Church was
anti-Christian. He did so to the end, as his last book, a
" Christian Plea," [3] clearly proves. He has, however, become
decidedly more Presbyterian. It was Presbyterian to say
[according to (1) and (7)] that " a congregation without

---

[1] In his " Animadversion," quoted
(in full) by Lawne, " Profane Schism,"
pp. 78-9, from a *private* document, so
Ainsworth complains.

[2] 1610.

[3] 1617. It is well to note that the
" Plea " therefore marks no sudden or
even quite recent change.

ministers cannot elect and ordain officers "; or, that one previously ordained by a bishop need not be re-ordained [the ground of (5) and (3)]; or, that the Romish baptism was a true sacrament, and so the Romish Church, in this respect, as well as its daughter the English Church, was not " apostate " [which accounts for (4) and (8)]; or that baptism, rather than conversion and voluntary covenant, was a sufficient condition of church fellowship [which explains (6)]. His change, however, in the direction of Presbyterianism is most marked in the matter of the eldership.

Curiously enough, Johnson himself was unconscious, or professed to be unconscious, of change. But Ainsworth could refer him to his own words in a former writing,[1] viz. :—

"A company of faithful people (though considered apart by themselves they be private men, yet) being gathered together in the name of Christ and joined together in fellowship of His Gospel, they are a public body, a church, a city and kingdom, and that of Jesus Christ, who is present among them to guide, bless, and confirm what they do on earth in His name and by His power. So that like as in a city the citizens—considered apart are private members—yet jointly together are the corporation and public body of that town: so is it also in the Church of Christ, whether it consist of more or of fewer, yea, though they be but two or three, so as they be joined together in the communion of the Gospel, and gathered together in the name of Jesus Christ, as before is said." Ainsworth quotes this in answer to what he considers the amazing statement that a Church cannot *be* without its officers, and that it is impossible to find in Scripture any witness to the contrary. Truly, thinks Ainsworth, Johnson and his followers have " lost that which they (once) had found, and let them take heed lest for not keeping it God deprive them of finding it any more." [2]

[1] His commentary (1595) on Arthur Hildersham's " Treatise of the Ministry," pp. 63-4.

[2] His " Animadversion," pp. 47-8.

Ainsworth's own view of what he deems the right "ancient" faith is this:—[1] "Men come unto Christ by belief; are joined unto Him and one to another by mutual covenant. The ministers of Christ are as *builders* of the House—by preaching the Gospel (and) laying first the foundation, Christ. Then upon Him, Christian people (are) God's building. But if (as often cometh to pass) the builders do refuse, yet the Lord *without them* putteth Christ for Head of the corner, and causeth the faithful to come unto Him, and maketh them His spiritual House to dwell in them, whose House they continue to be, *not (by) having officers alway among them,* but *by holding* fast their confidence and rejoicing of hope unto the end." Does he, then, depreciate the officers or elders? By no means. "The elders," he says,[2] "by directing the Church in the right way are as eyes to the body; by administering the sacraments and censures they are as hands; when they are sent on the Church's messages they are as feet; when they reprove sins they are as the mouth; when they are reproved for their sins they should be as ears; and so other Christians in their places and employments. And as God hath bestowed His graces upon any, so is He to be regarded of all without respect of persons. Neither should the elders be minded like Achitophel, and take it ill if at any time their counsel be not followed."

We have not space to state Johnson's position in detail. Suffice it to say that he took his stand, with the Presbyterians generally, on Matthew *xviii. 17.* As Ainsworth says: "For the Church's power now in controversy *only* Matthew xviii. 17 is dealt with by our opponents." And we can judge of Johnson's divergence from the Separatist standpoint, as well as of that standpoint itself, by his list of "Divers errors, abuses, and erroneous courses that by divers (viz., Mr. Ainsworth, Mr. Robinson, Mr. Jacob, Mr. Smith) have been gathered, received, pleaded for, and urged earnestly" about this matter.[3]

---

[1] His "Animadversion," pp. 47-8.
[2] Ditto, p. 41.
[3] "A Christian Plea . . . touching the Reformed Churches with whom myself agree in the Faith of the Gospel, &c.," pp. 306-16.

He enumerates thirty-six, of which the most relevant to our purpose are these :—

2. That "an elder cannot with good conscience govern and perform his duty in a Church that is persuaded so to walk " —*i.e.*, persuaded that the Church of Matt. xviii. 17 may be understood of the eldership. (His conscience will suffer from the temptation to tyrannise ?)

5. That "the people are to have voices in excommunications, and in judging of causes and persons "—as in election ot their officers.

6. That "in a controversy the sentence is to go out according to the number of the voices of the greater part of the people, though all the elders and other brethren be against them."

7. That "the greater part is the Church" in such a case, "although they be in error and though all the elders and other brethren be against them herein."

8. That the members of any one Church are to have voices in every Church where they come, in the elections and excommunications, &c.

9. That the government is popular by the multitude.

10. That the elders may not admonish a sinner, though obstinate in transgression (whereupon to proceed against him), without first taking the people's consent so to admonish and proceed with him.

14. That the people now are answerable to the elders of Israel then. (This can only mean, as Barrow and Ainsworth said, that as the ultimate power lay once with the elders, now it lies with the people themselves.)

15. That cases of sin and controversy between man and man are to be heard and judged by the Church on the Lord's Day, and as a part of God's worship. . . .

16. That the Church's government is not aristocratical.

17. That the elders may not hear and determine the cases aforesaid unless the people be present, although the parties and

witnesses be there ready to have their matters heard and judged.

21. That the people are the rulers properly and the governors of the elders.

26. That the order of saints or saintship in the Church is an order superior unto and above the order of officers, or of bishopric or eldership.

27. That the order of saints is an order of kings (which is the highest order in the Church) sitting upon the throne of David for judgment.

28. That suspension is a corruption and device of man.

31. That no good writers use the word "ecclesia" for the congregation of elders.

35. That seeing the elders are not called "Archontes" (rulers) in all the New Testament, therefore they are not to rule the Church of God.

36. That if the elders be stewards only over the servants, and not lords over the wise (i.e., the Church), then is not the Church to obey or submit unto them.

"These and other like errors, false doctrines, and sinful courses have been conceived and urged (says Johnson) . . . not all by any one, but some by one, some by others, their tongues being exceedingly divided among themselves about these things. By which also may appear how needful it is to search out the meaning of this Scripture, and carefully observe it, still looking unto Israel and the right understanding thereof what we can. And this the more, considering that some[1] are so very peremptory and stiffly conceited in their opinions concerning these things as (that) they fear not to make schismatical divisions and notorious scandals thereabout, contrary to the doctrine which we have learned of the prophets and apostles. For which cause they are to be marked and avoided of all that love the truth and seek their conversion and amendment."

Meanwhile Ainsworth, on his side, looked upon Johnson

[1] A marginal note indicates "some" to mean "Mr. Ainsworth and his followers."

and his abettors as making "common cause with our adversaries" (Mr. Some, Mr. Gifford, Mr. Bernard). And would that he could "reduce them again into the right way"! For "their straying from it is a reproach to the world, a scandal to the weak, dangerous to their own soul, and to *me* most dolorous. And my soul shall weep in secret for them, remembering our former amity and concord in the truth."[1] One cannot but sympathise with Ainsworth. For the issue was not a slight one. It involved, and still involves, the very being of a Congregational Church.

While, however, anxiously guarding, Ainsworth is careful to limit, the power of the people. This is a point to be noted. Bernard had imputed it as an "error" to the "Brownists" that they say "the power of Christ—*i.e.*, authority to preach, to administer the sacraments, and to exercise the censures of the Church—belongeth to the whole Church, yea, to every one of them, and not to the principal members thereof." He calls this "the A B C of Brownism." Ainsworth thinks it may be put rather "in the cress-cross row of Bernardism."[2] For Bernard himself is "the first that I ever heard to utter such a position." But he has mistaken the matter. "Christ's ruling power, which the Papists say is in the Pope, we say not (as this man calumniateth us) that it is in the body of the congregation, . . . nor that it is in the prelates, . . . nor (as the Puritans) that it is in the presbytery, . . . but that it is in Christ Himself." "The Word of God," indeed, "is given to all and every member of the Church to read and exercise privately; but publicly—in the Church—there is a double use (of it) in prophesy and in office (as the apostle distinguisheth, Rom. xii. 6, 7). The *office* of teaching is laid upon some few,

---

[1] "Animadversion to Mr. Richard Clyfton's advertisement," 1613 — Preface.

[2] Ainsworth's "Counterpoyson," pp. 174-5. This consists of three parts, of which part ii. (153-200 pp.) is "a brief answer to Mr. Bernard's book intituled 'The Separatist Schisme'" —1608. Bernard's reply—"directed against Mr. Ainsworth, the Separatist, and Mr. Smyth, the se-Baptist"— drew forth John Robinson's largest work, "A Justification of Separation," 1610.

chosen and ordained thereunto. In this office may no man intrude, or usurp it, without a lawful calling."[1] "Teaching in the way of prophecy (1 Cor. xiv.) is absolutely unlawful for all women in the Church; but men, so many as have the gift and ability from God, may all prophesy one by one."[2] Again, "that authority to administer the sacraments should belong to every one of the Church we utterly deny. . . . In our confession[3] he could not but see (unless he winked) this plainly expressed: no sacraments to be administered until the pastor, or teachers, be chosen and ordained unto their office." So, once more, "that everyone hath authority to exercise the censures of the Church we also deny; but hold that every member hath authority to rebuke his brother for sin; and if he repent to forgive him; if not, to take witnesses; if yet he repent not, to tell it to the Church, which Church hath Christ's power to judge all within the Church, and cast out from among them all wicked men. Now that everyone hath not this power, nor yet any member or members apart, we have plainly signified in our confession." . . . "So then for popular government (which Mr. Bernard would traduce us by), we hold it not, we approve it not; for if the multitude govern, who shall be governed? Christian liberty (which all have, 1 Cor. vii. 23; Gal v. 1), is one thing, the reins of government (which some have, 1 Cor xii. 28), is another thing." In fine, the Church elects its officers and controls their conduct by its free vote; but, once elected, it acts through them, yielding at the same time to their judgment all due observance. But the mainspring of power for people and officers alike is in the living presence of Christ. This is exactly the teaching of Barrow.[4]

If Ainsworth reflects that teaching most clearly and

---

[1] See "Confession of Faith," Articles 19, 20, 21.
[2] "Confession," Article 34.
[3] „ „ 24.
[4] "Counterpoyson," p. 178. Ainsworth refers here to Barrow's "Discovery, &c." He mentions also Henry Jacob, one of Mr. Bernard's "fellow ministers," as writing "much more soundly" on this point.

fully, the man, perhaps, who comes next to him in this respect is Robinson. It does not fall within my scope to do so, else it were interesting to trace with what entire consent Robinson takes up and reaffirms Barrow's positions one after another. Even in tone he often echoes him. Like Barrow, he does not mince his words when there seems occasion for plain speaking. He cares nothing that he may be called a "railer and scoffer." Nay, he defends Barrow himself, on this score, with as much heartiness as does Ainsworth. When Mr. Bernard, full of pious horror, produces a list of Mr. Barrow's blasphemies,[1] Robinson passes the list in review, and justifies every item of it. Like Mr. Ainsworth, he "will not justify all the words of another man, nor yet mine own"; but like Mr. Smyth, "because he knew not by what particular motion of the Spirit Barrow was guided to write those phrases he dare not censure him." And is not the following quite in Barrow's manner?—"For your very divine exercises of prayer, preaching, sacraments, and singing of Psalms, howsoever they be good and holy in themselves or, at least, have much good in them, yet in respect of the unhallowed communion, forged ministry, and superstitious order wherein these and all other things with you are ministered and exercised, they are liable to the heaviest censure Mr. Barrow hath put upon them. And for the most forward preachers in the kingdom—considering their unsound and broken courses in denying *that* in deed and practice which in word and writing they profess to be the revealed will of God and inviolable Testament of Christ binding His Church for ever, yea, and practising the contrary in the face of the sun (hindering them that would, persecuting them that do, defending themselves unconscionably)—" they do deserve a sharper medicine than haply they are willing to endure."[2]

[1] Quoted in Robinson's Works, Vol. II., p. 90 ff.

[2] Quoted in Robinson's Works, Vol. II., p. 93.

Robinson, then, no less than Ainsworth was, if not a disciple, yet an admirer and adherent of Barrow. I cannot recall anything in which he differed from him down to the year 1610; and, least of all, did he differ from him or Ainsworth in his view of the eldership. Mr. Bernard in the "Separatists schism" laid down the Puritan exposition of Matthew xviii. 16—that the church there means the elders—with the utmost assurance; and Robinson in his reply (1610) felt the point to be so important that he dealt with it exhaustively under twelve heads. Robinson's work came into the hands of Johnson, and made him angry. Especially did he resent what Robinson emphasized as most important—namely, "that the order of officers in the Church is an order of servants, and the order of saints an order of kings," and that the latter, therefore, is superior to the former.[1] In his "Answer touching the Division" (1611) between him and Ainsworth—Johnson drew special attention to this as something new and monstrous. For, says he,[2] "whereas we had learned and professed that Christ was the only King and Lord of His Church, and had left unto it among men but a ministerial government, and that all the multitude of the members, the saints, ought to obey and submit to the eldership in every Church: *now* we have lately been taught, that the people as kings have power one over another, and that the saints, being kings, are superior to their officers, because the order of kings is the highest order in the Church, &c." Robinson's reply—elicited, and afterwards published, by Ainsworth[3]—was to the effect, briefly, that Johnson had shifted the point, and perverted his meaning. The question was "about the *power*," not "about the *government* and *guidance* of the Church in the use of this power." The latter Robinson acknowledges is "peculiar to the officers," but the former is "common to all." The distinction is a very

[1] Works, Vol. II., p. 228 ff.
[2] Page 27.
[3] In his "Animadversion, &c.," pp. 111-117.

important one—is, indeed, "the main ground of our controversy." It may be illustrated, for example, from the procedure of the "civil government of our own land." "When a malefactor comes to be arraigned at the assizes or sessions he is to be tried by his country . . . which they call the jury, whose power and sentence is of such force as that the Lord Chief Justice himself, and all the Bench with him, cannot proceed against it, either for the quitting or condemning of the person; and yet the Bench governeth the whole action, and the jury is by them, according to law, to be governed." The Bench here stands for the elders, the jury for the Church. And, adds Robinson, "I wish the elders with whom we have to do would allow the body of the Church the like liberty at their sitting, as they call it, that is, at their spiritual sessions; or, rather, that they would better consider that they are as ministers to stand and serve, and not as lords to sit and judge." Further, he would have it understood that nowhere does he affirm—as Johnson "chargeth" him—"that the people are kings, or as kings, *one over another.*" What he has said is that "the saints are not kings for themselves alone, but for their brethren also; as they are not priests only for themselves, but for their brethren . . . much less" are they kings "over the officers, for government, in the external policy of the Church." "The plain and simple truth, then," is "that we call the saints kings" merely "as they are partakers of Christ's kingly anointing, by His Spirit, common to the head and the members, and so kings by participation, and endowed with kingly power for the conquering and subduing of the power of sin and Satan, not only in themselves, but in their brethren also, by the sword of the Spirit, the Word of God, which they are to minister unto them, as all other graces in their order."

This was the last interference on Robinson's part in the controversy. It was a most reluctant interference. But he

could not well help himself.[1]   At an early stage in the
" uncomfortable business " some thirty members of the
Amsterdam Church who differed from Johnson wrote re-
questing help from the Church at Leyden. They gave as
a reason that " Mr. Ainsworth was so sparing in opposing
Mr. Johnson's new doctrine (though always disliking it)
. . ." and " so loath to come to any professed and public
opposition with him," partly because " he rather hoped to
pacify " him " by moderation "; partly, too, because he feared
" to give any encouragement to the too violent oppositions
of some " on his own side. The help requested was that
the Leyden Church should send delegates to consider the
matter and give counsel. This they were not unwilling to
do, but first thought it well that the whole Church at Amsterdam should know the substance of what had been written to
them, and that the whole Church should invite them. No,
said the Church, ' we do not approve your coming though we
may permit it, and meanwhile we wish to see an exact copy of
the letter you have received from the thirty.' There was a
phrase, however, in the letter—Judges v. 23[2]—" which, applied
as it was, might · give offence."   So an exact copy was refused
until—refusal only leading to " oft and earnest " demands—it
seemed better " for their importunity " and for the ends in
view to grant it. In the end delegates came[3]—permitted " as
men use to permit that which is evil and which, indeed, they
could not hinder." After hearing the case, delivering their
Church's message, and reproving (" with some vehemency ")
what they judged evil on both sides, but specially on the side
of those " with whom we agreed in the things " controverted, the
result reached was (" on the motion of Mr. Johnson ") that such
members as could not walk with them " in peace of conscience—

[1] See " The Testimony of the
Elders of the Church at Leyden."
Robinson's Works, Vol. III., pp. 470-5,
quoted also by Ainsworth in his
" Animadversion," pp. 133-6.
[2] " Curse ye Meroz . . . because

they came not to the help of the
Lord, to the help of the Lord against
the mighty."
[3] Mr. Robinson being the chief of
the messengers sent. — Bradford's
Dialogue, p. 416.

there lying no other cause against them "—should be freely demitted (or transferred) to the Leyden Church, and *vice versa*. This motion, it would seem, embodied the message of the Leyden Church. The members of the Amsterdam Church "received it with general assent "; on the return of its delegates the Leyden Church ratified it; and, news of this being sent to Amsterdam, the Church there confirmed it "a second time." Thus Robinson hoped that a way of peace, if not an ideal way, had been found.

But it soon turned out otherwise. The Amsterdam Church announced a change of mind, and that a new motion had come to the front, a motion "to permit of a double practice among us, that those that are minded either way should keep a like course together, as we would do if we were asunder, according as the persons shall be that have the causes."[1] The Leyden Church resented such action as a breach of the agreement, "which we did and do repute as full and absolute." And as for the new motion, "we do not see how it can stand either with our peace or itself; but that it will not only nourish, but even necessarily beget, endless contentions when men diversely minded shall have business in the Church." There is, however, a middle way which might be held, "namely, that the matter of offence might first be brought for order, preparation, and prevention of unnecessary trouble unto the elders, as the Church governors . . . ; and after, if things be not there ended, to the Church of elders and brethren, there to be judged on some ordinary known day ordinarily, the admonition being carried according to the alteration practised and agreed upon by all parts. . . ."[2] It is interesting to find that this was the course actually taken at Leyden. For— Robinson and Brewster say—" so far as we remember, there never came complaint of sin to the Church since we were officers

---

[1] Letter of Church at Amsterdam to Leyden, Nov. 5, 1610.

[2] Letter of Church at Leyden to Amsterdam, Nov. 14, 1610.—Robinson's Works, Vol. III., pp. 467-8.

but we took knowledge of it before, either by mutual consent on both sides, or, at least, by the party accused."[1] But in so doing they appear to have acted on their own discretion. "We do not bind our brethren." If the Church objected they would not persist, and as a matter of fact when it came up before the "brethren" (doubtless at Robinson and Brewster's instance) as a middle and reasonable way which might be suggested to the Amsterdam Church, and formally adopted by themselves, there was some demur. "It is like," says their letter, "we for our parts shall *not* so practise in this particular." A flash of light surely on the jealous care with which the members generally guarded their "rights" even against leaders so trusted and loved as Brewster and Robinson. The suggestion came to nothing. In their reply the Amsterdam Church say, "the brethren differing from us (*i.e.*, Ainsworth's party) . . . will not yield to that middle course propounded in your letter." Nor will they "admit of" the proposed "double practice." In fact, they suspected (with good reason) that compliance would risk a surrender of the principle whose purity they felt bound to maintain.[2]

Robinson said no more. He lost all hope of doing good. His sympathies went entirely with Ainsworth—especially when the Johnsonians spoke of ceasing from "spiritual communion with him and his"—*i.e.*, of excommunication; spoke also of objecting to any of them who might be "demitted" to the Leyden Church being allowed to return and settle beside their former brethren even in the same city. He lamented the want of charity more than he deplored the absence of sound judgment on Johnson's part. For it made a return to kindly relations almost impossible: as he had "put them in mind," a "peaceable parting" leaves the door open to reunion, but "extreme straitness" now may bring abiding

Robinson's Works, pp. 473-4.   [1] Works, Vol. III., pp. 469. The "Animadversion," pp. 126-128.

alienation, besides making "themselves, yea, and us all, a byword to the whole world."

Robinson sought and pursued peace more and more as the years went by. He never came to question whether he had done right to separate from the Church of England. His "just and necessary apology, &c.," published so late as 1619, is proof enough of that; for here all the main points of his earlier plea are distinctly restated and upheld. But he grew weary of negation, of contending about the things he did *not* believe. He longed to discover points of communion rather than points of repulsion. He would fain draw far away from those who "make their differences as great, and the adverse opinion or practice as odious as they can, thereby to further their desired victory over them, and to harden their side against them." He had known too many of this type in Amsterdam. He felt, on the other hand, an increasing joy in being among those who "seek how and where they may find any lawful door of entry into accord and agreement with others."

He was always in favour of private communion with godly members of the Church of England, herein differing from Ainsworth. One of his correspondents, the Puritan Dr. Ames,[1] "learned Amesius," charged him with the contrary, and he admits that he had not always been consistent. He tells us that all the while he abode in England he himself and the people with him—generally—understood their separation to be only "from communion in the public worship, and administrations there," and "in this persuasion" never gave up "private communion."[2] He gave it up for a time afterwards, "finding them of other Churches with whom he was most nearly joined otherwise

---

[1] See Letters in Robinson's Works, Vol. III., pp. 85-89.

[2] *i.e.*, "Private prayer, thanksgiving, and singing of psalms, profession of faith, and confession of sins, reading or opening the Scriptures, and hearing them so read or opened, either in a family or elsewhere, without any Church power or ministry coming between."—Works III., p. 104.

minded for the most part. He gave it up through his vehement desire of peace, and weakness withal." He went so far even as to persuade himself, and argue against it. But he was therein "far from that certainty of persuasion which he had and has of the *common* grounds of the separation." Hence it came to pass that three years after Dr. Ames's letter—which may very likely have occasioned him more earnest thought than ever on the subject—we find him with mind and heart, where his heart has always been, on the side of charity. He is convinced, and says so, "that we who profess a separation from the English national, provincial, diocesan, and parochial Church and Churches, in the whole formal state and order thereof, may, notwithstanding, lawfully communicate in private prayer, and other the like holy exercises (not performed in their Church communion nor by their Church power and ministry), with the godly amongst them, though remaining, of infirmity, members of the same Church, or Churches, except some other extraordinary bar come in the way between them and us."[1] He is sure, moreover, that in favouring such communion neither does he "oppose" any "article of our confession," nor does he act contrary to the spirit of Barrow, and others. Thus "Mr. H. Barrow in the letter written a little before his death . . . to an honourable lady yet living, as he acknowledgeth her in her own person to have been educated and exercised in the faith and fear of God, so professeth he further, that he gladly embraceth and believeth the common faith received and professed in the land as good and sound; that he had reverend estimation of sundry, and good hope of many hundred thousands in the land, though he utterly disliked the present constitution of the Church." To the like effect is the "testimony" of the authors of the "Apology"; and so Penry in the "Confession" sent forth "a little before his execution." This is not to say, of course, that these leaders

---

[1] Works, Vol. III., p. 105.

of the separation did what Robinson commends, but only that their words may be taken to warrant it.[1] For, though " outward ordinances " are much, Christian character is more; and we must not so " please ourselves in " the former as to suppose that " in them piety and religion " do " chiefly consist." " The grace of faith in Christ, and the fear of God, the continual renewing of our repentance, with love, mercy, humility, together with fervent prayer and hearty thanksgiving unto God, for His unspeakable goodness, are the things wherein especially we must serve God." " And if God will be known, and honoured in all His creatures, yea, even, in the silliest worm that crawleth upon the earth, how much more in the holy graces of His Spirit vouchsafed to His elect, notwithstanding their failings of infirmity, especially in outward ordinances." We must beware, then, of over-valuing these, " howsoever great in themselves "—a danger to which we are the more liable, " considering our persecutions and sufferings for them." [2]

Robinson went another step under the lead of charity when he declared for the " lawfulness of hearing ministers of the Church of England." Paget in 1618 says[3] that he had "tolerated" his fellow-elder, Mr. Brewster, "for this long time" in that practice. His people agreed with him; for it had ever been his way to repress in them, so far as he could, "all sour zeal against, and peremptory rejection of, such as whose holy graces challenged better use and respect from all Christians."[4] When, therefore, the Church in London wrote to ask if they had " done well in retaining " a young woman whom some fierce spirits would have excommunicated because she had heard sermons in a parish church, although she had done so " without neglect of the Church whereof she was a member,"

---

[1] Barrow, Penry, Johnson, and Ainsworth certainly did not mean to sanction "private communion," even with "saints," so long as they remained in a false Church.

[2] Works, Vol. III., pp. 109, 110.
[3] Arrow Against the Separation of the Brownists, p. 28.
[4] Works, Vol. III., p. 353.

and had at once ceased to do so when forbidden, Robinson carried his whole Church with him in commending their action.[1]

The same letter of inquiry had been received previously by the Amsterdam Church—the result being lively "contentions." In fact that Church was concerned, or about to be concerned, with a similar case of its own. Someone, once a member of the London Church, was transferred first to Leyden, and then from there to Amsterdam. While in London the preaching of a parish minister had occasionally attracted him. This becoming known at Amsterdam, immediately led to trouble. What took place may be gathered from Robinson's letter addressed to the Amsterdam Church six months later than the one to the London Church.[2] The offender was cited before the Church and complaint made against him by the elders. They brought forward no witnesses—though both law and Gospel required the presence of two or three. They proceeded with him rather "by questions and interrogatories, tending to his prejudice." Finally, they cast him out. A minority, however, openly took his side and denounced so "inordinate and lawless" a course, with the result that they also were cast out. Efforts were made to obtain a reversal of the sentence, but were withstood on the ground that as "civil judgments once passed by the judge" are final, so should this be. The majority boasted, in a letter to the Leyden Church, that "they were able to make good their proceedings before God and men."

But Robinson was deeply shocked and grieved. He could not find a word to say for them. He lamented especially their ruthless abuse of the Church's last solemn instrument of discipline. In comparing excommunication with the sentence of a civil judge, they have forgotten, he said, "how grievous it was unto the body of you,

[1] Works, Vol. III., p. 382.   [2] September 18, 1624. Works, Vol. III., pp. 389-93.

and dangerous in itself, when some of place among you, a few years since, would pattern the government of the Church *now* by the government of the elders of Israel "; they have forgotten that " in spiritual judgments there is a further thing which the magistrate meddles not with—the repentance of the censured to follow in time, by God's blessing." For " the end of excommunication is not that the person might be excommunicated, but that repentance might follow." And surely in the present case, " considering the ground and carriage of the thing, the number of the persons opposite, and . . . the interest of all other churches in the business "— they might, at least, have been willing to revise their decision. But they are a people who reject all advice " in confidence " of their " own unerring judgment "; " since the death " of their " wise and modest governors " they have " laden the ordinances of God and the professors of the same " with " scandal and opprobry " in the eyes of all. In this disgrace, the Leyden Church has shared—has, in fact, as the Church " nearliest united unto " them shared in it very largely. But for the last time ! Henceforth Robinson and his people will cease to trouble them ; they will attempt no further persuasion of those " whose ears prejudice hath stopped "; they will merely " bewail their state," " which is indeed to be bewailed."

Robinson died in 1625, but while still full of the distress caused by this sad story, he penned the Treatise—"found in his study after his decease "—on " the Lawfulness of Hearing of the ministers in the Church of England." He thinks of three sorts of " opposites " who may read it. First are those " who truly desire and carefully endeavour to have their whole course, both in religion and otherwise, framed by the holy and right seal of the Word of God "; next are those " whose tender and scrupulous conscience makes them fearful and jealous of everything which hath in it the least appearance or show of evil, lest coming too near it they be defiled by it one way or other." Both these he hopes to persuade, but not the third. For this sort consists of

those whom he has " found carried with so excessive admiration of some former guides in their course as they think it half
heresy to call into question any of their determinations or
practices," and of those who . . . " think to cover and
palliate their own both grosser and more proper and personal
corruptions under a furious march not only against the failings,
but the persons also failing—of infirmity—in matters of church
order and ordinances."

The reference is obvious, and may partly explain (together
with the avowed reason that " some, though not many,"
even of the author's own Church, were " contrary-minded
to his judgment ") why the finders of the Treatise held it
back for nine years.   When, however, the same root of
bitterness which had poisoned the Amsterdam Church sprang
up in Leyden—" four or five " of its members rending the
Church because the rest would not consent to expel " two "
brethren who " upon some occasion heard some of the
ministers in England preach—it was deemed " high time " for
the Treatise to be published.[1]   And surely such " unused
example from the grave " must have been effectual for its
purpose !   His beloved people, to so many of whom the memory
of his life and words was a sweet and sacred possession, cannot
have refused to hear the voice which sounded from " the low,
last verge of life " and called them to remember that the " one
mystical body of Christ scattered far and wide throughout the
world " is more deeply united in " the same faith, hope, spirit,
baptism, and Lord " than it is divided by differences of " order
and ordinance " ; and that " He who would have us receive the
weak in faith, whom God hath received, would not have us
refuse the fellowship of Churches in that which is good for any
weakness in them of one sort or other."

[1] 1634.   Works, Vol. III., pp. 345-378.

Professor Arber and the Amsterdam Church.

PROFESSOR ARBER AND THE AMSTERDAM CHURCH.

Mr. Arber is a diligent man and a skilful editor. He has edited "20,000 pages of letterpress," and has done so generally with a sure eye to the points most essential or picturesque. I am only one of many students who feel grateful to him for much valuable assistance in threading the maze of our earlier and less known writers. This book,[1] however, shows that he has attempted too much. He would have his work accepted as "accurate" and "adequate;" as "impartial yet sympathetic;"[2] as original, to some extent; as explosive of "myths;" and as "a cool-headed rectification of opinions."[3] It is a large claim, and one's instant desire is to find it well founded. It would be so delightful to possess a volume with "nothing" in it which one will be "hereafter compelled to unlearn," and to "feel sure that, in respect to all its contents," one "is standing on the solid rock of truth."[4] But, alas! infallible books are very rare, and Mr. Arber's is not one of them. The very preface gives the reader pause, if he happens to have something more than a "general" knowledge of the subject. On page 8, for example, there is a list of "not a few notable facts" which will be found "in this volume." Perhaps the author does not mean to suggest that these facts are new, in the sense that he is the first to discover them. But if he does he is much deceived. Some of his facts do, indeed, turn out to be discoveries of his own—baseless enough as the

---

[1] Story of the Pilgrim Fathers : as Told by Themselves, Their Friends, and Their Enemies. 1897.

[2] Preface, p. 1.
[3] Preface, p. 8.
[4] Preface, p. 2.

sequel will show. As to the rest, "the first three are among the commonplaces of history; the payments to William Brewster as post on the great North road, and the entries in Zachary Clifton's Bible were published by Mr. Hunter in his 'Collections' as far back as 1854; the identification of John Smith, the se-Baptist, with John Smith, of Lincoln, was made many years ago by Professor Scheffer, of Amsterdam," while "the story of the Pilgrim Press at Leyden, and of the hunt after Brewster and Brewer, was given in fullest detail in Sir Dudley Carleton's Letters (1615-1620), and in the State Papers Dom. James I., vol. cx., 1619." These are the words of Dr. John Brown,[1] of Bedford, of whose existence Mr. Arber does not seem to be aware—to his own loss. To me, however, the first arresting sentence of the Preface [2] was this: "Especially must Governor Bradford's good-natured and optimistic estimates of the leaders of the English separation in Holland—Johnson, Clyfton, and Smyth—be considered as incomplete and misleading for reasons which will be found later on in this book." Turning to these reasons with great expectation, they seemed at first sight rather overwhelming, though even then one felt the absence of that "tabula rasa"[3] state of mind of which Mr. Arber makes his boast. But when these reasons were examined, with the authorities on which they rest, their weight began to lessen and ere long to "approach the point of zero." In fact, just here where the author is most confident that he has restored to us a true, however disenchanting, picture, has he succeeded in producing what I do not hesitate to call a caricature. In other words, it is a picture which has a certain resemblance to the truth, but is hardly less misleading than if it were utterly unlike. Persons who read his "Story" will gather an idea

---

[1] In a private letter to the writer. Dr. Brown's book on the Pilgrim Fathers was out eighteen months before Mr. Arber's, and is just that "adequate" "account, scientifically written but popular in form," which Mr. Arber says "does not exist."

[2] Preface, p. 3.

[3] Preface, p. 5.

of the earliest Congregational church about as near the truth as one might get of the early Christians from a perusal of Celsus. It is not that the author consciously distorts the facts. But there are facts which he misses; there are facts which he fails to apprehend; there are facts which he exaggerates; there is, above all, a lack of insight and imagination. Hence the effect of the narrative is still further to darken and discolour what was none too clear as it stood. Such, at least, is my conclusion. How far it is correct remains to be seen.

Meanwhile, before entering on this, the main purpose of the chapter, there are some other matters which call for a word of notice.

They occur mostly in the Introduction, and may serve as a preliminary test of Mr. Arber's competency for the task he has undertaken.

Thus : (1) More than once Mr. Arber mentions the " Holy Discipline." It is called a "craze," [1] and the date of its birth is given as November 20, 1572, when the first English Presbytery met at Wandsworth, in Surrey. It insisted, we are told, on the permanent necessity for the Church of "pastors, doctors or teachers, ruling elders, prophets, deacons, and widows or helpers, or deaconesses." [2] So far good. But Mr. Arber is aware that equally necessary to the discipline were [3]" Presbytery, Classis, Synod, General Assembly, and Moderator."

It was a scheme of government applying not merely to each particular church, but to all the churches collectively— a scheme by which " independent " action was systematically controlled. The distinction of a Congregational church was that it rejected such control. It might adopt the government by pastors, teachers, elders, deacons, and widows, but it would have nothing to do with the external rule of Presbyteries, Synods, and Assemblies. In this way it became not "a kind of exaggerated Presbyterianism," [4] but its mutilation. Johnson, for example, was a believer in the Holy Discipline

[1] Introduction, p. 25.   [2] Page 27.   [3] Page 28.   [4] Page 27.

19

until he read one of John Greenwood's books. This converted him to Independency. His Church, too, was independent, acknowledging no earthly authority higher than its own will. A follower of Cartwright or Travers would have said that here lay a chief cause of its troubles. But Mr. Arber ignores this distinction. He speaks of Whitgift being "fully determined to stamp out " " Separatism *or* the Holy Discipline." [1] He describes Johnson's church as [2] " the most notable English Christian community on the Continent, that was *completely* [italics his own] organised on the lines of the " Holy Discipine." His first comment on his story of that Church is : " Here, then, the ' Holy Discipline ' in actual practice utterly broke down." [3] Thus he has fallen into the vulgar error of confounding Presbyterian and Separatist.

(2) He says the Holy Discipline was [4] " so pivoted upon the eldership that if an elder went wrong . . . the system had no remedy." " Who was to watch the watchers ? " The answer is that the " Holy Discipline " might be, and was, " pivoted upon the eldership "; but not a Congregational church—not even the Amsterdam Church, which he has in mind. The remedy lay in its own hands. Johnson and Studley *tried* to make the eldership the pivot ; and in doing so, split the Church. For, as Ainsworth said—and Johnson also at one time—the very life of the Church was bound up with the contention that the " true matter of a church "—to quote John Smyth's words—are " the people."

(3) Again, one cannot but wonder at the following. Says Mr. Arber : " The question that any practical man of the world would put was, How could it (*i.e.*, Holy Discipline) possibly be financed ? Each isolated, voluntary association, fluctuating from month to month in numbers, was to pay three officers— the pastor, the teacher, and the ruling elder ; all of whom, being family men, must have enough to keep them and their families in decent respectability." [5] If this is meant to express the

[1] Page 8.   [2] Page 102.   [3] Page 120.   [4] Page 29.   [5] Page 129.

"theory" of a Separatist church it is absurd. If it is meant to describe the practice of the Amsterdam or Leyden Churches Mr. Arber should produce his evidence. There were, for example, in 1597, three ruling elders in the "ancient church" (later on there were four). Were these, with "their families," dependent on the church for maintenance? Or, if Mr. Arber, when he speaks of "the ruling elder," refers to *one* of them only, who was it? As to the Leyden Church, Robinson (like Johnson and Ainsworth) may have lived by the voluntary offerings of the people, but the only "elder" was Brewster, and did he do the same? Governor Bradford's words, quoted[1] by Mr. Arber himself, are decisive to the contrary. "After he (Brewster) came into Holland he suffered much hardship; after he had spent the most of his means, having a great charge and many children; and, in regard of his former breeding and course of life, not so fit for many employments as others were, especially such as were toilsome and laborious. But yet he ever bore his condition with much cheerfulness and contentation.

"Towards the latter part of those twelve years (1608-20) spent in Holland his outward condition was mended, and he lived well and plentifully. For he fell into a way, by reason he had the Latin tongue, to teach many students who had a desire to learn the English tongue, to teach them English. . . . And many gentlemen, both Danes and Germans, resorted to him, as they had time from other studies; some of them being great men's sons. He also had means to set up printing by the help of some friends; and so had employment enough." So writes Bradford, not even hinting that in thus working for his own support Brewster assumed a burden which rightly belonged to the Church.[2] We know, indeed, that the Separatist

---

[1] Pages 191-2.
[2] *Cf.* (1) "Pastors or leading elders . . . as being chiefly to give themselves to studying, teaching, and the spiritual care of the flock, are therefore to be maintained." (2) Mere ruling elders . . . being not to give themselves to study or teaching . . . have no need of maintenance."—*Prince*, describing the theory and practice of the Separatist Churches, quoted by Young, "Chronicles," p. 455 (Note).

leaders laid great stress on the duty of giving; and Johnson
seems to have done so to excess.   Thus the slanderous Lawne
reports that Johnson taught that " every man who brings not
up one-tenth of that which he getteth by his labour for
maintenance of the Church is a thief." [1]   And Johnson himself
says in his last book, that " it is the duty of all churches and
of the members thereof, every one according to his ability, to
give maintenance unto their ministers of and (as there is
occasion) to the elders also that rule the Church. [2]   But, besides
the fact that the duty of maintaining the elders is limited by
the words—" as there is occasion," i.e., when they are not able
to maintain themselves—there is nothing to show that this was
not one of Johnson's later private " heresies "—as what he goes
on to say, about the obligation of kings and magistrates to aid
in the maintenance of ministers and churches, certainly was.

3. Further evidence that Mr. Arber is not quite at home
in his subject is given by statements like the following :—" The
ancient exiled Church and the Gainsborough Church "—though
" constantly called Brownists "—" had little or nothing in
common with Browne " : [3] the fact being that they had nearly
everything, of real moment, in common with Browne.

Again, Johnson in holding " that the word church " in
Matt. xviii. 17 " meant only the eldership " was " maintaining
what is known as the Barrowist view of ecclesiastical polity,
from Henry Barrow." Ainsworth, on the other hand, " held
that it meant all the members of the society; maintaining what
is known as the Brownist view of ecclesiastical polity, from
Robert Browne " ; [4] the fact being that Browne's view was
likewise Barrow's, and passed from Barrow to Ainsworth,
who expressly claimed to be keeping in the " old way," while
Johnson's was the common Presbyterian view.

Then (5) lastly, Mr. Arber prints [5] the "seven articles," " in

[1] Profane Schism, p. 13.
[2] A Christian Plea, &c., p. 316.
[3] Page 38.
[4] Page 31.
[5] Pages 280-282.

which," as he truly says, "the Pilgrim Fathers strove, in order to conciliate the King and his Government, to minimise to the uttermost their differences from the Church of England as it then existed." They were subscribed by Robinson and Brewster, and sent to the Privy Council of England, whence they found their way to the Public Record Office, London. It was not a public, but essentially a private document; not "an exposition of faith," but "rather conditions of agreement." Hence, there was no occasion, one would think, to let it pass into the hands of outsiders; and one is surprised to read what Mr. Arber says, that "the above extremely able paper gave rise to a short controversy in print at the time." But the truth is, Mr. Arber has fallen into a curious and even *inexcusable* mistake. His account is, that the Rev. Thomas Drakes, Vicar of Harwich and Dovercourt, who died before March 18, 1618, very soon after the presentation of the above seven articles, published a reply to them, entitled, "Ten Counter Demands propounded to the Separatists against their Seven Demands," which work is now apparently totally lost. To it—adds Mr. Arber—appeared from the Pilgrim Press at Leyden the following reply :—" William Euring, an answer to the Ten Counter Demands propounded by T. Drakes, preacher of the Word at H. and D., in the county of Essex. Printed in the year 1619." It seems a suspicious circumstance that Drakes, in the title to his book, should call the seven *Articles* seven *Demands ;* the spirit of "demand" is so completely absent from them. This alone might have suggested to Mr. Arber that he was possibly on a wrong tack; and a due examination of Euring's "Answer" would have convinced him that he was. We say a "due examination" because, as he refers to the only known copy—the one in Dr. Williams's Library—it may be assumed that this has passed through his hands, and yet he has overlooked the fact that the "seven demands" against which Drakes propounded his "ten" *are given word for word in the Preface, and have absolutely no connection with the seven*

Articles. In fact, they are a *summary* of the Separatist position under seven heads, issued "some good space since." Drakes says Éuring has seen them, no doubt; but he does not answer them. He "had rather ask than answer . . . (as what bungler cannot better strike than fence?); and so his meaning is to set these his "Ten counter-demands against their seven demands, that so they might knock heads together to see whose is hardest." It appears, then, that Mr. Arber cannot have read the *Preface* in which these words and the seven demands occur, not to speak of the book itself.

Mistakes of this kind scarcely prepare one to accept his guidance, when he undertakes to lift the veil from the church at Amsterdam.

1. Mr. Arber applies strong language to the Amsterdam Church, and still stronger to its pastor (Francis Johnson, 1562-1618).

It is a "scandalous" church—a "community" that "consisted of knaves and dupes,"[1]—its history is "one of the saddest chapters in the annals of Protestantism," "nothing but a tissue of folly, wrong-headedness, and violence; of hypocrisy, wrangling, and immorality: so that its members became quite odious to the inhabitants of Amsterdam."[2]

When Robinson led his people away to Leyden, he did so not only in pursuit of peace, but also of purity, for moral pollution was "rampant"[3]; and it was Robinson himself who called the Ancient Church a "rebellious rout."[4] As to its pastor, Governor Bradford's estimate of his character is "charitable," but "perfectly untrustworthy."[5] Bradford gives us the "general impression that Johnson was a saint," whereas Mr. Arber is able to give abundant proof that he was "a most remarkable sinner."[6] He had "some good points, but many more bad ones."[7] "He was an arrogant, wrong-

[1] Page 101.
[2] Page 102.
[3] Page 102.
[4] Page 123.
[5] Page 105.
[6] Page 105.
[7] Page 105.

headed, irascible man; an unnatural son, &c.: anything, in fact, but a Christian gentleman."[1] In the interval between the excommunication of his brother (1599) and that of his father (1602), he was "steadily going from bad to worse."[2] By October of the latter year "he was a dead Christian," an "utter disgrace to our sacred faith, and what he afterwards said, preached, or wrote is not deserving of serious attention, from a spiritual point of view."[3] He is, in short, by this time, "a thoroughly bad man."[4] White-washing is said to be a fashionable process just now. We have here a reversal of it, with a vengeance. And we can only call such language reckless, unless Mr. Arber has ground for it which is clear and strong. He thinks he has. He finds it in Christopher Lawne's books (1612-13), which he considers "worthy of an implicit belief."[5] Of these there were two. Both came out in London under the licence of the Rev. Doctor Nidd, a chaplain to the Archbishop of Canterbury (Abbot); the one in July, 1612, the other in May, 1613. The title of the first was:—

"The Prophane Schisme of the Brownists or Separatists; with the impietie, dissensions, lewd and abhominable vices of that impure sect:

Discovered by
{
Christopher Lawne,
John Fowler,
Clement Sanders,
Robert Bulward;
}

lately returned from the companie of Master Johnson, that wicked brother, into the bosom of the Church of England, their true mother. 1612. Psalm lxxxiii. 16; Rom. xvi. 17."

The authors complained that the book was "corruptly printed"—with additions, omissions and alterations: the probability being that it contained things too libellous even for the Archbishop's chaplain to let pass.

[1] Page 105.
[2] Page 110.
[3] Page 112.
[4] Page 110.
[5] Page 112.

The second bore the title :—

"Brownism turned the inside outward. Being a Parallel between the Profession and Practice of the Brownists' religion. By Christopher Lawne, lately returned from that wicked Separation. Matt. xxiii. 27 ; Gen. xlix. 6."

Mr. Arber says "this work adds no new facts."[1] Perhaps so ; but it shows up convincingly the spirit of the writer, as we shall see.

Is Christopher Lawne a trustworthy witness ? He claims to be. "I have not written anything . . . but that which I can of my own knowledge, with good conscience, affirm."[2] He is a penitent man, devoutly thankful for his escape from so foul a "ditch," and eager "to stretch out a hand of help and comfort to those that yet lie" therein, and "especially to stay and strengthen some weak Christians that are inclining and looking"[3] toward it.

But (a) one is bound to say that it took him a long time to repent. Writing in 1612, for example, he weeps tears of compassion over the fate of Johnson the elder, and shudders at the base ingratitude of his son—a son who "drew his whole company to consent and approve" of the father's excommunication—an excommunication "given out upon so slight a cause; yea, so unjust a cause, while the father sought peace between his children"; done, moreover, against "such a father as had been at so great cost in bringing up his son to learning; . . . who also with so much labour, cost, and grief had sued to sundry judges and nobles in England for releasing of that son." But this had taken place ten years before. Lawne had seen it; had been among those drawn "to consent and approve" of it; had raised no protest apparently and felt no distress. Had he done so, and withdrawn at once, it would have been possible to believe in his sincerity. But to plead an

[1] Page 118.
[2] Preface to his Brownism Turned Inside Outward.
[3] Preface to Profane Schism.

aroused conscience after so long a period of connivance is rather too much.

(b) The same may be said in another respect. White [1] accuses specifically seven or eight persons: "one Castle," Robert Bayly, J. Nicolas, Christopher Bowman, Thomas Cannady, Francis Johnson, Studley, and "their teacher," Ainsworth. Against Castle is placed a charge of "cozenage"; against Nicolas a charge of borrowing and not paying; against Bowman a charge of "purloining half that which the magistrates of Naarden had given them weekly"; against Ainsworth a charge of being "stained with hypocrisy . . . spotted again and again with apostasy . . . a means to bring in false doctrines"; against Johnson the charge of unfilial behaviour toward his father. Only in the case of Bayly, Cannady and Studley are the charges of a kind strictly immoral. As to Cannady, White adds a postscript, in which he mentions, "on hearsay," a further charge so palpably slanderous and absurd as to render the first charge much more than doubtful; and, indeed, to suggest malice for the root of all. Certainly nothing else can explain what is said of Ainsworth. And admitting that Bowman, the deacon, was guilty of theft, it is one thing to steal half of what was given weekly (according to White), and another to steal half of a sum which (according to Johnson) was given once, and once only.[2] It is the difference between habitual crime and the committal (possibly under strong temptation) of a single offence. But this is by the way. The point to notice is that Lawne, *so far as the period before his expulsion is concerned, cites no new cases.*[3] Castle, Bayly, Nicolas, Cannady are dropped. Francis Johnson is still the unnatural son. Ainsworth is

---

[1] A Discovery of Brownism (1605). John Robinson speaks of White as "an ungodly apostate, whose accusations have been answered one by one." —Justification of Separation, p. 78 (edition 1610).

[2] In 1595.

[3] Richard Clifton, in his "Advertisement" (1612) concerning Lawne's book, says, "*As it is like White's,* it may be thought less needful to refute it point by point." Johnson had answered White in 1606.

mentioned in terms of comparative respect. Poor Bowman is still pilloried, as Judas, for his one offence—a sure sign that he is otherwise without open fault. Studley, indeed, is made to appear worse than ever. But here, again, the more definite and reiterated charges are White's—couched in White's own words. What is the inference as regards Lawne himself? Plainly that the vexation of his righteous soul in 1612 was due not to things happening before his eyes, but mainly to things which had happened (if at all) previous to 1605—things which either he did not believe when White wrote them, or chose hypocritically to wink at.

(c) We are inclined, then, to suspect the genuineness of so belated a repentance, especially in view of a further fact, the fact mentioned by Ainsworth, that Lawne and company "*first* declined to these our opposites."[1] Consider what that means. The controversy about the eldership began late in 1609, and reached its climax late in 1610. There was, one would have thought, every reason why Lawne should side with Ainsworth. He professes to be indignant, for example, at Johnson's tyranny in his government of the Church, but the vindication of the Church's authority was the object for which the Ainsworthians were contending. Again, he professes to be overwhelmed with horror of Studley, his character, his conduct as elder, his being retained in office; but Studley and Johnson stood together, and by the simple expedient of leaving with Ainsworth he would have escaped both. In spite, however, of his professed detestation of the men and their methods, he stands by them, and remains with them for more than six months after the Ainsworthians have seceded.

Then, at length, we hear of his conferring about his "doubts" with Master Paget, minister of the English (Episcopal) Church, sworn foe of the "Brownists."

Then we get sight (on July 9, 1611[2]) of a stormy encounter

---

[1] That is, the Johnsonian party of the Amsterdam Church.　　　[2] Profane Schism, pp. 4, 5.

between Lawne and company "with divers strangers and members of the English Church" on the one hand, and Johnson's Church on the other, whose meeting house they have invaded at the close of evening service. Lawne maintains a charge of "schism" against the Church generally, and "nominates one woman to be profane." Johnson replies ("flew in upon us," is Lawne's phrase), calling him and his "hypocrites," "Rabshakites," &c.

Then, finally, on July 28, 1611, Christopher Lawne is cast out "for railing, slandering, abusing, and despising the governors and the whole Church"; for charging them with schism; for leaving our communion and disclaiming our profession; for a letter sent to England, in which he wrote divers slanders of the elders and brethren.[1]

The sequel came as a matter of course.

Nothing more easy than to sweep up into a book whatever odds and ends of scandal he has read, heard or seen; nothing more to his taste than to garnish it with Studleyan "flowers of eloquence."[2]

He can re-edit White, so far as it may serve his purpose, which is principally to damage Studley and Johnson.

He can quote the pastor's brother (whose "testimonie" now seems incontestable), and produce (by the obliging assistance of Master Paget, who is now at his elbow) the Latin letter of the Amsterdam Churches to show up Francis in his true colours.

He can bring forth the articles "exhibited" against Studley at the time of the split in order to secure his deposition—a rich dish whether its ingredients be true or false.

He can recall how it has been said of "the ancient companie of the Brownists that were under the feeding (in Middelburg) of Browne himself" that "not one of them . . . continued faithfull, but became apostates. Not to speak of manifold curses that flew abroad in the time of

---

[1] Profane Schism, pp. 6, 7.   [2] Arber, p. 124.

Barrow, nor yet of the manifold curses which the companie of
the Brownists—remayning in London have oft layed upon one
another, one half devouring another at once." [1]

He can, thus, point the moral that the Brownist Church is,
and always has been, " a patcherie of a few schismatics." [2]   And
very opportune in this connection is what he can instance from
personal experience : how within the Church the brethren " do
oft except one against another for their doctrine, whereby
much heart-burning and strife is kindled betwixt them " [3]—how
Thomas Cocky and Jacob Johnson, " falling into variance one
with another, one of them brings in before the Church a list of
fifteen lies, wherewith he charged the other (Lawne is quite
sure about the "number," although the time was some years
ago).   The other again, to requite his pains, brings in, at the
next turn, against him, a list of sixteen lies.   Betwixt them
both they make up the sum of thirty-one lies." [4]   Still more
opportune is the scene of disruption and dissension now
transacting itself before the general eye.   He can make the
most of this—adding touches here and there to heighten the
effect : he can tell how " Fr. Johnson and his company are now
accursed and avoided by Mr. Ainsworth and his company—how
Mr. Ainsworth and his company are again rejected and avoided
by Mr. Johnson and his " [5]—how " the two houses where the
several factions of these two seditious captains do meet, being
in the same street, and within one house of another, are much
like unto those two wells Eseck and Silnah (Sedition and
Dissension), or strife and hatred " [6]—how having an " ecclesiastical suit about the kernel, which should be the people of God
and the true Church, so have they another civil contention
about the shell and the husk, who shall have the meeting-
house " [7]—how " Mr. Smith and his company are rejected " both

[1] Profane Schism, p. 63.
[2] Ditto, p. 8.
[3] Ditto, p. 58.
[4] Ditto, p. 83.
[5] Ditto, p. 62.
[6] Ditto, p. 26.
[7] Ditto, p. 26.

by Mr. Johnson and Mr. Ainsworth—how "Mr. Robinson and his company holding Mr. Johnson and his to be in Apostasie, by their own grounds must avoid them; and Mr. Johnson *him* again, for taking part with Mr. Ainsworth in his schism against" himself.[1]

All this is easy enough, especially with a Mr. Paget, or some one else, at hand to trim the style and arrange the matter—easy and very agreeable to a malicious mind. Nor need he fear that his story will be discredited: there are too many ears eager to welcome it, and too many grains of truth to make it plausible.

But even he might overreach himself. And he did. He did, for example, in his "Brownism Turned Inside Outward," of which Mr. Arber says it "adds no new facts." It certainly does not, except the fact which must be patent to any sober-minded reader, that it answers well to Ainsworth's description of a "lewd pamphlet," aiming "to disgrace the truth" and "sundry men's persons,"[2] but disgraceful mainly to himself.

Here are one or two extracts: "A most frailful and villanous pastor, a most simple and piteous teacher (Richard Clifton is meant), most careless and unright governors, most negligent and untrusty deacons; *there were no believers while I lived among them*, but a most haughty, proud, disobedient, dissembling and spiteful people."[3]

"Their pastor . . . is a man that loveth vice; he is foolish, unrighteous, unholy, intemperate; he is of life reproveable, as all the Churches of God do testify and so generally will be reported of; one that ruleth his own house dishonestly; he is immodest, haughty, proud, cruel, and un-natural; he is always careless and negligent over the flock, whereof he pretends to be overseer; with all unwillingness grudgingly, for maintenance; holding his office in respect of lucre, but doing his duty to never a soul."[4]

---

[1] Profane Schism, p. 62.
[2] Animadversion, &c., Preface.
[3] Brownism Turned Inside Outward, p. 6.
[4] Ditto, p. 11.

Again, "their doctor or teacher (Clifton) is a man unapt to teach (and unable to divide) the Word of God aright; and he delivers unsound and unwholesome doctrine (of schism) from the same. He is weak in the Scriptures, unable to convince his gainsayers, and careless to deliver his doctrine pure, sound, and plain, but with curiosity or affectation. . . . Those that have left their schism—to wit, C. L. (Christopher Lawne) and R. B. (Robert Bulward)—have sundry times gone unto him desiring conference but never could obtain it of him. [So we will lay upon him our lash of slander with the rest!] Many good Christians do lament his fall in the place (Babworth) where he lived in England, commending his innocent life, praying for his enlargement from his miserable schism, which God grant, if it be His will." [1]

(d) Yet this is the man whom Mr. Arber avers to be "worthy of an implicit belief"! Nay, Mr. Arber not only accounts Lawne a safe guide, but even draws conclusions for which even Lawne gives no sufficient warrant. I will mention three examples.   1. Lawne undoubtedly wished his readers to conceive of the Church under Johnson as utterly corrupt. But it is not his bare assertion to that effect, it is the facts he can produce which must decide our judgment. His bare assertion, however vehement and repeated, ought to count for nothing in view of his known animus. His facts *may* be incontestable. We have seen, however, that even his "muck-rake," diligently plied in every direction, could bring to light no proof whatever that the Church, as a whole, had grown worse during the years between 1605-10; nay, no proof that any new cases of immorality had sprung up at all. How gladly he would have described such if he had known of them! And when he had that last encounter with the Church, to which reference has been made, and when Johnson declared in the course of the

[1] Brownism Turned Inside Out, p. 13. Contrast, "he was . . . a reverend old man" . . . who "converted many to God by his faithful and painful ministry . . . sound and orthodox he always was, and so continued to his end."—Governor Bradford.

proceedings that "they were, by the mercy of God, the purest Church and the freest from corruptions . . . that he knew this day in the world,"[1] what more certain than that Lawne would have tried at least to prove the statement audaciously shameless had he been acquainted with numerous facts to the contrary? But, himself being witness, the only charges he then affirmed were a charge of "schism" and a charge which "nominated one woman to be profane"![2]

Surely it is a fair inference from such an argument " e silentio " that there was no "rampant" vice, and that Mr. Arber lacks even Lawne's support in saying that the Church was "corrupt and dead"[3] and that "matters went on for some years to come "[4] just as White had alleged.

Indeed, Mr. Arber seems to me to exaggerate even in what he says of Daniel Studley. I am far from exculpating him; the evidence, after the most charitable sifting, leaves him under a cloud. But I do say, bearing in mind, e.g., the countless "incredibilities" so diligently circulated against Anabaptists, that the evidence may stand in great need of sifting; I say that some of the charges are so absurd as to be selfrefuting, such as this: "Teaching his schollers (the little children which learned of him) not the songs of Sion, not the Psalms of David, but filthy, unsavourie, and rotten rimes; "[5] I say, further, that more than one of the (eight) articles[6] which take away Mr. Arber's breath, and drive him into mere ejacula-

---

[1] Profane Schism, pp. 4-6.
[2] Ditto.
[3] Story, &c., p. 120.
[4] Ditto, p. 120.
[5] Profane Schism, cap. vi.
[6] See Studley's answer in Richard Clifton's "Advertisement," pp. 115-125. Arber considers this "answer" "perfectly amazing," and Clifton a "fool" for printing it, because in it Studley "simply throws away his defence." But what he does is this: (a) He admits that as to two of the charges—(1) and (5)—his behaviour had been "bad" or "sinful" and "unseemly," but by no means what was supposed; (b) he admits as regards (2) "unsavoury words and unprofitable speeches"; (c) charges (3), (4), (5) he says are false; (d) charge (6) is "due to faction"; (e) charge (8) is "false and malicious." Moreover, as to charges (1) and (8), the worst of the series, Johnson (in 1606) says that (1) had been traced to White's wife, who had confessed herself the author; and that for (8) Studley had called White before the magistrates.

tions at " that unspeakable Studley," are of the vague, wild sort that arouse instant suspicion.

But Mr. Arber will entertain no suspicions. It is Lawne who speaks; and what Lawne has said is worthy of "implicit belief."

2. It is only as we remember this primary assumption that we can at all understand the section of his book which Mr. Arber heads "The fiendish cruelty of Richard Mansfield."[1]

(a) The reference is to what Lawne calls "a comparison between two notable Separatists, Daniel Studley, a Franciscan, and Richard Mansfield, an Ainsworthian."

(b) Lawne's object seems to be plain, viz., to convince the credulous reader that each branch of the " Separation " concealed and sheltered a "monster"; that Ainsworth retained among his prominent members a man who, in a somewhat different line, was as much a genius of iniquity as Studley.

(c) " The iniquitie of R. M. appeareth notable," as follows : by " cruel tasking, oppressing, and exacting the task imposed " on his servant-girl; "by hanging weights of lead upon " her " arms while she spinned, as though otherwise the work had been too light and easy; by " the inflicting a cruel punishment when the work was not accomplished "; " by shameful and vile manner of whipping her naked "; " by cruel nipping and pinching of her arms, hanging her up naked by her hands with cords, while he spent divers rods upon her . . . ; by making her spin " bombasine wool " so rigorously that she " hath often for fear eaten up the wool " . . . ; by compelling her to " sing songs of mirth immediately after " a " cruel whipping," alleging Scriptures in defence Exodus xxi. 20, 21 . . . and then (for anti-climax) by " falling asleep when Mr. Johnson and Mr. Ainsworth preached, and even at home in the midst of his prayer." Yet is he " stricter in the Separation, and makes greater show of holiness and piety than any." [2]

---

[1] Story, &c., p. 127.

[2] Profane Schism, cap. vi., pp 32-41.

That there was some slight kernel of fact to all this slanderous rubbish we may take for granted. There generally is in such cases. But how any unprejudiced critic can hesitate for a moment to conclude that here is a choice specimen of slander gone mad is well-nigh incomprehensible, especially taking into account one or two items which (though not of the technically immoral sort) are too bad to be quoted. Mr. Arber, however, is unappalled.

(d) Nay, he puts a worse face still on the case by speaking of the " unfortunate *maidens* " whom " this brute subjected to his atrocious indignities and unheard barbarities," whereas Lawne himself mentions but *one* maiden, and gives her name and age: D. Hanwell, 18 years of age—Richard Mansfield's household servant.

(e) Consider, too, the implied reflection, not merely on the Church, but especially on its pastor Ainsworth, with regard to whom no hint of moral laxness was ever breathed, in Mr. Arber's comment: " Had this monster been living now, his life would not have been worth five minutes' purchase outside a prison " ! Shall we not rather say that Ainsworth's silent tolerance of the man points rebuke alike at Lawne's mendacity and the too-easy faith of his apologist ?

3. Again, let us examine the section entitled, " The Ancient Church is an abomination to the citizens of Amsterdam." [1] Lawne is said to prove this by—

(1) The testimony of the Dutch Church concerning the Brownists. " When as they sent their messengers, with some questions, unto the Dutch eldership: they received this answer from them, That they did not acknowledge their assembly to be an ecclesiastical assembly, or a lawful church. And when Master Johnson and others of them were instant (urgent) to hear reasons of this answer from them : it was further answered, They would do it, if they saw it needful, or if they found anything that was worthy of answer." [2]

[1] Profane Schism, p. 128. [2] Page 21.

20

Now certainly repulsion, and repulsion in a tone of contempt, is manifest here.

But (a) those who repulsed can scarcely be described as "the citizens of Amsterdam" generally. They are the few men who made up the "eldership" of the Dutch Church.

(b) There is nothing in their answer to show that they declined dealings with the Ancient Church on the ground of its "immoral life," as Mr. Arber says. It is quite conceivable that the ground may have been doctrinal, or ecclesiastical, or personal even, in the form of some supposed grievance.

And that it was so we have the means of knowing. Ainsworth refers to the matter in his correspondence with Paget, pastor of the English Church. He complains of the treatment meted out by the Dutch eldership to the church of which he was teacher, as illustrating that exclusiveness was not confined to the latter; that if the latter (as Paget affirms, and Ainsworth denies)[1] did "disclaim and renounce" the "communion of all the churches of Christ," and "so gave offence to the godly in our country (England), as also to the godly magistrates, ministers, and people in this city," the spirit of the former was not, and never had been, a whit more charitable. In fact, says Ainsworth, the "Ancient Church" had always been scouted and scorned as in England so here—its character maligned, its principles misrepresented, its efforts to create a better understanding haughtily put down. Witness, for example, the chilling reception given to "our confession of faith dedicated" to the Universities of the Reformed Churches—although we on our part "had acknowledged" these to be "true churches" "upon the sight of their confessions."[2] Witness particularly the answer *given by the Dutch eldership to the questions mentioned by Lawne in his "infamous book."*[3] Neither Ainsworth nor Paget says what the questions were;

[1] An Arrow against the Separation of the Brownists, by John Paget (1618), p. 43.

[2] Ditto, p. 45.
[3] Ainsworth's expression. (Italics mine.)

but there can be little doubt, I think, that they were "feelers" after some common ground between the two churches. To which came the answer, first, "we do not acknowledge you to be a lawful church" at all; and then, to inquiries "Why?" a disdainful silence.

Paget, of course, justifies the Dutch Church, and would have done so most crushingly, had he been able, by a description of the Brownists' "immoral life." This, however, is what he says:—[1] "Might they (the Dutch Church) not have their reasons so to answer? Did they not discern your contentious disposition in other dealings before as well as afterward, when the deputies both of the Dutch and French Churches[2]—dealing with your eldership about the cause of Mr. John Johnson, to have stayed your pastor from the excommunication of his father, if it might have been—do yet testify that they could not get a plain or direct answer from you?" The situation is clear. John Johnson, the father, failing otherwise to control Francis, sought the interference of the elders of the Dutch and French Churches. He submitted the whole controversy to their decision. They wrote[3] to Francis and some elders of his congregation inquiring if they were prepared to do the same. They expected, but did not get, a "categorical" yes or no—Francis, perhaps, trying to make them understand that it was utterly against the first principles of his church to entrust the decision of its own private affairs to any outside authority. So they drew off, offended. And if

[1] An Arrow, &c., p. 55.

[2] G. Johnson says that he himself appealed to the "Reformed Churches," and that the "Dutch and French Churches were content to hear, try, judge and end the matter between us." He mentions also an interview between "Arminius and the Pastor" (F. Johnson), in which the former took the part of the Father and "talked in Latin" (Discourse, pp. 205, 31, 38).

[3] See their (Latin) letter printed by Lawne in "Profane Schism." It is signed by Joannes à Vinea, in ecclesia Gallobelgica, Minister Evangelii; Petrus Plancius, administer Evangelii; Jacobus Arminius, administer Evangelii in ecclesia Belgica; Simon Goulartius, administer Verbi in ecclesia, Gallobelgica. It is simply a "testimonium," given to John Johnson, at his request, stating that he had solicited their "counsel and help"; that they had offered to adjudicate in the matter; that F. Johnson and his elders would give them no "reponsum categoricum"; and that they had then ceased to interfere.

at any future time "the Ancient Church" shall, in its simplicity, make friendly overtures, the "answer" may be anticipated!   It will be a snub, delivered with keen relish. "We do not acknowledge your assembly to be a church.   *We* are an 'ecclesia,' *you* are a mere 'coetus.'"[1]   This is the whole story so far as the "testimony" goes which Mr. Arber quotes. There is "scorn," something like that of the High Churchman now for the Dissenting conventicle; but there is not a trace of outraged decency, nor does even Paget hint that there was. His strongest word is "contentious disposition."

(2) As to "the testimony of the magistracy of Amsterdam,"[2] it is amazing how its true character and drift can be mistaken.   Read in connection with Lawne's account of the suit entered against White in 1606,[3] what comes out clearly is this:—

(*a*) The magistrates were the burgomasters, and were (apparently) the same in 1606 and 1611.

(*b*) They were "members of the Dutch Church"[4]; probably, therefore, elders as well as magistrates, and certainly not predisposed to regard too favourably the suit of people whom their own Church (perhaps in their own person) had already disowned.

(*c*) The suit both *against Master White,* and about their meeting-house, is said to have been brought "in the name of the Church."[5]

(*d*) It was on this account, because "they sought to lay in their action in the name of the Church,"[6] that the magistrates repelled them.   "They would not receive complaint from them in the quality or name of a Church, or (in) the name of any elder or deacon, *but as from private men.*   The magistrates told them that they held them not as a Church but as a sect."[7]   The ground taken up is precisely that of the Dutch eldership; and,

---

[1] The terms employed in the Latin letter.

[2] Story, &c., p. 128.

[3] Quoted by Arber, p. 120.

[4] So says the "Testimony," p. 128.

[5] Ditto.

[6] Ditto.

[7] Ditto.

so far as it goes, is significant not of the suitors' bad character, but of the magistrates' intolerant arrogance.

(e) Owing to this attitude, on the part of the magistrates, the plaintiffs against White, never had a CHANCE OF PRESENTING THEIR CASE. The result was a thoroughly one-sided trial. Lawne implicitly confesses this. He says, "When Master White had once taken order by his attorney to answer the matter" and . . . had . . . "brought sundry witnesses before the burgomasters, which there did testify and by their oaths and depositions confirm the things which Master White had written," then the magistrates closed the case. Mr. White was "discharged, and had liberty from the magistrates to go for England, as his occasions or business should require."[1] What then? Had the suitors let judgment go against them by default? Had they, when brought to the point, been afraid or unable to proceed? By no means. Lawne admits that it was only "at length," after repeated attempts to get a hearing (attempts which he, of course, calls "troublesome and contentious"), that they "were content to let their suit fall, and ceased to proceed any further therein."[2] It was, in fact, a glaring case of injustice—done under the influence of ecclesiastical prejudice against people of whom (as of the Anabaptists) anything was credible. But Mr. Arber sides with the magistrates. He finds in the fact that they acted as they did, both in 1606 and 1611, corroboration of White's assertion that "there is no sect in Amsterdam, though many, in such contempt for immoral life as the Brownists are."[3] He finds, also, a proof that Lawne's charges "were perfectly crushing"[4] in the fact that the men who had failed to get justice, or a hearing, in 1606, did not endeavour "either individually or collectively" "to vindicate themselves . . . in a Court of Justice in 1612 and 1613."[5] He thinks they "dared" not do so. Such

[1] Story, &c., p. 120.
[2] Ditto, p. 120.
[3] Ditto, p. 128.
[4] Ditto, p. 115.
[5] Ditto, p. 115.

perverseness in one who claims to be nothing, if not impartial, is rather hard to bear.

4. There remains the case of Francis Johnson. Mr. Arber, we have seen, sums him up—at least from the end of 1602— " a thoroughly bad man."

When one reflects that he had still fifteen years of life before him, and that he went on writing, praying, preaching to the end, never seeming to be afraid or ashamed, although a hypocrite incarnate, this sentence of Mr. Arber's is very terrible. One remembers the early days, yet only ten years before, when for love of the truth which came to him at Middelburg through one of Barrow and Greenwood's writings, he gave up a " great and certain maintenance " (£200), and went to London, " to confer with the authors," " then in prison," and adjoined himself to the poor Separatists, and was soon afterwards committed to prison himself, and lay there for five years, and was then banished. Surely he was sincere so far—sincere and brave under circumstances the most trying. For long the fate of Barrow, Greenwood, and Penry stared him in the face, but he did not falter. Like them, he was ready to lay down his life.

Nevertheless, five years later, we must pronounce him " a thoroughly bad man," " a most remarkable sinner," " a dead Christian," " an utter disgrace to our sacred faith." It is a hard blow to one's belief in human nature —or rather in the saving and preserving grace of God ! Governor Bradford thought he knew him. He had some reason for thinking so. He lived within sight and sound of him for a year. And in after days, when he set down his clear and calm impressions of bygone events and persons, this was what he said of Johnson : " A very grave man he was, and an able teacher; and was the most solemn in all his adminis- trations that we have seen any ; and especially in dispensing the seals of the covenant, both baptism and the Lord's Supper." One pictures the scene : the plain meeting-house ;

the silent congregation, gathered about the Lord's Table; the pastor, always "very grave," seeming so to enter into the spirit of the service that his voice as he reads or prays, and his manner as he dispenses the "seals of the covenant," awe the soul by their solemnity. This, at least, was the experience of Bradford; and he did not see or suspect that the man who thus impressed him had been for years past "a dead Christian," an "utter disgrace to our sacred faith"! Of course, it may have been so. In the sphere of character semblance and fact are, alas! sometimes the poles asunder. It is not only in fiction that the like of Nathaniel Hawthorne's Arthur Dimmesdale exist. But before saying of any particular individual that *he* is such a man—a mere mask of goodness—we ought to be quite sure of our ground, if indeed we ever can be.

What, then, is Mr. Arber's ground in respect of Johnson? It is Lawne again. Lawne declares that "of all the Separation it is Mr. Johnson that hath the haughty eyes above them all."[1] This means, being interpreted, that Johnson was naturally masterful and inclined to be autocratic, a fault which others who had to do with him have recorded; and one which might drive him, on occasion, into very unchristian actions. But it is not a fault which proves its subject to be "thoroughly bad"— in some circumstances it might as easily prove him virtuous. Nor does Mr. Arber style Johnson "thoroughly bad" on this account.

What other ground is there? Well, there is the charge of conniving at the iniquities of Daniel Studley. This, however, assumes two things which have not been proved—that Studley was guilty to the extent alleged; and that Johnson was fully aware or convinced of his guilt. The utmost it is safe to say is that the pastor manifested toward his elder more and longer tolerance than was right, or than he would have shown, perhaps, toward a man less influential. And this implies, no doubt, that Johnson was not altogether the strong man he

---

[1] Profane Schism, p. 63.

seemed; that there was a flaw in his courage if not a twist in his conscience; but it fails to make him out "a thoroughly bad man." Indeed, if it be true as is reported, that what kept Studley in office during his last year (1611-12) was the popular vote; and that what cast him out in 1612 was Johnson's "free" hand,[1] he may not have been even weak. He may, that is to say, have begun to work for his removal as soon as his unworthiness became clear to him.

Where, then, lies the one clinching proof which will warrant Mr. Arber's sweeping denunciation? Simply here—the way "he treated his father and suffered him to be treated by his church."[2] Other accusation than this, of any definiteness, he brings none. Before 1597 Johnson, on the whole, had lived blameless. Even the expulsion of George Johnson in 1599 was, it seems to Mr. Arber, "richly deserved," and he will only say that "Francis committed an error in policy, in going so far as *publicly* to excommunicate his own brother. Some other way should have been found."[3] (Does Mr. Arber, by the way, suppose that the excommunication could have been PRIVATE, or that, if privately done, it would not soon have been publicly known, and the pastor have been an object of keen resentment for usurping, or letting the elders usurp, an essential function of the Church?) But then he went "steadily from bad to worse." And the proof is that he excommunicated his father, or, as Mr. Arber prefers to put it, "delivered" his father "over to Satan." This was the "perfectly unpardonable" act. It was an act, too, of "amazing impudence";[4] for the father "did not belong to his own community." Here, at any rate, Mr. Arber is wrong—absurdly so. For excommunication could, and did, only apply to those actually

[1] "That which the Popular Government could not then effect is now effected since that government was changed by Master Johnson."—A Shield of Defence, p. 37 (quoted by Arber, p. 123).

[2] Story, &c., p. 110.

[3] Ditto, p. 109.

[4] Ditto, p. 108.

members of the Church. The Separatists never dreamt of passing formal censures on outsiders. These "God would judge." And that Johnson, senior, could be "cast out," is completely demonstrative of the fact that he was "within." But still the act was "unpardonable." How do we know? Mr. Arber points us to the father's letter, and Lawne's comments, and the vain interposition of the Dutch elders. But was there nothing on the other side; were there no extenuating circumstances? I think there were. I think the act may be defensible, to say the least, if the father came over from England, *three years after George had been dealt with*, not merely, as he says himself, " to seek and make peace between " the two brothers and the Church, but mainly, as John Robinson declares, to " take the part "[1] of George, to rake up dying fires, and so render quiet life and work impossible. But, grant that the act was unpardonable, shall we for a single "unpardonable" offence confidently write down a man as " thoroughly bad "? It will go hard with most of us if such is to be the rule of judgment.

But there is no mercy for Francis Johnson!

Being a bad man, bad motives must be ascribed to all he does. Mr. Arber reads in Lawne, for example, how " Master Johnson brought Master Robinson's book (A Justification of Separation) against Master Bernard into their meeting-house (at Amsterdam), and there, before the congregation, made a solemn testification against the manifold errors[2] contained in it. . . ." And, at once, it occurs to him that here there is no genuine concern for what Johnson deemed the truth; but spite at " the exodus of the Pilgrim Church to Leyden, which would have greatly reduced his importance, if not his income."[3]

Again, the result of his quarrel with Ainsworth about

---

[1] Justification of Separation, pp. 55–6 (Edition 1610).

[2] His views about the superiority of the Church to the offices, &c.

[3] Story, &c., p. 123.

the eldership was to wreck his church, to make it homeless, and to drive it into exile. Surely a situation fraught with the anguish of despair to a man who was (as I read him) too ambitious of power, too confident of possessing the truth, too lacking in sympathy with other men and their views ; but not insincere, nor consciously untrue to his ideals. It is an issue to all his suffering and striving which comes home to one as something very pathetic ; as it did to Dr. William Ames when he wrote, " Think not evil ! if thou meanest well. We intend not to insult over him that is down, or to pursue a man that is flying of himself ; but to lend him a hand that knoweth not well which way to take. Master Johnson, indeed, is rather to be pitied than much opposed. We need but stand still as lookers on. He falleth willingly on his own sword." [1] An erring and defeated man he seemed to Dr. Ames, as did John Smyth to Ainsworth, and the Separatists generally to most onlookers.

But to Mr. Arber, Johnson's flight to Emden, and his misery, is the last act but one in a spiritual tragedy; is a vision of Nemesis dogging the steps of a hypocrite; is the prelude to *a final tearing-off of the mask.*

For,[2] says he, " now we come to the death-bed acknowledgment of Rev. Francis Johnson, that his whole life had been one long mistake."

At last, then, we are to have something "perfectly crushing." What is it ? It is the following letter from " Matthew Slade to Sir Dudley Carleton. Amsterdam, Saturday, 10-20 January, 1617-18.

" This day we have buried Master Francis Johnson, a man that hath many years been pastor of the Brownists ; and (having cast himself, and drawn others, into great troubles and miseries, for their opinions and schism) did, a few days before his death, publish a book, wherein he disclaimed most of his former singularities and refuted them. To which work

[1] Story, &c., pp. 125–6.   [2] Ditto, p. 129.

he hath also annexed a brief refutation of the *Five Articles.*" [1]

Now, is it not very remarkable that this *published* "death-bed recantation "—so certain to arouse feeling and comment—quite escaped general notice? Is it not strange that Matthew Slade should be the only one to hear about and report so sensational an occurrence? For certainly other reference than his there seems to be none. But what if Mr. Arber, in this case as in some others, has been the dupe of his own impulsiveness?

He says, in a note,[2] that the book containing the re-cantation "was probably published in the previous December, and therefore would bear the date 1617. It is certainly not ' A Christian Plea, &c.,' which Johnson published in that year. Even the title of this recantation is not known, so utterly has the book perished." And, in his preface,[3] he names it as one of the two books concerned with the history of the " Separation " which should " be sought for, without wearying."

But the searcher, I think, may spare his pains. The book will never be found; or, rather, it has never been lost, but has probably been in Mr. Arber's own hands. For almost as certain as he is that the book is *not* " A Christian Plea, &c.," so certain am I that it is.

My suspicion was aroused by the fact already stated (viz., complete absence of allusion to such a phenomenon); it was strengthened by the fact that Ainsworth should (in 1618) write "A Reply to the Pretended Christian Plea for the Antichristian Church of Rome, published by Francis Johnson, A.D. 1617," but betray not the faintest acquaintance with a production, by the same pen, still more recent and

---

[1] Mr. Arber adds to the last words, *Five Articles,* a query (? Synod of Dort), as if he did not know that the Synod of Dort was not convened till November, 1618.
[2] Story, &c., p. 129.
[3] Ditto, p. 9.

alarming; it was confirmed by a slight examination of the
" Christian Plea " itself.

The full title of this book is :—

" A Christian Plea conteyning three Treatises—

" (1) Touching the Anabaptists, and others mainteyning
some like errours with them (pp. 1-220) ;

" (2) Touching such Christians as now are here commonly
called Remonstrants or Arminians (pp. 221-244) ;

" (3) Touching the Reformed Churches with whom myself
agree in the faith of the Gospel of our Lord Jesus Christ (pp.
244-323) : made by Francis Johnson, pastor of the Ancient
English Church now sojourning at Amsterdam, in the Low
Countreyes.

" Printed in the yeere of our Lord 1617."

Now what calls for notice, and appears to me decisive of
the question, is (1) this—that the second teatise " concerns
some points which touch not only the Anabaptists, but
such other Christians, also, as are called Remonstrants," or
Arminians, these, namely :—

God's decree of Election.

God's decree of Reprobation.

General Redemption.

Free Will or Power in ourselves unto good since
the Fall.

The Perseverance of the Saints.

On these (the famous Five Points) the Arminians contested
the regnant Calvinism, and Johnson entered the lists to defend
the latter, as he had always done. But the treatise numbers
only twenty-three pages, and might fitly be described by
Matthew Slade as a " brief Refutation " "annexed " to the
main work.

(2) In the other two treatises—particularly in the third—
Johnson does make concessions which might well give rise to
the rumour (and rumour, or a casual glance, may be all Slade
had to go by) that he had retracted or " disclaimed most

of his former singularities "—*i.e.*, the characteristics of his Separatism. Thus, for example:

(*a*) He calls it[1] "a great error . . . to think that baptism had in the Church of Rome, or other apostate Churches, is not to be regarded." On the contrary, he holds that the Church of Rome, since it "baptizes with water in the name of the Father, the Son, and the Holy Ghost," and, at the same time, "professes all the articles of the Christian Faith contained in the Apostles' Creed, the Nicene, the Athanasian," is, so far, a true Church.

(*b*) He gives a wide extension to the term *Teacher*,[2] making it include not only those who teach in "particular Churches," but also "such as do either in the schools and Universities interpret the Scriptures and train up students in theology," and, indeed, any one anywhere "who instructs the people in religion and all duties of godliness, common or special, as there is just occasion."

(*c*) He leaves it to be discussed " by the Word of God " whether Teachers are to be raised up extraordinarily; or, having an ordinary calling, should be sent out by princes; or should be "allowed by the Universities and governors thereof," or should be "designed by particular Churches," or should be "approved by the pastors and presbyteries of one or more Churches." A far cry this from Henry Barrow.

(*d*) He argues (again contrary to Barrow) for suspension[3] (as preliminary to excommunication), considering it to be "like that keeping of persons in ward, whereof we read in Lev. xxiv. 12; Numb. xv. 24, till it manifestly appear that the parties suspended are to be cut off and cast out of the congregation."

(*e*) He thinks it[4] "doth lie upon kings and all other magistrates (within their dominions, cities, and jurisdictions) to have special care—in the matter of maintenance—of the estate

[1] Christian Plea, p. 27.
[2] Ditto, p. 279.
[3] P. 303.
[4] P. 316.

of the ministers and Churches under them, after the example
of Hezekiah and Nehemiah."

(*f*) He inclines to the opinion that [1] "the remnants and
monuments of idolatry (altars, images, garments, temples, &c.) "
need not be " all done away," as Ainsworth, &c., maintained, and
that such things are not to be made a reason for separation or
even condemnation.   Let there be a common endeavour " to
grow up in the truth and to nourish mutual love and peace one
with another, and (what they can) to have communion in the
things whereof both are persuaded, or wherein they shall not
themselves personally offend and partake with other men's
sins."

Then, finally and specially, there is the exposition [2] (quite
in a Presbyterian sense) of Matt. xviii. 17, and in connection
with this a narration of divers (thirty-six) errors, abuses, and
erroneous courses " which Messrs. Ainsworth, Robinson, Jacob,
Smith, &c., have gathered, received, pleaded for, and urged
earnestly "— a list of differences with old colleagues which
would be certain to give a superficial reader the impression that
he had turned his back alike on them and on his earlier self.

On the whole, however, he had not.   He still sees good
cause to separate from the Church of England ; he still resents
" any other strange ecclesiastical power and authority " being
" interposed   between "   " a   particular   church "   with   its
" pastors " and " the Arch-Pastor Jesus Christ "[3]—which is
the kernel of the matter.

But he has changed, and in some respects broadened.   He
has become representative of those Brownists " who separate
from the Church for corruptions and yet confess both it and
Rome to be a true Church."[4]   He has resumed certain of the
views which he used to hold at Middelburg.   He is, therefore,
nearer than he was to the " Reformed Churches," and writes his

----

[1] P. 318.
[2] Pp. 306–16.
[3] P. 251.

[4] Paget's " Arrow against the Separation of the Brownists," preface.

"Plea"—as the wording of the title would suggest—in the hope of opening a way to communion with them of a closer kind than formerly seemed to him possible or desirable. It is, accordingly, rather of the character of an eirenicon than a recantation—at least, it is such a recantation as Mr. Arber applauds[1] in John Robinson.

We conclude, then, that Mr. Arber crowns his unfair censures of Johnson with the cruellest cut of all. We say that Johnson was never a bad man—unless to be sometimes arrogant and passionate and harsh and narrow is to be bad. We say that the signs, so far as they go, point not to his having grown worse but rather better as the years went by—more calm and self-restrained and tolerant. We say, lastly, that we are prepared to rest this judgment on the style, drift, and spirit of the book[2] which he wrote when the subduing sense of the end may have been already upon him, and which is the only "recantation" he ever made.

5. In general support of Lawne, Mr. Arber cites Rev. John Paget and John Robinson.

Paget was a Puritan, one of the Forward preachers. He settled in Amsterdam ten years later than the Ancient Church (1607). As Ainsworth says, "Our Church is before yours, being through God's mercy scattered and established first, and you coming after, gathered a people and erected a ministry in this city by us. . . ."[3]

In doing so, Paget "communicated with many learned English, Scottish, Dutch, and French, who," says he, "gave us counsel and help in our endeavours";[4] but he ignored the existence of the Ancient Church. When Ainsworth complained of this slight, he said in defence, that he did right to ignore so exclusive a body.

[1] Story, &c., chap. xxiii., pp. 174–188.
[2] Compare it, e.g., with his "Certayne Reasons and Arguments Proving that it is not Lawful to Heare or have any Spirituall Communion with the Present Ministerie of the Church of England," 1608.
[3] Quoted at p. 37 of "Arrow against the Separation of the Brownists," by Paget.
[4] Ditto, p. 43.

Paget's church flourished to his own satisfaction. "The hand of God was with us, the reformed churches gave us the right hand of fellowship, the hand of the Christian magistrates furthered our enterprise; divers who left your church and went to the Dutch did come to us; many more have come since."[1] On the other hand, he took it for a clear sign of God's anger against "the Brownists" that "three or four hundred" of them "have brought forth more apostate Anabaptists and Arians sometimes in one year than 10,000 members of the Reformed Dutch Churches in this city have done in ten years or more."[2] In fact, the spirit which persecuted the Separatists in the home-land embodied tself in the English Church of Amsterdam. As Ainsworth says in effect—like mother like daughter.

Among those whom Paget welcomed into his fold were " C. Lawne, Fowler, and others,"[3] concerned in what Ainsworth calls "that charitable libel," which appeared under their name. Ainsworth speaks of them as "your proselytes"[4] : not merely welcomed, then, but also enticed. "Some of them," he adds, "have stood in election to bear office among you."[5] Unable to give literary form to their libels, they have not lacked a "penman."[6] Someone in the English Church—the manner of reference pointing to Paget himself—has been all too ready to do this office for them. Moreover, Lawne's book is not the only one which has appeared. Others of like character, "disguised" but not so far as to conceal authorship, have issued from the same source.

In short, Paget has made a "dead set" at the Ancient Church from the first. To cherish into a flame the embers of discontent, and allure the discontented to the refuge of his own congregation, has been a pleasant, and has seemed to him a pious work. Could he have scattered the nest of

[1] An Arrow, &c., p. 43.
[2] Ditto, preface.
[3] Ditto, p. 3.
[4] Ditto, p. 36.
[5] Ditto, p. 3.
[6] Ditto, p. 3. Cf. p. 36, Lawne, "the first pretended author of that book."

schismatics by the arm of the law, he would have done it gladly. But, failing this, he has used such means as came nearest to hand. Any foul weapon was clean enough for his purpose. Nay, it was easy to persuade himself that the foulest story about people so detested was true, and that "great fruit" might come "from publishing the personal sins of them that continue in error."

About Ainsworth nothing could be gathered to his moral detriment. Even he, however, had evinced his frailty, and although Thomas White has long ago drawn attention to the fact, it is well to refresh the public memory. So he writes[1] :—"You are noted to have turned your coat and changed your religion five several times :—

(1) Being of our religion, and a member of the Church of England, you forsook that Church and separated.

(2) Being separated you did again in London—being in the hands of authority—yield to join with the worship and ministry of the Church of England.

(3) After this you did again slide back into the separation, and renounce the Church of England.

(4) After this, when you were in Ireland and in some danger of punishment for your scandal, you did again return into the communion renounced by you (whether feignedly or unfeignedly I leave unto yourself to consider).

(5) After this you change your profession again, and fall back into separation and stick now presently in this schism.

This (if true) was rather ancient history, seeing that Ainsworth had been (as Paget tells us[2]) twenty years in Amsterdam, and had during that period been only too consistent in "sticking" to his principles. But it is a slight contribution to "the dunghill of slander,"[3] in which the Separatists might, perhaps, be buried; and that is enough.

---

[1] An Arrow against the Separation of the Brownists, p. 91.
[2] Ditto, p. 119: "You have lived more than twenty years as a neighbour unto the Reformed Churches."
[3] John Robinson's phrase.

Paget, then, does not seem a likely witness to keep Lawne's credit in countenance.

But instead of adding further comment of my own, let me quote Ainsworth's calm and surely "perfectly crushing" rebuke.

"And upon this occasion I shall put you in mind (Mr. Paget) of that which in part appeareth in this your writing (An Arrow against the Separation of the Brownists), and more fully in the disguised pamphlets that come out of your congregation: how you take a special delight, and think it for your (ad)vantage, to upbraid men's differences; to rake into particular men's sins and infirmities, yea, though they be repented of; and to blazon them abroad to the world, for the discredit of the cause which they profess or have professed. If the arrows of the Almighty did stick fast in you, and you felt your own misery, you would not write after this manner. . . . If the contentions and particular sins, I say not of all Christendom, but of England and the churches in the Netherland, or the like—which you acknowledge true churches—were thus blazoned, what a sink of ill-savour would be smelt? And are there no personal sins amongst yourselves may we think, that you take such a course? If God herein should reward you according to your works, where should you appear? I counsel you, therefore, to take a better course. Error may be refuted by the Word of God, without any such leaven of maliciousness; and the truth needeth no such fleshly means to maintain it. If you like not of this counsel you may walk on in the light of your fire, and in the sparks that you have kindled, but my soul shall not come into your secret, though I shall not cease to wish your welfare, so long and so far as I may.[1] November 9, 1617."

We turn, lastly, to John Robinson's witness.

In a certain passage[2] of his "Justification of Separation,"

---

[1] An Arrow against the Separation of the Brownists, p. 381.

[2] Vol. II., pp. 259-60 (Ashton's edition).

Robinson says "that if iniquity be committed in the Church, and complaint and proof accordingly made, and that the Church will not reform or reject the party offending, but will, on the contrary, maintain presumptuously and abet such impiety—that then, by abetting that party and his sin, she makes it her own by imputation, and enwraps herself in the same guilt with the sinner. And, remaining irreformable (either by such members of the same church as are faithful, if there be any, or by other sister churches), wipeth herself out of the Lord's church-roll, and now ceaseth to be any longer the true Church of Christ. And whatsoever truths or ordinances of Christ this *rebellious rout* still retains, it but usurps the same, without right unto them or promise of blessing upon them; both the persons and sacrifices are abominable unto the Lord."

Here Mr. Arber (*suo modo*) rushes to the conclusion that Robinson had a picture before his mind of Studley and the Ancient Church, so that by 1610 "he had come to regard" that church "as a rebellious rout."[1] Of course this may have been the case if Robinson really thought of the Amsterdam Church as Mr. Arber does. But then that is the question at issue. And Mr. Arber has overlooked two facts :

(1) That such a church, a mere "rebellious rout," was one with which another church could only have retained communion on pain of "enwrapping herself" "in the same guilt." Yet in this same year Robinson let his church be consulted on the differences about the eldership, and let a deputation be sent as well as letters with a view to preserving peace.[2] Indeed, he never severed fraternal relations —not even in the extremely severe letter of 1624, where mention is made of "differences and troubles" which, "since the death of your wise and modest governors," "have laden

[1] Story, &c., p. 123. [2] Robinson's Works, Vol. III., pp. 466–475 (Ashton's edition).

the ordinances of God and professors of the same " "with scandal and opprobry." For this, too, is addressed " to our beloved, the elders and Church at Amsterdam," and is signed, " your loving brethren, the pastor and Church at Leyden." [1]

(2) But possibly more conclusive still, both as to this particular question and as to the merits of the case generally, is the fact that Robinson wrote thus in 1614 :—[2]" There passed out, some time since, a defamatory libel under the names of Charles Lawne and three other, his brethren in evil, but *certainly penned by some other persons*,[3] whose greater knowledge did arm their cruel hatred the more to hurt, . . . against whom and whose friends, durst I use the same liberty in publishing to the world *their personal corruptions which I know, and could soon learn by the testimony of honester men than these informers*,[3] they who have written of others what hath pleased them, should read that which would not please them, of their own, if not of themselves. But God forbid! My desire is rather to pacify than to alienate affections. . . . Besides, in following their course I should, for the faults of a few corrrupter persons, wrong the credit of many honest and innocent men, for whose sakes, I would rather cover the others' failings, than for them blemish the credit of the rest."

Then, of the " accusations " in the libel he says: " Though they were all true, *as I know some of them to be wholly false, and others impudently published by such as were themselves chief agents in them*,[3] yet did no more concern me, and the Church with me, than did the abuses in the Church at Corinth, the Church at Rome."

Finally, of " the publishers of those accusations " he says, they " cannot be unsuspected of any reasonable man ; being such generally as are both enemies to our profession, and have either for their unfaithful apostasy, or other scandalous

[1] Robinson's Works, Vol. III., p. 393.
[2] Ditto, pp. 95–99 (preface to " Of Religious Communion)."
[3] Italics mine.

sins, or both, been cast out of the Church, and excommunicated. Now, as for the former, it is truly and commonly said that no person, running away from his master, will easily speak well of him; so doth experience confirm it, for the latter, that scarce any condemned in any court, how justly soever, but will complain either of the malice of the evidence, or ignorance of the jury, or injustice of the judge. Condemned persons must repair their own, by ruinating the credits of their judges."

With which judgment, based on personal knowledge of the facts and persons involved, as also on the dictates of common sense, it is hard to see how a " cool-headed " man can fail to agree. And so we leave the matter.

APPENDICES

APPENDIX I.

[SEE NOTE I. AT END OF CHAPTER I.]

The Scholar of Oxford.

OF course, since the writer of "Master Some laid open in his true colours, &c.," was the "clerk of Oxford" against whom Barrow girds so strongly, it is plain that Dr. Dexter cannot be right in (conjecturally) assigning the book to Greenwood.[1] Since, moreover, the writer was Job Throckmorton, an extract or two may serve to show how extremely probable is the conjecture that he—Penry's friend—had a share in the writing of the Tracts. If the following does not "smack" of Marprelate it would surely be very hard to say what does.

. . . "That clothead of Sarum [*i.e.*, Dr. Bridges, Martin's butt] to go away with a whole fardle of errors and absurdities, and not to say black was his eye." [2]

"This John of Beverley told the young man that doubtless he was not baptized, if that dull-headed, dogbolt priest baptized him." [3]

"And methink I should see some reverent bishop, or other, on his knees before Her Majesty as one loath to speak, good man, but only that the heinousness of the case doth thereunto force him, as it were, against his will; and therefore he begins, I warrant you, with a sigh or two fetched from the very depth of his bowels, in this sort: 'O madam, you may see now what your Puritans are come to . . . that your Majesty is not christened!'" [4]

"And so peradventure father John Elmar should kiss Kate no more in the pulpit while he lived—and what a shrewd loss were that?" [5]

Dr. Some's "foul, gross, and more palpable absurdity than ever the ignorant Welshman perpetrated. Will you see how unresistibly I can bring this gear about? Then lay down your books awhile. Give ear—

Ubi non ecclesia, ibi non vocatio,
Ubi non est vocatio, ibi non est ministerium,
Ubi non est ministerium, ibi non sacramentum.

ergo subjoined.

Will you have it in English now? For I'll never dissemble you. I do by my Latin as that sweet babe of Sarum doth by his Greek and Hebrew—beg and borrow here a patch and there a patch, as the dictionaries that come in my way do yield me sustenance. And if anything happen to be false, then it was either Chard,[6] my printer's, fault, or else my dictionary was not the last edition, or else my candle wants snuffing." [7]

---

[1] History of Congregationalism, Bibliography. "In writing which (so decidedly does it, in parts, seem to differ in style from other books bearing Greenwood's name) I am persuaded Barrow had a considerable hand." But J. G., being Penry's friend and Barrow's opponent, the argument turns against Dexter.

[2] p. 34.

[3] p. 11.

[4] p. 56.

[5] p. 65.

[6] Chard was one of Bridge's printers.

[7] p. 86.

APPENDIX II.

The Earliest Separatist Manifesto.

REASON is shown [in chronology of Barrow's writings, Appendix III., p. 338, § (b)] for believing that "A Brief Summe, &c.," which finds place in the 1605 edition of the "Plain Refutation," was first published in 1588; and it may be taken as, perhaps, their earliest "manifesto" on the part of the Separatists. It is very short, and is here given in full:—

"A Brief Summe of the causes of our separation, and of our purposes in practice [withstood by G. G., defended by H. B., as followeth— this was added when Barrow added his reply]:—

"We seeke above all thinges the peace and protection of the Most High, and the kingdome of Christ Jesus our Lord. 2. We seeke and fully purpose to worship God aright, according as He hath commanded in His most holy Word. 3. We seeke the fellowship of His faithfull and obedient servants, and together with them to enter Covenant with the Lord, and by the direction of His Holy Spirit, to proceed to a godly, free, and right choise of ministers and other officers by Him ordeyned to the service of His Church. 4. We seeke to establish and obey the ordinances and lawes of our Saviour *Christ* left by His last will and Testament to the governing and guyding of His Church, without altering, changing, innovating, wresting, or leaving out any of them that the Lord shall give us sight of. 5. We purpose (by the assistance of the Holy Ghost) in this faith and order to leade our lives, and for this faith and order to leave our lives, if such be the good will of our Heavenly Father, to whom be honor and glorye. Amen.

"6. And now that our forsaking and utter abandoning of these disordered assemblies as they generally stand in England, may not seeme strange nor offensive to any man that will judge or be judged by the Word of God, we alledge and affirme them heinously guiltie in these four principall Transgressions.

"1. THEY worship the true God after a false manner, their worship being made of the invention of man, even of that man of sinne, erronious and imposed upon them.

"2. FOR that the prophane, ungodly multitudes, without exception of any one person, are with them received into, and reteined in the bosome of the Church.

"3. FOR that they have a false Antichristian ministerie imposed upon them, reteined with them, and mainteined by them.

"4. FOR that these Churches are ruled by, and remaine in subjection unto an Antichristian and ungodly government, cleane contrarie to the institution of our Saviour CHRIST.

"When these things stand thus, let him that readeth consider."

APPENDIX III.

Chronology of Barrow's writings (and Greenwood's).

So far as it goes the evidence of Robert Stokes and Robert Bowle contained in the Egerton Papers[1] gives the most exact information. They were two of the group examined in March, 1593. They appeared before Justices Popham, Anderson, Egerton, and Stanley on the 19th.

Certain facts disclosed by their evidence are these:—

(1) Stokes found the money. "The several impressions" of the books he got printed "cost him about £40."

(2) The place of printing was Dort (in Holland), and the printer "one Hanse."

(3) Bowle and Stokes worked hand-in-hand. At one time both are at Dort together negotiating with Hanse; at another they are in London intriguing with the prisoners, supervising MSS., furtively distributing copies of the printed books; now Stokes alone is the "instrument" at Dort, now Bowle alone; now Bowle brings them over into England, now Stokes; and the latter's "clock (i.e., cloke) bag," seems to have been in active use with each.

(4) There were only three of the "books" which came into anything like a wide circulation during the writers' lifetime, or even before the end of the century. These were—(a) "A Collection of Slanderous Articles," and (b) Greenwood's "Answer to George Gifford's Pretended Defence of Read Prayers," both printed about April, 1590.[2] Five hundred copies of each, says Stokes, were brought into England, and "200 or 300 given" to Barrow and Greenwood for distribution; (c) "A Collection of Certain Letters, &c.," printed about midsummer, 1590—500 copies in all—and 200 or 300 brought into England.[3] The later "books"—and the more important —were intercepted, or did not emerge from the MS. state. Just a few copies were all that found their way among the "brethren." It is of consequence to bear this in mind.

(5) Stokes' connection with the printing ceased after the seizure of the "Brief Discovery, &c.," in the spring of 1591—except possibly as secret "informer" to the Prelates. He "fell away" in the autumn, and—to have done with him—it may be added that when the Church became formally constituted under Johnson it publicly cast him out. This

[1] Printed for the Camden Society, 1840. Pp. 167-179.

[2] Stokes (March 19, 1593) says he caused these to be printed about this time three years. But as the former includes a conference held on April 13, 1590, they cannot have been in the printer's hands before the end of April.

[3] Greenwood says (March 11, 1593), that he has heard that the price of these three was 8d. each, and that 1,000 of them were printed. Perhaps he means 1,000 of them altogether.

appears from Thomas Settell's evidence (April 5, 1593)—" He also saith
that he was at the excommunication of Robert Stokes, and the words
were pronounced by Francis Johnson, their pastor." [1]

1589.   I.—1589. " A TRUE DESCRIPTION OF THE VISIBLE CONGREGATION OF
THE SAINTS UNDER THE GOSPEL, ACCORDING TO THE WORD OF
TRUTH."

This was the " little thing of one sheet " which Stokes printed before
anything else, i.e., before March, 1590.

It was reprinted (at least it is bound up) with " an apology or defence
of such true Christians as are commonly, but unjustly, called Brownists "
. . . 1604. (British Museum.)

It was reprinted again in 1641—" in the time of this hopefull Parliament, for the good of God's people, which desire that Christ may raigne in
His own ordinances." (Memorial Hall Library.) From this edition I
have quoted the title, but the title as given in the edition of 1604 is more
correct, viz., " A True Description out of the Word of God of the Visible
Church." [2]

In some notices of the " little thing " Johnson, Penry, and others are
mentioned as writers of it with Barrow. [3] But the date disposes of
Penry and Johnson at any rate. For neither was a " Separatist " before
1592 ; and the " tract " is " Separatist " unmistakably.

II.—" A COLLECTION OF CERTAIN SCLANDEROUS ARTICLES GIVEN OUT BY
THE BISHOPS AGAINST SUCH FAITHFULL CHRISTIANS AS THEY
NOW UNJUSTLY DETEYNE IN THEIR PRISONS, TOGETHER WITH
THE ANSWEARE OF THE SAIDE PRISONERS THEREUNTO. ALSO
THE SOME [SUM] OF CERTAINE CONFERENCES HAD IN THE
FLEETE ACCORDING TO THE BISHOPS BLOUDIE MANDATE WITH
TWO PRISONERS THERE."   [Dr. Williams's Library.]

1590, circ.   1590 [about April]. Printed at Dort [500 copies] at the charge of
April.   Robert Stokes, and conveyed by him into England.

The contents :—(a) Preface by the Editor [Stokes ?] 3 pp.

(b) Letter " to owre loving friends, Mr. Archdeacon Mullins, Mr. Doctor
Andros [Andrews], Mr. Cotton, Mr. Hutchinson, and the rest of the
Preachers in and about London within named." Dated 25 February,
1589–90 ; signed John Lond [Aylmer], John Herbert, Edw. Stanhope
Rich. Cosen.

(c) " A briefe of the positions holden by the new sectorie of recusants "
—twelve in number.

(d) List of the prisoners and of the preachers appointed to visit them.

(e) " Brief answeare to such articles as the Bishops have given out in
our name "—an introduction and answer to the " positions " seriatim. 7 pp.

(f) " The brief summe of a conference had the 9 day of the 3 moneth

---

[1] Harleian MSS. 7.042, p. 35.
[2] See Appendix IV.
[3] Thus, Dexter's title for it in his
Bibliography is " A description of the
visible Church, written by Barrow,
Johnson, Penry, and others." This
need not mean that he himself would
include Penry and Barrow.

between Mr. Hutchinson Archdeacon, and me, John Greenwood, prisoner in the Fleet, having been kept close now a year and an half by the Bishops' sole commandment. . . ." 5 pp.

(g) "The summe of the second conference had betweene Mr. Hutchinson and me, John Greenwood, the 17 day of the third moneth." 5 pp.

(h) "The summe of the conference had in the Fleet the 18 of the 3 moneth betwixt Mr. Hutchinson and Dr. Androes of the one partye, and Henry Barrow close prisoner[1] there on the other. . . ." 13 pp.

(i) "A summe of such cheif poynts as were handled in the second conference betwixt Mr. Hutchinson, Dr. Androes on the one parte, and John Greenwood and Henry Barrow prisoners in the Fleet, on the other partie, upon the 13 of the 4 moneth." 5 pp.

(k) "A breif answeare to certayne sclaunderous articles and ungodly calumniations sparsed abrode by the BBs and theire adherents against diverse faithfull and true Christians her Majesties loyall and lovinge subjectes to colour theire owne ungodly and tyrannicall dealing with them and to bring them into hatred both with Prince and people." (These articles are different from the "Positions" already answered— though the same in number and not unlike in general character. *Those* were a private "schedule" for the Preachers' guidance, *these* had been "sparsed abrode"; and are so expressed as to evoke the greatest amount of prejudice.) 9 pp.

At the end: "Expect theyr other conferences with all possible speed."

III.—"AN ANSWER TO GEORGE GIFFORD'S PRETENDED DEFENCE OF READ PRAIERS AND DEVISED LITOURGIES, WITH HIS UNGODLIE CAVILS AND WICKED SCLANDERS, COMPRISED IN THE FIRST PARTE OF HIS LAST UNCHRISTIAN AND REPROCHFULL BOOKE, ENTITULED A SHORT TREATISE AGAINST THE DONATISTS OF ENGLAND." "BY JOHN GREENWOOD, CHRIST'S POORE AFFLICTED PRISONER IN THE FLEET FOR THE TRUTH OF THE GOSPELL." *1590, circ. April.*

[Dr. Williams's Library.]

Printed[2] at same time and place as (2); 500 copies, conveyed into England by Stokes; 200 or 300 given to Barrow and Greenwood "for dysposytion."

In his preface Greenwood gives the outline of an earlier writing by himself on the same subject, which, being "carried abroade by such as desired true instruction," was intercepted, and "fell into Mr. Gifford's hands."

When the treatise was republished, in 1603, the editor [F. Johnson?] refers to this, and says: "if by any means that first of his come into thy handes, be thou entreated, for the truth's sake, eyther thyself to publish it, or to deliver it to such as will; that so the whole matter and carriage of it may better appeare to all men, for the further manifestation of the truth in this behalf." I am not aware that the lost MS. has ever been recovered.

[1] "Two yeares and well nye an half," says Barrow, later

[2] Stokes's Evidence, March 19, 1593.

The 1603 edition suggests Francis Johnson as editor by the fact that the Introduction is in the style of Johnson, and that both this and the body of the treatise are apparently in the same type [old English] as "Master Francis Johnson's answer to Master H. Jacob's defence of the Church and ministry of England" (1600), interspersed, in like manner also, with sentences in Roman type. Another circumstance points the same way. The 1603 edition has an appendix entitled, a "*Fewe observations of Mr. Giffard's last cavills about stinted read prayers and devised Leitourgies.*" This appendix is wanting in the 1590 edition—naturally, as it was written later. But it appears to have been printed together with [Barrow's] Plain Refutation, &c., and [Greenwood's] Brief Refutation, in 1591—the volume which brought about Johnson's conversion to Separatism. Hence in retaining that volume he retained the "observations," and might be expected to add them to the "treatise" [of 1590] which dealt with the same subject.

IV.—CONFERENCES AND LETTERS, &c.

[The full title-page is missing in the copy I have consulted—in Dr. Williams's Library.]   Preface 2 pp.

1590,
Summer.

(a) "The summe of the conference betwixt Mr. Thomas Sperin and me, Henry Barrow, upon the 14th of the third moneth in the Fleet. . . ." 15 pp.

(b) "The summe of a conference had betwene Mr. Sperin and Mr. Egerton of the one side, and Henry Barrow and John Greenwood of the other side, in their chamber . . . in the Fleet, upon the 20 of the third moneth, 1590." 15 pp.

(c) Correspondence of Barrow and Greenwood with Mr. Egerton. Seven letters, April 12 to May 11, 1590.

(d) "The summe of a confuse conference had the 3 of the 4 moneth, betwixt Mr. Sperin and Mr. Cooper, John Greenwood and Henry Barrow in the Fleet." 18 pp.

(e) Eleven "arguments" which "were more than a yeare and an halfe since delivered to Mr. Cartwright, Mr. Travers, Mr. Charke and Mr. Floyde," and "which still remaine upon them unanswered." 4 pp.

These five pieces—which give the other conferences that were to be expected "with all possible speed"—were printed in the summer of 1590. Stokes says they were printed at his charge, but Bowle was the agent, and brought them from Dort into England. He "delivered sundry copies to one Mychens." "500 in all."

V.—"THE FIRST PART OF THE PLATFORME, PENNED BY THAT WORTHY SERVANT OF JESUS CHRIST, AND BLESSED WITNES OF HIS MOST HOLY ORDINANCES TO THE LOSSE OF LIFE, MR. HENRY BARROWE."   [Dr. Williams's Library.]

The Platform is included in a longer writing with this title-page:—

"MR. HENRY BARROWE'S PLATFORM,

Which may serve as a Preparative to purge away Prelatisme: with some other parts of Poperie.

1590,
September
13?

Made ready to be sent from Miles Micklebound to much-beloved England. Together with some other memorable things. And, a familiar Dialogue, in and with the which, all the severall matters conteyned in this booke, are set forth and interlaced. After the untimely death of the penman of the foresaid Platforme, and his fellow-prisoner; who being constant witnesses in points apperteyning to the true worship of God, and right government of His Church, sealed up their testimony with their bloud; and paciently suffred the stopping of their breath, for their love to the Lord—Anno 1593.

Printed for the yeare of better hope—[*1611 at end*].

Micklebound [otherwise quite unknown] says truly that the Plat form "sheweth principally two things. The first, that "all false and anti-Christian ministeries [yet reteyned in the land] ought by the Prince's-authority to be rooted out." The second, that "[by like authority] their anti-Christian and idolatrous livings ought to be converted to [charitable] civil uses: and are not to be given or appropriated to God's true ministerie for the maintenance thereof: neither ought it to receive the same."

Desiderius [Micklebound's imaginary interlocutor] says: "You call the writing the first part, &c., which implieth a second likewise. But is there so?"

Miles: "I never saw it; but I hope ere my return I shall see Amsterdam and Leyden, where I shall make diligent inquiry among the people there." Farther on he speaks more positively: "I know not where to have it, neyther doe I think that ever it was finished. For the adversary Prelats thought better to finish the authors' lives." What the second part was to treat of is stated by the authors themselves [for Greenwood is coupled with Barrow, though the latter alone did the writing]—it was to show how the changes advocated in the first part "should be effected, what the true ministry of Christ is, how it should be created and brought in."

Desiderius asks: "To whom was this work presented?"

Miles: "As I have heard, to the Right Honourable Sir William Cecill, Knight, Baron of Burleigh, Lord High Treasurer of England, &c."

Desiderius: "They in their writing have praised his wisdome, but had he preserved their lives from the violence and cruelty of the Prelates, that would have praised his virtue."

As to the date of "Platform," a sure clue is found in a letter addressed to Burghley by Barrow and Greenwood which is printed with it. The letter is dated "from the Fleet this 13 of this 9 moneth." But what year? Well, the writers say we have "had no exercise to our bodies, ayre, or other things needfull, even for the preserving of life this *three yeares* in effect." Thus the date would be September 13, 1590.

Desiderius says: "I pray you tell me the reason why they printed not this Platform heretofore, and that especially against the King's Majestie's First Parliament in England; for that was the time, then was the hope."

Miles: "Had his Majestie any Arch or Lord Bishop in all his kingdome of Scotland? Were not all put downe? And who would not then have thought but the like worthy work should have been done in England, after his Highnes coming thither, to have brought those kingdomes and countries into Christian uniformitie? This was their hope . . . ."

Desiderius: "But how know you they stayed the printing of the Plot (i.e., Platform) against the Prelates, upon any such desire, hope, or consideration as you mentioned?"

Miles: "I had speech with Mr. Francis Johnson, one of the pastors of that people, who came with other his assistants to make their humble sute to the King, and were readie to enterteyne conference with the Prelates, that His Majestie might the more perfectly have understood the innocency of their cause, and the evilnes of their adversaries; andthat same party [viz., F. Johnson] told me, if they should print the aforesaid Platforme, he thought it would give offence, and bee very ill-taken, inasmuch as it was thought that the King and Councill would doe something of themselves for the abolishing of Bishops, &c. And so they patiently waited to see what would be done."

Not paged, but there are 46 pp. of the Platform.
9 pp. of the Letter.
Large print, duodec.

VI.—"A BRIEFE DISCOVERIE OF THE FALSE CHURCH.
'*As the mother such the daughter is.*'—*Ezek. xvi. 44.*
1590."

Three thousand copies were printed at Dort in the early months of 1591 [1590, we must remember, would extend to March 25, 1591] and seized at Flushing and Brill. Stokes bore the charge. Arthur Byllett was "examiner," or reader of the proof.[1] *All* the copies were not confiscated as the one we quote is a 1590 edition, and we hear of others—thus Daniel Studley deposed that he had two copies "after they were printed from Arthur Byllet," and that he gave one (perhaps the two) to John Gwalter 263 pp., 4 introduction. [Dr. Williams's Library.]

The book was republished in 1707 [London] under the title "A Brief Discovery of the False Churches, wherein the rights of the Christian Church are further asserted by the Holy Scriptures. Done from an. authentic MS. written in the reign of Queen Elizabeth by Henry Barrow, a member of the Honourable Society of Gray's Inn, who suffered death for his nonconformity to the Church of England." The changes from the original are abundant, and, as Dexter says, "unwarranted." The following, taken from the last pages of the book, will suffice to show this:

1707 [reprint].	1590 [original].
Seeing also that the Reformation of most of the Protestant Churches, in the state they are now in,	. . . Seing also evē[2] by this little search and superficiall view we have takē[2] of the present estate, and pretended reformation of this their Church of England, all things

---

[1] "Print" is Stokes's word.   [2] ē = en.

1707 [*reprint*].

is far from being completed, being [at the best] but enclining to the primitive and ancient defections from Christ's first institution, it behoveth

the chosen people of God who wait for the appearing of our Lord Jesus Christ to preserve their bodies and souls in purity . . .

1590 [*original*].

appeare to be out of frame, stil in the olde corruption, and (at the best) but enclining to the primitive and ancient defections from Christ's Testament, nothing being aright or according to the will of God amongst them: seing we find all those Scriptures that have foreshewed of Antichrist and his proceedings, truely fulfilled amongst them, al the markes of that painted deceitful harlot, the false and malignant Church, to be fownde upon them; as also all the vials of God's wrathfull judgments to be poured forth upon them, and al their doings. Finally, seing God vouchsafeth both to discover, and to call al men forth out of *Babilon*, by proclaiming of his glorious Gospel, and yet offreth more grace before he let fal the heavy milstone of his finall indignation upon them al to grind them to dust, and to presse them to the bottome of hel, being ready to receave all that come forth unto him, to esteeme, guide, and defend them as his deare children. It behoveth

al such, in whome is any care of their owne salvation, any feare of God, or love of that appearing of our Lord Jesus Christ to preserve their soules and bodies pure from the idolatrie and abhominations of the false Church . . .

VII.—"A PLAINE REFUTATION OF MR. GIFFARD'S BOOKE, INTITULED, A SHORT TREATISE GAINST THE DONATISTES OF ENGLAND.

Wherein is discovered
{
1 The forgery of the whole ministerie,
2 The confusion
3 False worship
4 Anti-Christian disorder, of these Parish assemblies, called the Church of England.
}
(i.)1590-91.

Here also is prefixed *a summe of the causes of our separation and of our purposes in practise*, which Mr. Giffard hath twise sought to confute, and hath now twise received answer, by Henry Barrowe. (ii.) 1588?

Here is furder inserted a brief refutation of Mr. Giff. supposed consimilitude betwixt the Donatistes and us. Wherein is shewed how his arguments have been, and may be by the Papists more justly retorted against himself and the present estate of their Church. By Jo. Greenwood. (iii.) 1590-91.

Here are also annexed a few observations of Mr. Giff. his last reply, not printed heretofore: *as the other aforesaid were in the yeare 1591.*" (iv.) Jan., 1592?

[Dr. Williams's Library.]

22

"An advertisement to the reader" at the end of Barrow and Greenwood's epistle dedicatory [to Sir Wm. Cecil] tells us that these Treatises [with the exception of the "Few Observations"] were intercepted "some while since" and are "now [1605] republished"—by whom is not said.

(a) In his examination March 20, 1593, Greenwood was required to identify a "book" containing (i.), (iii.), and also "A few observations of Mr. Gifford's last cavils about stinted read prayers and devised Leitourgies," which last must be carefully distinguished from (iv.). Hence it appears that these three were printed together in one volume 1590-91.

(b) No. (ii.).—viz., "A Briefe Summe of the causes of our separation and of our purposes in practice withstood by G. G., defended by H. B. as followeth" [a booklet of 20 pp.], if not printed earlier than 1591 was written earlier, as early even as 1588. For [on p. 3] Barrow says it is twenty-nine years since the existing Church order, which he calls the yoke of Antichrist, was set up, *i.e.*, since the early summer of 1559, when the Act of Uniformity came into force. But this *booklet* is later than the "Briefe Summe" itself: it is Barrow's "*defence*" of it against Gifford's answer to it. The "Briefe Summe" is quoted verbatim as introductory to the rest, and was a "leaflet" intended probably for general distribution. Perhaps it was the earliest thing which Barrow [and Greenwood?] wrote. We quote it in the Appendix. [See Appendix ii.]

A better idea of the 1605 volume is given by the volume itself than by the editorial title-page.

1. "The Epistle to the Right Honourable Pere and grave Counsellor Sir William Cecill, Knight of the most noble order, Baron of Burleigh, Lord High Treasurer of England, &c." 5 pp.

2. Preface. "Wisdome to the Reader from the Father of lights to discerne of these times, and to judge of themselves what is right. . . ." 12 pp.

3. "A Briefe summe of the causes of our separation, and of our purposes in practise, withstood by G. G., defended by H. B. as followeth." 20 pp.

4. "A Plaine Refutation of Mr. Giffard his reprochful Booke, intituled, A short treatise against the Donatistes of Englande, &c." 188 pp.

5. "A Briefe Refutation of Mr. George Giffard, his supposed consimilitude betwene the Donatists and us, &c." 28 pp. Jo. Greenwood signed at the end.

6. "A few observations to the reader of Mr. Giffard his last replie"—23 pp.—a reply, it appears, "to certaine intercepted books of ours," meaning, no doubt, the "*Plain*" Refutation and the "*Brief*" Refutation which, on their publication in 1591, had fallen into the hands of the authorities. The opening sentences disclose the writer and the date:—"The Prelates of these tymes, not having such power as their predecessors to murrther the faithfull servants of Christ openly, have together with the learned of their clergie taken a more secret course, to make them away in their prisons and there to burie them as it were alive. . . . Among others Mr. Greenwood and *myself* have thus been entreated by them. Now albeit we

are and have been four years and three months without tryal or relaxation, kept by the Prelates in most miserable and streight imprisonment. . . ."

Barrow, therefore, was the writer,[1] and the date would be early in 1592. For on March 15, 1590, he had been close prisoner for two years and well-nigh a half. When he wrote the "Epistle Dedicatory" to the intercepted volume, he had been close prisoner for "more than three years," which brings us, say, to January, 1591; and then if we take "more than" as equal to the "three months" we reach January, 1592, for the "Observations." This does not mean that they were printed then. The 1605 editor says distinctly that "they were not printed heretofore." He found them in manuscript.

These Treatises—a "Plain" and a "Brief" Refutation *minus* Barrow's "few observations of Mr. Giffard's last reply," but *plus* Greenwood's "few observations of Mr. Giffard's last cavills"—formed one of the two volumes taken at Flushing and Brill in the spring of 1591. But [perhaps] a year later a second printing of the volume was attempted— this time at Middelburg, in Zealand. And here comes in the well-known story of Francis Johnson: how he was at the time "a preacher to the Company of the English [Merchants] of the Staple at Middelburg"; how "he was so zealous against this [Separatist] way as that [when] Master Barrow and Master Greenwood's Refutation of Master Gifford *was privately in printing in this city*, he not only was a means to discover it, but was made the [English] Ambassador's instrument to intercept them at the press, and see them burnt"; how he "surprised the whole impression, not suffering any to escape, and then . . caused them all to be openly burnt, himself standing by until they were all consumed to ashes"; how "he took up two of them—one to keep in his own study, that he might see their errors; and the other to bestow on a special friend, for the like use"; how he was "so taken, and his conscience was troubled so as he could have no rest in himself until he crossed the seas, and came to London to confer with the authors."[2] If Johnson was the editor in 1603 of Greenwood's answer [with his "Few Observations"] it is likely that he was also the editor in 1605 of these Treatises [with Barrow's "Few Observations"]. Who, indeed, more likely, seeing that he had them in his possession, and had studied them to such advantage himself? In this light his counsel to the "*Good Reader*"[3] to "read and ponder them with judgment and indifference"; and to "receive them" so far and "no furder" than they agree with the Word of God gains a special interest.

VIII. The only other authentic writings of Barrow, so far as I know, are:—(a) The private Letter,[4] in December, 1590, to one Mr. Fisher, which, as it seems, was intercepted. [Strype quotes[5] from it, but does not say

---

[1] His name is printed on the last page.
[2] Bradford's Dialogue in Young's Chronicles, pp. 424-5.
[3] The phrase occurs again in the advertisement to the 1603 vol.

[4] Printed in the Separatists' "Apology" (1604), B. M.
[5] Whitgift, Bk. iv., c. xi., p. 414-5.

where he has seen it.]   Barrow owned to two other letters which were produced at his examination [March 20, 1592-3], the one beginning "Brother R., your letter of the 12th"; the other beginning, "So honour hath been."   These, too, had miscarried.

(b) The Petition to the House of Commons, occasioned by the arrest of Separatists on April 3, 1592 [preserved by Miles Micklebound].

(c) Probably [judging from the style] the Petition to the Lord Treasurer presented some time earlier than the last in the same year.[1]

(d) His petition to the Attorney-General Egerton for a conference . . . and his address [for the same] to the Council, entitled "A motion tending to unity."   Strype[2] puts these at the beginning of 1593 ["soon after executed," he says of the writer].

IX. The following has been attributed to Barrow—by Dexter among others, who draws from its defence of "Martin" a part of his argument for Barrow's authorship of the Tracts :—

"A Petition directed to Her Most Excellent Majestie, wherein is delivered :

1. A mean how to compound the civil dissension in the Church of England.

2. A proofe that those who write for Reformation do not offend against the statute of 23 Eliz. c. 2; and, therefore, till matters be compounded deserve more favour, &c."

There is no author's or printer's name, and no date; but 1590, as Dexter conjectures, must be near the mark.

The writer says :—"I do not *now* write either to pull down bishoprics or erect presbyteries."   But he says as means to that end "a free national or provincial Council at home were much to be wished, so that the bishops and their followers did not overrule the rest.   . . ."

His reasons for advocating such a Council are these :—

1. The laws expect a further Reformation of the Church.

2. The defenders of our common cause expect it.

3. The defenders of the State of Bishops expect it.

4. The suspicious and doubtful handling of the controverted matters imply some need of reformation and conference.

5. So do the testimonies of learned men.

6. On the other side, all these "pursuers of reformation have had great inducements to enforce the eldership."

It is "further reformation" and the "eldership" that he wants.   He is a Puritan, therefore, and cannot be Barrow.

We come to the same conclusion from his sympathetic references to Martin Marprelate.   For example,[3] "When Martin, senr., speaks of 100,000 hands" [and "saith that these so many together would strike a great stroke" (p. 16)], here he merely "exhorts lords, gentlemen, and people of England to become joint suitors to Her Majesty that in every parish there may be a preacher so near as may be; that there may be quiet

---

[1] Strype's Annals, vol iv., pp. 127-130.   [2] Annals, vol. iv., p. 239, ff.   [3] P. 44.

meeting for debating controversies, and power to sue a bishop at King's Bench when they act unlawfully. . . ."

Dexter would identify the writer with Martin himself, and some of his words are intimate enough to warrant the inference, or, at least, to make it probable that he knew him well. Thus, " In saying that Dr. Bridges [for writing against Reformation] would shortly have twenty fists about his ears more than his own," he meant that they would " exercise hands in writing " against Bridges.

But if the writer was Martin, what we have found to be his ecclesiastical position shows that Martin could not have been Barrow, though he might well have been Penry, or, what is perhaps more likely, Penry is the writer, and is here defending his friend Throckmorton.

The two editions of "a True Description . . . of the visible Church."

WE give here the 1641 reprint of "A True Description," collated with the first edition of 1589. The former is in the Memorial Hall Library. The latter is in the British Museum, 4103 C 2.

Additions to the original text are marked by square brackets.

Omissions and alterations are noted in the margin.

The Scripture references are omitted and the spelling modernised.

A True Description *of the Visible Congregation of the Saints under the Gospel, according to the Word of Truth.*[1]

As there is but one God and Father of all, one Lord over all, and one Spirit, so there is but one Truth, one Faith, one Salvation, one *Congregation;*[2] called in one hope, joined in one profession, guided by one rule, even the word of the Most High.

This *congregation,*[3] as it is universally understood, containeth in it all the elect of God that have been, are, or shall be; but being considered more particularly, as it is seen in this present world, it consisteth of a company and fellowship of faithful and holy people, gathered in the name of *Jesus Christ,*[4] their one[5] King, Priest, [6] Prophet; worshipping Him *according to His Word,*[7] being peaceably [8] governed by His officers and laws; keeping the unity of faith in the bond of peace and love unfeigned. *Most excellent and glorious things are spoken throughout all the Scriptures of this congregation.*[9]

It is called the City, House, Temple, and Mountain of the Eternal God, the chosen Generation, the holy Nation, the peculiar people, the Vineyard, the Garden enclosed, the Spring shut up, the sealed Fountain, the Orchard of Pomegranates with sweet fruits, the Heritage, the Kingdom of Christ, yea, His Sister, His Love, His Spouse, His Queen, and His Body; the Joy of the whole earth. *To this holy society and blessed fraternity is the covenant*[10] and all the promises [11] peace, of love, and of salvation, of the presence of God, of His graces, of His power, and of His protection.

If this congregation[12] be considered in her parts, it shall appear most beautiful, yea, [13] wonderful, and even ravishing the senses to conceive, much more to behold, what then to enjoy so blessed a communion! For behold! her King and Lord is the King of Peace and *Lord of Glory*;[14] she enjoyeth [15] holy and heavenly laws; [15] faithful and vigilant pastors; [15] sincere and pure teachers; [15] careful and upright *elders*;[16] [15] diligent and trusty deacons; [15] loving and sober relievers; [16]

Margin notes (1589 EDITION):

[1] out of the Word of God of the visible Church.
[2] Church.
[3] Church.
[4] Christ Jesus.
[5] only.
[6] Adds—"and."
[7] aright.
[8] Adds—"and quietly."
[9] Most joyful, excellent and glorious things are everywhere in the Scriptures spoken of this Church.
[10] To this Society is the Covenant, &c.
[11] Adds—"made of."
[12] And surely if this Church.
[13] Adds—"most."
[14] Lord himself of all glory.
[15] governors.
[16] Adds—"and a most."

1589
EDITION.

humble, meek, obedient, faithful, and loving people; *every stone living, elect and precious, having his beauty*,[1] his burden, and his order; all bound to edify one another, exhort [admonish], reprove [encourage], and comfort one another; *loving*,[2] as to *the members of their own natural body, faithful as in the sight and presence of God*.[3]

No office here *must be*[4] ambitiously affected, no law wrongfully wrested or wilfully neglected; no truth hid or perverted. Every one here hath freedom and power (not disturbing the [peaceable] order of the *congregation*)[5] to utter his complaints and griefs, and freely to reprove the transgression and errors of any without exception of persons.

Here is no intrusion or climbing up another way into the sheepfold than by the holy and free election of the Lord's holy and free people, and that according to the Lord's ordinance, humbling themselves by fasting and prayer before the Lord, craving the direction of His Holy Spirit, for the trial and approving of [their] gifts, &c.

Thus they[6] *proceed* to ordination, by fasting and prayer, in which action the Apostles [or first messengers of Jesus Christ], *using*[7] laying on of hands, *thus*[8] hath every one of the people interest in the election and ordination of their officers, as also in the administration of their offices, upon transgression, offence, abuse, &c., having *a special*[9] care unto [the] unviolable order of the *congregation*,[10] as is aforesaid.

In this congregation[11] they have holy laws as limits and bonds, *which are to be put in execution that they may be precisely kept and at no hand transgressed. These Laws are so complete that they direct them in all things, especially in the choice*[12] of every officer, what kind of men, *they*[13] will have [and how they must be qualified].

Their pastor must be apt to teach, no young scholar, able to divide the Word [of God] aright, holding fast that faithful Word [of truth] [14] that he may be *able to inform, exhort, admonish, and rebuke with*[15] wholesome doctrine, and to convince *those*[16] that *oppose it*.[17] He must be a man that loveth goodness, *of good report, who* [undecipherable] *unreprovable as God's steward, one that ruleth his own household well, lest he be unfit to rule in the congregation of God*;[18] he must be modest, humble, meek, gentle, and loving; [he must be a man] of great patience, compassion, labour, and diligence; he must always be careful and watchful over the flock whereof the Lord hath made him [an] overseer, with all willingness and cheerfulness, not holding his office in respect of persons, but doing his duty to every soul [committed to his charge] as he will answer *to*[19] the chief *Pastor*[20] of our souls in the great day of his accounts.

(1) *Their teachers also must be*[21] apt to teach, able to divide the Word of God aright.[22] He must be mighty in the Scriptures, able to convince the gainsayers, and careful to deliver his doctrine pure, sound, and plain, not with curiosity or affectation, but so that it may edify the most simple, approving it to every man's conscience. He must be *holy in his conversation*,[23] one that can govern his own household. He must be *sober*,[24] humble, temperate, modest, gentle, [and] loving, &c.

[1] every stone has his beauty.
[2] lovingly.
[3] their own members faithfully as in the eyes of God.
[4] is.
[5] Church.
[6] Adds—"orderly."
[7] used.
[8] Thus.
[9] an especial.
[10] Church.
[11] Likewise in this Church.
[12] which it is lawful at no hand to transgress. They have laws to direct them in the choice.
[13] the Lord.
[14] Adds—"according to doctrine."
[15] able also to exhort, rebuke, improve with.
[16] them.
[17] say against it.
[18] he must be wise, righteous, holy, temperate; he must be of life unreprovable as God's steward; he must be generally well reported of, and one that ruleth his own household under obedience with all honesty, &c.
[19] before.
[20] Shepherd.
[21] Their Doctor or Teacher must be a man . . .
[22] Adds—"and to deliver sound and wholesome doctrine from the same, still building upon that same groundwork."
[23] of life unreprovable.
[24] of manner sober.

1589
EDITION.

Their elders must be of wisdom and judgment, indued with the Spirit of God, able to discern between cause and cause [1] and accordingly to prevent and redress evils, always vigilant, and *endeavouring*[2] to see the statutes, ordinances, and laws of God, kept [and executed] in the Church, and that not only *by all the particular members for their part of obedience, but that they also see the officers do their duties.*[3]

These *officers*[4] must be likewise unreprovable [in their conversation], governing their own families orderly; they must also be sober, gentle, modest, loving, temperate [&c.].

(2) Their deacons must be men of honest report, having the mystery of [5] faith in a pure conscience [and], indued with the Holy Spirit; they must be grave, temperate, not given to excess, nor to filthy lucre.

Their widows or relievers must be women of sixty years of age at the least, for avoiding of inconveniences; they must be well reported of for good works, such as have nourished their children, such as have been *harborours*[6] to strangers; diligent and serviceable to the saints, compassionate and helpful to them in adversity, given to every good work, continuing in supplications and prayers, day and night.

These officers must first be duly proved, then if they be found blameless, [let them] administer, &c.

Now as the persons, gifts, conditions, manners, life and proof of these officers are[7] set down by the Holy *Spirit*,[8] so are their offices limited, severed and *diverse*.[9]

The pastor's office is to feed the sheep of Christ in [the] green and wholesome pastures of his [blessed] Word, and lead them to the still waters even to the pure fountain and river of life; He must guide and keep those sheep, by that heavenly sheep-hook and pastoral staff of the word [of truth], thereby drawing them to him, thereby looking into their souls, even into their most secret thoughts, thereby discerning their diseases, and thereby curing them; applying to every disease a fit and convenient medicine, and according to the quality and danger of the disease, *giving*[10] warning to the Church, that they may orderly proceed [in all the censures] to excommunication. Further, he must by this [11] sheep-hook watch over and defend his flock from ravenous beasts, and the wolf, and take the little foxes.

The teacher's office being already described,[12] his special care must be to build upon the only true ground-work, gold, silver, and precious stones, that his work may endure the trial of the fire, and by the light of the same fire, reveal the timber, hay, and stubble of false [and corrupt] teachers; he must take diligent heed to keep the Church from errors; and further he must deliver his doctrine so plainly, simply and purely that the Church *may be edified*,[13] and grow up unto Him which is the Head, Christ Jesus.

The office of the *elders being*[14] expressed in their description, their special care must be [as well] to see the ordinances of God truly taught and *administered*,[15] as well by *the preaching elders, according to their duty, as that the remnant members of the Church perform their parts of obedience*

1 Adds—"between plea and plea."
2 intending.

3 by the people in obedience, but to see the officers do their duties.
4 Men.

5 Adds—"the."

6 harborous.

7 is.
8 Ghost.
9 divers.

10 gives.

11 Adds—"his."

12 The Doctor's office is already set down in his description.

13 may increase with the increase of God.
14 Ancients is.

15 practised.

1589
EDITION.

willingly and readily.[1] It is their duty to see the congregation holily and quietly ordered, and no way disturbed by the contentious, disobedient, froward, and obstinate, [yet] not taking away the liberty of the least [who stand for the maintenance of the truth once given to the saints], but upholding the right of all, [and] wisely judging of times and circumstances. They must be ready assistants to the pastor and teachers, helping to bear their burden, but not intruding into their office.

[1] by the officers in doing their duty uprightly as to see that the people obey willingly and readily.

The deacons' office is faithfully to gather and collect by the (ordinance of the *congregation*[2]) the good and benevolence of the faithful ; and, by the same direction, diligently and trustily to distribute them according to the necessity of the saints ; *further*,[3] they must enquire and consider of the proportion of the wants, both of the officers, and other poor [saints], and accordingly relate unto the Church, that *provision and relief may be made in due time, according to the Church's power and their necessity*.[4]

[2] Church.

[3] . Further.

[4] that provision may be made.

The widow's office[5] is to minister to the sick, lame, weary, and diseased such helpful comforts *and refreshments as be most needful*[6] by watching, *attending*,[7] and helping them [at all times, especially when they can least help themselves : likewise] [8] they must show good example to the younger women in sober, modest, and godly conversation, avoiding idleness, vain talk, and light behaviour.

[5] The relievers' and widows' office
[6] as they need.
[7] tending.
[8] Adds— "further."

These officers, though they be *diverse*[9] and several, yet are they not severed, lest there should be a division in the body but . . . [undecipherable][10] same care one of another, jointly doing their several duties, [in their places] to the service of the saints, and to the edification of the [mystical] body of [Jesus] Christ, *until*[11] we all meet together *in unity of faith unto a perfect measure of the fulness of Christ*,[12] by whom all the body being thus coupled and knit together every joint for the furniture thereof, according to the effectual power, which is in the measure of every part, receiveth increase of the body, unto the edifying of itself in love, neither can any of these offices be wanting without grievous lameness and apparent deformity of the body, yea, violent injury to the head, Christ Jesus. [In this Church is the heavenly harmony of the exercise of Prophecy, where the variety and diversity of God's gifts and graces in His saints are manifested, according to the gifts and abilities, that God hath given unto them, to the murall edification, exhortation, and comfort one of another and the rest of the body . . . and the whole. Which exercise of Prophecy is the first ordinance that the Lord commanded, and commended in His Church, under the Gospel, exhorting all His saints to the same, as the most special and excellent gift, yea, and most needful at all times, but especially when the pastor and teacher are either taken away by death, imprisoned, or exiled.]

[9] divers.
[10] they are as members of the body having the
[11] till.
[12] in the perfect measure of the fulness of Christ.

Thus this *Heavenly army of the militant saints*[13] is marshalled here on earth by these officers, under the conduct of their *most glorious and great General, Jesus Christ*,[14] that victorious Michael : *thus*[15] it marcheth in this most heavenly order and gracious array against all enemies, both corporal and *spiritual* ;[16] peaceable in itself as Jerusalem, terrible to the enemy as an army with banners, triumphing over their tyranny with patience, [over]

[13] Holy army of saints.
[14] Glorious Emperor Christ.
[15] . Thus.
[16] Ghostly.

[1] with dying.

their cruelty with meekness, and over death itself *by rejoicing in suffering, with joy unspeakable and glorious.*[1]

Thus through the blood of that spotless Lamb, and that word of their testimony, they are more than conquerors, bruising the head of the serpent; yea, through the power of His word they have power to cast down Satan like lightning, to tread upon serpents, and . . .[2] [undecipherable] thing that exalteth itself against God [and His blessed Son Jesus Christ]. The gates of Hell and all the principalities and powers *in*[3] the world, shall not prevail against it. *Moreover,*[4] he hath given [to] them the keys of the Kingdom [5] that whatsoever they bind *on earth, according to His Word,*[6] shall be bound in heaven, and whatsoever they loose on earth shall be loosed in heaven. Now this power which Christ hath given *to*[7] His Church, and to every member *thereof,*[8] to keep it in order, He hath not left it to their discretions and lusts, to be used or neglected [nor yet made more, less, or otherwise] *as* they will; but in His last will and testament he hath set down both an order of proceeding and an end to which it is used.

[2] scorpions: to
cut down strong-
holds and every-
thing.
[3] of.
[4] Further.
[5] Adds—"of
heaven."
[6] in earth by his
word.
[7] unto.
[8] of his Church.

If the fault be private, holy and loving admonition and reproof is to be used, with an *earnest*[9] desire and *inward*[10] care to win their brother; *but*[11] if he will not hear, yet to take two or three other brethren with him, whom he knoweth [to be] most meet for that purpose, that by the mouth of two or three witnesses every word *might*[12] be confirmed; *and*[13] if he refuse to hear them, then to declare the matter to the Church, which ought, [in love to God and the party and hatred to the sin], [14] sharply to reprehend, gravely to admonish, and lovingly to persuade the party offending, showing him the heinousness of his offence and the danger of his obstinacy, and the fearful judgments of the Lord.

[9] inward.
[10] earnest.
[11] . But

[12] may.
[13] And
[14] Adds—
"severally and."

Notwithstanding all this, the Church is not to hold him as an enemy, but [15] pray for him as a brother [and exhort him with the spirit of meekness], proving if at any time the Lord will give him repentance, [and bring him out of the snare of the devil] for this power is not given them to the destruction of any, but to the edification of all. . . . [Undecipherable][16] power of the Lord Jesus, with the whole congregation, reverently in prayer to proceed to excommunication, that is, to the casting [of] him out of their congregation and fellowship, covenant and protection of the Lord, for his disobedience and obstinacy, and committing him to Satan, for the destruction of the flesh, that the spirit may be saved in the day of the Lord Jesus, if *it*[17] be His good will and pleasure.

[15] Adds—"to ad-
monish him and."

[16] If this prevail
not to draw him
to repentance,
then are they in
the name and . . .

[17] such.
[18] Further.

Then[18] they are to warn the whole congregation and all other faithful [people] to hold him as a heathen and publican, and to abstain themselves from his society, as not to eat or drink with him, &c., unless it be *those which*[19] of necessity must needs, as his wife, [20] children, and family; yet these, ([as well as others] if they be members of the Church) are not to join with him in any spiritual exercise.

[19] such as.
[20] Adds—"his."

If the offence be public, the party is publicly to be reproved and admonished; if he then repent not, to proceed to excommunication as aforesaid.

The repentance of the party must be proportionable to the offence; *that is,*[1] if the offence be public, [the repentance must be] public; if private, [the repentance must be] private, *humble,*[2] submissive, sorrowful, unfeigned, giving glory to the Lord.

There must *be great care had*[3] of admonitions [and reprehensions] that they be not captious, or curious, finding fault where none is; neither yet in bitterness or reproach, [nor deridingly to insult, as if themselves were without fault] for that were to destroy *rather than save*[4] our brother; but they must be carefully done with prayer going before; they must be seasoned with truth, gravity, love, and peace.

Moreover, in this Church is *a special*[5] care to be had [6] of offences; the strong ought not to offend the weak, nor the weak to judge the strong, but all graces here are given to the service and edification of each other in love and long suffering.

In this *congregation,*[7] [though it consist but of two or three] is the [word of] truth purely taught, and surely kept; here is the Covenant, the *seals*[8] and promises, the graces, the glory, the presence, the worship of God, &c.

[So] *into this blessed Church which is heaven upon earth, there ought not to enter any*[9] unclean thing, [and if any creep in and be discovered, to be speedily removed,] neither whatsoever worketh abominations or lies, *ought to enter, but only such as be of holy conversation, and whose names are written*[10] in the Lamb's book of life. But without this *congregation,*[11] [and heavenly society] shall be dogs and enchanters, and whoremongers and murderers, and idolaters, and whosoever loveth and maketh lies.

FINIS.

Printed in the time of this hopeful Parliament, for the good of God's people, which desire that Christ may reign in His own ordinances. 1641.

1 Vis. :
2 humbled.
3 great care be had.
4 and not to save.
5 an especial.
6 Adds—" by every member thereof."
7 Church.
8 Sacraments.
9 Into this Temple entereth no . . .
10 . But they which are writ . . .
11 Church.
1589.

APPENDIX V.

The Separatists' Seven Questions.

THE following are the "seven questions" which Mr. Arber [pp. 280-2 of his "Story of the Pilgrim Fathers"] has mistaken for the "seven articles" sent by the Church of Leyden to the Council of England. They are quoted verbatim by Will Euring in the preface of his answer to Mr. Thomas Drakes's "Ten Counter Demands."

Euring [1619] says they were "propounded" by the Separatists "some good space since."

Question I.—Whether the Lord Jesus Christ have in His last will and testament given unto and set in His Church sufficient ordinary offices, with their callings, works, and maintenance, for the administration of His holy things, and for the ordinary instruction, guidance, and service of His Church to the end of the world, or no?

Question II.—Whether the offices of Pastors, Teachers, Elders, Deacons, and Helpers be those offices appointed in the testament of Christ? or whether the present ecclesiasticall offices of Arch-Bishops, Lord Bishops, Suffragans, Deanes, Priests, Vicars, Arch-Deacons, Prebendaries, Canons, Gospellers, Petty-Canons, Epistlers, Virgerers, Queristers, Organ-Players, Parsons, Curates, Chancelors, Commissaries, Proctors, Registers, Apparitors or Sumners, Churchwardens, Doctors of Divinity, Questmen or Sidemen, Deacons or Half-Priests, Chaplins or House-Priests, Clarkes, Sextons, and the rest now had and retained in the Cathedrall and Parishionall Assemblies of the land, be those offices appointed in Christ's last will and testament, or no?

Question III.—Whether the calling and entrance into the ecclesiasticall offices last before named, with their administrations and maintenance, now had and retained in England, be the manner of calling, administration, and maintenance which Christ hath appoynted for the offices of His Church, or no?

Question IV.—Whether every true Church of Christ be not a company of people called and separated out from the world and false worship and waies thereof by the word of God and joyned together in the fellowship of the Gospel by voluntary profession of the faith and obedience of Christ.

Question V.—Whether the Sacraments, being sealles of the righteousnes which is by faith, may be administered unto any other but to the faithfull and their seed, or in any other ministry or manner than is prescribed and appointed by Jesus Christ the Apostle and high priest of our profession? And whether they be not otherwise administered in the parish assemblies of England this day or no?

Question VI.—Whether the booke of Common Prayer, with the feasts, fasts, stinted prayers, holly dayes, and leiturgy prescribed therein and used in the assemblies, be the true worship of God commanded in His word, or the devise and invention of man for God's worship and service.

Question VII.—Whether all people and churches without exception be not bound in religion only to receive and submit unto that ministry worship and order which Christ, as Lord and King, hath given unto and appointed in his Church: or whether any may receive and joyne into another devised by man for the worship and service of God, and consequently whether they that joyne to the present ecclesiasticall ministry worship and order of the Cathedrall and Parishionall Assemblies can be assured by the word of God, that they joyne to the former, ordayned by Christ, and not to the latter, devised by man for the worship and service of God?

INDEX OF REFERENCES.

A—CONTEMPORARY.

Ainsworth (Henry), *Counterpoyson* (1608), 240, 272

———— *Defence of Holy Scripture, &c. . . . against . . . John Smyth* (1609), 250-251

———— *Animadversion to Master Richard Clyfton* (1613), 256, 257, 266-268, 271, 274, 301

———— *Certain Notes of his Last Sermon* (1630), 259

Apologie or Defence of such true Christians as are commonly called Brownists (1604), 76-79, 254, 339

Bacon (Francis, Lord), *Observations on a Libel* (1591), 9, 62

Bancroft (Richard), *Survey of the Holy Discipline* (1593), 11

Barrow (Henry). See Appendix III. for full list

———— *Letter to Cartwright Travers, &c.* (1588), 93-94

———— *A True Description out of the Word of God of the Visible Church* (1589), 36, 108

———— *A Collection of, and Answers to Certain Slanderous Articles* (1590), 99, 121

———— *Plain Refutation of Mr. Giford* (1590), 5, 20 *note*, 85, 92, 99, 103, 105, 125-129, 148-149, 153

———— *A Brief Discovery of the False Church* (1590), 5, 85, 91, 93-95, 97-98, 102-105, 108, 110-111, 114-115, 117-118, 120-122, 127-130, 143-144, 149-150

———— *Platform* (1590, pub. 1611), 144

———— *Supplication to the Queen* (1590), 58-59

———— *A Few Observations to the Reader of Mr. Gifford's Last Reply* (1592, pub. 1605), 21, 33

Canne (John), *Necessitie of Separation* (1634), 154

Conferences with Barrow and Greenwood (1590), 10, 14, 34, 42, 43-57, 92-93, 98-101, 103 *note*, 106, 115, 153

Confession of Faith of certain English People living in Exile (1596), 221

Clyfton (Richard), *Advertisement* (1612), 227, 233, 297, 303 *note*

Cooper (Thomas), *Admonition to the People of England* (1589), 165, 171, 174

D'Ewes' Journals (1593), 62, 79, 224

Dighton (Thomas), *Certain Reasons of a Private Christian against Conformity to Kneeling, &c.* (1618), 121

Egerton Papers, the (1593) (Camden Society's Publications), 35, 37, 75, 76, 331, 333

Euring (William), *Answer to Mr. Thomas Drakes* (1619), 293-294, 348-349

Examinations of Barrow and Greenwood (1586), 16-21, 24 *seqq.* 119

Fairlambe (Peter), *Recantation of a Brownist* (1606), 224

Foxe, *Book of Martyrs*, 23

Harleian MSS., 4, 9, 33, 58, 67-71, 74, 75, 225, 234, 332

Hooker, *Ecclesiastical Polity*, 131, 153-154, 188

Johnson (Francis), *Answer to Master Henry Jacob* (1600), 131, 229-231, 237, 238, 265

———— *An Inquiry and Answer of Thomas White, his Discovery* (1606), 243

———— *Certain Reasons and Arguments, &c.* (1608), 319 *note*

———— *Answer touching the Division, &c.* (1611), 274

Johnson (Francis), *Christian Plea* (1617), 131. 258, 268, 292, 315-318

Johnson (George), *A Discourse of Some Troubles at Amsterdam* (1603), 227, 228, 238-240, 243, 244, 307

Lawne (Christopher). *Profane Schism* (1612), 154, 227, 234, 240, 256, 292, 296, 298-301, 303-305, 307 *note*, 311

———— *Brownism Turned Inside out* (1613), 296, 301, 302

Marprelate Tracts, the (1588), 53 *note*, 83-85, 165, 171

Miles Micklebound in Barrow's Platform (1611), 64, 80-81, 120-121, 128, 144, 221, 243, 254, 335-336

Paget (John), *An Arrow against the Separation of the Brownists* (1618), 131, 225, 232, 256, 261, 306-308, 319-322

Robinson (John), *Justification of Separation* (ed. 1610), 297, 313. *See* Works ii.

Robinson (John), *Works* (Ed. Ashton), 117, 120-121, 226, 228, 236, 240, 241, 249, 251, 259-261, 271, 273-284, 322-324

Smyth (John), *The Differences of the Churches of the Separation* (1608), 211, 216-217, 250

———— *Parallels, Censures, Observations* (1605), 248

———— *Retraction of his Errors* (c. 1613), 248 *note*, 253-254

Some (Robert) *Godly Treatises* (1588-1589), 26, 85

Throckmorton (Job). *Master Some Laid Open in his Colours* (1590), 84, 329

Udall (John) *Demonstration of Discipline* (1588), 140

———— *Deotrophes* (1588), 147

White (Thomas), *Discovery of Brownism* (1605), 243-245, 297

Whitgift (John), *Works* (Parker Society's Publications), 188-197, 339

B—LATER.

Adeney (Professor), *The Church in the Prisons* (Tercentenary Tracts, I.), 106

Allen, *Christian Institutions*, Introduction

Arber (Professor), *Introductory Sketch to the Marprelate Controversy*, 15, 22, 35, 84

———— *Story of the Pilgrim Fathers*, 79, 229, 240, 243, 245, 248, 249, 250, 252, 259 *note*, 289-296, 302-305, 308-309, 812-315, 319, 323

Arnold (Dr.), *Fragment on the Church*, Introduction

Axon, *Henry Ainsworth, the Puritan Commentator*, 232-233, 258

Barclay, *Inner Life of the Religious Societies of the Commonwealth*, 206, 210, 248 *note*, 252-254

Beard, *Hibbert Lectures* (1883), 212, 213

Briggs (Dr. C. A.), *The New Testament Doctrine of the Church* (American Journal of Theology, Jan. 1900.), Introduction

Brown (Dr. John), *The Pilgrim Fathers*, 246, 249

Caird (Principal), *University Sermons*, Introduction

Davidson (Dr. Samuel), *The Ecclesiastical Polity of the New Testament*, Introduction

———— *Autobiography*, Introduction

Dexter, *Congregationalism as seen in its Literature*, 14, 82, 85, 251, 329, 332

Dictionary of National Biography : art. "Francis Johnson," 229

Encyclopædia Biblica : art. "Church," Introduction

Froude, *History of England*, 24, 206

Fuller, *Church History*, 206

Gage, *History and Antiquities of Suffolk*, 3

Heath, *Rise of Anabaptism*, 202 *passim.*

Jessopp (Dr. Augustus), *Norwich (Diocesan Histories)*, 176

Macaulay, *Essay on Burghley*, 7, 31

Mackennal, *Story of the Separatists*, 229

Mullinger, *History of the University of Cambridge*, 5-7, 11, 166, 188

Neal, *History of the Puritans*, 11, 59, 61, 141, 146, 180

Paget (Dean), *Introduction to the Fifth Book of Hooker's Ecclesiastical Polity*, Introduction

Prothero, *Select Statutes*, 161, 223

Rogers (Dr. Guinness), *John Robinson* ('Tercentenary Tracts, IV.), 34

Strype, *Annals*, 31 *note*, 72-73, 161, 164, 170 *note*, 172, 173, 178-179, 180, 226, 340

———— *Life of Aylmer*, 4 *note*, 10 *note*, 60 *note*

———— *Life of Whitgift*, 59, 169, 177-178, 181

Tayler, *Retrospect of the Religious Life in England*, 139, Introduction

Van Braght, *Martyrology of the Churches of Christians commonly called Baptists* (Hanserd-Knollys Society's Publications), 206

Wakeman (H. O.), *The Church and the Puritans*, 135

———— *History of the English Church*, 136

Walton, *Life of Hooker*, 153, 167, 185

Wood (Anthony), *Athenæ Oxonienses*, 74

Young, *Chronicles of the Pilgrim Fathers* (for Bradford's *Dialogues*), 8, 80-82, 224, 225, 232, 233, 237, 238, 241-242, 244, 245, 246-248, 255, 258, 259 *note*, 291, 302, 339

INDEX.

A

Act to retain the Queen's Subjects in Obedience, the (1593): enjoins banishment to the Separatists, 222

Acton, 3

Admonition to the People of England, Cooper's, 163

Ainsworth, Henry: life of, and arrival in Amsterdam, 232 and *note*; character of, and election as teacher, 233; versifies the Psalms, 234-236; approves the excommunication of George Johnson, 240; attacked by White, 244; writes an answer to Smyth, 250-251; quarrel of, with Johnson, and separation, 254-257, *cf.* 300; gains possession of old meeting-house, 257; last years of, 258; Biblical studies of, *ib.*; after history of his Church, 259; his last sermon, *ib.*; his account of Johnson's doctrinal changes, 266-268; his theory of the eldership and agreement with Barrow, 268, 271-272, 278; his "old" view of the Church, 292; controversy of, with Paget, 306; answers Johnson's *Christian Plea,* 315; answers Paget, 322

————, other references to, 131, 225, 228, 238 note, 242, 253, 297. *See also* Index of References

Aldgate, palace near, 33, 70

Aldrich, 11

Ames, Dr. William, 279-280; quoted, 314

Amsterdam, the Ancient Church at, 41, 42, 120; its origin, 226; connection of, with the London Church, 227-228; organisation of, completed, 233; details of services of, 234-236; troubles begin in, 238 and *note*; Johnsonian quarrels in, 239-242; troubles of, with new-comers, 243-245; troubles of, with John Smyth and his followers, 249-253; Ainsworth's secession from, 254-257; petition of, to James I., 254; has to give up old meeting-house, 257;

removes to Emden, *ib.*; return of, and death of Johnson, 258; dissolution of, *ib.*; doctrines of, primarily based on Barrow's, 265; Confession of Faith and Apology of, *ib.*; question of the Eldership in, 276-278; intercourse of, with Leyden, *ib.*; intolerance of, 282; maintenance of elders in, 291; statements of Arber concerning, *see* Arber; repulsed by Dutch Church, 305-306; and by the magistrates, 308-309, *cf.* 257; hostility of John Paget to, 319-321

Amsterdam, the Dutch Church at: refuses to acknowledge the Ancient Church, 305-308; appealed to by John Johnson, 307 and *note*

————, the Scotch Presbyterian Church at, joined by Ainsworth's Church (1701), 259

Anabaptists, the, and Barrow, 112-113, 128, 209-210, 215-216; Whitgift and, 195-196; and the Peasants' War, 201-203; early principles and hardships of, 203-205; power of, nearly destroyed, 205; later persecution of, 206; treatment and opinions of, in England, 206-208; valuable doctrines of, 208-209; their theory of the Prince unique, 210-212; insist on principle of toleration, 212-215; baptismal theory of, 217. *See* Mennonites, *and* Smyth, John

Anderson, Justice, 75, 331

Andrews, Dr. Lawrence: conference of, with Separatists, 45-48; *see also* 32, 39, 43, 92-93, 98

Andrews, Robert, 44

Answer to George Gifford's Pretended Defence of Read Prayers, 36, 333-334

Answer to Master Jacob, Johnson's, 230, 334

Answer to Cartwright, Whitgift's, 195

Apologie or Defence of such true Christians as are called Brownists, An, 265

Apostolic Church, the, Barrow on, 121

Arber, Dr.: confuses the Holy Discipline with Separatism, 289-291; the assertion of, concerning maintenance of elders discussed, 290-292; mistakes the Seven Demands (q.v.) for the Seven Articles, 293-294; on Johnson and the Amsterdam Church, 294-295, 309, 311-314; relies on Lawne, 295, 302 passim; on the character of Studley, 303; on Lawne's account of Richard Mansfield, 305; on Johnson's last work, 315; on Robinson's testimonies, 323

Articles, the twenty-four, 193; the Seven, sent from Leyden to the English Council, 293; the Five, of the Arminians against Calvinism, 316

Aylmer, Bishop of London, 3, 19, 20, 174 note, 179 and note; condemns Barrow, 22, 24; Barrow's opinion of, 29, 38; issues mandate for conference with sectaries, 39; other references to, 48, 65, 165, 166, 173, 329

B

Babworth, 302

Bacon, Francis Lord, 3; remarks of, on Barrow, 4; on the Separatists, 62

Bacon, Sir Nicholas, son of the Lord Keeper, 3

Badkin, 40, 41

Baker, Sir Richard, widow of, 169

Bancroft, Bishop, 48, 54

Baptism, Barrow's views concerning, 110-114; difference with Penry on, 84, 112, 114; among the London Separatists, 237; Francis Johnson on, 317

Barbary, 224

Barrow, 3

Barrow, Henry: his birth, family, connections, 3; at Cambridge, 4; at court, 7; conversion of, 8; member of Gray's Inn, 9; and Greenwood, 14-15; his knowledge of the London Separatists, 14 note; visit to Greenwood, and arrest of, 15; first examination of, 16-19; second examination of, 19; third examination of, 20-21; indicted at Newgate Sessions, 21; charged under statute made against Papists, ib.; sent to the Fleet, 22; "lamentable petition" of, 23-24; fourth examination of, before Council, 24-30; imprudent conduct of, 25; asks for a conference, 28; account of his imprison-

ments, 32-33; reputed to be dangerous, 33; did not write the Marprelate Tracts, ib., 82-85; fifth examination of, 34; obtains copy of the "sparsed articles," 85; writings of, in prison, ib.; their publication, 85-88, cf. 331; permitted to be with Greenwood, 39; party in third conference with Hutchinson and Andrews, 45-47; in fourth conference with same, 48; in fifth conference with Sperin, ib.; in sixth with Sperin and Egerton, 49; correspondence of, with Egerton, 50-52; last conference of, with Sperin and Cooper, 53-54; life of, in prison, 57-58; supplication of, to the Queen, and letter to Mr. Fisher, 59, cf. 339; petitions of, 62-63; probable author of the Supplication to Parliament (1592), 64; appeals to Attorney-General Egerton, 72-73; address of, to Council, 73-75, cf. 340; trial of, 75; writes his Apologie to a kinswoman, 76; execution of, 79; stories concerning, 80-82; legacy of, 224; other references to, 265, 272

———, his doctrine of the Church, 91-133, cf. Introduction. See Scripture, Spirit, Ministry, Prophecy, Discipline, Supper, Baptism, Worship

——— and the Reformists, 135-157.

See Presbyterians, Lecturers

——— and the Bishops, 161

——— and the Anabaptists, see Anabaptists

Barrow, Thomas, 3; family of, 4 note

Barrowist, the term, 222 and note

Bayly, Robert, 297

Bedlam, Garden House near, 42

Bellot, Arthur, 71, 76 note, 225

———, Scipio, 76

Bernard, Richard, 246, 248 and note; his Separatist Schism referred to, 271-274 passim

Bickley, Thomas, Bishop of Chichester, 163, 167

Bill against Barrowists and Brownists, a, 79

Billot, see Bellot

Bilson, Bishop, letter of, to Burghley, 173

Bishops, Barrow on, 100; the Elizabethan, 161-181; position of, in the State, 161-162; character and learning of, 164-166; subservience and worldliness of, 166-181

Blackwell, Francis, 258

Blethyn, Bishop of Llandaff, 175
Bowle, see Bull
Bowman, Christopher, wedding of, 33; career of, 41, 69 note. See also 155, 227, 238 note, 297
Boyes, Widow, 238. See Johnson, Mrs.
Boys, Edward, 69-70
Bradford, Mr., the martyr, 185
Bradford, Governor, story of Barrow told by, 80; his character of Ainsworth, 232-233; on the deaconess of the Amsterdam Church, 237-238; trustworthy in his account of Johnson, 242; at Amsterdam, 245, 294. See Index of References
Brewster, 281; life of, in Holland, 291; subscribes Seven Articles, 293
Bridges, Dr., 329, 341
Brief of Positions holden by the New Sectorie of Recusants, the, 35
Bright, Dr., 45
Broomal, William, 86
Brown, Dr., letter of, quoted, 288
Browne, Robert: career and influence of, 12-14; treatises of, 14 note; repudiated by Barrow and Greenwood, 51, 54, cf. 154; his theory of the word church, 292. See also 11, 106, 210, 299
Brydwell, 38, 86-87
Bryghts, George, 86
Buck, Daniel, 237 and note, 244; his description of Separatist Sacraments, 237; quoted, 238
Buckholt, assembly of Anabaptists at, 205
Buckhurst, Lord, 24
Bull, Robert, 37, 75-76, 331
Bullingham, Bishop of Gloucester and Bristol, 165, 168, 173
Bures, Anne, wife of Edmund Butts, 3
————, Henry, 3
————, Judith, wife of Aylmer, 3, 4 note
————, Mary, 3
Burghley, Lord: 3, 138, 193; examines Barrow, 25-30; Macaulay on, 30; character of, 31; and the Puritans, 63-64, 67; desires the reprieve of Barrow and Greenwood, 80; influence of, 171
Burroughs, Edith, 40, 237 note
Burying, Barrow's view of, 120
Bury St. Edmunds, 13
Butts, Edmund, son of Sir William, 3
————, Agnes, daughter of Edmund, wife of Sir Nicholas Bacon, 3, 79 note

C

Caius, Dr., see Cambridge
Calthorpe, Mr., 44
Cambridge, Barrow's opinion of, 5; description of, by Travers, Cox, Whitgift, ib.; account of, by Dr. Caius, 5-6; Puritanism in, 11-12
Campen, 224
Campion, 73
Canadine, Thomas, 42, 297
Cannady, see Canadine
Canne, John, 259; his Necessitie of Separation, ib.
Cartwright, Thomas, 11, 26, 60, 138, 152, 290; his Directory of Church Government, 126; and Whitgift, 152, 186, 195
Chaderton, Dr. William, 27 and note
Chancewell, the, 229
Chandler, John, 24
Chard, a printer, 329
Charke, Mr., 152
Charlbury, 43
Chief Justice, the Lord, 20
Church, the Amsterdam; see Amsterdam. So Gainsborough, Leyden, &c.
Church, the, definition of, by Hutchinson, 47; by Sperin, 48-49; Barrow's doctrine of, 91-127, 292, 342-349; Whitgift's theory of, 188-196
Church Buildings, Barrow on, 129-131
Churches, the Separatist, relations of to the world and to each other, 123-127
Civil, the, union of, and the ecclesiastical, 49
Civilians, disagreement between, and the Bishops, 20; at Barrow's third examination, 20 note
Classes, Presbyterian, 139
Clare Hall, Cambridge, 4, 6
Clarke, William, 41, 85, 87
Clerke, John, 58, 225, 226; escapes to Holland, 229
Clink, the, 16, 40, 41, 68, 69, 230
"Clock-bag," Stokes's, 37
Clyfton, Richard, 233, 253; his account of Divine Service in Amsterdam, 233 seqq.; character of, given by Lawne, 101-102; death of, 258 note. See Index of References
Cocky, Thomas, 236, 300
Collection of Certain Letters, &c., A, 36, 75
Collection of Certain Slanderous Articles, A, 13, 35-36, 75
Collier, George, 41, 44, 86
Conference at Lambeth, 141-142

Conferences, the seven Puritan, 43-50, 53-54; character of, 54-57. *See* Hutchinson, Andrews, Egerton, Sperin, &c.
Cooper, Bishop, 162-163; *Admonition of*, 163; learning of, 165
Cooper, Mr., 44; dispute of, with Greenwood at the last Conference, 53
Corpus Christi College, Cambridge, 10
Cosin, Dr. Richard, 18 *note*; at Barrow's first examination, 18
Cotton, John, reference of, to John Smyth, 246-247
Cotton, Mr., 39
Council, the Privy, address to, 73-75; the Seven Articles sent to, 293
Counter, the (Poultry), 40-41; (Wood Street), 40-41, 68, 86
Cox, Richard, Bishop of Ely, 167; dispute of, with Lord North, 177-178; quoted, 5.
Crane, Nicholas, 24, 86
Cycely, Barrow's maidservant, 37

D

Deaconess of the Amsterdam Church, the, 237-238
De diversis gradibus ministrorum Evangelii, Saravia's, 43
Demands, the Seven, *see* Questions, the Seven
Demonstration of Discipline, Udall's, 138
Denck, Hans, 208
Denford, William, 41
Dering, 11, 138
Description of the Visible Church, the True, 36 and *notes*, 332, 342-347
Dexter, Dr., and Barrow's authorship of the Marprelate Tracts, 34, 82-85
Directory of Church Government, Cartwright's, 125
Discipline, Barrow on, 104-108; Presbyterian theory of, different, 105
Discovery of the False Church, a Brief, 37-38, 58, 75, 336-337
Discourse of Some Troubles at Amsterdam, George Johnson's, 227 *note*
Drakes, Thomas, and his *Ten Counter-Demands*, 293
Dort, printer's house at, 35, 37, 331

E

Edwards, John, 33, 70
Egerton, Mr., 44, 52 *note*; conference of, with Barrow and Greenwood, 49, 106; correspondence of, with Barrow, 50-52

Egerton, Thomas, Lord Ellesmere, and Barrow, 71-73; reports result of trial to Lord Keeper, 75-76
Eldership, the, question of, 267-278; Ainsworth on, 268, 270-272; opposed by Johnson upon, 269-270; at Leyden, 277-278
Elizabeth, Queen, Court of, 7; " lamentable petition " to, 23-24; supplication to, 59; letter of King James to, 60; supports Whitgift before Parliament, *ib.*; stays Barrow's execution, 77-78; Burghley speaks to, on behalf of Barrow and Greenwood, 80; inquires after Barrow, 80-81; Barrow on the baptism of, 112, *cf.* 76-77; ecclesiastical position of, 135-136; her charge to Whitgift, 139; urges on the bishops, 162; subserviency of bishops to, 166-170; keeps bishoprics open, 170; address to, on behalf of pluralities, 176-177; regarded as the fount of law, 193; Whitgift regards heresy as treason against, 194
Emden, 257, 314
Emmanuel College, Cambridge, Puritan origin of, 11
Euring, William, his answer to Drakes, 293, 348
Excommunication, discussion on, 49; Barrow on, 105-108

F

Fairlambe, Peter, recantation of, 155
Ferdinand, King of Moravia, edict of, 204
Few Observations to the Reader of Mr. Gifford's Last Reply, A, 33, 62, 338-339
Field, John, 186
Finch, Mr., speech of, 222 *note*
Fisher, Mr., Barrow's letter to, 59
Fleet, the, description of, by Bishop Hooper, 22-23; Barrow sent to, 22; his account of, 23-24; prisoners in, 40-41; marriages in, 58
Fletcher, Richard, Bishop of Worcester, 80, 167, 168-170; pluralist, 175
Floyde, Mr., 152
Forrester, James, copyist for Barrow, 37-38 and *note*, 42; examination of, 75
Fox, George, anticipated by Barrow, 118; *Inner Life* of, 209
Fox's house in Nicholas Lane, *see* Nicholas Lane

Francis, John. 41, 86
Frankenhausen, Massacre of, 201
Frankfort, 43
Freake, Bishop of Norwich, disorderliness of, 179

G

Gainsborough, Church at, 246; John Smyth at, 248-249; removal of, to Amsterdam, 249
Gallebrand, Edward, 164
Gardiner, Mr., 155
Gatehouse, the, 40, 87
Gifford, George, 151 *note*; writings against, *see* Appendix III.; *see* also *Plain Refutation of*, &c.
Godly, Henry, house of, 70
Godwin, Thomas, Bishop of Bath and Wells, 164, 167, 168
Goodman, Dr., Dean of Westminster, 225
Grave, Edward, 71
Gravet, Mr., 38 *note*
Gray, Lord. 142
Greenwood, John, 10, 69, 152; at Cambridge, 12; and Browne, *ib.*; and Barrow, 14-15; indicted at Newgate Sessions, 21; sent to the Fleet, 22; imprisonments of, 31-32; at large and rearrested (1592), 33; collects letters with Barrow, 37; permitted to be with Barrow, 39; first conference of, with Hutchinson, 44; second conference of, 45; party in fourth conference, 48; in sixth conference, 49-50; conference of, with Egerton, 50-52; last conference of, 53-54; his refutation of Gifford, 61, 333-334; apprehension of, 68; trial of, 75; execution of, 79
Grindal, Archbishop, 139, 167
Grove, Edward, 155
Gualter, John, 87

H

Hacket, 60 and *note*
Hause, printer at Dort, 36, 37, 331
Harrison, Robert, 13
Hart, 73
Hatton, Sir Christopher, 24, 178 *note*; shows ignorance of Greek at examination of Barrow, 29
Hayes, Luke, 87
Helwys, Thomas, 248 and *note*; goes to Amsterdam with Smyth, 249; forms a church with him, 251; refuses to join the Mennonites, 252; forms Arminian Church in London, 253

Helwys, Ivan, 249
Heresy, Whitgift's view of, 194
High Commission, the Court of, 187, 193
Hoffmann, Melchior, teaching of, 205, 207
Hogsden, the *Antelope* at, 71
Holder, Judith, 243
Holland, emigrants to, 224
Holy Discipline, the, 141, 289-290
Holy Discipline of the Church, Travers's, 138
Hooker, 131 *note*
Hopewell, the, 229
Howland, Bishop of Peterborough, 167, 172; a pluralist, 175
Hughes, Bishop of St. Asaph, a pluralist, 174
Hull, Mr., goes with Barrow to the Clink, 16
Humphreys, 138
Hutchinson, Mr., 43; conference of, with Separatists, 32, 34, 39, 44-48
Hutton, Matthew, and the Archbishop of York, 172
Hutton, William, 44

I

Ireton, Mr., house of, 70
Islington, rector of, and Browne, 14

J

Jackson, Richard, 86
Jacob, Henry, intercourse of, with Francis Johnson, 229-232; influenced by Robinson, 232; his congregation in Southwark, 227, 228, 259
James, King of Scotland: intercedes on behalf of Cartwright, 60; King of England: petition to from Amsterdam, 254
James, Dr., 173
Johnes, Anthony, 87
Johnson, Francis: his view of church buildings, 131; examined by the Dean of Westminster, 225; arrives in Amsterdam, 227; still recognised as pastor by the London Church, 228; details of his experiences in England, 228-229; controversy of, with Henry Jacob, 229-232; quarrels with his brother and father, 238-241; answers White, 243; relations of and quarrel with Ainsworth, 254-257; leads remnant to Emden 257; return of, and death, 258, 314; Presbyterian tendencies

of, 266-270, 276 *passim*; and Robinson's reply to Bernard, 274; his want of charity, 278; and the maintenance of ministers, 292; his view of the Church, *ib.*; Bradford's character of, 310; Arber's charges against, 311-315; his *Christian Plea*, 316-319, *cf.* 266

———, other references to, 68-69, 245, 289-290, 297, 310-311, 331, 339

Johnson, George, 225, 229 and *note*; escapes to Amsterdam, *ib.*; quarrels with Francis in London, 238-239; renews quarrel in Amsterdam, and is cast out, 239-240

———, Jacob, 236, 241, 300

———, John, letter of, against his son Francis, 240-241; excommunication of, *ib.*, 312-313; appeals to the Dutch Church, 307

———, Mrs. Francis, her dress irritates George, 239; Bradford's account of her and it, 242

K
Keake, Edmund, Bishop of Rochester, 166
Knewstubbs, 138
Kniveton, George, 41, 69 and *note*, 227
Knollys, Sir Francis, attacks legal "superiority" of bishops, 60. *See* also 61, 74, 138, 177

L
Lacy, of Gray's Inn, 19
Lane, Walter, 40
Lathrop, John, 228 *note*
Latimer and the Anabaptists, 206
Lawne, Christopher, 227, 245, 320, 324; complains of rhymed Psalms, 234; his writings, 295-296; his slow recantation, 296, 298; his intercourse with Paget and expulsion from the Amsterdam Church, 257, 299; his slanders, 299-302; silent concerning the years 1605-1610, 302-303; his attacks on Studley and Mansfield, 303-305; his account of the proceedings against White, 309
Lawson, Mrs., 53 and *note*
Leake, Bishop, a pluralist, 175
Lecturers, the rise of, 146-147; Bishops' treatment of, 147; Barrow's hostility to, 147-151
Lee, Nicholas, 69; Penry at the house of, 71
Legate, Thomas, 42, 86
Leicester, Earl of, 138, 142

Leyden, the Church at, 120, 291, 324; its conference with the Amsterdam Church on the question of the Eldership, 276-278
"Luck," Barrow reproves Andrew for using the word, 48
Luther and Toleration, 212-213

M
Magistrates, the Amsterdam, 257, 308-309
Mansfield, Richard, 304-305
Marprelate Tracts, the, authorship of, 34, 35, 82-85, 188
Marriage, civil, Barrow's view of, 120
Marsh, Edmund, 87
Mason, William, 234 *note*
Menno, 206, 209
Mennonites: the Waterlander, 210; in Amsterdam, 252
Meynard, Widow, 86
Micklebound, Miles, 81, 335
Micklefield, Thomas, 155
Middelburg, 12, 14, 224
Middleton, Marmaduke, Bishop of St. David's, 165
Millenary Petition, the, 138, 154
Millet, John, house of, in Hertfordshire, 71
Ministers: unlawful, 54, *cf.* 100; maintenance of, 115-116, *cf.* 270, preparation of, 116-117
Ministry, the, Barrow's divisions of, 97; and theory concerning, 98-101, 119-120; *cf.* Eldership, the question of
Mollins, Archdeacon, 39, 40, 43
Montgomery, Dr., and the Deanery of Norwich, 176
Morrice, Mr. Attorney, motion of, in Parliament, 61
Morrison, John, 140
Morton, Mr. Secretary, 247
Motion Tending to Unity, A, 73
Münster, 203, 205
Munter, Ian, 252
Münzer, Thomas, not an Anabaptist, 202
Musculus, 11
Mychens, 87

N
Naarden, 224
Newgate, 39, 40, 41, 86
Nicholas Lane, 38; election of church officers in, 69; school at the house of Fox in, 229 *note*
Nicholas, J., 297
Nidd, Dr., 295

North, Lord, and the Bishop of Ely, 178

Norwich, 13

O

Oaths, Barrow on, 48

Onyon, Katherine, 225

Ordination and Recognition, growth of, in the Congregational Church, 120

Overton, William, Bishop of Coventry and Lichfield, 164 ; a pluralist, 174

P

Padry, 38, 86

Paget, John : on Barrow's view of church buildings, 181; his intercourse with Lawne, 298-299 ; his career in Amsterdam and hostility to the Ancient Church, 319-321; attacks Ainsworth, 321-322

Parker, Robert, on the Brownists, 154

Parker, Archbishop, petition against the injunctions of, 11 ; and Corpus Christi College, 12 ; admonition of, concerning preachers, 146

Parkhurst, Bishop of Norwich, 161, 164, 179-180

Parliament and the Puritans, 60-61

Peasants' War, the, 201

Penry, John, 26, 33, 138, 225, 280, 341; his journey to London and capture, 70-71 ; no relations between, and Barrow, 83-85; his answer to Dr. Some, ib.; last letter of, 223-224

Perne, Dr., 186

Peterhouse, Cambridge, 27

Petition directed to Her Majesty, a Puritan, 85, 340-341

Petitions, see Separatists, Pluralism

Philippes, Thomas, alias Morice, letter of, quoted, 79-80

Philips, Edward, 81 and note, 155

Piers, John, Archbishop of York, 163-164, 166, 172

Plain Refutation of Mr. Gifford, 30, 32, 58, 75, 337-339

Platform, Barrow's, 58, 62, 334-336

Pluralism : of Elizabethan bishops, 174-177 ; Parliamentary petition against, 176 ; address of clergy concerning, 176-177

Popham, Justice, 75, 331

Prayer-Book, the, 136

Presbyterian church government, Barrow and, 125-126, 143-144

Presbyterians, the, 138-142; called Reformists by Barrow, 142; Barrow's indictment of and argument for their separation, 143-153 ; position of, after Barrow's death, 153 ; logical outcome of their teaching, 154-156; confused by Mr. Arber with Separatists, 289-290. See Holy Discipline, the

Prince, the, Barrow's view of ecclesiastical powers of, 128-129 ; of the personal standing of, 129 ; Whitgift's view of position of, in the Church, 191 ; Anabaptist theory concerning, 210-212

Proctor, Mr. Penry's, 85, 114. See Throckmorton, Job

Profane Schism, Lawne's, 295

Prophecy, Barrow on, 102-104 ; at Amsterdam, 236

Psalms, metrical, sung in Amsterdam, 234-236

Puckring, Sir John, petition of, 170 note

Puritan preachers, aid the bishops against the Separatists, 42, 153

Puritans, the, divisions of, in the Church, 137, 139. See Presbyterian, Separatist

Pym, 138

Q

Questions, the Seven, 293-294, 348-349

R

Raglande, 24

Raines, 229

Raleigh, Sir Walter, speech of, on the Separatists, 62, 79 note

Ratcliffe, Penry at, 71

Redgrave, 3

Reeve, Thomas, 87

Reformists, the, see Presbyterians

Remonstrance, the, 138

Reynolds, Dr. John, 74 and note, 138 ; reported opinion of, concerning Barrow and Greenwood, 80

Rich, Lord, 10 note, 14

Rippon, Roger, his epitaph, 40

Robinson, John, 118, 120, 249 ; writes to the London Church, 226, 228, 282; approves excommunication of George and John Johnson, 240-241; his letter to Ainsworth's congregation, 259 ; follows and defends Barrow, 273 ; his reply to Bernard, 274, 313 ; and to Johnson, 274-275 ; and the question of the Eldership at Leyden, 277-278; in favour of private communion with members of the English Church, 279-281 ; declares it lawful to hear ministers of the Church of England, 281-284 ;

his grief at the intolerance of the Amsterdam Church, 282-283; maintenance of, in Leyden, 291; subscribes the Seven Articles, 298; keeps up a connection with Amsterdam, 323-324; opinion of, on the *Profane Schism*, 324-325. *See* Index to References
Rochford Hall, 14
Roper, Christopher, 41
Row, Widow, 86

S

Sacraments, Separatist, 237
St. Alban's, sign of *Christopher* at, 70
St. Andrew-in-the-Wardrobe, parish of, 15
St. Benet's, Cambridge, and Browne, 12
St. Botolph's, Boston, 246
St. Bride's, parish church of, 47
St. John's College, Cambridge, scandal of, 11
Sampson, 138
Sandys, Bishop, his quarrels with Whitgift and Aylmer, 178-179
Saravia, Dr., 38 *note*, 43
Scambler, Bishop of Peterborough, a pluralist, 175, 179
Scriptures, the, Barrow's absolute reliance upon, 91-93
Scrooby, the Church at, 120, 247, 248
Sectary, discussion upon the definition of, 47
Separatists, the: their number, 62; petition of, 62-63; Supplication of, 64-67; arrest of, *ib.*; attack upon and third petition of, 68; scholarship of early, 118; influence of, 154-155; condition of London Separatists (1593), 221; main body of them go to Amsterdam, 226; London congregation of, lasts until 1624, 227-228. *See* Jacob, Henry; Amsterdam, Ancient Church at; Ainsworth, &c.
Settle, Thomas, 33, 40, 67, 69, 71, 85, 332
Shepherd, Keeper of the Clink, arrests Barrow, 16
Shipdam, Barrow's birthplace, 3, 10, 14
Slade, excommunication of, 238 *note*
Slade, Matthew, letter of, on Johnson's death, 314
Smels, George, 41
Smith, William, 74 *note*
Smyth, Andrew, 37-38
————, John, 42, 211; his early life, 245; preacher in Lincoln, 245-246;

at Gainsborough, 248-249; goes to Amsterdam, 249; secedes from the Ancient Church and writes the *Differences of the Churches*, 249-251; forms a new church, 251; seeks to join the Mennonites, 251-252; quarrels with Helwys, 252; his character, 253-254; his *Retraction*, *ib.* *See* Index of References.
Smyth, Quintin, 41
Some, Dr. Robert, his career and intercourse with Barrow, 26-27; his *Godly Treatises*, 26 and *note*, 35, 44, 84-85
Southwark, congregation at, 227, 228, 289
Sparkes, 141
Sparowe, John, 44
Spenser, 138
Sperin, Thomas, 44; conferences of, with Barrow, 48-49, 53, 99-101, 115
Spirit, the, accepted by Barrow as interpreter of Scripture, 92-93
Stanhope, Dr., 40, 41, 65
Stanley, Justice, 331
Starsmore, Sabin, 259 *note*
Statute, against Recusants (1581), 21-22; against seditious books, 75
Stephens, Thomas, 87
Sterrell, William, letter to, 79
Stokes, Robert, agent of Barrow, 85-86; recants, 61; examination of, 75, 331; cast out by Johnson, 331
Stratford-at-Bowe, 70
Studley, Daniel, 37-38; helps Barrow to print the *Brief Discovery*, *ib.*; *see* also 40, 67, 69; elected elder, 69; examination of, 75; escapes to Holland, 229; active in disputes, 239; interferes in the Norwich Church, 243 *note*; attacked by White, 243, 297; supports Johnson against Ainsworth, 255; attacked by Lawne, 303; his answers, 303 *note*; deposition of, 257
Suckling, Dr., 176
Supper, the Lord's, Barrow on, 108-110; among the London Separatists, 237
Supplication to the Queen, A, 56
Suspension, Barrow's view of, 108

T

Thesaurus, Cooper's, 163
Thorneby, 16
Throckmorton, Job: his defence of Penry, 84-85, 339, 341; his baptism, 111-112, 114

Tomson, Henry, 86
Travers, 5, 11, 138, 141, 152, 290

U

Udall, John, 60, 138
Umberfield, Richard, 87
Universities, the, deprecated by Barrow, 117-118

V

Vestianan Controversy, the, 11
Visible Church, the, *see Description, the True of*

W

Walsingham, Sir Francis, 142
Wandsworth, first English Presbytery at, 139, 289
Ware, 16
Waterer, Roger, 42; messenger between London and Holland, 227 *note*
Watson, a pursuivant, 16
Wheeler, Richard, 85
White, Thomas, arrives in Amsterdam, 243; his *Discovery of Brownism*, 243-245; his accusations renewed by Lawne, 297; account of the proceedings against, 308-309
White Lion, the, 87
Whitgift, Archbishop: examines Barrow, 16-21, 24; Barrow's opinion of, 29; issues order for conference with sectaries, 39; Barrow's description of, 59; independence of, 61; gains possession of Barrow's books, 75; insists on the execution of Barrow, 79-80; reported words of, concerning Barrow and Greenwood, 81; and the

Presbyterians, 139-142; learning of, 166; his quarrel with Sandys, 178-179; his life, 185-186; his hatred of the Puritans increased by his controversy with Cartwright, 186-187; his attack on Puritanism, 187; hated by the Puritans, *ib.*; the good points in his character, *ib.*; moderation of, attested by Wotton and Hooker, 188; his ecclesiastical polity, 188-197; his definition of the Church, 188; and theory of Church government, 188-190; his apology for the Church of England, 190-191; considers the Prince as keystone, 191; an Erastian, 191-192; regards the will of the Queen supreme, 193; and heresy as treason, 194; his hatred of the Anabaptists, 195-196
——— other references to, 5, 9, 11, 38, 113, 136, 142, 167
Wickham, William, Bishop of Lincoln, 245
Willcocks, Thomas, 186
Worship, Public, Barrow's apostolic view of, fetters his spiritual view, 121-122 with *note*; Separatist features of, 122-123

Y

Yonge, Justice Richard, 24, 65; charges Barrow, 27, 65
Young, Bishop of Rochester, a pluralist, 175; his domestic expenses, 181

Z

Zurich, 43
Zwingli and the Anabaptists, 203

LONDON:
IGHT AND SONS, PRINTERS,
FETTER LANE, E.C.

Lightning Source UK Ltd.
Milton Keynes UK
UKHW020616020320
359617UK00011B/349

9 780461 551433